URBAN ANTHROPOLOGY

THE CROSS-CULTURAL STUDY OF COMPLEX SOCIETIES

Urban Anthropology

The Cross-Cultural Study of Complex Societies

Richard Basham

UNIVERSITY OF SYDNEY

 MAYFIELD PUBLISHING COMPANY

To George DeVos
and Alan Dundes—
whose influence is more real
than apparent

Library of Congress Catalog Card Number: 78-51942
International Standard Book Number: 0-87484- 393-6

Manufactured in the United States of America
Mayfield Publishing Company,
285 Hamilton Avenue,
Palo Alto, California 94301

This book was set in IBM Baskerville by TypArt
and was printed and bound by Haddon Craftsmen.
Sponsoring editor was C. Lansing Hays, Carole Norton supervised
editing, and Meryl Lanning was manuscript editor. Michelle Hogan
supervised production, the book was designed by Nancy Sears,
and photo editor was Brenn Lea Pearson.

Photo credits: cover and ch. 3, Peter Menzel/Stock, Boston;
Introduction, Jeroboam/David Powers; ch. 1,
David A. Krathwohl/Stock, Boston; ch. 2, United Nations;
ch. 4, George Cohen/Stock, Boston; ch. 5, Ira Kirschenbaum/Stock,
Boston; ch. 6, Richard Basham; ch. 7 and 8, George Malave/Stock,
Boston.

Contents

Preface

This book is a product of more than a decade of interest and research in urban anthropology. I was initially attracted to the study of anthropology by its cross-cultural perspective of human cultures. Monographs on such diverse topics as Azande witchcraft, New Guinea cargo-cults, and the Black Carib were endlessly fascinating to me in my undergraduate years: as a fledgling anthropologist I was proud of the work of those who preceded me. Yet I was also troubled by anthropology's emphasis on primitive and peasant peoples to the virtual exclusion of urban and industrial societies.

Anthropologists clearly were performing a necessary and urgent task in studying and pre-serving rapidly changing, often vanishing traditions. Still, it seemed their almost exclusive concern with "primitives" had persisted long after such a singularity of purpose was justified. Indeed, since most of anthropology's primitive constituency had already vanished by the mid-1960s, it then seemed to me fully possible that anthropology in time could become merely a custodian of vanished traditions preserved in verbal formaldehyde.

I carried this concern with me when I became a graduate student at Berkeley in the mid-1960s. There I found numerous courses emphasizing primitive and peasant societies but no regular, formal courses in urban anthropology. Consequently, I undertook a program of individual reading courses in the subject under the aegis of Professor James N. Anderson, who provided willing and able guidance even though at that time the subject was somewhat peripheral to his interests. These reading courses, coupled with numerous formal seminars in Psychological Anthropology chaired by Professor George DeVos, and in Folklore with Professor Alan Dundes, formed the core of my graduate coursework and prepared me for dissertation research on French-English relations in Canada. They also alerted me to a rapidly emerging literature on the anthropology of urban and complex societies.

The last decade has seen a phenomenal growth of interest in urban anthropology. Indeed, it is probable that most anthropological work today is being done in urban and complex societies; certainly this will be the case in the future. Courses titled "Urban Anthropology" and "Anthropology of Complex Societies" have proliferated in American universities in recent years. Yet despite the tremendous interest, no truly comprehensive urban anthropology textbook has yet appeared. This text is intended to help fill the void by offering both an introduction to the field and suggestions for future research.

I have already acknowledged my debt to Professors James N. Anderson, George DeVos, and Alan Dundes. I also owe a great debt to C. Lansing Hays of Mayfield Publishing Company for his combination of enthusiastic encouragement and subtle pressure, to Meryl Lanning for her skilled editing, and to Professor Gordon W. Hewes of the University of Colorado, Boulder, for his example of scholarly breadth and integrity. During much of the time when I was engaged in writing *Urban Anthropology,* I worked closely with a good friend and former graduate student, David DeGroot, who served as a receptive listener and perceptive critic and read this text many times in manuscript. I hope he gained as much from his reading courses with me as I did from our lengthy discussions and debates.

Finally, I welcome and encourage suggestions for improving this text. I should also very much appreciate receiving copies of any papers and articles pertaining to urban anthropology which you may wish to send me.

Department of Anthropology
The University of Sydney
Sydney, N.S.W.
Australia

Introduction

In recent years, a major shift in anthropological research has led away from an almost total concern with primitives and peasants toward the study of complex societies. Upon reflection it is clear that it could hardly be otherwise. Today, there are few truly primitive peoples or peasants who have not been profoundly affected by urban influences. Anthropology as a living, active profession, not merely a keeper of the verbal formaldehyde of vanished life styles, must accommodate itself to the reality of a world that has undergone radical transformation since the early days when anthropology styled itself as the study of primitive peoples.

Introductory anthropology textbooks invariably begin by informing the student that anthropology is "the study of man," and that in America the field is segmented into four major subfields: (1) sociocultural anthropology, the study of human customs and societies; (2) archaeology, the study of human prehistory; (3) linguistics, the study of language; and (4) physical anthropology, the study of human physiology. With so exhaustive a scope, anthropology holds the promise of providing a truly comprehensive view of man. But the novice to the field quickly discovers that such broad definitions have been severely narrowed, by anthropologists themselves. For most anthropologists and nonanthropologists, anthropology has really meant the study of "primitive," or, at least, non-Western peoples; the study of "civilized" and Western populations has generally been ceded to the field of sociology.

This preoccupation of anthropologists with primitive and non-Western peoples does not lie in the theoretical foundations of the field itself. Whether viewed from the perspective of the cultural anthropologist, with his concern for the study of learned, socially transmitted behavior, or of the social anthropologist, who concentrates upon the organizing elements of human societies, the proper focus of sociocultural anthropology *is* all humanity.

In this study of human cultural diversity, anthropologists have long concerned themselves with the manner in which human cultures adapt to their particular environments—environments which include not only natural geographic conditions, but other cultures. Thus, unlike most other animals which must develop physiological responses to environmental change, man has the capacity for developing learned behavioral, or cultural, responses.

One universal human adaptive response has been the elaboration of family and kinship systems that socialize humans during their long childhood and give them a sense of orientation in later life. Not surprisingly, many anthropologists have focused primarily on kinship and social organization. Indeed, in primitive societies social organization and kinship systems are virtually the same; only in more populous agricultural societies do the requirements of social organization really begin to exhaust the resources of kinship. Here, social position is typically based either upon birth-ascribed positions of caste or ethnicity or upon achieved positions of class. Equally important in the development of anthropology as the study of cultural adaptations, kinship, and social organization has been the problem of how individuals are transformed into cultural beings who fill societal roles.

In recent years, many anthropologists have turned their attention to the study of cities and advanced societies. Partly this has been in recognition of the fact that anthropology's primitive "constituency" has largely disappeared, and that peasant peoples everywhere have been profoundly influenced by urban traditions. But for most, the impetus to study more complex societies has come from a sense that the actual scope of anthropological concern had grown too narrow, that anthropology did not place enough emphasis upon studying the kinds of societies in which most people live today.

Although still a relatively new field, urban anthropology has already contributed greatly to our knowledge of cities. It has added a crucial comparative dimension to urban work that views the city as a recent form of societal organization that must be approached from both historical and cross-cultural perspectives.

The contribution of urban anthropology has not been a uni-directional one in which only urbanists have profited from the anthropologist's broadened perspective on human society. Urban anthropologists have extended the traditional research concerns of anthropologists and uncovered a significant body of information on rural-urban migration, the function of kinship in the city, the adaptation and adjustment of humans in densely populated environments, and the effects of urban settings upon cultural pluralism and social stratification. Most important, the growing interest of anthropologists in complex societies has reaffirmed the claim of anthropology to concern with all human cultures and societies, whether "primitive," "peasant," or "complex."

The questions that this book will discuss and attempt to answer center on the issues of why people migrate to cities, and what happens to them and their traditions at this most complex level of human social organization. The first chapter considers the differing research interests and methods of sociologists and anthropologists in the study of cities and complex societies. Chapter 2 is about the origin and spread of cities. In chapter 3, the incredibly rapid growth of cities throughout the world, and the motivations for the rural-urban migration largely responsible for such growth, is considered.

Chapter 4 treats the modifications undergone by traditional family and kinship systems in cities and industrializing societies. Common urban dilemmas such as crime, overcrowding, and inadequate housing, and how urbanites throughout the world have coped with them, is the subject of chapter 5. Chapter 6 focuses upon the systems of social classification and stratification common to complex societies; it attempts to assess whether cities, as is often believed, tend to promote the rejection of birth-ascribed categories in favor of those based upon individual achievement. In chapter 7, the various techniques which urban anthropologists have developed for studying large-scale societies are assessed. And finally, chapter 8 draws some conclusions on the state of urban anthropology and offers suggestions for its future.

Often a particular topic, such as "squatter settlements," will be under focus, and the discussion will be based upon examination and comparison of certain of its various facets. But in the chapters on kinship in the city and urban social stratification and pluralism (4 and 6) the setting of the discussion will be detailed tours of the world's major cultural areas. The purpose for this is twofold: (1) the changes brought about by urbanization are too intricately intertwined with traditional family and social organization to permit their ready removal from context—for example, the effects of urban life upon Indian and American families are best first considered within their particular cultural contexts; (2) it is hoped that the reader will enjoy and profit from the background discussion of various cultures which such an approach necessitates.

In moving to larger-scale societies, anthropologists have been forced to reconsider the benefits and limitations of the traditional methodology. In the past, ethnographic work has depended upon the development of close rapport with a relatively few informants from whom anthropologists have attempted to construct descriptions of entire cultures. Such an approach can work quite well in communities of a few hundred or even a few thousand people. But what happens to anthropological methods in cities of tens of thousands or even millions of people?

Many urban anthropologists have chosen to emphasize the traditional intensive ethnographic approach known as *participant-observation*. In doing so they have often abandoned the effort to capture the entirety of a city, in favor of description of particular ethnic or occupational groups. Others have attempted to study particular problems such as interethnic relations across entire societies. But studies of urban and complex societies need not be undertaken at sacrifice to either participant-observation or holism; they can be built on modifications of both. Anthropologists working in cities and complex societies must extend their scope beyond informant interviews and develop some of the skills of the social historian and analyst of current affairs. They must learn to take full cognizance of written materials, including surveys, historical studies, and novels, realizing that these materials, an indispensable part of the holistic conception of a complex society, are often even more significant than information gained from the lips of an informant. The urban anthropologist must take these materials into account, yet still participate in the society to gain the additional dimension of emotional understanding of the lives and interaction of its members. Herein lies the essential challenge for anthropologists working in cities and complex societies: to grasp the realities of groups of perhaps millions of people without sacrificing the vivid description which characterizes the best traditional ethnographic research.

Most anthropological work in the future will undoubtedly be undertaken in cities and complex societies. But there is not yet, and there may not be, agreement on how to conduct anthropology in cities. There is no "notes and queries" to guide urban ethnographers such as exists to study less complex societies. Nevertheless, urban anthropology is no longer in its infancy, and some attempt is needed to provide order and coherence to it. Such is the goal of this book. As you read it I hope you, too, will be attracted to the challenge of understanding complex human cultures and societies.

The Study of Urban
and Complex Societies

With the world's rapid urbanization during the past several decades, historians, political scientists, urban planners, and others have been attracted to the increasingly important cross-cultural study of urban and complex societies. Most notably, sociologists, with their long-standing interest in the study of urbanism, and anthropologists, with their grounding in comparative study of the world's peoples, have increasingly devoted themselves to systematically studying the significance of the spread of more complex forms of social organization. Urban anthropology, if it is to be truly comparative, cannot limit its scope to research conducted solely by anthropological methods or by those who identify themselves as anthropologists; familiarity with the work of other urban specialists, especially sociologists, is essential. In this chapter, some sociological contributions to comparative urban studies will be briefly traced, and the reasons for anthropologists' growing interest in complex societies and the paths that interest has taken will be discussed.

URBAN SOCIOLOGY

Not surprisingly, sociologists were first to turn toward the systematic analysis of urban societies. Ferdinand Tönnies' famous distinction between *gemeinschaft* and *gesellschaft* patterns of interaction,[1] and Emile Durkheim's notion of *anomie*,[2] were rooted in theoretical assumptions about what constitutes the essence of urban and non-urban life. Max Weber offered an historical sociology of ancient and medieval Western and non-Western cities in his work *The City*, in an effort to trace the evolution of cities and provide an historical platform for contemporary urban research.[3]

More important to the later development of urban anthropology, however, was the sociologist Louis Wirth's classic essay of 1938, "Urbanism as a Way of Life." Wirth suggested that urbanism could best be approached from three inter-related perspectives: (1) as a physical structure, (2) as a system of social organization, and (3) as a set of attitudes and ideas and a "constellation of personalities." Although he touched upon each of these approaches, his contribution to urban theory has been greatest in its speculations about the characteristic influences of urban life on social organization and attitudes. Noting that urbanites usually "meet one another in highly segmental roles," Wirth constructed a widely accepted theory of urbanism. Urbanites, he says,

> are, to be sure, dependent upon more people for the satisfaction of their life-needs than are rural people and thus are associated with a greater number of organized groups, but they are less dependent upon particular persons, and their dependence upon others is confined to a highly fractionalized aspect of the other's round of activity . . . The contacts of the city may indeed be face to face, but they are nevertheless impersonal, superficial, transitory, and segmental. The reserve, the indifference, and the blasé outlook which urbanites manifest in their relationships may thus be regarded as devices for immunizing themselves against the personal claims and expectations of others.
>
> The superficiality, the anonymity, and the transitory character of urban-social relations make intelligible, also, the sophistication and the rationality generally ascribed to city-dwellers. Our acquaintances tend to stand in a relationship of utility to us in the sense that the role which each one plays in our life is overwhelmingly regarded as a means for achievement of our own ends. Whereas, therefore, the individual gains, on the one hand, a certain degree of emancipation or freedom from the personal and emotional controls of intimate groups, he

loses, on the other hand, the spontaneous self-expression, the morale, and the sense of participation that comes with living in an integrated society.[4]

Urban life, in other words, Wirth argued, is characterized by impersonal, instrumental contacts which tend to free individuals from the strong controls of such primary groups as the extended family. But this freedom of individual action comes at cost of a loss of sense of collective security.

Robert Redfield adapted Wirth's formulation of the characteristics of urban life to his *folk-urban* continuum, by characterizing the *urban* pole in Wirth's terms and the *folk* pole as its opposite— small, isolated, homogeneous, and traditional communities which were economically self-sufficient and had only a rudimentary division of labor. The rural-urban continuum seemed logical enough and for a time enjoyed wide acceptance among social theorists. Both Redfield and Wirth have been criticized, however, for ethnocentrism in their assumption that ideal-type patterns which they isolated as characteristic of Western cities and rural areas can readily be generalized to non-Western societies,[5] and for facile extension of their analysis of urban social systems to the level of individual personality characteristics. As Oscar Lewis argued, in remarking that "some of the description of the modern urbanite reads like another version of the fall of man . . . according to Wirth's theory both the carriers of knowledge and progress (the elite and the intellectuals) and the ignorant slum dwellers have a similar urban personality, since presumably they share in the postulated urban anonymity."[6] In fairness to Redfield and Wirth it should be noted that both later came to regard their conceptions of urbanism and the folk-urban continuum as "working hypotheses," which unfortunately have yet to be subjected to a serious test.[7]

It would be inappropriate in a text on urban anthropology to devote extensive space to purely sociological research. But, sharing similar interests, each field has had strong impact on the other. Sociological research is often associated with the use of *survey techniques* which study a particular topic in depth by covering relatively large population samples through interviews or questionnaires. The hallmark of anthropological research is intensive *ethnographic* research involving a few informants with the goal of understanding an entire cultural tradition. Traditional sociology studies many individuals to develop an understanding of specific concerns, while anthropologists rely upon the development of deeper relations with a few individuals to study a whole tradition. Although both fields have maintained much of their discrete approaches, a great deal of methodological blending has occurred so that anthropologists often behave like sociologists and vice versa.

It is worthwhile to briefly consider the approaches of urban sociological research which have been most important to the fields of urban sociology, urban anthropology, or both: *The Chicago School of Urban Ecology, The Community Study Approach,* and *Interactionism.* The community study approach is most "anthropological" in the traditional sense, especially as evidenced in Whyte's *Street Corner Society,* while interactionism offers the most fruitful suggestions for future urban anthropological research.

The Chicago School of Urban Ecology

A major contribution to urban sociology has come from the "ecological" studies of Robert E. Park and his students at the University of Chicago. Rather than theorize in the abstract upon urban life, the "Chicago School" grounded its research in demographic and census information as well as interviews and historical data. Park was fascinated with the tendency of cities to develop such *natural areas* as slums, ethnic neighborhoods, vice areas, and exclusive residential sections. In the collection of essays edited by him and E. W. Burgess entitled *The City,* the principals of the Chicago School outlined the grafting of an ecological analogy to the study of urban life. In this union, cities may be thought of as ecosystems which require energy to maintain their structure and which are segmented into natural areas subject to laws of residential succession.

The concept of succession as an explanation of changing residential patterns in urban neighborhoods was best developed by Otis Dudley Duncan and Beverly Duncan in *The Negro Population of Chicago.* In the years after World War I, as blacks migrated north to job opportunities in Chicago, extensive black ghettos began to develop. In analyzing the formation and spread of ghettos the Duncans noted that, once substantial proportions of blacks—10 percent or more—had entered an area, the area almost always increased its black population. They identified four stages of residential succession: (1) *penetration,* in which blacks began to move into an area previously inhabited by whites, (2) *invasion,* which occurred when the number and proportion of blacks became sufficiently great to indicate imminent black dominance in the area, (3) *consolidation* of the neighborhood into an all-black area, and (4) *piling-up,* in which the density of settlement increased as more blacks moved into the neighborhood. Perhaps the most interesting conclusion drawn from this study of residential succession was that

> despite the increase in congestion in the piling-up tracts and the undoubted deterioration of living conditions in many respects, there was no decline in the levels of several characteristics indicative of socioeconomic status or standard of living, e.g. educational attainment, white-collar employment, homeowner-ship, and dwelling units with central heating and mechanical refrigeration . . . Areas in which one or another kind of social problem is localized at a given time are likely to retain such a problematic character for a period of years, even if, in the meantime, the population in these areas has undergone considerable turnover. Or, to state the point in the language of theory, *the residential structure of an urban community is in good part independent of the racial makeup of the community's inhabitants.*[8]

The Chicago School produced a vast literature on cities and their social problems.[9] Certain studies, such as Thrasher's *Gang* and Wirth's *Ghetto,* remain landmarks in urban research. Most of the later work spawned by the ecological analogy, however, seems to have focused upon the classification and statistical reworking of census data for their own sake. What began as an attempt to ground urban theory in actual research, in time took its own refuge from the uncertainties of fieldwork through minute reworking of census statistics. Such studies, no matter how carefully conducted, seem sterile to those who seek an understanding of the lives of the city's inhabitants.

The Community Study Approach

Partly in reaction to the abstract empiricism of the later Chicago School, many sociologists undertook community studies reminiscent of traditional anthropological research. One of the earliest and most detailed efforts was led by W. Lloyd Warner, an anthropologist who attempted to merge an ethnographic perspective gained in fieldwork among Australian aborigines with information gathered from formal interviews for his study of a New England City, *Yankee City.* With numerous co-workers and assistants, Warner produced an impressive multivolume record of Yankee City's industrial and social structure. But few others have been able to amass Warner's resources or have felt such an extensive effort justified in their own studies. Consequently, sociologists have tended to follow the model of ethnographic research laid down by anthropologists, and have restricted themselves either to small communities of a few hundred or at most a few thousand people[10] or have studied clearly demarcated communities within larger cities.[11]

One of the earliest of the urban community studies, Caroline Ware's *Greenwich Village, 1920-1930,* was conducted with such an acute awareness of the problems which encumber urban survey research that it seems current even forty years after its publication. Greenwich Village has had a distinctive character since its first days in the early 1800's, when it was a thriving village on the outskirts of New York City. Expansion of the metropolis gradually led to incorporation of "the village" at the center of the city, although the separate pattern of its streets (laid out at a diagonal to those of the city) and the special character of its inhabitants has kept it somewhat distinct from New York City proper.

In gathering material for her monograph, Ware encountered the gamut of frustrations common to urban research. Obtaining basic demographic information was made difficult by the fact that census tracts and administrative districts often did not coincide with the boundaries of the community itself, necessitating great effort to construct the commonest kinds of social data such as school statistics and assessed housing valuations. Contact with an unbiased community sample was made difficult by the fact that certain people were suspicious of her research and unwilling to be treated as "white rats," while others who were more eager to cooperate were often atypical in their high level of education or their behavior. Many were too busy and too disinterested to become involved. As these problems are frequently encountered in all urban research, Ware's improvisations to cope with them are worth discussing in detail.

An initial survey of Greenwich Village pointed out a gulf between the local population of ethnically grouped tenement dwellers and newcomers who had moved into the village after some of its older homes had been renovated. To reduce social complexity to a manageable level in an area inhabited by significant numbers of Italians, Irish, Jews, and other groups, individuals were set in relation to their adherence to traditions of their groups:

> Certain key features of each group pattern were selected and used as touchstones. In respect to each pattern, characteristics were chosen which represented either end of the scale of conformity—the first and last feature to be abandoned by someone abandoning the ways of the group—and were used as

short cuts which made it possible to eliminate many questions.
For example, if a Catholic is married outside of the Church, it
is not necessary to look at the frequency with which he attends
Mass or at much of anything except whether he sends for a
priest on his deathbed, while if he goes to confession every
month it is probably safe to assume that he observes the Holy
Days of Obligation. If a Jew fails to have his son circumcised,
it is hardly necessary to inquire whether he keeps a strictly
Kosher house, and if he refrains from cooking on the Sabbath,
he is pretty sure to have his son confirmed.[12]

By using such basic "litmus tests" of adherence to group tradition, a
great deal can be assumed about an individual without undertaking
the impossible task of eliciting the whole range of experience,
attitudes, and behavior from every member of the community. The
researcher is freed to engage in a deeper, more thorough study of
group traditions and to more closely investigate the significance of
individual variations for future social change.

In order to ground her observations in a villagewide sample,
Ware distributed interview schedules through the mail. Return rates
were low, indicating a probable bias of selection in those who
returned the questionnaire, made all the more significant by the fact
that much of the population was illiterate or semiliterate in English.
Door-to-door interviewing proved too time-consuming for one person
to undertake: too few people were at home or willing to spare
leisure time. Consequently, Ware decided to use interviewers. Aside
from the problem of finding conscientious individuals willing to
faithfully carry out their tasks, there was the question of what type
of interviewer to choose. In general, "interviewers were selected for
each contact on the basis of their ability to elicit the particular type
of information sought, which meant, in general, those who were as
closely identified as possible with the group studied." Thus, "in
selecting college students to investigate street-corner loafers, those
whose own backgrounds were similar were chosen in preference to
boys from more refined localities. A red-haired Irish girl 'with the
map of Ireland written all over her face,' was sent to draw out even
second and third generation Irish."[13] Ware was conscious of the
problem that use of an "insider" can entail: he is often unaware of
the significance to a nonparticipant of assumptions so basic to him
that he neglects to notice them. When possible in certain formal
settings—such as interviews with church officials—where an outsider's
queries would be given respectful consideration, she attempted to use
someone "who is sufficiently of the group to recognize implications

and is at the same time either detached and articulate or in some way outside the group as well as inside it."[14] One such interviewer, a Jewish college student who had grown up in an Italian neighborhood, was particularly valuable.

Finally, Ware faced the crucial problem of ordering and making sense of data gathered from many diverse sources. She noted that "the practice used in some studies of presenting excerpts of material apparently on the assumption that the reader is in a position to interpret the material, fails to recognize the basis necessary for interpretation and relieves the author of a responsibility which is rightly his. Nobody is in so good a position as he to analyze and interpret the material."[15] Ware acknowledged that urban sociology, like history, must rely simply upon a reasonable critique of the evidence at hand. Like historians, the urban sociologist is

> constantly dealing with materials of just this type, never uniform or complete, never produced under controlled conditions, always subject to the bias of recording and the accident of preservation, and always complicated by the problem of whether a silence shelters a commonplace or something which does not exist. Everything, quantitative and qualitative, has here been regarded as evidence and has been treated accordingly. It has been tested and discounted for bias, examined for internal consistency, and subjected to external checks, weighed for completeness and searched for the meaning of omissions.[16]

Of all research conducted by urban sociologists, none seems more familiar to anthropologists in conception and undertaking than William Foote Whyte's ethnography of an Italian slum, *Street Corner Society*. Upon receiving a fellowship from Harvard for three years of unrestricted research, Whyte decided to study "Cornerville," his name for a big-city slum. Initially, he determined that the task would require a team of at least ten men; his advisor "poured cold water on the mammoth beginning," fortunately without dampening his enthusiasm.

The problem was how as an outsider to begin the study of an Italian slum. Whyte was from "a very consistent upper-middle-class background . . . very far removed from the life"[17] of Cornerville and was naturally apprehensive about how to gain entry into what was not only a community of foreigners but one with a reputation for racketeering as well. After an amusing false start in which he tried to establish community contact by picking up a girl in a hotel and was nearly thrown down the stairs by her male companion, he visited a social worker at a local settlement house who introduced him to "Doc," a prominent member of a local gang.

> As I remember it, I said that I had been interested in congested city districts in my college study but had felt very remote from them. I hoped to study the problems in such a district. I felt I could do very little as an outsider. Only if I could get to know the people and learn their problems first hand would I be able to gain the understanding I needed.
>
> Doc heard me out without any change of expression, so that I had no way of predicting his reaction. When I was finished he asked: "Do you want to see the high life or the low life?" "I want to see all that I can. I want to get as complete a picture of the community as possible." "Well, any nights you want to see anything, I'll take you around. I can take you to the joints—gambling joints—I can take you around to the street corners. Just remember that you're my friend. That's all they need to know. I know these places, and, if I tell them that your're my friend, nobody will bother you. You just tell me what you want to see, and we'll arrange it."[18]

With entry gained into a sector of the community, Whyte rented a room with an Italian family and began several years of participation in community life, focusing on the contrasting groups of "corner boys" and "college boys"[19] and on racketeers and politicians. One of the most interesting observations to emerge from his research was the fact that the social hierarchy of peer groups was closely related to such group activities as bowling. After studying Doc's gang, "the Nortons," Whyte constructed a sociogram of its hierarchy and member relations.

The sociogram of course represented Whyte's conception of group relations and was not explicitly recognized by the members themselves. But a year after the period of the sociogram, the Nortons held a bowling contest to climax the season. When the scores were tabulated the bowlers ranked as follows.[20]

1. Whyte (outsider bowling with the Nortons)
2. Danny
3. Doc
4. Long John
5. Mike
6. Joe
7. Mark (outsider)
8. Carl
9. Frank
10. Alec

While the agreement between group ranking and bowling scores was not perfect, there was a clear division between scores of the leaders—

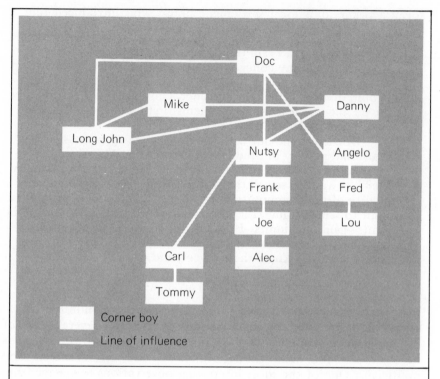

FIGURE 1

Position of boxes indicates relative status. (Reprinted, by permission, from Whyte, 1943:13. Copyright University of Chicago Press.)

Doc, Danny, Mike, and Long John—and the followers, Frank, Joe, Carl, and Alec. Prompted by this "coincidence," Whyte checked the season records and noticed that there was a close correspondence between social position and bowling performance which had "developed because bowling became the primary social activity of the group . . . [and] the main vehicle whereby the individual could maintain, gain, or lose prestige."[21] Bowling performance itself seemed not to be a determinant of social position, but rather the reverse:

> When Doc, Danny, Long John, or Mike bowled on opposing sides, they kidded one another good-naturedly. Good scores were expected of them, and bad scores were accounted for by bad luck or temporary lapses of form. When a follower

threatened to better his position, the remarks took quite a different form. The boys shouted at him that he was lucky, that he was "bowling over his head." The effort was made to persuade him that he should not be bowling as well as he was, that a good performance was abnormal for him. This type of verbal attack was very important in keeping the members "in their places."[22]

In bowling, as in other activities, Whyte found it was necessary not only for the leader to win, but for the follower to lose in order for both to continue as members of the group.

Today, more than three decades after its publication, *Street Corner Society* retains an immediacy and ethnographic freshness which should make it mandatory reading for all students of urban and complex societies.

Interactionism

By far the most fascinating response to the lifeless empiricism of the later Chicago School has come from Erving Goffman's microstudies of human interaction. Earlier sociologists recognized the importance of focusing upon the content and process of individual behavior,[23] but none approached the brilliance brought by Goffman to the study of microsociology. In *The Presentation of Self in Everyday Life* (1956), Goffman defined and analyzed human interaction in terms of dramaturgical metaphor. Human behavior, he suggested, can be viewed as a series of performances of parts, played singly or in teams, the character of which varies according to the nature of the audience, the context or region of the performance, and of course the line being put forward.

Goffman's work is much too broad and variegated to discuss in detail here. However, as Gerald Berreman says in a personal communication, "to consider oneself literate in contemporary social science one must be familiar with the work of Erving Goffman." The interested student is strongly encouraged to refer to Goffman's own works[24] and, for an example of the applicability of a Goffman-esque perspective to ethnographic work, to Berreman's monograph *Behind Many Masks.*[25]

The use of dramaturgical analogy to understand human behavior is not new; indeed, the word "person" has its root in the Latin *persona,* meaning "mask." In acting our parts as social beings, we inevitably assume roles the content of which is largely culturally ascribed and thus somewhat beyond control if, for example, one wishes to avoid losing face for an incompetent performance of the role he performs in daily life. We often find ourselves in situations in which we behave contrary to true inclination in order to avoid being thought unlearned. One may not order a certain wine in an exclusive restaurant for fear of looking foolish by mispronouncing its name— or one may take a proffered sip of a California wine of recent vintage so as not to appear ignorant of established ritual, rather than say to the wine steward, "You and I both know that California wines are highly consistent in their quality; and we both know that this particular popular wine is prepared, bottled, and sealed in such a fashion that there is not the slightest chance that it has gone bad."

In his story "Shooting an Elephant," George Orwell records how a crowd of Burmese pressed him inexorably to shoot an elephant that had run wild while in heat and killed a coolie but that had calmed down by the time Orwell arrived. The crowd, excited by the prospect of the kill, waited for him to act, as the sole representative of the British Empire on the scene. To return to town after having marched out with an elephant gun and "two thousand at least" Burmese would have invited ridicule. Slowly and with great reluctance Orwell lay on the ground, positioned himself, and fired his rounds. Afterward, he reports,

> there were endless discussions about the shooting of the
> elephant. The owner was furious, but he was only an Indian
> and could do nothing. Besides, legally I had done the right
> thing, for a mad elephant has to be killed, like a mad dog, if its
> owner fails to control it. Among the Europeans opinion was
> divided. The older men said I was right, the younger men said
> it was a damn shame to shoot an elephant for killing a coolie,
> because an elephant was worth more than any damn Coringhee
> coolie. And afterwards, I was very glad that the coolie had been
> killed; it put me legally in the right and it gave me a sufficient
> pretext for shooting the elephant. I often wondered whether
> any of the others grasped that I had done it solely to avoid
> looking a fool.[26]

A framework particularly relevant to the study of human interaction is Goffman's division between *front* and *back* regions. In single or group performances before an "audience," we characteristically distinguish between two regions: one where the performance is given, the front region; and the other, in which performers can relax beyond sight or hearing of the audience, secure in the knowledge that they do not have to keep up role appearances. In restaurants a rigid division is generally made between the front region of the dining room and the back, where the food, and the performance, is prepared. Often the conditions under which food is cooked and the casualness of the back region directly contradict the performance under way in the front. Segregation of the two areas is essential if customers are not to be repulsed and the restaurant is to remain in business.

Different cultures may define frontstage and backstage dimensions differently. I remember vividly a dinner in a newly opened Japanese restaurant in San Francisco a number of years ago. The grace of the staff and the location and furnishings of the restaurant suggested that it had been designed for a clientele of gourmets. Only the enormous roach unveiled in the platter of rice when the waitress removed its cover contradicted the performance. Quickly and deftly she brushed the roach to the floor, put the platter back on the table, and returned to the kitchen to bring the rest of our dinner. My companions sat in disbelief as she continued to serve us, until one finally demanded a new plate of rice. Her response was to carry the plate into the kitchen and probably, after an appropriate interlude, simply return it. Her "mistake" in performance lay in so casually accepting the roach's presence—as her American counterpart might have done in the kitchen but not in the dining room.

The value of Goffman's work to urban anthropologists lies primarily in his emphasis upon the subtle observation of role playing in human interaction. As we shall see, urbanites especially are constantly called upon to present fragmentary aspects of themselves to strangers or others who know them only as inhabitants of discrete occupational or ethnic categories. By carefully attending to role expectations and the leeway accorded to role performances, the researcher can develop an understanding of the roots of urban social structure.

URBAN ANTHROPOLOGY

Although the division of human populations into those most suitable for either anthropological or sociological study may lack theoretical justification, the history of the two fields has given it a certain legitimacy. During the last decades of the nineteenth century both anthropology and sociology, together with most of today's social sciences, were engaged in the process of defining their proper domains. The concerns of the earliest sociologists and anthropologists were often broad, evidenced by such works as sociologist Emile Durkheim's *Elementary Forms of the Religious Life,* dealing with religion among Australian aborigines, and anthropologist Edward M. Tylor's observations of Londoners.[27]

Curiously, what seems to have given greatest impetus to the geographical separation of the two fields is anthropology's concern with the variety of human cultures and societies. Tylor's early conception of culture as "that complex whole which includes knowledge, belief, art, law, morals, custom, and any other capabilities and habits acquired by man as a member of society" provided a definition that meshed easily with the concerns of early anthropologists in reconstructing the history of human culture.[28] In tracing the evolution of societies, anthropologists sought information on the presence and absence of specific culture traits among the world's peoples. In the process, a non-Western focus came to dominate debates over the plausibility and significance of their reconstructions. At first most of these theoretical controversies were grounded in the reports of travelers, missionaries, and others who had lived among non-Western peoples. In time, the evolutionist's preoccupation with the diversity of human customs gave rise to a new generation of anthropologists more concerned with discovering and recording the plasticity of human behavior than with reconstructing uncertain culture histories. When these anthropologists went "to the field" to record and describe, they turned not to the peasants and urbanites of Europe's nation-states, but to non-Western populations, and especially to the systematic description of the so-called primitive peoples who had played so prominent a role in the speculations of European anthropologists and philosophers about the nature of man.

As anthropologists directed themselves toward primitives, so, too, did sociologists carve out a niche with an implicit evolutionary base: the study of modern European societies. So strong was social evolutionary thought during the formative period of anthropology and sociology that another discipline, folklore, nearly succeeded in carving a wedge between the two. For a time it seemed that anthropology was destined to become the study of primitives, sociology the study of civilized peoples, and folklore the study of peasants. The folklorist Arnold van Gennep devoted much of his life to delineating this field as the study of the customs "of peasants and rural life, and their remains in industrial and urban milieux."[29] Failure to achieve his aim was not the result of lack of research, in which he was quite prolific. He neglected to produce a body of student-disciples who could occupy academic positions and propagate his notion of folklore's proper scope. Consequently the natural terrain of the folklorist was gradually consumed, in non-Western regions by anthropological research in peasant communities, and in the West by "rural sociology."

Until recently, few anthropologists were disturbed by relegation of their field to the study of non-Western communities. Not only was there no shortage of research opportunities, there seemed too much research to be done. In America, a relative handful of anthropologists operating from Chicago, Berkeley, Columbia, and a few other schools were confronted with the major task of recording entire cultures from the recollections of aged American Indians who could still remember when their community traditions had not been radically altered by contact with whites. For European anthropologists the colonial empires seemed to promise inexhaustible research vistas, and the need for recording rapidly vanishing life ways did not seem so pressing. Except, perhaps, for the difficulty of obtaining funds for research projects, it was a golden age for anthropologists.

Only the exhaustion of research opportunities with American Indians—or at least a sense of increasingly diminished returns—and the outbreak of World War II led American anthropologists increasingly to study complex societies. Margaret Mead wrote of wartime America in *And Keep Your Powder Dry*; and as part of the American war effort Ruth Benedict produced a monograph of Japanese culture, *The Chrysanthemum and the Sword,* based on information gleaned from interviews with interned Japanese-Americans and from published material about Japan. After the war, Hortense Powdermaker continued research for *Hollywood, the Dream Factory,* which turned anthropological techniques toward American popular culture and its heros. "My field techniques," she explained,

> had some similarities to and some differences from those I had used on an island in the Southwest Pacific and elsewhere. As in other communities, I had to establish and maintain the same role: that of a detached scientist . . . I took the inhabitants in Hollywood and in the South Seas seriously, and this was pleasing to both. To me the handsome stars with their swimming-pool homes were no more glamorous than were the South Sea aborigines exotic. All, whether ex-cannibal chiefs, magicians, front-office executives, or directors, were human beings working and living in a certain way, which I was interested in analyzing.[30]

Still, work in complex and especially in Western societies generally remained a sideline for anthropologists.

World War II and its aftermath accelerated the dismantling of the great colonial empires. For Western anthropologists the transfer of governments from colonial administrations to elites of the new nations had little effect initially. Most were able to continue their work as before, although not, perhaps, with the same freedom of movement and sense of security of the colonial period. Gradually, however, decolonization has begun to shift the attitude toward anthropologists on the part of rulers of these newly independent nations. Most important, those in power in the "third world" have come to view foreign scholars in general as a potential threat to the impressions of life in their nations that they, the elites, wish to foster abroad. For anthropologists an additional problem has arisen. As significant numbers of elites began to travel to the West for university education and, more recently, as universities have begun to proliferate throughout the third world, these elites have discovered a truth that has irritated them: anthropologists study "primitives" and sociologists study "civilized" peoples. Some have come to regard the presence of an anthropologist in their country—unless he is studying people the elites themselves consider primitive—something of an insult. Consequently, while sociologists have often gained ready acceptance, those trained in the study of non-Western populations have sometimes found themselves in disfavor or have been forced to pass as sociologists.

Short of becoming "house" anthropologists, virtually spokesmen for official government positions, anthropologists can do little about the natural desire of some ruling groups to restrict research and distort conclusions in their favor. But, in the face of increasing disenchantment of much of the world at being thought "primitive," anthropologists can only blame themselves. However logical our concentration upon primitive and peasant populations may once have been, the violation of our own requirement that the study of human behavior and social organization must be grounded in all human societies now returns to haunt us at a time when our primitive constituency is vanishing. If anthropology is not to become little more than a modern version of classics, we must make it clear to all, *especially to those we study,* that anthropology never really was devoted to the study of primitive peoples, but that anthropologists were forced as much by necessity as by desire to try to describe as best they could many soon-to-be-extinct cultures.

Anthropological Research Methods:
Participant-Observation and Holism

From long concern with the preservation and analysis of alien cultures came the hallmarks of anthropological methodology: *participant-observation* and *holism*. True ethnographic fieldwork demands that the researcher live among the people he studies and participate as fully as possible in their lives. Participant-observation, though it can yield a detailed day-to-day understanding of a society, is not an easy task. Properly undertaken it requires great effort on the part of the ethnographer—to learn the language and the details of customary behavior of his new people, for example. After months at the very least of feeling marginal and alien, he gradually begins to learn how to behave like those of the group he is studying. His understanding will never be that of a native, but in time the confusion he first experienced will fade as the internal logic of the culture becomes clear.

The need once felt by anthropologists to record as much as possible of the life ways of a group under study led to holism, or the attempt to study each society in its entirety. Although this perspective emerged at first in ethnographic fieldwork, it quickly became a basic tenet of anthropological theory. Bronislaw Malinowski, often credited with the development of long-term ethnographic fieldwork, returned from the Trobriand Islands of Melanesia (where he had been forced to live out World War I) with a wealth of detail concerning Trobriand traditions. With reflection, Malinowski realized that adequate explanation of a Trobriand custom's existence had to be based on the function it performed, in providing a livelihood for the Islanders or in synthesizing their understanding of their lives.[31] He and other "functionalists" and "structural-functionalists" felt that little could be gained by studying isolated culture traits. What is the point of recording that the bow and arrow is found among African bushmen and American children, if the functions of the instrument for providing food in the former instance and as a plaything in the latter are not emphasized? And, as Benedict complained, early "armchair" anthropologists tended to illustrate their arguments by "bits of behaviour selected indiscriminately from the most different cultures . . . the discussion builds up a kind of mechanical Frankenstein's monster with a right eye from Fiji, a left from Europe, one leg from Tierra del Fuego, and one from Tahiti, and all the fingers and toes from still different regions."[32]

Functionalism gave anthropologists additional theoretical incentive to attend to the whole of the cultures they studied in search of clues that might provide understanding of seemingly unrelated traditions and even unlock entire world views. Taken together, participant-observation and holism have come to define the anthropological perspective and have enabled anthropologists to provide vivid and insightful ethnographies of the world's peoples.

The Anthropology of Urban and Complex Societies

It is a commonplace that the world has grown smaller, but in a very real sense it is true. Regular daily flights around the world make it possible to reach almost any place on earth from any other in a day or two. American and British popular songs can be heard, and pirated records and tapes bought, in Hong Kong, Bangkok, and Singapore almost as soon as they are released in the West. When Neil Armstrong first set foot on the moon, hundreds of millions of people—some of whose parents may have been informants to anthropologists investigating primitive or peasant cultures—followed the landing with the same fascination shown by Americans.

So fast and far-reaching have been changes in the past several decades that it is impossible to find any population that has not been profoundly touched by them. Indeed, the changes have come so quickly that the "ground rules" of anthropological research have changed nearly overnight. No longer is it possible to treat communities as isolated entities, as everywhere the impact of the outside has become too great to ignore. Anthropologists working in peasant communities now find significant numbers of their villagers absent working in cities or even other countries. When these migrants return they bring with them city goods and city ways.

During the 1950's and 1960's, anthropologists began to yield increasingly to the realities of modern life and communication and to recognize the crucial role that cities have come to play in today's world. In consequence, the peculiar deviation of the field's past, away from a total view of humanity, has begun to be rectified; and "urban anthropology"—or, as it is often called, the "anthropology of complex societies"—has been added to the existing anthropological literature on primitives and peasants. More and more anthropologists have turned to research in Western societies, in efforts to study aspects of their own traditions with some of the intensity once reserved for alien peoples.

Most anthropological work in the future will undoubtedly be undertaken in urban and complex societies. Yet, important as these "new" research arenas have become, they still retain in the minds of many anthropologists something of a questionable and "pop" status. Many British social anthropologists have engaged in urban work since World War II, and the study of complex societies has long been an important part of British African research. But urban anthropology seems to have crept up gradually and almost unnoticed in America, only to spring upon the scene in the late 1960's and early 1970's. Almost any American-trained urban anthropologist will reveal that he is an urban anthropologist self-taught. Even just a decade ago, when I was a graduate student at Berkeley, structured seminars or courses in urban anthropology were not available. Today courses proliferate in North American universities, and many anthropologists who began their careers studying peasant or tribal groups now consider themselves "urban anthropologists."

Born of a holistic tradition of participant-observation forged in tribal and village societies, what becomes of the anthropologist in the city and in complex societies? Is there, indeed, a role for him in an urban setting? If so, what is it?

Many anthropologists attracted to urban research by virtue of the current growth of interest in urban problems have chosen to emphasize the participant-observation approach, limiting the scope of their studies to sectors of the city inhabited by individuals with whom they have come in direct contact. This approach, which can best be seen as an attempt to analyze city life on a tribal level, is exemplified by such works as Elliot Liebow's excellent study of the life style of black street-corner men in Washington, D.C., *Tally's Corner*,[33] and Whyte's *Street Corner Society*;[34] and by the concern with social networks in the work of J. Clyde Mitchell and other social anthropologists.[35] There is an even more profound extension of the participant-observation formula in city life in the work of Oscar Lewis, who chose to concentrate upon individual and family perspectives of lives lived in urban poverty and in so doing entered the realm of biographical narrative.[36] Excellent as many of these studies are, the vividness of their portrayals, which comes from almost total reliance upon transplanting the participant-observation technique to the city, is gained at cost of holistic perspective. Emphasis on the "tribe," or family, has given us only a fragment, albeit an engrossing one, of the urban mosaic.

But the sacrifice of holistic perspective has not been total. Anthropologist W. Lloyd Warner brought to his dissection of an

American city in the early 1930's the perspective of a recent sojourn among Australian aborigines.[37] His approach combined an emphasis upon understanding the reality of social interaction as seen in the minds of the city's inhabitants with a concern for grasping the reality of the city as a whole. For him, the parameters of study were not limited by the rigors of participant-observation, but were extended to include all he had gained that was relevant to the problem at hand.

Studies of urban and complex societies included today under the rubric "urban anthropology" need not be undertaken at sacrifice to either of the field's major tenets, but may be built firmly upon both, taking cognizance of the necessary modifications that are exigencies of urban work. Anthropologists, especially in dealing with literate urban populations, must extend the scope of their concerns beyond the level of oral utterance and develop some of the skills of the social historian and analyst of current affairs. Essential to urban work is the utilization of written materials including census studies, newspapers, and polemical texts—as well as the realization that they are at least as important, as an introduction into the preoccupations and shared beliefs of a people, as information gained from an informant. But the urban anthropologist, especially if he is working in a society with a long history of literacy, must not only take written materials into account, he must still learn the language of the group and enter into the society as fully as possible in order to gain the vivid dimension of emotional understanding of the lives and interactions of its members.

The very scale of a city, with its diverse peoples and life ways, almost precludes total comprehension; obviously, a concession to its immensity must be made. If this concession is not to be at the expense of methodology, then it must be one of limitation of scope. Anthropologists, like all others approaching urban aggregations, must yield to the immensity of the world before them and reduce their focus to some degree. Thus, while one may not limit himself to the study of a single urban tribe, he must limit himself to a particular topic, whether it be economic, religious, or social, that concerns the city's people.

Although an extensive literature has been amassed in the anthropological study of urban and complex societies, it has not yet been systematically organized. The problem of bringing order, hence legitimacy, to the area is complicated by the fact that much valuable work on urban forms has been done by sociologists, economists, geographers, political scientists, and historians. Discipline boundaries in urban work have sometimes become so permeable as to have disappeared altogether. So much valuable work has been done by nonanthropologists on Western and non-Western cities and their inhabitants that past thoughts of what should properly constitute the subject matter and methods of anthropologists seem now to be of a different order. Even a definition of urban anthropology as "what urban anthropologists do" will not suffice; it is not only what they do that counts, but what *interests* them in the performance of these duties.

But urban anthropology is not nearly so fragmented as it sometimes seems. Most of the research done by individuals who call themselves urban anthropologists and most of the work of nonanthropologists that they consider relevant to their own—which together comprise urban anthropology—has quite clearly, and quite naturally, evolved from concerns common to more traditional anthropological work in smaller-scale societies. Probably the most consistent focus of anthropologists throughout the discipline's history has been on the cross-cultural study of kinship and marriage customs. From the earliest anthropological writings of Bachofen, Morgan, and Tylor up to those of the present, investigation of systems of marriage, descent, and postmarital residence have served as basic points of ethnographic and ethnological orientation.[38] Indeed, many university students have probably left introductory anthropology courses convinced that anthropology *is* the study of kinship.

Of almost equal importance to the growth of the field has been the study of the adaptation and adjustment of individuals to the requirements of their culture, a concern best reflected in the work of Mead, Benedict, Kardiner, and DuBois.[39] And, coupled with the concern with kinship has been the study of social organization, which, in the most primitive societies, is largely regulated through kinship. In larger, more complex, societies, however, the maintenance of social order requires elaboration of extrakin systems of social organization based upon allocation of position through either birth-ascribed or achieved criteria. Finally, the question of how best to describe particular cultures so as to compare them has always been at the core of anthropological debate.

Urban work has not moved anthropologists to different theoretical and methodological realms, but has reflected and reworked those which already existed. The continuity between traditional anthropology and the anthropology of urban and complex societies is the basis of this text, which will demonstrate how traditional anthropological topics (such as kinship, the place of the individual in society, the acculturative impact of contact between cultures, and the way in which accurate descriptive ethnographies amenable to cross-cultural comparison can best be achieved) have been transplanted to urban research settings. Only anthropology's concern with motivations for rural-urban migration is truly peculiar to *urban* anthropology; and even here, study of the effect of migration upon traditional societies is a part of anthropology's long concern with contact between different cultures and with acculturation. Even the problem of scale and how ethnographers can cope with large populations is merely a compounding of a dilemma that anthropologists have always faced: how accurately do their informants portray the culture as a whole?

Urban anthropology is an exciting field—as much to the novice as to the professional—and one as productive of insight into the human condition as any other. Although many of its concerns remain within the tradition of past anthropological research, urban anthropology is not merely an extension of the study of primitive and peasant societies. As we shall see, urban life can have profound and far-reaching influences upon traditional societies, and urban anthropology has already begun to effect our thinking about the meaning and utility of such basic anthropological concepts as "culture" and "society."

Anthropologists have long argued that we can understand what it is to be human only by observing mankind wherever he is found. It is appropriate that anthropologists, themselves products of urban traditions, have finally discovered that urbanites are equally as exciting and important to study as were primitive peoples in days gone by.

⊛ NOTES

1. Tönnies (1963) saw the feudal, *gemeinschaft* society as characterized by intimate interpersonal relations and collective activity, in contrast to the impersonal, contractual bonds of the capitalist or *gesellschaft* society.
2. Durkheim (1951), in his classic study *Suicide*, suggested anomic suicide as one of his major etiological types, such suicides being characteristic of those who live in isolated, personal worlds, having lost touch with society's influence.
3. Weber 1958.

4. Wirth 1938:12-13.
5. See Hauser 1965.
6. Lewis 1965a:496-497.
7. Wirth 1956:173-174, quoted in Hauser 1965:506-507.
8. Duncan and Duncan 1957:16, 18.
9. For a brief introduction to the literature of the Chicago School, see Park and Burgess 1925 and Burgess and Bogue 1967.
10. See West 1945; Gallagher 1961; Vidich and Bensman 1968.
11. See Ware 1935; Whyte 1943; Gans 1962; Kornblum 1974.
12. Ware 1935:429.
13. Ware 1935:431.
14. Ware 1935:432.
15. Ware 1935:433.
16. Ware 1935:432-433.
17. Whyte 1943:280.
18. Whyte 1943:291.
19. Whyte found that one of the most relevant contrasts between the two was that "both the college boy and the corner boy want to get ahead. The difference between them is that the college boy either does not tie himself to a group of close friends or else is willing to sacrifice his friendship with those who do not advance as fast as he does. The corner boy is tied to his group by a network of reciprocal obligations from which he is either unwilling or unable to break away" (1943:107).
20. Whyte 1943:21.
21. Whyte 1943:23.
22. Whyte 1943:24.
23. See especially Mead 1934 and Cooley 1902.
24. Goffman 1959, 1961, 1971, 1973a, 1973b.
25. Berreman 1962.
26. Orwell 1973:195.
27. See Lowie 1937:69.
28. Tylor 1874, vol. 1:1.
29. van Gennep 1924:29.
30. Powdermaker 1950:3-4.
31. See Malinowski 1922, 1944.
32. Benedict 1959:49.
33. Liebow 1967.
34. Whyte 1943.
35. Mitchell 1969.
36. Lewis 1961, 1965b.
37. Warner 1963.
38. Bachofen 1861; Morgan 1870; Tylor 1889.
39. Mead 1928; Benedict 1959; Kardiner 1939; DuBois 1944.

◉ REFERENCES

Bachofen, J. J.
   1861   Das mutterrecht. Basel: Benno Schwabe.
Benedict, Ruth
   1946   The chrysanthemum and the sword: Patterns of Japanese culture. New York: Houghton Mifflin.
   1959   Patterns of culture. Boston: Houghton Mifflin. (Original 1934.)
Berreman, Gerald D.
   1962   Behind many masks: Ethnography and impression management in a Himalayan village. Ithaca, N.Y.: Society for Applied Anthropology, monograph 4. Reprinted in G. D. Berreman, Hindus of the Himalayas. Berkeley: University of California Press, 1972.
Blair, Eric [pseud. George Orwell]
   1973   Shooting an elephant. Reprinted in W. G. Bennis et al., eds., Interpersonal dynamics. Homewood, Ill.: Dorsey Press.
Burgess, Ernest W., and Donald J. Bogue, eds.
   1967   Urban sociology. Chicago: University of Chicago Press.
Cooley, Charles H.
   1902   Human nature and the social order. New York: Charles Scribner's Sons.
Davis, Fred
   1973   The cabdriver and his fare: Facets of a fleeting relationship. Reprinted in W. G. Bennis et al., eds., Interpersonal dynamics. Homewood, Ill.: Dorsey Press.
Du Bois, Cora
   1944   The people of Alor: A social-psychological study of an East Indian island. Minneapolis: University of Minnesota.
Duncan, Beverly
   1967   Variables in urban morphology. In E. W. Burgess and D. J. Bogue, eds., Urban sociology. Chicago: University of Chicago Press.
Duncan, Otis Dudley
   1959   Human ecology and population studies. In P. Hauser and O. D. Duncan, eds., The study of population. Chicago: University of Chicago Press.
   1961   From social system to ecosystem. Sociological Inquiry 31:140-149.
Duncan, Otis Dudley, and Beverly Duncan
   1957   The Negro population of Chicago: A study of residential succession. Chicago: University of Chicago Press.
Durkheim, Emile
   1947   The elementary forms of the religious life. Glencoe, Ill.: The Free Press. (Original English trans. 1915.)
   1951   Suicide. Glencoe, Ill.: Free Press. (Original 1897.)
Gallagher, Art, Jr.
   1961   Plainville fifteen years later. New York: Columbia University Press.
Gans, Herbert J.
   1962   The urban villagers: Group and class in the life of Italian-Americans. New York: Free Press.

Goffman, Erving
    1959   The presentation of self in everyday life. New York: Doubleday Anchor. (Original 1956.)
    1961   Asylums: Essays on the social situation of mental patients and other inmates. New York: Doubleday Anchor.
    1971   Normal appearances. In E. Goffman, Relations in public. New York: Harper Colophon.
    1973a   On face-work: An analysis of ritual elements in social interaction. Reprinted in W. G. Bennis et al., eds., Interpersonal dynamics. Homewood, Ill.: Dorsey Press.
    1973b   On cooling the mark out. Reprinted in W. G. Bennis et al., eds., Interpersonal dynamics. Homewood, Illinois: Dorsey Press.

Hauser, Philip M.
    1965   Observations on the urban-folk and urban-rural dichotomies as forms of Western ethnocentrism. In P. M. Hauser and L. F. Schnore, eds., The study of urbanization. New York: John Wiley and Sons.

Hughes, Everett C.
    1943   French Canada in transition. Chicago: University of Chicago Press.

Kardiner, Abram
    1939   The individual and his society. New York: Columbia University Press.

Kornblum, William
    1974   Blue collar community. Chicago: University of Chicago Press.

Lewis, Oscar
    1961   The children of Sanchez. New York: Random House.
    1965a   Further observations on the folk-urban continuum and urbanization with special reference to Mexico City. In P. M. Hauser and L. F. Schnore, eds., The study of urbanization. New York: John Wiley and Sons.
    1965b   La vida. New York: Random House.

Liebow, Elliot
    1967   Tally's corner: A study of Negro streetcorner men. Boston: Little, Brown.

Lowie, Robert
    1937   The history of ethnological theory. New York: Holt, Rinehart, and Winston.

McKenzie, R. D.
    1925   The ecological approach to the study of the human community. In R. E. Park and E. W. Burgess, eds., The city. Chicago: University of Chicago Press.

Malinowski, Bronislaw
    1922   Argonauts of the western Pacific. New York: Dutton.
    1944   A scientific theory of culture. Chapel Hill: University of North Carolina Press.

Mead, George Herbert
    1934   Mind, self and society. Chicago: University of Chicago Press.

Mead, Margaret
    1928   Coming of age in Samoa. New York: Morrow.
    1942   And keep your powder dry: An anthropologist looks at America. New York: Morrow.

Mitchell, J. Clyde, ed.
1969   Social networks in urban situations: Analyses of personal relation-
        ships in Central African towns. Manchester: Manchester University
        Press.
Morgan, Lewis Henry
1870   Systems of consanguinity and affinity of the human family. Wash-
        ington: Smithsonian Institution.
Orwell, George. See, Eric Blair
Park, Robert E., and E. W. Burgess, eds.
1925   The city. Chicago: University of Chicago Press.
Powdermaker, Hortense
1950   Hollywood, the dream factory: An anthropologist looks at the
        movie-makers. New York: Harper and Row.
Steffans, Lincoln
1957   The shame of the cities. New York: Hill and Wang. (Original 1904.)
Thrasher, Frederic M.
1963   The gang. Abridged ed. Chicago: University of Chicago Press (Original
        1927.)
Tönnies, Ferdinand
1963   Community and society. C. P. Loomis, trans. and ed. New York:
        Harper and Row. (Original 1887.)
Tylor, Edward B.
1874   Primitive culture: Researches into the development of mythology,
        philosophy, religion, language, art, and custom (2 vols.). Boston:
        Estes and Lauriat. (Original 1871.)
1889   On a method of investigating the development of institutions: Applies
        to the laws of marriage and descent. Journal of the Royal Anthro-
        pological Institute of Great Britain and Ireland 18:245-272.
Van Gennep, Arnold
1924   Le folklore: Croyances et coûtumes populaires françaises. Paris:
        Stock.
Vidich, Arthur J., and Joseph Bensman
1968   Small town in mass society. Princeton: Princeton University Press.
Ware, Carolyn
1935   Greenwich Village, 1920-1930. New York: Harper and Row.
Warner, W. Lloyd, et al.
1963   Yankee City. Abridged ed. New Haven: Yale University Press.
Weber, Max
1958   The city. New York: Free Press. (Original 1921.)
West, James. See Withers, Carl
Whyte, William Foote
1943   Street corner society. Chicago: University of Chicago Press.
Wirth, Louis
1928   The ghetto. Chicago: University of Chicago Press.
1938   Urbanism as a way of life. American Journal of Sociology 44:1-24.
1956   Community life and social policy. Chicago: University of Chicago
        Press.
Withers, Carl [pseud. James West]
1945   Plainville, U.S.A. New York: Columbia University Press.

The Origin and Evolution of Cities

2 The clustering of men into cities is a relatively recent phenomenon. Although humans have inhabited the earth for over a million years, cities only began to appear about 5,000 or 6,000 years ago. The earliest cities were tiny by today's standards—the population of the first Sumerian cities seems to have ranged from 7,000 to 12,000, and Ur probably had no more than 25,000 people within its walls during the third millennium B.C.[1] Many inhabitants of these cities were full or part-time farmers who resided in the city itself or at its periphery but gained their living through working outlying fields.

Initially, cities were scarcely larger than the farming villages that preceded them. What differentiated cities from villages was the presence of monumental religiogovernmental buildings, of writing, and of artisans, merchants, officials, and priests who were not directly involved in food-producing activities.

Two issues, especially, have concerned researchers of early urban forms: (1) What ecological and cultural factors led men to cluster in permanent settlements and eventually develop larger, internally differentiated communities, or cities? (2) Was the idea of the city invented once or twice or more and diffused elsewhere, or did cities develop independently in most or all ancient urban centers?

THE DEVELOPMENT OF EARLY CITIES

With the possible exception of some early coastal Peruvian fishing settlements that resembled cities, co-residence of sufficiently large populations to justify the designation "urban" seems to have required the presence of agriculture. Ethnographic and archaeological evidence indicates that plants have everywhere been at least as important a source of energy as meat in the diets of hunters. These plants, however, grew wild and were gathered, rather than planted by humans. Undoubtedly, this was not because humans were ignorant of the fact that planted seeds would produce food, but because nomadic conditions did not favor agriculture. Even if nomads wandered in the same territory and could return regularly to their fields, the women of the group could still glean an equal amount of food to what might be grown. Since it appears that the lives of hunters and gatherers were far from the quick and brutal existences that many civilized peoples have imagined—indeed, hunters were generally quite healthy and leisured, as the collection of food required only a three-hour day, or a twenty-one-hour week[2]—it is evident that the development of agriculture required some inducement for humans to remove cereal grains from their natural environment and prepare and tend fields.

Several hypotheses have been advanced to explain why humans first shifted from gathering to producing edible plants. It can probably be assumed that the transition was made in response to environmental and population pressures which demanded the development of greater food supplies from a limited territory than was possible through hunting. In Mesopotamia the shift to agriculture appears first to have occurred among groups that inhabited the hilly flanks of the Fertile Crescent, where wheat, barley, and oats grew naturally and were later transplanted to the much richer, and easier to farm, alluvial soils of the floodplains.[3]

Whether the so-called food-producing revolution began in upland areas or was the result of the confinement of groups to river banks in arid regions, the development of agriculture provided the potential for concentration of much larger populations than had theretofore been possible.[4] Equally important, although agriculture did not reduce the total amount of time spent in productive activity over that expended by hunters, it made storage of food easier and freed farmers from actual farming during much of the year. In Mesoamerica, the planting of corn and protecting of fields with fences against cattle (which only became a problem after the Spanish conquest) required some 143 to 161 man-days, while recent calculations from Mesopotamia suggest that a maximum of 249 man-days a year of agricultural labor was needed to provide for each family unit.[5] Just as agriculture permitted the production and storage of food surpluses, the limited period required for productive labor made it possible for agricultural peoples to devote large amounts of time to such communal activities as the building of temples and other public buildings or warfare.

In early agricultural populations, both the potential for production of food surpluses that could support a nonproductive urban population and annual blocks of time for collective labor were available. But farmers do not tend to produce a surplus unless there is a demand for it, nor do they or any other segment of a population willingly devote leisure time to difficult labor or warfare without strong inducements to do so.[6] It is clear that while agriculture and a favorable environment are prerequisites of city development, something more is needed. As Sjoberg has enumerated them, the requirements for the emergence of cities are: (1) a favorable ecological base, (2) a relatively advanced agricultural and nonagricultural technology, and (3) *a complex social organization with a well-developed power structure.*[7] The latter was especially important to the formation of cities and to the later emergence of states: in order for the city to exist at all peasants had to be made to pay taxes or tribute. Since the early city produced little that could be exchanged for surplus production or peasant labor, peasants had to be persuaded to contribute time and labor to its support.

In the earliest cities religion provided the focal point for the collection and redistribution of peasant tribute, and cities themselves developed around temples devoted to the city-god and other deities. Priests vested with the authority of gods were undoubtedly able to exact labor and payments to the temple with a minimum of protest from believing peasants. The position of the priests was reinforced by ecological instability in both Mesopotamia and Mesoamerica. By directing cult activity toward assuring crop and animal fertility and the regularity of seasons, priests proclaimed control over the source of peasants' greatest anxieties.[8] Early temples typically had large granaries located within their grounds, and the earliest writing of temple scribes was concerned not with philosophical or religious questions but with the more mundane keeping of temple accounts. In some Mesopotamian cities fishermen also offered a substantial share of their catch to the city temple. Records tell of fish offerings so large that they were obviously destined for others beyond the group of priests and their retainers. Evidently, the temples served both to stimulate and to redistribute the surplus of farmers, fishermen, and often herders as well.[9]

Acquisition of surplus food by religious practitioners also permitted them to support artisans who worked on the temples and homes of the upper class and produced the world's earliest consumer goods. Pottery, monumental art work, and implements made of iron, copper, and bronze were made for public buildings and the personal use of priestly and civil elites. Merchants, too, became permanent community fixtures as peasant surplus production provided the underpinning for stable systems of trade. With the ability to support greater numbers of craftsmen, the division of labor became progressively more marked. Specialized subdivisions of boat and transport (wheeled carts) carpenters appeared. Access to such innovations as carts, however, was quite limited; their widespread use as a labor-saving device, for example, seems to have come over a thousand years after they were first introduced for religious and military purposes.[10]

Life for the elites seems to have been quite leisurely. Early texts from the first dynasty of Ur provide evidence that rulers enjoyed the services of large retinues of servants: gatekeepers, cooks, cupbearers, male and female slaves, harem officials, and so on.[11] As their wealth grew, religion alone proved insufficient to protect them from periodic peasant resistance and the continual threat of semi-nomadic groups at the edges of the city's hinterlands. Nor, of course, was religious belief sufficient to thwart invasions launched from neighboring cities whose citizens and peasants had their own gods.

The increase in agricultural production which occurred as farmers transplanted grains from hillsides to lowland valleys and eventually to irrigated areas carried with it two important consequences. (1) Increased production and a sedentary life encouraged absolute population growth. (2) The shift from uplands to low-lying valleys that could be irrigated meant that the total area of desirable arable land in any given region was greatly restricted, since land suited for irrigation was limited to lowland river areas and preferably to the river's delta. In effect, population increased as new and more productive agricultural techniques greatly reduced the size of areas most suitable for habitation. In the circumscribed valley regions in which the earliest cities developed, the gradual filling up of the best agricultural land extended the hinterlands of riverine cities to the point where neighboring peoples came into direct competition for land. Thus, even before irrigation systems were well developed in the extensive canal pattern which later came to dominate in what Karl Wittfogel calls "hydraulic societies,"[12] warfare over land had become commonplace among cities. For the victor the spoils included not only the right to alienate certain parcels of land, but, increasingly, political control over conquered peoples and the receipt of tribute that could only be paid by greater productive efforts on the part of the vanquished. Victorious elites gained the labor of those they had defeated, both directly as slaves and indirectly as tributaries.[13]

The spoils of war and the need to protect the city inevitably enhanced the position of warriors. Everywhere the power of the priestly elite was at first shared with, and later lost to, a new elite that owed its position to the need to defend the city. The priests remained in their religious positions, where they provided the rationale for the city's integrity and thus justification for military excursions. In the periods of militaristic polities during the third millinium B.C. in Mesopotamia and about 1,200 years ago in central Mexico, warrior-kings first emerged to lead these city-states. At first kings seem to have been regarded as great men but not gods. The temptation to fuse the power of the military with the respect owed to a god, however, was irresistible. Divine warrior-kings arose to rule over subjects who were considered absolutely removed from them by their status as human commoners. The inevitability of the transition of power from priest to warrior to divine king is evident in that it was not only common to the early Near Eastern states—the pharaohs of Egypt providing a prototype for divine kingship—and the ancient and modern societies of India, Southeast Asia, China, and Japan, but was also developed independently in Mesoamerica. There Maya priests first lost prominence to their own warriors and then were supplanted altogether by an Aztec empire whose later rulers enjoyed a "divinity" and position above that ever accorded European kings.[14]

THE DIFFUSION OF URBAN LIFE

About 3,000 B.C., cities began to appear outside the Fertile Crescent of the Tigris-Euphrates region. The earliest of these non-Mesopotamian cities arose in the Nile Valley of Egypt, where the local population had long been settled in small agricultural villages. Egypt quickly developed a succession of strong states led by god-kings known as pharaohs, who were both political heads of state and the chief religious leaders. The cities contained impressive public and religious buildings, large communities of priests and scribes who added significantly to the mathematical and calendrical knowledge of the day, and artisans who worked first in copper and later (circa 2,000 B.C.) in bronze.

The development of cities in the Nile Valley seems to have been based upon that of the earlier Mesopotamian cities, although Egypt must have possessed all of the necessary bases for urban development and undoubtedly would have "invented" cities independently if the nearby Mesopotamian model had not been available. The relative ease with which such inventions as bronze-making diffused across spatial and cultural boundaries has long been established. What is less certain is whether such a complex "invention" as a city, with its systems of writing, division of labor, and governing hierarchy, can actually diffuse like an item of material culture or a simple technological process. Certainly, as Paul Wheatley suggests, the "mere knowledge of city life diffusing through a folk society" could never have been "sufficient to induce the generation of urban forms."[15] However, for a region such as the Egypt of the day, which stood on the threshold of urbanism, the introduction of certain crucial inventions was apparently enough to hasten natural urban development. The assumption that urbanism diffused from Mesopotamia—suggested by the close proximity of the two regions and the 500-year time lag between the appearance of the first Mesopotamian and Egyptian cities—is reinforced by evidence that some of the earliest Egyptian cylinder seals and architectural styles were borrowed from Mesopotamia, and that the early pictographic writing of Egypt suddenly changed to a well-developed writing system without passing through a transitional stage.[16]

Still later, nearly a millennium after the emergence of cities in the Fertile Crescent, the first cities appeared east of Mesopotamia in the Indus River valley of present-day Pakistan. Here an advanced civilization centered around the twin cities of Harappa and Mohenjo-Daro, whose identical material culture and ground plan has intrigued archaeologists in that it suggests that the two cities and the empire they surveyed were united under a single ruler. Here again, proximity to the so-called cradle of civilization, and the fact that neighboring Mesopotamia had had cities for over a thousand years, suggests that a folk society on the threshold of urbanism may have been stimulated to develop cities by the diffusion of writing, technology, and administrative knowledge from the Fertile Crescent.

It does seem likely that the Egyptian and Indus civilizations owed a major debt for their development to Mesopotamia. But the origins of the earliest Chinese cities are much more in dispute. Our knowledge of the prehistory of East and Southeast Asia is relatively scanty in contrast to that of the Middle East. In part this is because of the lack of extensive archaeological research in the area. Historians have had to rely on classical Chinese historiography, and many of its texts seem to exaggerate the antiquity of early dynasties and distort events according to political expediencies of the day. In part, too, our understanding of regional prehistory has been restricted by political events and even climatic factors—the moist climates common to much of East and Southeast Asia quickly destroy fabrics, wood, and earthworks which would be preserved in the drier Middle East.

Clear evidence of Chinese cities does not occur until the beginning of the Shang dynasty, around 1600 B.C., with the appearance of large, socially stratified settlements enclosed by protective mud walls. The ruler's residence was located in the center of the city and surrounded by the houses of artisans who, among other activities, worked bronze and produced porcelain pottery. A form of the present-day Chinese script existed, consisting of approximately 3,000 characters of which 1,000 can still be read today. Although Chinese ideographic writing has always been more cumbersome than phonetically based alphabetic systems, the fact that today's newspapers usually have a vocabulary of some 3,000 characters, and scholars command at most only 8,000, suggests that the literati of the day were able to express themselves within the framework of the available characters.[17]

The emergence of Chinese cities seems to have been almost solely the result of internal developments, although it is apparent from certain technological traits borrowed from Turkish peoples that they did not develop in complete isolation from their predecessors. The character of cities in China and of Chinese civilization itself was so distinct from Middle Eastern forerunners that it can be said that cities developed independently in China.[18]

But only in Mesoamerica does certain evidence exist for independent city development. By the beginning of the Christian Era cities had already developed in the Yucatan Peninsula. The ease with which maize could be grown, and its high caloric yield, provided the basis for the development of a series of city-states presided over by rulers chosen from the religious elite. Together with priests, city residents included military and civil officials, soldiers, merchants, artisans, and slaves taken as part of the booty of war. Priests and scribes in these cities developed fairly accurate calendars and conceptualized the mathematical concept of zero. The similarity of urban social types and of the organization of indigenous hierarchies in Mesoamerica—though developed without outside influence—with those of Egypt and Mesopotamia is especially interesting. Here there is parallel evidence for the commonly noted assumption that the elaboration of social hierarchies and the elaboration of cities seem to inevitably accompany one another.

Redfield and Singer have suggested a useful distinction between *primary urbanization* and *secondary urbanization* as (1) the development of cities as a natural outgrowth of the cultural traditions of their surrounding hinterlands (primary urbanization) and (2) the grafting on of an urban tradition as the result of foreign influence (secondary urbanization).[19] Strictly speaking, primary urbanization seems to have occurred only twice in human history, in Mesopotamia and in Central America. All other urban development owes its existence in varying degrees to outside influence. It can be useful, however, to extend the concept of primary urbanization—as Redfield and Singer do—to include urban traditions that owe their principal formative forces to elaboration of a pre-existing folk tradition rather than to outside influence. Cities of secondary urbanization, on the other hand, have been established as the direct outgrowth of the expansion of empire.

City building has principally been associated with the wax and wane of empires. As an empire expands, it increases the scope of its hinterland and the surplus available to the people at its center in the form of tribute or particularly favorable trade arrangements. Maintenance of empire requires the development of outposts to oversee newly conquered territory; these outposts may in time develop into cities in their own right. Many of the major cities of Europe—among them London, Vienna, Belgrade, and Paris—began as forts and regional administrative centers of the Roman Empire.

In addition to their functions of political and economic control, such cities of secondary urbanization also serve as centers of diffusion of technological and other knowledge. As early as the time of the first competition between Sumerian and Akkadian city-states conquered peoples yielded to their colonizers by becoming bilingual and acculturating to their traditions.[20] Similarly, expansion of the influence of Athens and other Greek city-states was most clearly manifest in the establishment of colonial city enclaves on islands and along much of the coast of the Mediterranean and Black seas. Those exposed to urbanizing influence at the margin of the Greek Empire gained knowledge which they sometimes fused with generally more warlike traditions—as did the Macedonian Alexander the Great— to the benefit of the spread of metropolitan culture. Or, more commonly, they absorbed its administrative and technological knowledge and then turned to construction of their own empire (as did Rome), or toward destruction of the metropolitan empire itself, as did the semiurbanized "barbarians" who later dismembered the Roman Empire.

One of the ironies of an empire is that it carries within itself the seeds of its own destruction.[21] At the outposts established to maintain control over conquered territories there is usually a shortage of administrative personnel, so that locals must be trained to help administer the empire. In exposing locals to the inner workings of the more sophisticated administrative and technological structure of the society that conquered them, a process is begun that ultimately reduces the differences between the two peoples and provides the subjugated with the skills they need to assert their independence.

Nowhere can this internally destructive process more clearly be seen than in the course of European colonial history during the past several centuries. After the fall of the Roman Empire, cities such as Paris and London declined to little more than villages, which they remained for centuries. Contact through trade with the Islamic city-building tradition, and the very real threat that Islam would sweep Christian Europe, helped revive dormant European cities. In the late Middle Ages, Europe was confronted by Muslim control of Spain and Muslim armies on the outskirts of Vienna. This threat not only helped unite a seriously divided Europe—and in the process greatly advanced the development of nation-states—through anti-Muslim crusades, it also exposed the rather rustic Europeans to far more sophisticated Muslim traditions, and to universities that were the best of their age. Not surprisingly, the European cities most exposed to Islamic influences were the first to partake in the Renaissance: Florence, Venice, and Genoa, for example, which served as entrepots for East-West trade, were the first to emerge from the so-called Dark Ages. The Iberian Peninsula, which had long been under Moorish dominance, was the first region to gain an ultramarine empire. Indeed, the year 1492 marks not only Columbus' voyage of discovery, but also the time at which Islam was finally driven from Spain.

The European voyages of discovery were motivated largely by desire to remove Eastern trade in spices and other luxuries from control of Arab merchants who exacted high prices for their merchandise. During the Middle Ages, Arabs became the world's middlemen as their trading networks extended from European ports through India to present-day Indonesia. Such major Arab cities as Baghdad, Cairo, and Tunis were situated at strategic transfer points of East-West trade where sea and land routes joined.[22] The success of the Iberians in capturing this trade, by circumventing the Arabs through the Portuguese capture of Malacca and Goa and the Spanish development of Manila, led to the rapid decline and dwindling population of many Middle Eastern cities.

The Iberians gained only a momentary edge over the rest of Europe. Their successes encouraged the French, British, and Dutch to seek their own empires. The bullionist monetary philosophies of the day, which measured a nation's wealth in terms of its reserves of precious metals, seem to have encouraged the Spanish and Portuguese to concentrate on extracting metallic wealth from their empires. Instead of developing the productive sector of their economies, they focused upon administration of their empires. Consequently, their consumer demands had to be met by other countries, helping to build the industries of northern Europe and set the foundation for the Industrial Revolution, which permitted the English to dominate much of the globe.

The process of natural expansion and wane of empires can most recently be seen in the post-World War II decline of European colonialism. The colonial experiences of peoples throughout the world carried them from an initial period of fearful submission to European technological superiority to gradual mastery of their colonizers' secrets. Competition between the major European colonial powers forced them to spread their manpower more thinly among numerous colonies and to rely strongly upon trained local administrators, who in time rose to contest the dominance of their colonizers. It is no accident that many anticolonial movements of this period were led by individuals who had been steeped in the culture of the metropole, often through study in London or Paris. Of numerous leaders who fit this pattern, Gandhi and Ho Chi Minh are obvious illustrations.

URBAN TYPOLOGIES:
PREINDUSTRIAL AND INDUSTRIAL CITIES

A number of scholars have attempted to formulate typologies that distinguish among cities, either on the basis of their function in relation to their hinterlands and to other cities or on their technological level. Weber distinguishes between *consumer* and *producer* cities;[23] Redfield and Singer segment their typology into (1) *pre-Industrial Revolution,* pre-Western expansion cities and (2) *post-Industrial Revolution,* post-Western expansion cities.[24] Each of these is subdivided into types: preindustrial includes such *administrative-cultural cities of the literati and indigenous bureaucracy* as Peiping, Lhasa, and Kyoto and *cities of native commerce* like Bruges, Marseilles, and early Canton; postindustrial includes *cities of the world-wide managerial and entrepreneurial class*—London, New York, Singapore—and *cities of modern administration*, such as Washington, New Delhi, and Canberra.

Perhaps the most commonly accepted of all city typologies is that advanced by Gideon Sjoberg, which distinguishes between *pre-industrial* and *industrial* cities on the assumption that the character of basic modes of production has profound ramifications on human social relations.[25] Thus, *preindustrial cities* usually have their base in agricultural hinterlands that rely upon human and animal labor to produce surpluses to feed the urban population; the partial exceptions are those cities which by virtue of their location function chiefly as entrepôts for trade. Only a small proportion, at most 15 percent of the total population, can reside in cities and not participate directly in food-producing activities. The need for such cities to focus on control and exploitation of their agricultural hinterlands gives them a feudal character marked by sharp, castelike distinctions between social classes and low social mobility, and by clear divisions of labor. Preindustrial cities must of necessity have a literate elite to coordinate religious, military, public works, and trade activities. This elite, composed of high religious, political, and military functionaries as well as large landowners and a few wealthy merchants, tends to be bound together by kinship and frequent face-to-face relations, which help maximize the effectiveness of their control. The mass of the urban population are employed as merchants, artisans, and unskilled laborers. Still lower in the social hierarchy are outcaste and slave populations, which perform such services as clearing the city's streets of refuse and carting away human excrement.

The centers of preindustrial cities are usually occupied by central religious and public buildings and serve as the chief locale for residences of the elite. In contrast to the prevailing pattern in industrial cities, commercial buildings and homes of the lower classes are located away from the center and extend to its periphery. A striking feature of preindustrial cities is that members of the same occupation cluster in a small area, often lining a single street. Thus, if one wishes to buy such items as gold jewelry or a coffin, a single shopping trip will suffice to view what is available. Prices, too, although based on bargaining, are given greater standardization by such centralization: merchants know the quality and selling prices of their competitors' products, and customers know that if a price seems high they need only threaten to walk to another shop. In general, economic activity in preindustrial cities is poorly developed. As labor is cheap and plentiful most people are underemployed, so that several individuals may share a task that one of them could easily perform.

Kinship and family ties are of great importance to residents of preindustrial cities. Marriage is typically conceived of as a relationship between two kindreds as much as between individuals. There is little or no emphasis on romantic love as found in industrial societies, where increased economic freedom of both men and women reduces control by their kindred over marital decisions and makes romantic love a condition considered necessary for stable marriage.[26] Within the family and the society as a whole, women are clearly subordinate to men, as are younger people to their elders. This is especially true of the upper classes, the women of which are often confined to their homes. Lower-class women, on the other hand, typically have more freedom and play a more important role in economic life.

In contrast to the preindustrial city, *industrial cities* rely upon machine technology and inanimate sources of energy to absorb many of the tasks formerly performed by hand. Ideally, in Sjoberg's schema, industrialization reinforces the distinctiveness of the individual as position is gained more by virtue of ability and acquired training than through personal contacts. Associated with more flexible and less well-defined industrial class systems that emphasize individual achievement, conjugal (nuclear) families function with relative independence from larger, extended families. Women are able to find employment on a more equal basis with men. Social norms, in general, are likely to be less prescriptive and more permissive, so that the individual has more freedom.

Sjoberg's division of cities into preindustrial and industrial types has received a mixed reaction from other sociologists and anthropologists. Certainly any researcher who has worked in today's preindustrial or industrializing cities is struck by the acuteness of his insights. But some anthropologists have objected to the implicit evolutionary character of the typology,[27] while others have questioned whether or not "there really are any substantial number of ways in which 'pre-industrial cities' are a homogeneous phenomenon."[28] Sjoberg was aware that he was advancing a "constructed type" and noted that "not all preindustrial cities demonstrate every structural pattern that we isolate."[29]

What most troubles researchers, however, is whether there are so many exceptions to the constructed type that its utility is destroyed. An equally important concern is whether the distinctive characteristics of Sjoberg's type are really peculiar to preindustrial cities. Industrial cities, too, often display so-called "preindustrial" traits. In employing forty criteria supposedly diagnostic of pre-industrial cities, Southall found that fourteen apply wholly or in part to American industrial cities. For example: the behavioral norms of urban lower-class Americans are far different from those of the elite; upper-status groups occupy the key governmental positions; "ethnic quarters" exist in the black ghettos of most inner cities; formal educational institutions tend to perpetuate rather than help remake the social order; and sexual division of labor remains important. The problem is not that Sjoberg's criteria for distinguishing preindustrial from industrial cities are wrong, but that they are graded continua rather than absolutes.[30]

WHAT IS A CITY?

"The concept of 'city' is," as V. Gordon Childe has remarked, "notoriously difficult to define."[31] Implicit within this chapter is the assumption that we all know what a city is and when something is not a city. As usual, however, things become less certain once we leave the realm of common-sense definitions. Cities have been defined according to numerous criteria—among them relative size and population density, relation to surrounding territories, and occupational and role differentiation of their inhabitants—but no brief, single definition has been advanced that satisfies all scholars. Though his definition is inadequate today, Childe's is one of the most useful attempts to distinguish between the earliest cities and older or contemporary villages. Early cities, he said, were:

1) more extensive and densely populated than previous settlements

2) inhabited by full-time specialist craftsmen, transport workers, merchants, officials, and priests

3) supported by tithes or taxes of primary producers

4) marked by monumental public buildings

5) possessed of a ruling class of priests and civil officials whose responsibility it was to plan and organize their activities as well as to reassure "the masses that the sun was going to rise next day and the river would flood again next year (people who have not five thousand years of recorded experience of natural uniformities behind them are really worried about such matters!)"

6) centers where writing was first developed and where

7) a leisured literati was able to develop and elaborate systems of arithmetic, geometry, and astronomy

8) artisans gave new dimensions to artistic and craft expression

9) regular trade was established and raw materials for local industry and cult activities were imported

10) specialist craftsmen were provided both with the necessary raw materials for their crafts and security based on residence rather than kinship.[32]

But even the smallest villages in an industrial society today have literate populations; and larger villages often have full-time specialists such as mechanics and storekeepers who do not support themselves through agriculture. Even more frequently, small-village-size populations subsist through trade and tourism or the extraction of minerals from the earth. In America, television, radio, telephones, electricity, and even supermarkets are found in small villages. The visitor to the Thai town of Aranyaprathet, on the Cambodian border, encounters a sea of television antennas mounted high enough on roofs of stilted wooden houses to receive *Bonanza* and other programs from Bangkok. Even in the nations of Southeast Asia where, according to preindustrial "primate city" patterns, the second largest city is a mere town, the fusion of rural and urban worlds has made it increasingly difficult to isolate distinctively urban characteristics.[33]

Probably few researchers would disagree with Horace Miner's definition of a city as a center of dominance,[34] or with Aidan Southall's use of the "density" of role relationships as an index of urbanization.[35] Such definitions, like Childe's, tell us a great deal about the nature of cities but are difficult to translate into absolute criteria. Not surprisingly, many students of urbanism have come to favor a criterion based on actual population size—of 20,000 or 50,000, or more—when research necessitates an arbitrary distinction between cities and smaller units. As with other definitions, however, a distinction between urban and nonurban communities based on population alone has drawbacks. The Yoruba, for example, have long lived in city-sized communities, but their social structure is based on descent and age groups and the practice of near-subsistence agriculture.[36] Since, generally, there is little disagreement over whether a given community is a city, we can leave marginal cases to those who feel something is to be gained by making a distinction. As Southall says in discussing the religious centers of Tikal and Angkor, "the question as to whether they are 'true' cities or not can be left to those who know what the significance of the answer would be."[37]

Today most "urban" anthropologists recognize the pervasiveness of urban influences in nearly all societies. It is not surprising, therefore, that many have suggested that our proper concern should not be with cities as such but with complex societies, in which cities and their hinterlands are interwoven into tight political and economic webs. In such societies mass communications help bridge the traditional experiential distance between urban and rural peoples, so that even inhabitants of relatively remote regions often display a cosmopolitan outlook unknown in the past. Certainly, few would quarrel with the need to study both cities and the complex societies in which they are found.

NOTES

1. Childe 1950; Sjoberg 1960:36-37.
2. Pfeiffer 1972; Sahlins 1972:21.
3. Braidwood and Howe 1962; Darlington 1970; Flannery 1965.
4. Agriculture was independently developed in Mesoamerica and Mesopotamia and probably in Southeast Asia as well. The process at first undoubtedly involved human efforts to aid the growth of wild plants (by raking the soil, scattering seeds, and removing weeds), only gradually becoming routinized into true agriculture. As such, the development of agriculture also probably occurred independently within large zones in Mesoamerica, Mesopotamia, and Southeast Asia, rather than only once in one location in each major region. See Braidwood and Howe 1962.
5. Adams 1966:42.

6. Polanyi, et al., 1957:320-339; Adams 1966:45-46.
7. Sjoberg 1960:27.
8. Adams 1966:122.
9. Adams 1966:50.
10. Adams 1966:126-127.
11. Adams 1966:143.
12. Wittfogel 1957.
13. Carneiro 1970.
14. Adams 1966:25.
15. Wheatley 1971:7.
16. Sjoberg 1960:40.
17. Eberhard 1971:22.
18. Eberhard 1971:17; Wheatley 1971:6-9.
19. Redfield and Singer 1954.
20. Gelb 1960.
21. See Sjoberg 1963.
22. Hamdan 1962.
23. Weber 1958:68-70.
24. Redfield and Singer 1954.
25. Sjoberg 1960.
26. See Sjoberg 1960:151-154.
27. Uzzell and Provencher 1976:20.
28. Smith 1973:164.
29. Sjoberg 1960:21.
30. Southall 1973:98.
31. Childe 1950:3.
32. Childe 1950:9-16; quotation on 13.
33. In 1955, for example, before Vietnam experienced the tremendous growth of its urban populations that came with American involvement in its war, the Saigon-Cholon metropolitan area had 16.3 times the population of the next largest city, Hue (Linsky 1969). Today, the population of Bangkok-Thonburi is approximately 30 times that of Thailand's second city, Chiang Mai.
34. Miner 1967:5-10.
35. Southall 1973.
36. Lloyd 1973.
37. Southall 1973-87.

 REFERENCES

Adams, Robert McC.
    1966   The evolution of urban society: Early Mesopotamia and prehispanic Mexico. Chicago: Aldine-Atherton.
Bascom, William
    1959   Urbanism as a traditional African pattern. Sociological Review 7:29-43.
Braidwood, Robert J., and Bruce Howe
    1962   Southwestern Asia beyond the lands of the Mediterranean littoral. In R. J. Braidwood and G. R. Willey, eds., Courses toward urban

life. New York: Wenner-Gren Foundation for Anthropological Research, Viking Fund Publications in Anthropology, no. 32.

Cahnman, Werner J.
1966   The historical sociology of cities: A critical review. Social Forces 45:155-161.

Carneiro, Robert L.
1970   A theory of the origin of the state. Science 169:733-738.

Childe, V. Gordon
1950   The urban revolution. The Town Planning Review 21:3-17.

Darlington, C. D.
1970   The origins of agriculture. Reprinted in D. E. Hunter and P. Whitten, eds., Anthropology: Contemporary perspectives. Boston: Educational Associates.

Eberhard, Wolfram
1956   Data on the structure of the Chinese city in the pre-industrial period. Economic Development and Cultural Change 4:253-268.
1971   A history of China. Berkeley: University of California Press.

Flannery, Kent V.
1965   The ecology of early food production in Mesopotamia. Science 147:1247-1256.

Frankfort, H.
1950   Town planning in ancient Mesopotamia. Town Planning Review 21:98-115.

Fryer, D. W.
1953   The "million city" in Southeast Asia. Geographical Review 43:474-494.

Gelb, Ignace J.
1960   The function of language in the cultural process of expansion of Mesopotamian society. In C. H. Kraeling and R. M. Adams, eds., City invincible: A symposium on urbanization and cultural development in the ancient Near East. Chicago: University of Chicago Press.

Hall, John Whitney
1955   The castle town and Japan's modern urbanization. Far Eastern Quarterly 15:37-56.

Hamdan, G.
1962   The pattern of medieval urbanism in the Arab world. Geography 47:121-134.

Horvath, Ronald J.
1969   The wandering capitals of Ethopia. Journal of African History 10:205-219.

Hoyt, Homer
1966   Growth and structure of twenty-one great world cities. Land Economics 42:53-64.

Linsky, Arnold S.
1969   Some generalizations concerning primate cities. In W. E. Moore and N. J. Smelser, eds., The city in newly developing countries. Englewood Cliffs, N.J.: Prentice-Hall.

Lloyd, Peter C.
1973   The Yoruba: An urban people? In A. Southall, ed., Urban anthropology. New York: Oxford University Press.

Miner, Horace
    1967   The city and modernization: An introduction. In H. Miner, ed., The city in modern Africa. New York: Praeger.

Pfeiffer, John
    1972   How man invented cities. Reprinted in D. E. Hunter and P. Whitten, eds., Anthropology: Contemporary perspectives. Boston: Educational Associates.

Polanyi, Karl, et al.
    1957   Trade and market in the early empires. Glencoe, Ill.: Free Press.

Redfield, Robert, and Milton Singer
    1954   The cultural role of cities. Economic Development and Cultural Change 3:53-73.

Sahlins, Marshall
    1972   Stone age economics. Chicago: Aldine-Atherton.

Sjoberg, Gideon
    1960   The preindustrial city. New York: Free Press.
    1963   The rise and fall of cities: A theoretical perspective. International Journal of Comparative Sociology 4(2):107-120.

Smith, Robert J.
    1973   Town and city in pre-modern Japan: Small families, small households, and residential instability. In A. Southall, ed., Urban anthropology. New York: Oxford University Press.

Southall, Aidan
    1973   The density of role-relationships as a universal index of urbanization. In Southall, ed., Urban anthropology. New York: Oxford University Press.

Uzzell, J. Douglas, and Ronald Provencher
    1976   Urban anthropology. Dubuque, Iowa: William C. Brown.

Weber, Max
    1958   The city. D. Martindale and G. Neuwirth, trans. and ed. New York: Free Press.

Wheatley, Paul
    1971   The pivot of the four quarters: A preliminary enquiry into the origins and character of the ancient Chinese city. Chicago: Aldine Publishing Company.

Witmer, John
    1962   Study of the ancient city of Damascus in the light of present urbanistic problems. Ekistics 13:177-181.

Wittfogel, Karl A.
    1957   Oriental despotism: A comparative study of total power. New Haven: Yale University Press.

Yazaki, Takeo
    1973   The history of urbanization in Japan. In A. Southall, ed., Urban anthropology. New York: Oxford University Press.

Rural-Urban Migration and the Growth of Cities

3 For most of the five or six thousand years that cities have existed, only a small minority of the population of any society has actually resided in them. Real growth in the urban portion of the world's population is an outcome of processes which began with the Industrial Revolution and have only in this century led to widespread urbanization of the world's population. Today, almost all the "developed" industrial nations of Europe and North America, along with Japan and Brazil, are essentially urban societies, and urban populations of the "developing" nations of South America, Africa, and Asia are experiencing tremendous growth.

For a phenomenon that began relatively recently in human history, urbanization has been amazingly rapid. Although it required 79 years for urban concentration in cities of 100,000 or more to grow from 10 percent to 30 percent of the total population of England and Wales, the same degree of urban concentration required only 66 years to achieve in the United States, 48 in Germany, 36 in Japan, and 26 in Australia.[1] Such urban growth has been principally the result of rural and small-town populations migrating to urban centers, not the consequence of high birthrate levels within cities; for urban birthrates are invariably lower than those of the countryside. Indeed, city populations throughout history have rarely even reproduced themselves.

In the past, the relatively low birthrates characteristic of urban areas have been accompanied by high deathrates resulting from the vulnerability to disease of large populations living in close proximity without modern sanitary knowledge. The black plague, for example, regularly ravaged European cities during the Middle Ages, forcing urbanites to flee to the country. London's water in the mid-nineteenth century came mainly from wells and rivers heavily contaminated by runoff from sewers and graveyards. As a result, cholera and other intestinal disorders were endemic. Life expectancies were low: in 1841 the average life expectancy in London was 36 years and in Liverpool and Manchester only about 26, compared to 41 for England and Wales as a whole.[2] Today, of course, people everywhere have learned basic sanitary measures, such as boiling possibly contaminated water, and urban life expectancies now generally equal or surpass those of rural areas. Still, the dramatic growth of the world's cities in the twentieth century—Mexico City, for example, grew from 470,000 people in 1910 to 7,115,000 in 1968—provides striking illustration that recent migration has been the most significant part of urban growth.

People throughout the world have begun to literally race to cities. That much is certain. What lies beneath the gross demographic statistics of urbanization, however, is not so clearly understood. Why are so many people opting for urban lives? Are cities magnets that somehow draw those of the hinterlands to their lights through employment and cultural opportunities, or are they merely the receptacles of rural and small-town populations that have been forced to emigrate by the deterioration of rural conditions and opportunities? Are people "pulled" to urban centers by the excitement of possibilities offered by the city, or are they "pushed" from rural and small-town lives which they prefer but are forced to abandon by lack of opportunities?

Such questions are stated easily but not so readily answered. Human motivations can often be observed only indirectly. Not only is it difficult for the investigator to develop the rapport necessary to gain truthful answers from large numbers of people, but they themselves often understand only incompletely the factors underlying

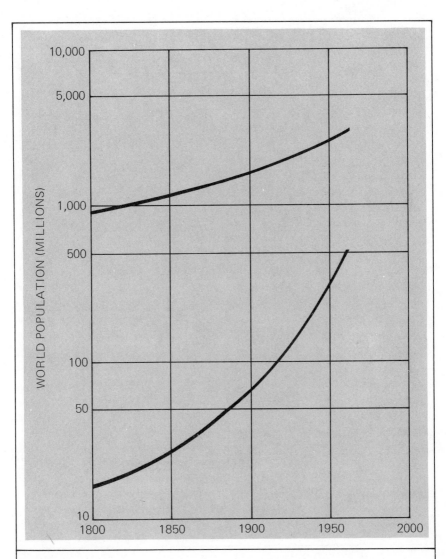

FIGURE 2

Rapid urbanization of the world's population is evident in this comparison of total population (upper curve) with the population in cities of more than 100,000 inhabitants (lower curve) over more than a century and a half. The use of cities of 100,000 or larger to define an urban population shows a close correlation with other definitions or urbanism. (Reprinted, by permission, from Kingsley Davis [1965:7], "The Urbanization of the Human Population," copyright 1965 by *Scientific American*, Inc., all rights reserved.)

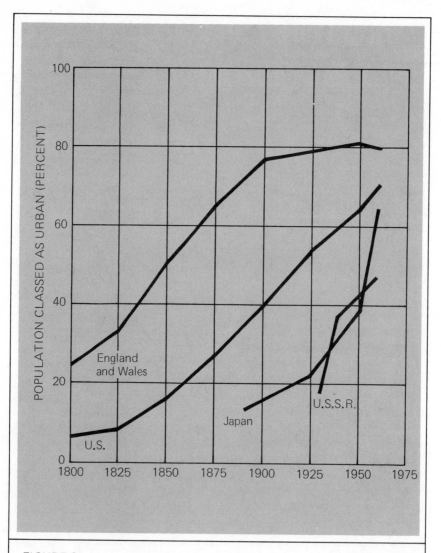

FIGURE 3

Industrialized nations underwent a process of urbanization that is typified by the curves shown here for four countries. It was closely related to economic development. The figures for 1950 and 1960 are based on a classification that counts as urban the fringe residents of urbanized areas; that classification was not used for the earlier years shown. (Reprinted, by permission, from Kingsley Davis [1965:10], "The Urbanization of the Human Population," copyright 1965 by *Scientific American, Inc.*, all rights reserved.)

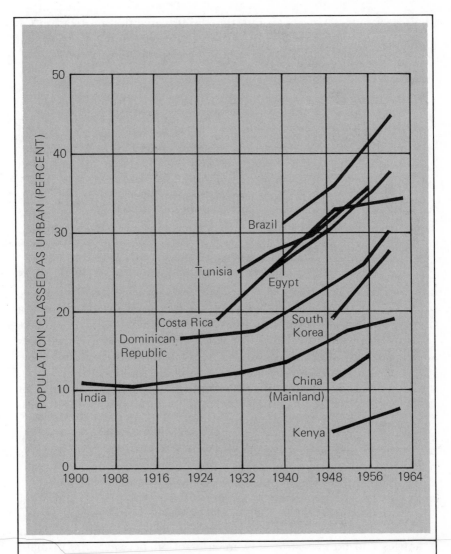

FIGURE 4

Nonindustrial nations are undergoing a process of urbanization that is typified by these curves. The process started much later than in the industrialized nations, as can be seen by comparing this figure with the one on page 60 and is attributable more to the rapid rise of total population in these countries than to economic development. (Reprinted by permission, from Kingsley Davis [1965:11], "The Urbanization of the Human Population," copyright 1965 by *Scientific American*, Inc., all rights reserved.)

their decisions. Answers to questions of urbanization motivation not only require a great deal of sensitive observation and reflection, but they are also unlikely to be clear-cut.[3]

PRIMARY AND SECONDARY URBANIZATION

The growth of cities at the expense of rural areas has been one of the most impressive events of the past few hundred years and especially of the last half-century. But the process of urbanization has not by any means had the same cultural meaning for all the world's peoples. In Europe, especially, those who have left their homes for cities have essentially moved from rural versions of the same urban tradition into which they have migrated. Others in much of the rest of the world have left rural regions to enter cities organized after foreign ideas, principally as the result of European colonialism.

In an article entitled "The Cultural Role of Cities," Redfield and Singer suggest the terms *primary urbanization* and *secondary urbanization* to distinguish between the development of cities as a natural outgrowth of the traditions of which they are part (primary urbanization), and the grafting onto a civilized or precivilized folk society of an urban tradition as the result of foreign influence (secondary urbanization). In cases of primary urbanization, a non-civilized folk society is transformed into two basic components—an urban center and a peasant hinterland—through indigenous forces. Such a city tends to elaborate on pre-existing "little traditions," codifying them into the more sophisticated "great tradition" of the urban literati. The city becomes the focal point of the nation's religious, legal, aesthetic, and moral life. The countryside, although it is the source upon which cultural elaboration is based, is viewed by both city and rural peoples as a pale and somewhat vulgar imitation of its urban center. Such a relation between the city and its hinterland can clearly be seen in the recent past of most Southeast Asian countries and still exists today in interaction between the primate city of Bangkok and the up-country areas of Thailand.

When migrants move from rural areas and small towns of a society which is urbanized in the primary fashion, they shift residence from one to the other aspect of the same whole. In leaving the folk tradition they enter a more complex version of their own culture, one which is strange but not alien. In such societies integration of city and countryside is great, and the hinterlander can sense the essential unity of his tradition.

In secondary urbanization, unity between city and countryside ceases to rest upon both communality of moral tradition and economic interest, as economic concerns overwhelm all others. The reality of concentration of power and wealth in the hands of members of another culture tends to undermine the value of pre-existing traditions and the status of those who cling to them.

The secondary urbanization of European colonialism has spread a common technical order to elites of the colonized world. It has provided new scientific and bureaucratic world-views that non-Westerners have had to internalize in order to advance in their own restructured societies. In such societies, members of the old elites who have not adapted to new realities—in failing, for example, to provide Western education to their children—have been displaced by those not so fully committed to the past. Migration to the city in these societies carries with it many possible meanings and consequences. The migrant is likely to find others from rural areas who have come to the city with values akin to his own, and he may even find a residual elite which still ministers to vestiges of the former great tradition. But it will be apparent even to his rural eyes that real economic and political power no longer rests with those who share his basic world-view, but with local, "Westernized" civil servants and local and foreign technocrats.

For most non-European populations, migration to cities thus means movement not merely from a relatively less complex, less hierarchical society to one which is more highly structured, but also to one which is qualitatively different. Yet, despite the fact that most of the world has been affected by foreign-influenced urban centers, much of traditional culture often coexists with the new technologies; this is most notably the case in Japan.

CITYWARD MIGRATION: THE "PUSH" FACTOR

Anthropologists, like other social scientists, often assume that cities are populated primarily by migrants who have been "pushed" to leave their rural and small-town homes as the result of economic hardship, rather than "pulled" by the attraction of urban opportunities. This is hardly surprising, considering the emphasis placed by many ethnographers on the corporate solidarity of primitive and peasant societies. What *is* surprising is the fashion in which an essentially rural bias has often directed interpretation of the polar concepts of *rural push* and *urban pull* so as to reduce the latter concept to insignificance.

Strictly speaking, neither notion is clear-cut. Both represent extremes of a continuum such that any urbanizing situation will necessarily be a mixture of the two, albeit to varying degrees. Rarely are there situations of such obvious rural push to cities as in certain areas of the Vietnamese countryside subjected to saturation bombing during the war. Rare, too, are situations of undiluted urban pull in which the attraction of rural prosperity that provides little or no push is outweighed by employment and cultural opportunities of the city.

In "Urbanization and Urban Conflict in Southeast Asia," Hans-Dieter Evers speaks of push factors as more important than pull factors in the rural-urban migration of the region, "as industrialization is slow and relatively few people are drawn into the urban areas through job offers."[4] But few migrants to any city are likely to have firm job offers before migration. Yet most expect to find ready employment. (Michael Whiteford has shown that only one-sixth of migrants to the barrio of Tulcan in Popayán, Columbia, had managed to secure employment before arrival, although nearly half were able to find jobs within a week, on their own or through a network of kinsmen and acquaintances.[5]) In stressing as evidence of rural push the low level of industrialization and especially, the lack of job offers, Evers places too great a demand on the city pull side of the equation by ignoring the fact that in most rural and small-town areas of Southeast Asia employment is available. More important, in countries such as Thailand, Burma, and Malaysia and in Indonesia's outer islands, ample rural-to-rural migratory opportunities still exist in the form of virgin lands heretofore unopened to agriculture. Clearly, if migrants choose to direct themselves toward urban rather than other rural opportunities—especially in the absence of job offers—they do so because they are attracted by a conception of what awaits them in the city.

That rural push factors are often primary in the decision to migrate, however, seems certain. Ireland, during the potato famines of the nineteenth century, was undoubtedly a region in which population pressures and the relative absence of rural-to-rural migratory opportunities far outweighed any attractions of American cities in influencing individuals to emigrate to the United States. Similarly, Hong Kong's New Territories illustrate a setting in which opportunities for rural-to-rural migration are strongly restricted. In the New Territories, lack of available land and the political reality of the

People's Republic of China across the border assure that any out-migration from native villages will be either toward the cities of Victoria or Kowloon or out of the British Crown Colony altogether.

In his study of the village of San Tin and its Man lineage, of whose members the entire village population has been comprised since their settlement there in the fourteenth century, James Watson discovered that long-range effects of the transfer by the imperial Chinese government of their land to the British in 1898 forced many Man to abandon their traditional homeland. For most villages in the New Territories, settled by emigrants from China, the attachment to Hong Kong has meant relative prosperity through a shift from traditional rice cultivation to vegetable farming for Hong Kong's burgeoning population. For the ancient village of the Man, however, the shift from rice to vegetable farming (made necessary by the importation of cheap, high-quality, Thai rice) resulted in a serious economic bind. The village is situated on a low peninsula surrounded by near-sea-level paddy fields and fish ponds and is irrigated by brackish water which is adequate for rice but unsuitable for vegetables. Consequently, the Man were neither able to shift production to newly profitable vegetable gardening nor to continue at their previous economic level by producing rice; rice prices were falling as those of all other commodities, including rural labor costs, were rising. Pressures were such that by 1962, in Watson's words, "San Tin's agricultural economy had collapsed completely, and the Man had to find another way to make a living."[6]

Pressured to leave their homeland, yet suited to only the most menial employment in Kowloon, villagers chose to leave Hong Kong altogether and seek employment in Europe. During the late 1950's and 1960's emigrant Man carved a niche for themselves in England's booming Chinese restaurant business, and emigration became an accepted way of life. Today, San Tin is a village of "professional emigrants" whose residents enjoy a relatively high standard of living—not through their own agricultural efforts, but in consequence of the remittances sent home by out-migrants and sums brought to the village by returning migrants. The self-description of one of Watson's informants captures perfectly the reality of their lives: "In some villages everyone grows rice for a living, but in San Tin we are all emigrants. That's what we do best."[7] While it is clear that the attraction of wages in the foreign restaurant trade exert a strong pull, it is likely that such a pull would never have been successful in attracting large numbers of Man emigrants—or even perhaps have been discovered to exist—were it not for the strong pressures to emigrate created by the particular circumstances of the home com-munity.

The presence of alternative rural opportunities do not always determine the relative weight of push and pull factors behind decisions to emigrate. Colonial situations have frequently provided a pressure to leave the countryside that is only indirectly linked to the lack of rural economic opportunities. In the former French colony of Niger in Africa, for example, the imposition of a head tax, payable in cash, to support the colonial government helped press much of the population into the urban-based cash economy. The need to meet colonial taxes at first led many young men into seasonal migratory labor to aid their families and later, with the gradual shift to a cash economy, to pay bride prices and acquire material possessions.[8] An excellent example of push orientation can be seen among the Papago Indians of Arizona, in the work of Robert A. Hackenberg and C. Roderick Wilson. The Papago migrate seasonally away from their desert reservation in order to gain adequate supplies of food and other necessities, supplementing the low productivity of the reserva-tion, and to attempt to maintain stable home communities. This pattern of migratory wandering undoubtedly existed as a part of Papago culture long before the first contact with Europeans.

In recent times, however, the stress on such *circular migration*, in which the migrant remains an integral though frequently absent member of the community, has declined in favor of permanent, *linear migration* of the Indian toward incorporation in the larger American society. A detailed statistical analysis of Papago population movement reveals that approximately 48 percent of those born before 1900 remained sedentary, choosing not to migrate, while 25 percent migrated in a circulatory fashion, returning to and regard-ing the reservation as their home. Twenty-three percent followed a linear, or permanent, out-migratory pattern. In contrasting this earlier group with those born between 1930 and 1939, it is evident that a major shift in residential and migratory patterns took place. Only 24.3 percent of the younger group remained sedentary and 20.2 percent were circulatory, while fully 46.5 percent were perma-nent out-migrants. Such an out-migrant level would in itself seem sufficient to lead to the "stagnation, deterioration, and eventual death" of the source community, which Hackenberg and Wilson fear.[9] Unfortunately for the survival of the Papago community, the level of desertion is actually even higher: 9.1 percent of those born during the 1930's—in contrast to only 3.7 percent of the pre-1900 group—have followed an *oscillatory* migratory pattern in which the

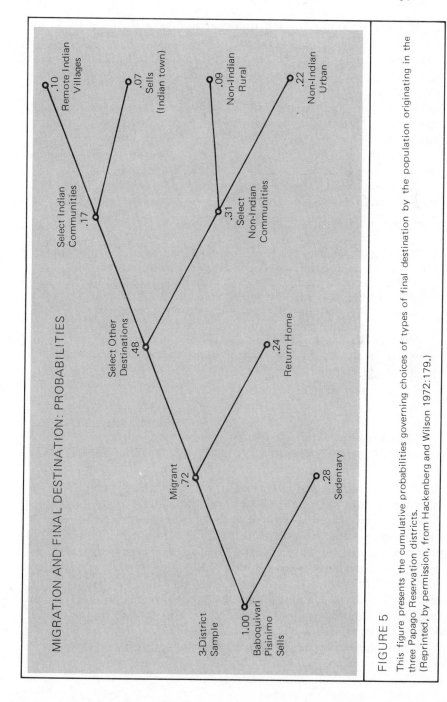

FIGURE 5

This figure presents the cumulative probabilities governing choices of types of final destination by the population originating in the three Papago Reservation districts.
(Reprinted, by permission, from Hackenberg and Wilson 1972:179.)

migrant left his home village for more than a year, then returned only to leave again, this time permanently.

That push is a more crucial factor than pull for the Papago seems clear from the fact that, for now at least, of those who do migrate permanently, 21 percent choose to settle in remote, non-Papago Indian villages, and 19 percent choose non-Indian rural residence; only 15 percent settle in the Sells Indian agency town on the reservation. Only 46 percent of those who move away permanently settle in non-Indian urban settings where eventual prospects for employment, for their children if not for themselves, are greatest.

In summarizing their Papago research, Hackenberg and Wilson offer a conclusion which applies to all those pushed to migrate by harsh conditions in their homelands:

> the picture of the Papago which emerges from this study is one of reluctant migrants who are detached from home communities by economic necessity rather than by the thirst for upward mobility . . . The enjoyment of cultural pursuits can become an unattainable luxury as population increases, resources are consumed, and income diminishes. Many Papago, perhaps a majority, can no longer afford to "enjoy their culture," because it has become unproductive of the necessities of life.[10]

TENSIONS OF RURAL, PEASANT, AND SMALL-TOWN SOCIETIES

Rural and small-town idylls die hard. Redfield's classic studies of the Mexican peasant villages of Chan Kom and Tepoztlan are paradigms of the implicit notion that small-scale societies, with their necessarily less complex structures and hierarchies, function more smoothly than large societies. The tenor of his studies is captured in this discussion of an informant's autobiography that appears in *A Village that Chose Progress: Chan Kom Revisited*. "It is the Golden Rule, applied very locally, rather than any general principle that all men are born equal, that guides Chan Kom. 'The peace and tranquillity of all beings on earth,' wrote Don Eus, 'depends solely on respecting the rights and reasonable nature of one's neighbor as one's self; this is the old law of our Lord God.' "[11]

Such descriptions of Chan Kom, and their counterparts for Tepoztlan, might have remained as the whole of the record had it not been for Oscar Lewis' suspicions that Redfield's view was one-sidedly rosy. Redfield found cohesiveness:

... I looked at certain aspects of Tepoztecan life because they both interested me and pleased me. I saw the almost ritual meaningfulness to the Tepoztecan of his daily work; I saw the delight taken in preparations for the many festivals and the pleasure, solemn but deep, at their consumation; I saw the pride the people had in their little mountain-walled country, so long inhabited, so deeply grown into their thoughts and feelings.[12]

In the same community, Lewis saw tension. He reported that "Tepoztecans view people as potentially hostile and dangerous, and their typical reaction is a defensive one." Far from open, warm, and cooperative he found them

... not an easy people to get to know, for they are not outgoing or expressive. Most interpersonal relationships are characterized by reserve and carefully guarded behavior. The man who speaks little, minds his own business, and maintains some distance between himself and others is considered prudent and wise ...

In Tepoztlan the motives of everyone are suspect, from the highest public officials of the nation to the local priest and even close relatives. It is assumed that anyone who has power will use it to his own advantage. Honest government or leadership is considered an impossibility; altruism is not understood. The frank, direct person, if he exists anywhere in the village, is thought to be naive or the greatest rogue of all, so powerful or so shameless as to have no need to conceal his actions or thoughts. Friendships are few. To have friendships outside the extended family is not a Tepoztecan ideal, nor is there a long tradition of a "best friend."[13]

George Foster, after decades of work in Mexico, concluded that peasants traditionally view their world in terms of "an image of limited good," dominated by the cognitive orientation that "all of the desired things in life such as land, wealth, health, friendship and love, manliness and honor, respect and status, power and influence, security and safety, *exist in finite quantity* and *are always in short supply.*"[14] If, indeed, such a perspective is characteristic of peasants, its implications for our understanding of rural-urban migrations are profound. If peasants carry within them an image of limited good *and the system is closed, "it follows that an individual or a family can improve a position only at the expense of others."*[15] If, on the other hand, the system is not closed—so that members of the community have access to wealth or other "good" gained outside its boundaries—then their prosperity may be envied, but it cannot reasonably be concluded that others have been deprived by their success. The ambitious individual who leaves his village for success in the city earns prosperity and, among his fellow villagers who stay behind, respect albeit tinged with envy. The man of ambition who chooses to focus his efforts on the village as his arena for personal and familial gain courts not only as great a risk of failure as does his migrant counterpart, for opportunities in a peasant village usually *are* restricted, but also the likelihood that he will incur strong resentment. *"Without economic opportunities,"* Foster concludes, *"the striving for material gain is a disturbance to the existing social order, since it means plunder of wealth from others."*[16]

Descriptions of peasant communities as centers of individuality and uncooperativeness, of repressed hostility and malicious gossip, are by no means limited to Mesoamerica. In one of the most insightful studies of a peasant community ever conducted by an anthropologist, Herbert P. Phillips discovered that a great deal of mutual suspicion and distrust lay beneath the superficial tranquillity of interpersonal behavior in the Thai village of Bang Chan. In contrast to stereotypes of rural communities, especially Asian, frequently held by Westerners, Phillips found a great fear of the overt expression of interpersonal tensions and a marked degree of instability in marital, kin, and friendship relations. So unstable and amorphous was the kinship structure that Phillips felt constrained to confess that

> I feel that any attempt to bring descriptive order to Bang Chan kinship does violence, in the very process of ordering, to the reality of what is being described. This is said neither out of a sense of inadequacy nor apology, but simply to underscore the fact that kinship relationships in Bang Chan are considerably more unpredictable, inconsistent, and chaotic than our descriptive modes typically admit, and that any coherent discussion of them must unavoidably involve an element of reification . . . What is perhaps most distinctive of this flux is the sense of uncertainty that surrounds it—a state that is easily tolerated by the villagers. Often during the course of field work we would enter a home looking for a particular informant only

to be told that he had left for Bangkok or for another village; for how long his wife or child did not know: "maybe he will be back next week or next month; it is not certain."[17]

Recently, in a superbly developed and controlled comparative study of four East African peoples, Robert B. Edgerton concluded that the farming groups studied displayed attributes that "consistently relate to a central core, or theme, that might be called 'interpersonal tension'."[18] Comparing herders and farmers of the Hehe of Tanzania, the Kamba and Pokot of Kenya, and the Sebei of Uganda through a combination of ethnographic description, interviews, and projective techniques, Edgerton found that the mode of economic adaptation had an effect upon interaction. In three of the tribes, the agriculturalists were clearly "more anxious and more hostile than the pastoralists of that tribe," while in all four groups "the pastoralists are more direct in their actions, and more open with their feelings, than their farming counterparts."[19] A short section of Edgerton's ethnographic summary of Pokot farmers illustrates the character of some agricultural villages.

Tamkal Valley was a lush green enclosure, surrounded by massive, cloud-covered peaks that were streaked with glistening waterfalls. The Pokot farmers had opened some of this land to cultivation and had dotted it with their conical huts, but much of the valley was still covered with green shrubs and trees. It was a cool place, without many insects, or large animals, and relatively free of disease. It was so beautiful, that it was all one could do to believe that the people who lived in this place were unhappy. But to look at these people was to remove all doubt.

Both men and women worked in Tamkal, sometimes hard, grubbing in the fields, cutting back brush, getting hot and dirty. The women sometimes sang when they worked, and chatted, but they often grumbled too. And the men were very often drunk and in bad temper. This set the tenor of Tamkal; the people were moody and dour. They quarreled, and they were violent. Their expressions were very often set in a scowl, and not even the children seemed to laugh very much. Not that Tamkal was quiet. It was noisy, but the shouts were joyless or angry. Two women seemed unable to meet at the river to fetch water without quarreling about something, and men not only quarreled, they fought, and even bit each other. They were an argumentative lot, and their arguments sometimes led to violence.[20]

All of this is not to argue that rural life is necessarily unpleasant, only that traits supposedly urban such as lack of societal integration and the presence of shallow interpersonal relations, have their counterparts in rural areas. In themselves, cities and their hinterlands are neither inherently attractive nor inherently alienating. If either one is viewed as a superior place of existence it can only be in the mind of the individual making the judgment. Redfield himself, in a reflective essay prompted by Lewis' sharply conflicting description of Tepoztlan, admitted as much. "There are hidden questions," he felt,

> behind the two books that have been written about Tepoztlan. The hidden question behind my book is, "What do these people enjoy?" The hidden question behind Dr. Lewis' book is, "What do these people suffer from?" . . . There is no one ultimate and utterly objective account of a human whole. Each account, if it preserves the human quality at all, is a created product in which the human qualities of the creator—the outside viewer and describer—are one ingredient.[21]

Although Redfield's point that one tends to see what one looks for in any society is well taken, the reports of Foster, Lewis, Phillips, and Edgerton of interpersonal tensions in peasant communities are reflected in dozens of ethnographies. Clearly, rural areas are not necessarily as idyllic as they have often been portrayed. Even making allowance for the importance of cultural differences in such varied regions as Africa, Mexico, and Southeast Asia, it appears that peasants *do* behave as if they subscribed to Foster's "image of limited good." And if this is so, then it is obvious that migration to cities may often have an important function in permitting an individual access to improved life opportunities, without undermining the acceptance he needs in order to call his village or small town "home." Thus, the motivations of such migrants are likely to be greatly influenced by pull factors. The relative potential of the city to provide economic opportunity without provoking excessive hostility, either at home in one's village or in the city itself, is likely to weigh heavily in the decision to migrate, especially in situations when migrants are already relatively prosperous, well-educated, or otherwise prepared for the challenge of the city. When push factors, caused by dearth of rural opportunity, predominate they are characterized by "unselected" migration, in which there is little or no discernible adaptive superiority for city life (represented by higher levels of education or other skills) in the migrant population over those who stay behind.

"CITY LIGHTS":
THE CITY AS A POINT OF ATTRACTION

Even the peasants of Redfield's Mayan village of Chan Kom did not view the life ways of the city as wholly alien to their conception of the good life. While it was clear to villagers that there was much to be wary of in the city—even the apparent benefit of knowledge brought by books was mixed with the realization that somehow "where there are so many books, there are also many troubles"[22]—they were acutely aware that cities represent focal points of a "progress" that is frequently to be desired. Thus, their scepticism and fear of the urban life which most knew only secondhand from those who had visited Mexico City and the Yucatan city of Merida was tempered with a sense that "progress" meant an adoption of certain benefits which the city alone could provide.

The idea is widespread that cities provide paths to wealth. Although the ease of success always seems exaggerated in the minds of potential rural and small-town emigrants, large cities with their relative concentration of wealth evidence that prosperity in cities is at least possible. The dream of success, despite the frequent reality of failure, is the heart of most decisions to emigrate.

But the pull of the urban dream is frequently associated with a desire to enhance one's status back home. Thus, as Leonard Plotnicov describes in his study of emigration to the town of Jos, Nigeria:

> The country boy goes to the city. He is looking for fame and fortune—or at least a job. But the farm remains "home"—his family, his roots, and possibly even his heart are there. He swears he will not desert the old people or the old ways: he will send back money; he will write; he will visit; he will renew his ties; and when he has made his fortune he will return to spend the remainder of his life in the bosom of his family.[23]

Such a goal was clearly the chief motivation behind the immigration to British Malaya of Chinese and Indians, who invariably saw themselves as temporary sojourners in its cities, tin mines, and rubber estates. Their intention apparently was to spend a few years or even decades away from their homelands in order to return and buy land or retire with relative wealth. That the dream was often abandoned is evident from the presence today in the Malay Peninsula of large Indian and Chinese communities, descendants of those who left home "temporarily."

In Nigeria, in Malaysia, in the industrialized nations of the world, the goal of the emigrant's triumphant return has seldom been achieved, because of either failure to flourish in the city or the gradual dimming of ties and obligations to his former home. The problem is often, as Plotnicov so well expresses it, that "coming home with dignity is not cheap." The Nigerian dream fails for two reasons. (1) Those who remain behind expect and in fact demand continual remittances from their urban kin;

> ... the natures and demands of the home ties themselves make friction easy and the accumulation of wealth difficult. Since first loyalty must be to homeland and family, requests for money cannot be easily refused—and they start early. Money that might become investment in a business or savings in a bank is spent instead on traditional gifts to chiefs and elders, gifts or support for relatives (some rather distant), help during illness or for lawsuits, and educational expenses for young male relatives.
> The heaviest requests from home fall upon those with most apparent success—professionals, traders, clerks, skilled workers. The wealthier of these I spoke to took pride in their ability to meet their obligations, even if it meant financial strain. The poorer complained of "family parasitism" and stated defensively that they preferred to live at a distance. But even they kept writing to the family and tried to meet at least some of the requests.
> What happens if a city dweller doesn't send money home? It becomes obvious that he has abandoned his people and the simple rural virtues and been corrupted and seduced by that Babylon, the city. Pleading poverty is not a good defense: anybody who can't make money in the city must obviously be weak in character, dissolute, lazy, spendthrift, incompetent, and generally useless.[24]

Moreover, (2) those who leave the world of the village for the city tend to become alienated in time from their former surroundings, so that ". . . the village people are . . . distrustful and jealous of those who have 'followed the Europeans.' One may return home to visit, and most . . . do so, but to return home permanently is . . . courting disaster. 'They like you to come back for a few months,' one man explained, 'but if you stay for good they will poison you'."[25]
Thus the pull of the city to which migrants originally yielded with the expectation of continuing obligations to their kin tends to become even stronger through time as the gulf grows between them

and those who remained behind. Some of this sense of distance and ambivalence is captured in the words of Shamu, a truck driver who had lived in Accra, Ghana, eleven years when he confided to Peter Gutkind that:

> The town is like strong drink because if you start living here you can't get away. You always want more and more. At times you get drunk, very badly, and then you want to run away to the village and sleep for a whole week. But then you wake up and you talk to your old friends and you find that they have done nothing all the time you have been away. They have done nothing but sit and talk and do a little in their gardens. So you are ready to run away again and you say to yourself: Do not get drunk on the city again. But you do get drunk and the drink is very strong but it also tastes good until you wake up the next morning and you feel bad and sad. But you don't have to drink in the city every day. You can also do better things. But you must have money.[26]

Of all the world's regions, that of the overcrowded subcontinent of India would seem most likely to provide unidimensional substantiation for rural push theories. N. V. Sovani notes that

> A common and widely accepted view about rural-urban migrants in Asian countries is that they are "pushed" rather than "pulled" into the urban areas. This results in rural underemployment and distress being replaced by urban unemployment, overcrowding and economic distress. To this is added the conventional view of the rural migrant to the city as handicapped in every way in the new environment, required to adjust to a totally different environment away from home, etc. and therefore overwhelmed by the urban circumstances. As a result he has to start very low on the economic ladder and finds it difficult to move up there because of the unequal competition he meets from his city-born competitors.[27]

So widely accepted is this view, he complains, "that it takes quite an effort even to notice the evidence that does not fit into this picture." Careful analysis of census information over time indicates that the growth pattern of India's cities cannot be predicted by the simple assumption that population pressures in the hinterlands force migration to the cities. On the contrary, the evidence suggests that urban growth is not always directly related to general population growth. While the total Indian population continued to grow at approximately the same rate during the 1950's as it had during the previous decade, rural-urban migration actually fell from 8.2 million during 1941-1951 to 5.2 million during 1951-1961, a decline of 37 percent. Additional evidence suggests that in-migrants are not necessarily less successful than local residents. Rates of unemployment, for example, are lower among migrants than among permanent residents. This is undoubtedly explained by the ability of in-migrants to return home if they fail to find urban employment—a fact suggesting that urban pull is probably more useful in explaining Indian migratory patterns than is rural push. As Sovani notes, urban migration in India ". . . is not such a blind phenomenon as results in over-migration to urban areas because of the rural 'push'. The movement seems to be more cautious and discerning and reversible. It seems a carefully calculated move and retreat is an integral part of it."[28]

K. C. Zachariah's study of migration to Bombay confirms Sovani's analysis for India as a whole. That rural push is not an adequate explanation of migration to Bombay is evident in the fact that the 1931 census report documented "an unprecedented exodus from Bombay to rural areas . . . (as) textile mills closed down, unemployment became widespread and many former in-migrants were said to have returned with their dependents to their native villages."[29] Comparative analysis of Bombay census statistics 1941-1951 and 1951-1961 again confirmed that "an accelerated rate of rural population growth, increasing rural density, and rural unemployment had not pushed out a larger number of migrants from rural areas to cities," evidence interpreted by Zachariah to mean that, "the fact that the expected exodus had not occurred may indicate that sufficient 'pull' from the cities was lacking and that these 'pulls' may, in general, be more important to cityward migration that the 'pushes' at the origin."[30]

In Mexico, as in India, the attraction of the city's potential apparently weighs more heavily than lack of rural opportunity. The majority of the peasants of Tzintzuntzan who leave their village and migrate to Mexico City do so quite willingly. In Robert V. Kemper's estimation, "they come to *buscar la vida,* to search for life."[31] The essential attraction of the city, of the "city lights" phenomenon, is seen in their perception, naively exaggerated as it may be, of the city as a center of opportunity. Nowhere is this orientation more clearly expressed than in the Thematic Apperception Test (TAT) protocol gathered by Kemper from a successful twenty-six-year-old school-teacher who had arrived in Mexico City as a teenager. His response to a portrait of a boy sitting on the doorstep of a log cabin was this story:

A boy of very humble birth grew up in the countryside. He
didn't know about a very different aspect of life: life in the
city. One time, his parents took him to the capital, and he was
surprised by the active way of life there: he saw new things, saw
children of his age who were totally different in looks, in
clothing, and in happiness—all stemming from living in the city
where modern comforts are available. This picture stayed in his
mind. Upon returning to the countryside, he spent his days
thinking about how he might come to live like those children
he had seen in the city; but around him he saw only animals,
plants, and poverty—and time passed without his achieving his
desires. So, he demanded that his parents let him go live in the
city. Finally, after a long time he got his wish. As a result he
became happy, dressed well, and enjoyed his work. He managed
to become someone who didn't lack the necessities of modern
life. And above all, in the city he improved and developed
himself.[32]

BEYOND PUSH AND PULL:
CITYWARD MIGRATION AS A
MULTIDIMENSIONAL PHENOMENON

The polar concepts of rural push and urban pull are useful in ordering
our thinking toward the problems of urbanization. Clearly, however,
they are alone too simplistic a representation of complex migratory
processes upon which to base comprehensive and universal, or even
particularistic, theories of urban growth. A better understanding of
the increasing urbanization of much of the world's population can
come through detailed analysis of: (1) types of urban migration and
(2) cultural, economic, and personal motivations for such population
movement.

Although a variety of cityward migration categories have been
proposed,[33] the division of populations by Hackenberg and Wilson
into *sedentary, circulatory, oscillatory,* and *linear* individuals is useful.[34] In studying rural and small-town to urban migration, the
sedentary individual can be defined as one whose pattern of movement is primarily restricted to his home territory, with occasional
visits to ritual and ceremonial locations. *Circulatory* individuals are
those whose pattern of movement has taken them at least once, and
often many times, to an urban setting for extended periods, but who
currently reside in their home communities; their principal goal of
migration is to gain sufficient savings to permit extended residence

at home. *Oscillatory* migrants resemble circulatory ones in that they have left their homes for extended periods and returned; but they are either unable or unwilling to remain in their native communities, and they leave to settle permanently in the city. Finally, *linear* emigrants are true rural-to-urban migrants in the sense that they leave their homes never to return.

The usefulness of such a typology can be seen in reflection upon some of the cases in this chapter. Most migrants represented in Plotnicov's study of Nigeria and in our discussion of Chinese immigrants to Malaya began their careers with the intention of becoming circulatory individuals but found themselves quickly transformed into oscillatory or even linear ones by virtue either of the difficulties of return or of their successful adaptation to urban life.

It is clear that the goal of return is common. Yet few migrants are able to achieve the circulatory dream of eventual permanent return as successfully as have the Mohawk Indians of the Caughnawaga Reserve near Montreal. Few Mohawk ever accepted farming as a way of life—in the 1870's it was estimated that only 52 men in a population of 1,300 farmed full time—and the reservation offered no other economic opportunities. Fortunately for the Mohawk, however, work as bridge-builders on the Canadian Pacific Railroad earned them employment and the reputation as surefooted and competent construction workers. Soon men began to travel to New York City to gain the generous wages paid to high-steel workers. Yet despite their success, and even what superficially looks like permanent residence in their Brooklyn homes, "Brooklyn must be considered as the turn-around stop on a round-trip journey . . . for example, no Mohawk has ever been buried in Brooklyn." The Mohawk, unlike the majority of the world's migrants who began with a circulatory dream, have succeeded and "in a fundamental sense . . . have never left home."[35]

Linear migration may, like its oscillatory counterpart, either represent a response to success in the city or a desire to escape from the countryside, but it may also result paradoxically from failure. The belief of ready success in the city is sometimes so strong that those whose who fail in their quest for riches are reluctant to admit defeat to their fellows. The repeated theme of exaggerated big-city future and unwillingness to admit failure undoubtedly functions to restrict circulatory migration below levels that would exist if pride and personality type did not contribute so much to decisions to shift residence. Just as fear of the uncertainties of urban life limits cityward migration, so does reluctance to admit failure hold those who come to regret the decision to depart for the city.

As patterns of migration are not uniform, neither are motivations. Individuals and groups choose to migrate for varied reasons, many of them only incompletely understood by those involved. Clearly, economic motivations rank first among reasons ordinarily advanced for urban or any form of migration. In his study of immigration to Santiago, Chile, Juan Elizaga found, not surprisingly, that approximately 60 percent of the immigrants interviewed disclosed that search for work was the principal factor pressing them to migrate; another 10 percent listed a desire to further their education as primary—a goal probably also motivated by economic considerations.[36] Often peasant and village peoples live too far from schools, especially post-primary schools, for children to gain an education that will assure them of literacy, much less prepare them for non-agricultural employment. Families who wish to provide their offspring with secondary education are forced to send them to live with city relatives or to migrate to a city themselves. Similarly, access to hospitals and medical care is nearly always restricted to towns or cities of some size, so that families with a member who needs extended medical care must make comparable provisions.

One especially useful generalization related to both economic and motivational factors of cityward migration and to this discussion of push and pull is the fact, noted by Everett Lee, that migrants who respond primarily to pull (or in Lee's discussion, *plus*) factors at their destination tend to be positively selected, while those who respond primarily to push or "negative" factors at their point of origin tend to be negatively selected, if at all.[37] In other words, when pull predominates, individuals tend not only not to be under any real pressure to migrate, but in fact they tend to be more highly educated and skilled than nonmigrants, although frequently not as skilled as those native to their point of destination.[38] Studies have also shown that the more skilled a migrant is, the more likely he is to travel long distances to find a location where his skill is in demand.[39] In contrast, those who migrate in reaction to negative pressures at the point of origin are least selective of destination according to job opportunities. They may either be among the least skilled and least well-situated members of their communities, or have been subject to general expulsive political pressures or severe economic pressures (famines, for example) such that the emigration involves individuals of all social levels and skills.

Personality, too, is a crucial selective factor in migration. Lee, in "A Theory of Migration," remarks that "there are personalities which are resistant to change—change of residence as well as other changes—and there are personalities which welcome change for the sake of change. For some individuals, there must be compelling reasons for migration, while for others little provocation or promise suffices."[40] Kemper concurs from his study of migrants from the village of Tzintzuntzan to Mexico City that it is "the meek, the less ambitious and adventurous, the rigid traditionalists . . . who stay in Tzintzuntzan."[41]

Age and sex are often important factors in determining who migrates. Generally, research on migrants has shown that people between the late teens and early thirties are more migratory than those of other ages, undoubtedly because this is when individuals are less likely to be married and have children or to be completely committed to residence in one locale. Men, too, are generally more likely to engage in solitary migration to cities than are women. This is especially true of initial periods of city development, when men migrate in search of work and leave their wives and children behind, as has been the case in the Zambian copper belt. Women who do enter such cities with exaggerated male/female ratios usually come as wives or prostitutes. Over time, however, the ratio tends to narrow as "respectable" employment opportunities open for women, especially as domestic help.

Where women do not themselves migrate, it must be remembered that the departure of male relatives frequently adds to their burden, they take over agricultural work previously performed by men. As Judith-Maria Buechler reports from research in Spain's northwestern province of Galicia, single women are often prevented by their families from working outside the home but are actually forced to increase their efforts at home "to perform a holding operation" on the land for migrant husbands. "They, like women in many parts of the world make it possible for *others*, primarily men, to engage in wage labor which is often associated with migration."[42]

Knowledge of the city, and especially knowing or being related to people within it, is often a precondition for emigration. The first few individuals from any community who move to a city must be adventurous and adaptable if they are to succeed. Later migrants can and do depend upon them. In discussing urbanization among Mixtec Indians, Douglas Butterworth provides a description that, for its particular geographical and cultural setting, holds true as much in Africa and South and Southeast Asia as it does in Mexico.

The first to settle permanently in Mexico City went directly
there from Tilantongo fifteen years ago, after having previously
spent three years in the capital city as a boy with his father.
The informant made the move from Tilantongo principally for
economic reasons. Upon arriving in Mexico City he worked as
an unskilled laborer in various jobs for three years until he
gained employment with a large firm in the city as an unskilled
laborer. He advanced in the company until he attained the
position of supervisor of general services . . . Since he has risen
to his present position, the man has found employment for
twenty-one other migrants from Tilantongo with his firm, and
become the informal leader of a large segment of the
Tilantongueños now residing in the capital city . . . The majority
of the migrants from Tilantongo arrive, usually without notice,
at the doorstep of a relative or compadre already established in
the mushroom slum of the city. The initial visit is generally
looked upon by the migrants as a "trial" . . . If employment is
obtained, however, they generally stay in Mexico City,
returning to Tilantongo only to fetch their family . . . [43]

That previous urban experience is sometimes crucial to the decision
to migrate is evidenced by studies suggesting that it is those who
have already left the land and who reside in small towns, rather than
truly "rural" people, who are most likely to form the bulk of
migrants to larger cities.[44] Sometimes this takes the form of "step
migration," in which migrants reside in a small town, often as
members of its middle class of merchants or skilled workers, before
moving to a larger city with better employment and educational
opportunities.

Finally, in assessing factors underlying urbanization we must be
aware of important ways in which the world's diverse cultures temper
otherwise uniform "laws" of migration. Some societies are structured
in a fashion that makes it relatively easy for an individual to leave
his family and surroundings and migrate, while others inhibit such
migration, especially if it may be permanent. Thai society, for
example, is frequently characterized as a "loosely structured" one
in which all relationships—even with one's parents and siblings—are
largely voluntary.[45] Interpersonal ties tend to be relatively brittle
and prone to severance. Even the Thai form of Buddhism, known as
Theravada or Hinayana Buddhism, stresses the responsibility of every
individual for his own destiny and his destiny alone. Thus, in general,
for a Thai the decision to migrate or not is a personal one in which
perception of his own welfare is usually primary, not a decision in

which strong pressures towards group and family cohension predominate.

Chinese religion, traditions, and even law, in contrast, have habitually discouraged emigration. Through the fusion of Confucianism, Taoism, and Mahayana Buddhism, Chinese folk religion places great emphasis upon loyalty to one's family and ancestral land. So strong has been this pressure to remain at home—a pressure codified at the level of international population movements to provide penalties for those who dared emigrate from China, especially if they carried females with them[46]—that those who have migrated have generally done so because they themselves were marginal, or because their families' economic lot was such that they undertook to find employment in Chinese cities or abroad as an act of piety in which the sacrifice of leaving the village helped permit their kin to remain at home.

The growth of cities through rural-urban migration is a process neither so simple as many scholars—operating under the Rousseauian assumption that people from rural or small towns would leave home only in the face of severe hardship—would have it, nor so complex that cross-cultural uniformities, or universal laws, cannot be found. As always, men operate from their own personal and cultural backgrounds to reach what seems to be the best decisions for their lives. That they only imperfectly understand their positions and glimpse their futures is what provides much of the complexity and challenge of attempting to understand their behavior.

 NOTES

1. Davis 1965:9.
2. Davis 1965:12.
3. I use the term "urbanization" either to refer to a proportionate increase in the urban as compared with the rural population of a society, or to the actual process of migration to the city. It is important to note, however, that the term is also often used to refer to the diffusion of urban forms (knowledge, behavior, economic structure, and so on) to rural areas and to the effects of urban contact upon the personal adjustment of individuals. See Lampard 1965 and Little 1974.
4. Evers 1975:778.
5. Whiteford 1975.
6. Watson 1974:204.

7. Watson 1974:205.
8. Van Hoey 1968.
9. Hackenberg and Wilson 1972:172.
10. Hackenberg and Wilson 1972:185.
11. Redfield 1950:164.
12. Redfield 1956:135.
13. Lewis 1960:87-88, 90.
14. Foster 1965:296; emphasis his in this and following quotations.
15. Foster 1965:297.
16. Foster 1965:309.
17. Phillips 1965:29-30.
18. Edgerton 1971:274.
19. Edgerton 1971:108.
20. Edgerton 1971:101-102.
21. Redfield 1956:136.
22. Redfield 1950:145.
23. Plotnicov 1965:18.
24. Plotnicov 1965:21.
25. Valdo Pons quoted by Plotnicov 1965:22.
26. Gutkind 1974:74.
27. Sovani 1966:142.
28. Sovani 1966:150-151.
29. Zachariah 1966:360.
30. Zachariah 1966:361.
31. Kemper 1974:80.
32. Kemper 1974:81.
33. Ravenstein 1885; Lee 1966.
34. Hackenberg and Wilson 1972:175.
35. Blumenfeld 1965:20, 21.
36. Elizaga 1969:345.
37. Lee 1966:56.
38. Balán 1969; Simmons and Cardona G. 1972.
39. Shaw 1975:51.
40. Lee 1966:51.
41. Kemper 1974:84.
42. Buechler 1975:209.
43. Butterworth 1962:261-262.
44. Balán 1969; Elizaga 1969; Simmons and Cardona G. 1972.
45. Embree 1950; Phillips 1965.
46. Purcell 1951:254.

REFERENCES

Balán, Jorge
    1969   Migrant-native socioeconomic differences in Latin American cities:
            A structural analysis. Latin American Research Review 4, 1:3-29.
Blumenfeld, Ruth
    1965   Mohawks: Round trip to the high steel. Trans-Action 3, 1:10-21.

Breese, Gerald, ed.
  1969   The city in newly developing countries: Readings on urbanism and
          urbanization. Englewood Cliffs, N.J.: Prentice-Hall.
Buechler, Judith-Maria Hess
  1975   The Eurogallegas: Female Spanish migration. In D. Raphael, ed.,
          Being female. The Hague: Mouton.
Butterworth, Douglas S.
  1962   A study of the urbanization process among Mixtec migrants from
          Tilaltongo in Mexico City. América Indigena 12:257-274.
Caldwell, J. C.
  1968   Determinants of rural-urban migration in Ghana. Population Studies
          22, 2:361-377.
Cohen, Abner
  1969   Custom and politics in urban Africa: A study of Hausa migrants in
          Yoruba towns. Berkeley: University of California Press.
Cohen, Ronald, and John Middletown, eds.
  1970   From tribe to nation in Africa. Scranton, Pa.: Chandler.
Coppa, Frank, and Philip C. Dolce, eds.
  1974   Cities in transition. Chicago: Nelson-Hall.
Davis, Kingsley
  1965   The urbanization of the human population. In Cities: A scientific
          American book. New York: Alfred A. Knopf.
Du Toit, Brian M., and Helen I. Safa, eds.
  1975   Migration and urbanization: Models and adaptive strategies. The
          Hague: Mouton.
Edgerton, Robert B.
  1971   The individual in cultural adaptation. Berkeley: University of Cali-
          fornia Press.
Elizaga, Juan C.
  1969   A study on immigrations to greater Santiago (Chile). In Gerald Breese,
          ed., The city in newly developing countries. Englewood Cliffs, N.J.:
          Prentice-Hall.
Embree, John F.
  1950   Thailand: A loosely structured social system. American Anthro-
          pologist 52:181-193.
Evers, Hans-Dieter
  1975   Urbanization and urban conflict in Southeast Asia. Asian Survey 15,
          9:775-785.
Fava, Sylvia, ed.
  1968   Urbanism in world perspective. New York: Thomas Y. Crowell.
Foster, George
  1965   Peasant society and the image of limited good. American Anthro-
          pologist 67:293-315.
Geiser, P.
  1967   Some differential factors affecting population movement: The Nubian
          case. Human Organization 26, 3:164-177.
Goldstein, Sidney
  1971   Interrelations between migration and fertility in population re-

distribution in Thailand. Bangkok: Chulalongkorn University Institute of Population Studies.

Gutkind, Peter C. W.
1974   Urban anthropology. New York: Barnes and Noble.

Hackenberg, Robert A., and C. Roderick Wilson
1972   Reluctant emigrants: The role of migration in Papago Indian adaptation. Human Organization 31:171-186.

Hance, William A.
1970   Population, migration, and urbanism in Africa. New York: Columbia University Press.

Herrick, Bruce H.
1965   Urban migration and economic development in Chile. Cambridge, Mass.: MIT Press.

Jackson, J. A., ed.
1969   Migration. Cambridge: Cambridge University Press.

Kemper, Robert V.
1974   Tzintzuntzeños in Mexico City: The anthropologist among peasant migrants. In George Foster and Robert V. Kemper, eds., Anthropologists in cities. Boston: Little, Brown.

Kerri, James N.
1976   "Push" and "pull" factors: Reasons for migration as a factor in Amerindian urban adjustment. Human Organization 35:215-220.

Kuper, Hilda, ed.
1965   Urbanization and migration in West Africa. Berkeley: University of California Press.

Lampard, Eric E.
1965   Historical aspects of urbanization. In O. M. Hauser and L. F. Schnore, eds., The study of urbanization. New York: John Wiley and Sons.

Lee, Everett S.
1966   A theory of migration. Demography 3:47-57.

Lewis, Oscar
1951   Life in a Mexican village: Tepoztlán restudied. Urbana: University of Illinois Press.
1953   Tepoztlán restudied: A critique of the folk-urban conceptualization of social change. Rural Sociology 18, 2:121-134.
1960   Tepoztlán. New York: Holt, Rinehart, and Winston.

Little, Kenneth
1974   Urbanization as a social process: An essay on movement and change in contemporary Africa. London: Routledge and Kegan Paul.

Mabogunje, Akin L.
1968   Urbanization in Nigeria. London: University of London Press.

MacDonald, L. D., and J. S. MacDonald
1968   Motives and objectives of migration: Selective migration and preferences toward rural and urban life. Social and Economic Studies 17, 4:417-434.

Meadows, P., and E. H. Mizruchi, eds.
1969   Urbanism, urbanization and change: Comparative perspectives. Reading, Mass.: Addison-Wesley.

Milone, P. D.
    1964   Contemporary urbanization in Indonesia. Asian Survey 4, 8:1000-1012.
Phillips, D. G.
    1959   Rural-to-urban migration in Iraq. Economic Development and Cultural Change 7, 4:405-421.
Phillips, Herbert P.
    1965   Thai peasant personality. Berkeley: University of California Press.
Plotnicov, Leonard
    1965   Nigerians: The dream is unfulfilled. Trans-Action 3, 1:18, 21-22.
Purcell, Victor
    1951   The Chinese in Southeast Asia. 2d ed. London: Oxford University Press.
Rabinovits, F., and Felicity M. Trueblood, eds.
    1971   Latin American urban research. Vol. 1. Beverly Hills: Sage Publications.
Radcliffe-Brown, A. R.
    1952   Structure and function in primitive society. London: Oxford University Press.
Ravenstein, E. G.
    1885   The laws of migration. Reprinted in Bobbs-Merrill Series in the Social Sciences no. S-482.
Redfield, Robert
    1940   Tepoztlán: A Mexican village. Chicago: University of Chicago Press.
    1950   A village that chose progress. Chicago: University of Chicago Press.
    1956   The little community: Peasant society and culture. Chicago: University of Chicago Press.
Redfield, Robert, and Alfonso Villa Rojas
    1934   Chan Kom: A Maya village. Washington, D.C.: Carnegie Institution.
Redfield, Robert, and Milton Singer
    1954   The cultural role of cities. Economic Development and Social Change 3, 1:53-73.
Romm, Jeff
    n.d.   Urbanization in Thailand. New York: Ford Foundation International Urbanization Study.
Rosser, Colin
    n.d.   Urbanization in tropical Africa. New York: Ford Foundation International Urbanization Study.
Shaw, R. Paul
    1975   Migration theory and fact: A review and bibliography of current literature. Philadelphia: Regional Science Research Institute.
Simić, Andrei
    1973   The peasant urbanites: A study of rural-urban mobility in Serbia. New York: Seminar Press.
Simmons, Alan B., and Ramiro Cardona G.
    1972   Rural-urban migration: Who comes, who stays, who returns? The case of Bogota, Columbia, 1929-1968. International Migration Review 6:166-181.
Sovani, Nilkanth Vithal
    1966   Urbanization and urban India. New York: Asia Publishing House.

Sternstein, L.
    1971   A first study of migration in the greater Bangkok metropolitan area. Pacific Viewpoint 12, 1:41-67.
Van Hoey, Leo
    1968   The coercive process of urbanization: The case of Niger. In Scott Greer, et al., eds., The new urbanization. New York: St. Martin's Press.
Watson, James L.
    1974   Restaurants and remittances: Chinese emigrant workers in London. In George Foster and Robert V. Kemper, eds., Anthropologists in cities. Boston: Little, Brown.
Whiteford, Michael B.
    1975   Reaching for the good life: A comparative analysis of urban adaptation. Paper presented to the 74th annual meeting of the American Anthropological Association, San Francisco, California.
Zachariah, K. C.
    1966   Bombay migration study: A pilot analysis of migration to an Asian metropolis. Reprinted in Gerald Breese, ed., The city in newly developing countries. Englewood Cliffs, N.J.: Prentice-Hall, 1969.

Kinship in the City: The Impact of Urbanization and Industrialization on Family Ties

4 As the most basic building block of human society, kinship has always been a major concern of anthropologists. Indeed, one of the most fruitful approaches to the study of any society is to begin with a study of its kinship system, and attempt to discover how and to what degree it provides a basis for social organization and the structuring of human interaction. Not surprisingly, a major concern of urban anthropological and sociological research of the past several decades has been to discover what if any impact urbanization has upon the nature and functioning of families. Many have suggested, for example, that the shift of the world's societies from predominantly rural and agrarian to modern urban and industrial ones has had profound effects on family and kinship systems.

Louis Wirth, in his classic essay "Urbanism as a Way of life," provides one of the most explicit statements of the commonly assumed connection between urbanism and family life:

> The distinctive features of the urban mode of life have often
> been described sociologically as consisting of the substitution
> of secondary for primary contacts, the weakening of bonds of
> kinship, and the declining social significance of the family ...
> the low and declining urban reproduction rates suggest that the
> city is not conducive to the traditional type of family life,
> including the rearing of children and the maintenance of the
> home as the locus of a whole round of vital activities. The
> transfer of industrial, education, and recreational activities to
> specialized institutions outside the home has deprived the
> family of some of its most characteristic historical functions ...
> The family as a unit of social life is emancipated from the
> larger kinship group characteristic of the country, and the
> individual members pursue their own diverging interests in
> vocational, educational, religious, recreational, and political
> life.[1]

Others, both sociologists and anthropologists, have seconded
this assumption that kinship, especially the extended family, becomes
relatively unimportant in modern urban societies. Talcott Parsons
speaks of the importance of the "isolated conjugal family" of husband, wife, and children as the "normal 'household' unit" of today's
American society, the isolation of which he feels stands "in strong
contrast to much of the historic structure of European society where
a much larger and more important element have inherited home,
source of economic support, and specific occupational status (especially a farm or family enterprise) from their fathers."[2]

Neil Smelser, in concluding his detailed and impressive study
Social Change in the Industrial Revolution, discusses the impact of
industrialization on the functions of the family. Whereas in preindustrial times and in the first few decades of the Industrial Revolution families generally formed a cohesive residential and economic
unit—such that children frequently worked side by side with their
parents—the pressures of industrialization gradually led to a situation
in which family members were separated for long periods during the
day. If the worker refused to accept isolation from his family he
could not properly support them. If, on the other hand, one or both
parents accepted industrial employment, such noneconomic functions
as child-rearing suffered.[3] In time, the effects of industrialization
helped lead to a thorough reorganization of the family as a "more
specialized agency" than it had been in preindustrial times.[4]

Taken together, (1) the assumed decline of the importance of
traditional extended kinship networks in favor of the isolated conjugal

family and (2) the shift of the family's role away from a productive economic, affective, and socialization unit to one concentrating on "emotional gratification and socialization"—the latter function partly usurped by formal educational systems common to modern societies— have been seen by many as either a crucial precondition or a direct result of the industrialization of society.

Both extended kinship systems and family patterns that insist upon unity of familial functions rather than division of the family's roles are assumed by many to retard the development and function- ing of modern societies. The progress of such societies is thought best aided by the presence of isolated human units free to develop skills and exercise geographic and social mobility without the hindrance of concern for extended kin. In essence, these theories assume that the presence of strong emotional ties to an all-encompassing kin group prevents an individual from maximizing his economic potential by making him reluctant to move to another region for better em- ployment or higher education. And, should he attempt to achieve beyond his kin's status, it is assumed that his social mobility will be impeded by his kinsmen's demands to share in his success.

These arguments have a compelling logic that most of us who are products of middle-class levels of a largely urban and industrialized society will intuitively accept. Progress in a modern society *does* seem to emphasize the importance of nonfamilial socialization in systems of formal education and in occupational advancement, and to place a premium on friends rather than kin in meeting our needs for com- panionship. The assumption, too, that the isolated nuclear family— relieved of many of its earlier functions—is a necessary concomitant of advanced societies seems logical enough.

But the reality of familial adaptation to modern urban life may not be nearly so simply as many assume. In examining the proposi- tion that the role of the family has shifted, several issues complicate the matter:

1) Has the family actually undergone change, or is the assump- tion that familial patterns have shifted an incorrect reading of the past?

2) Assuming that there has been an historical shift in the character of the family, what evidence do we have to con- clude that this is the result of urbanization, industrialization, or modernization?

3) If, indeed, urbanization, industrialization, or modernization does lead to alteration in the functions of kinship, is this a

universal phenomenon or merely one that is subject to the character of particular cultural traditions?

Investigation of these issues is critical in understanding the impact of urbanization on social organization. In order to reach meaningful cross-cultural generalizations, however, we must carefully weigh evidence from the world's societies. In the remainder of this chapter available information from the industrialized West (including French Canada), as well as Yugoslavia, India, Southeast and East Asia, Latin America, and Sub-Saharan Africa will be considered before conclusions are drawn on the role of kinship in urban settings. In these sections the reader is urged to compare areas and to attend closely to the different cultural settings of each.

THE EFFECTS OF WESTERN URBANIZATION
AND INDUSTRIALIZATION ON FAMILY STRUCTURE

Most research on whether the extended family is undergoing a break-down in significance in the industrialized West has concluded that urban dwellers generally maintain non-nuclear and non-conjugal kin ties. Elizabeth Bott, Young and Willmott, and Raymond Firth have emphasized the importance that extended family ties still retain in the lives of many citizens of London.[5] Morris Axelrod has reported that over three-quarters of those he studied in Detroit see their relatives at least once a month; and Marvin Sussman argues that "the evidence of the viability of an existing kinship structure carry-ing on extensive activities among kin is so convincing that we find it unnecessary to continue further descriptive works in order to establish the existence of the kin network in modern urban society."[6]

Just as urbanization per se has not apparently led to extinguish-ing kin contacts, neither has rural-urban or intercity migration. A core aspect of the hypothesis that the conjugal family is most congruent with modern industrial society is that its formation is favored by migratory processes which such societies tend to encourage. Often, especially in highly developed societies in which the division of labor is maximized, individuals are forced to migrate from their homes in order to gain employment appropriate to their skills. Logically, a society that places little emphasis on maintaining large kin groups would facilitate such migration, as the individual would feel relatively free to pursue his best employment opportunities; but the degree to which such mobility is actually characteristic of even American society is uncertain. Bert Adams concludes that "proximity, not separation is the rule, with actual geographical isolation from kin being characteristic of only a small portion of the population"; and that professional and managerial families are those most commonly isolated from their kin, although even here proximity rather than isolation remains the rule.[7]

Ted Jitodai, in an analysis of data from the University of Michigan's Detroit Area Study, discovered only minimal differences in maintenance of extended kin relations between natives of Detroit and migrants from rural or urban (other than Detroit) origin. Thus: the white collar sample revealed that 48 percent of native males (53 percent of women) saw relatives weekly; so did 36 percent (37 percent of women) of the interurban migrants, and 44 percent (41 percent of women) of the rural migrants. The differences between migrant and native maintenance of kin contact are even less significant for blue collar natives, interurban migrants, and rural migrants: 49 percent, 49 percent, and 43 percent, respectively, for male respondents.

When the sample was reviewed according to length of time spent in the city, the importance of kin groups became even more apparent, especially for interurban migrants. Only 11 percent of male interurban white collar migrants who had lived in Detroit for less than ten years maintained weekly face-to-face contacts with their kin, while 42 percent of rural migrants who had resided there for a similar time had such contacts. This substantiates the assumption that rural individuals are most likely to migrate to cities where they have kin, while urbanites are more willing to risk solitary or nuclear-family residence in a new city. For those of the white collar sample who had resided in the city for over twenty-five years, however, Jitodai discovered something rather surprising: long-term interurban migrants were more likely than rural migrants to have frequent interaction with relatives. Fifty-two percent of the long-term interurban migrants reported weekly contacts with relatives, in comparison with only 47 percent of the rural migrants.

Jitodai suggests two possible interpretations: (1) Interurban migrants who fail to establish extended kin networks over time leave the city, while those who enmesh themselves in kin remain, a hypothesis that reinforces the view of kinship ties as a hindrance to geographical mobility. (2) A more plausible and suggestive possibility is that young urban dwellers focus their concern on social mobility—accepting the geographical mobility often entailed—seeking only later, as their careers near a peak, to rejoin their relatives and to coalesce kin ties. Such a hypothesis suggests that kin may be important emotionally to modern urbanites but may take a temporary back seat to priorities critical in rising as far as possible occupationally. When maximum occupational achievement is approached and it becomes apparent that no further geographic moves are necessary, one can turn to consolidating kindred and especially to moving in parents, who are by now beyond working age.[8]

Many of Jitodai's insights into migratory patterns in Detroit were suggested by the earlier work of Eugene Litwak, which directly countered Parsons' concept of the congruence of the isolated nuclear family and the requirements of industrial society. Litwak argues that a modified extended family is compatable with advanced, democratic societies, on the basis of a survey of 920 white, mostly middle-class women living in Buffalo, New York—a group who theoretically should have minimal extended familial ties. He suggests that: (1) modified extended families actually promote the geographic mobility of their members, to aid them in social mobility; (2) extended family identification does not disappear as a result of such mobility, but continues despite the loss of face-to-face contact; and (3) as migrant members of the family near their peak earning powers, a "geographic coalescence" tends to take place as some members of the family reunite.

The assumption that modified extended families frequently act in favor of geographic mobility is well documented for many of the world's rural-urban migrants, where the family aids the young adult to migrate hoping that he will prosper and share his prosperity with relatives. That American families frequently accept, and even demand geographic mobility for their offspring is clear by the importance placed upon sending children to college; a locality is frequently chosen that should maximize career success later rather than maintain close proximity to the family. Supporting the assumption that identification with extended family does not prevent nuclear families from migrating, Litwak found that those geographically distant from kin are as likely as those who live nearby to be strongly identified with relatives; and that individuals most closely identified with their extended families, as opposed to their nuclear families or to non-kin, were actually *more* likely to leave their city and nearby relatives. In summary, Litwak suggests that:

> When individuals are moving ahead occupationally, those who are psychologically close to their families are much more mobile than those who dissociate themselves from their families (47 per cent and 22 per cent, respectively, are mobile). In contrast,

among people at their career peak, the extended family oriented are no more mobile than the non-family oriented (12 and 11 per cent, respectively).[9]

Litwak suggests—in contrast to the example he describes for the middle-class extended family of family-assisted mobility, maintenance of extended family identification aided by letters and telephone, and eventual family coalescence—that manual workers may tend to follow an alternate pattern. Occupational success for them may be directly related to job seniority, indicating a negative association between social and geographic mobility.

Surprising as it may seem in the light of commonly held assumptions, research on the relations of class and kin networks suggests that upper classes are more likely to maintain viable and extensive kinship networks than lower classes. This apparently does not result from the greater dependency of those of higher status on their kin, nor from any lesser likelihood of having extensive bodies of friends—indeed, the opposite is more generally true, as those of higher classes tend to have a broader range of interpersonal contacts—but from the fact that they have greater financial resources to allocate to the maintenance of emotionally important kindred ties.[10]

Not all research on kinship in American society has rejected Parsons' assumptions. Helen Codere, reporting the results of research into the genealogical knowledge of Vassar students, noted that "as a system of social organization and interpersonal relations, kinship is minimized in the United States." The data, she asserts, in direct contradiction to much of the literature of the past several decades, describes

> a kinship system that is localized in the immediate family, lacking in historical depth, lacking in reciprocities between age-mates, and equals, impoverished in opportunities for knowledge about people, and weakened by the rejection of relationships. These same conclusions, somewhat more generally phrased, are familiar to all students of American society and to reflective people living in it; but that they should arise so directly and forcefully from the data and methods of a geneaological study of a group of high socioeconomic status was unexpected.[11]

The majority of Codere's sample of 200 students came from families with only two children, and fully 70 percent had only one or two other siblings. Each was asked to construct as extensive a family genealogy as possible, indicating the name and relationship of each relative. Even taking into account that the students had few relatives in descending generations—that is, their own children, children's children, or children of siblings or cousins—the actual size of known kindred was small, ranging from 11 to 73 individuals for an average of only 30 to 33. Faced with such small genealogies, with some of their members deceased, many students betrayed "some sense of isolation and anxiety about really knowing so few relatives and having such a small backing of kinfolk . . . they often asked for some assurance that their genealogies were not abnormal in this respect and were relieved when they later heard the cumulative results and averages."[12]

Although Codere apparently assured her students that their small kinship universes were typical of Americans, other research suggests that this is not actually the case. Coult and Habenstein, in extensive research on kinship in Kansas City, found that the average respondent could *name* 104 relatives and knew specifically of the existence of 44 more. About 70 of the total of 148 were consanguineal, or blood relatives, and 77 were affines, related through marriage. Blue collar females had average kin universes of 200, followed by blue collar males with 153, white collar females with 109. While analysis of the data produced some interesting differences between white collar and blue collar individuals—white collar women tended to emphasize patrilineal relatives, while blue collar women were most familiar with their mothers' kin; white collar respondents were most knowledgeable about their lineal kin, while the blue collar sample tended to extend their recognized kin laterally (for example, cousins)—even the relatively small universes of the white collar males greatly exceeded the attenuated kinship knowledge of Codere's Vassar students.[13]

Thus, American research data from examination of the hypothesis that importance of kinship declines in modern industrialized urban society, has generally produced evidence of larger kin networks than that hypothesis would lead us to believe exist. Indeed, in some cases research suggests that extended kinship may actually be of greater significance to the lives and careers of members of the upper and middle classes (who should presumably be best adapted to the requirements of the modern urban milieu) than it is to those of the lower classes. On the basis of much of the research data, we could reasonably hypothesize that nuclear families who can call upon financial and emotional resources from kin outside their boundaries may be more perfectly adapted, for example, to the premium placed by industrial societies upon the individual's aquisition of costly and extended education.

But certain problems inherent in the research (largely a by-product of survey techniques) make it unwise to concur fully with Adams' premise that the coup de grâce has been given to the view that the nuclear family is isolated from kin in modern society.[14] Most research suffers from being limited to determining whether extended kinship ties are maintained in industrial society, rather than focusing on the more salient issues of the character and intensity of those ties. It is quite likely, for example, that kin ties retained through letters, telephone, and occasional visits may provide emotional or financial aid in emergencies, yet still lack some of the supportive intensity of ties with kin residing in the immediate area. In a world based more and more upon friends and business associates, the maintenance of extended kin ties may serve to provide a permanence that can always be relied upon, rather than to provide day-to-day emotional support.

Coult and Habenstein have pointed out that much of the controversy surrounding Parsons' "isolated nuclear family" hypothesis is evidently the result of a blurring of two separate issues: the use of extended families to form corporate groups, and the functioning of non-nuclear kin ties as a basis for construction of interactional dyads. If American kinship patterns are examined from the first criterion of group solidarity, then "it is clear that Parsons is correct in characterizing the American kinship system as one being composed of isolated nuclear families having a high degree of separation and autonomy even between the families of orientation and the family of procreation of the same person." Corporate responsibility for one's kin is in other words generally limited to members of a single household. But Americans recognize kinship as an important basis for interpersonal affiliation beyond the nuclear family. "We think it sufficient to point out," Coult and Habenstein conclude,

> that from a group *membership* perspective Parsons has correctly characterized the American nuclear family as "isolated" and that from a *dyadic relationship* perspective Sussman and Litwak have been equally correct in maintaining that the family is "non-isolated." (It is our opinion, however, that if all societies were classified on a scale of isolated-non-isolated in relation to dyadic affiliation the American family would prove to be closer to the isolated end of the continuum than the families of most other groups. For example, Eskimo families would be classified as "isolated" in terms of the group membership criterion, but their degree of affiliation with non-nuclear family kinsmen appears to be much higher than that of Americans.)[15]

William Goode, surveying worldwide changes in family patterns, acknowledges arguments against the decline of the extended family, yet concludes "that most family systems of the world are moving toward a conjugal system."[16] In his view, industrialization creates several largely inescapable points of pressure on traditional kin structures:

1) the physical movement often required by industrial systems does tend to reduce intensity of contact among family members despite compensatory communication possibilities (for example, telephone, letters)

2) industrialization frequently results in the differential success of kin, so that the development of varying tastes and life styles drives a wedge between them, inhibiting free interaction

3) many of the family's former functions of protection, education, credit, and so on, have been removed from it and vested in the agencies and organizations of industrialized society

4) industrialization promotes an ideology of achieved, as opposed to ascribed or birth-related, status such that there is less to be gained occupationally by submission to the desires of kin

5) high levels of occupational specialization make it much less likely statistically that members of one's kin will be able to provide jobs that suit one's particular skills.[17]

From the American literature it appears that a modified Parsonian hypothesis can be advanced: *the long-term trends of both urbanization and industrialization appear to increase the residential and emotional importance of conjugal families, and to give to the formation of close extranuclear ties some of the voluntary character of friendships.*

Providing further support for such a hypothesis, Murray Strauss found that in a sample of 448 married women in Minnesota, farm wives had greater interaction with their kin than did urban wives; kinship interaction was lower for higher-income wives; kinship interaction was lowest among the urban white-collar group. "In fact," Strauss reports, "wives in the urban middle-class families had less than half the kinship interaction of the wives in the low income farm families."[18] Additionally, in a comparison of such vectors of "modernity" as planning for the future and educational expectations for children, a strong association was discovered between frequency of interaction with kin and "nonmodern" psychological traits, such that the greater the kinship interaction, the lower the achievement values and educational aspirations for children and the less emphasis was on planning and innovation in homemaking.

An interesting historical dimension has been added recently to the Parsonian argument, with the discovery that relatively isolated nuclear families may have been common in England and America *before* the Industrial Revolution and are thus perhaps better viewed as a precondition to, rather than a consequence of, the urbanization and industrialization of the two countries.[19] Michael Anderson's study of nineteenth-century Lancashire cotton towns demonstrated, for example, that the frequency of extended families did not decline in the city but was modified from the "stem" family characteristic of farm areas to a transitional pattern in which married offspring reside with their parents until they can afford to develop an independent residence. In reality, the temporary residence of children with their parents in urban settings may not have been far removed from the typical rural family, which also began as a nuclear family and extended as a son married and had children, only to eventually become nuclear again with the death of his parents.[20]

One of the most interesting of the various historical studies of the family is Frank Furstenberg's "Industrialization and the American Family: A Look Backward," which attempts to reconstruct American family life during the past century from written accounts of European visitors to the new nation, rather than from the census or parish records upon which many earlier studies were based. Using this source lacks some of the rigor of previous studies but has the advantage of providing a more revealing, human account of the family's recent past. Furstenberg's hypothesis is that "although industrialization may have placed added strains on the family, the extent to which the industrial system affected the family has been greatly exaggerated. Further, I contend that not only did strains exist prior to industrialization, but some of these very tensions in the family may have facilitated the process of industrialization."[21] He examined many accounts of the American family taken from the first half of the nineteenth century, a period before America had industrialized, during which less than 16 percent of the labor force was engaged in manufacturing and construction industries.

Noting that free mate selection and the notion of romantic love are often associated with weakened control of family elders in industrialized societies,[22] Furstenberg provides compelling data suggesting that "free choice of mates was the prevailing pattern as well as the social norm" during this early preindustrial period. Isidore Lowenstern wrote in 1842 that "a very remarkable custom in the United States gives girls the freedom to choose husbands according to their fancy; practice does not permit either the mother or father to interfere with this important matter."[23]

One of the most notable characteristics of early American society, and one that has continued, was the relatively great freedom enjoyed by young unmarried people. Unlike the European societies from which the visiting commentators came, the America they wrote about seemed to have confidence in its youth even to the extent that adolescents of opposite sexes were permitted to be alone without fear that they would engage in sexual activity. Coupled with premarital freedom, however, was a strong pressure to marry at an early age, a fact noted by several travelers: "They marry very young; in fact, in no rank of life do you meet with young women in that delightful period of existence between childhood and marriage, wherein, if only tolerably well spent, so much useful information is gained, and the character takes a sufficient degree of firmness to support with dignity the more important parts of wife and mother."[24]

The pressure to marry and the rapid change from freedom that it often entailed was observed by many commentators, among them de Tocqueville and Murat. The latter remarked that after marriage the woman was put away "on a shelf."[25] Whatever the reasons for coupling relative freedom with early marriage—and a reasonable hypothesis is that the first almost required the second if illegitimate births were to be avoided—it is quite likely that the potential for boredom and frustration was maximized for American women. In Furstenberg's opinion, this may have been a significant feature of the American family that aided industrialization, as it "may have encouraged women into the labor market when the possibility arose some decades later."[26]

Another important observation of foreign travelers of the period concerned lack of closeness in the American family. This may have been partly because families to which the travelers were most exposed were often engaged in operating hotels and boarding houses; but a consensus existed that "husbands neglected their wives for business."[27] On parent-child relations, Frederick Marryat remarked that "there is no endearment between the parents and children; none of that sweet spirit of affection between brother and sister," while Michael Chevalier, in noting and accepting as fact the relative absence of "family sentiment," hypothesized that "the temporary weakness of family sentiment was one of the necessary results of the general dispersion of individuals by which the colonization of America has been accomplished."[28]

Finally, the journals of early visitors to the United States continually remarked upon the state of American youth. Agreeing that children were well cared for, most travelers were also amazed by the permissiveness that characterized childrearing in America. Again, Marryat summarized the general reaction when he wrote, "Everyone who has been in the United States must have perceived that there is little or no parental control."[29] British travelers, too, were struck by the precocity of the "enthroned" American child, who treated his parents as companions.[30] It appears that children of the era were subject to most of the same pressures to assert early independence as are American children today, if not more so, and apparently they held parental authority in much the same light regard.

Furstenberg's study is vulnerable to the criticism that families with whom most travelers came into contact were urban and probably largely middle class. Thus much of what the visitors describe may have been the result of the influence of urban life on the family. But his conclusions that "changes in the American family since the period of industrialization have been exaggerated," and that some of the tensions and character of families of the period "may have eased the adaptation to an industrial society," are worthy of serious consideration.[31]

Equally important to the issue of influence of urbanization and industrialization upon the family, however, is the fact that the open frontier of nineteenth-century America was an atypical one that renders comparisons with most other areas of the world problematic. In contrast to Great Britain, France, and most of Europe, for example, pressures toward strong rural family stability may have been reduced by the opportunities for young adults to find farmland away from their families and thus gain their independence.

HOW CULTURE INFLUENCES THE EFFECTS
OF URBANIZATION AND INDUSTRIALIZATION
ON EXTENDED KIN NETWORKS

Parsons' hypothesis that a strong congruence exists between a society's degree of industrialization and its emphasis on the structurally nuclear family provoked a great deal of research to test the accuracy of the assumption. Although superficially the hypothesis seems straightforward, amenable to objective verification or rejection, in reality it is multifaceted, encompassing such issues as the associations between urbanization and industrialization, urbanism and extended kinship networks, urban migration and maintenance of kin ties, and extent of kin network and social class.

While industrialization implies a level of social organization only found in societies with a well-developed urban base, our knowledge of urbanization in much of the non-Western world demonstrates that urban centers can and do develop outside industrial economies. The impossibility of separating the effects of urbanization from industrialization in the West, however, requires care in generalizing findings from industrialized to nonindustrialized societies. Even if we accept the thesis that, in undergoing massive urbanization and industrialization, the significance of large-scale kin networks has been diminished in the United States, caution must be used in generalizing this experience to other cultural traditions. In part this is because urbanization and industrialization have not necessarily occurred contemporaneously outside the United States, and especially outside the Western world, and therefore cannot be so readily considered as a unit. But another factor, the influence of cultural variation upon the adaptation of kinship systems to urbanization, must be considered. It is probable that, even if a worldwide shift toward conjugal systems is in process, the transition will not occur everywhere in the same manner or time.

To grasp the varying impact of urbanization and industrialization upon the family in various cultural traditions, it is worthwhile to survey the research from several different regions.

French Canada

One of the clearest examples of the tendency to maximize cultural differences in kinship studies is provided by Phillipe Garigue's article "French-Canadian Kinship and Urban Life," which appeared in the *American Anthropologist* in 1956. In analyzing the extent of kinship knowledge of 52 mostly middle-class individuals residing in Montreal, he discovered that the mean number of relatives whose name and/or sex and kin relation were recalled was 215, ranging from 75 to 484. In view of Codere's earlier discovery of recognition networks of only 30 to 33 kin in a survey of 200 American college students aged 17 to 20, Garigue remarked that there appeared to be marked cultural differences between French Canadians and Americans. Although college students—because of their age, consequent lack of descending generations, and assumed emphasis on upward mobility and non-kin-based relations—probably represent the extreme of minimal kinship recognition in America, the difference is still impressive.

Garigue considered that "one of the most widely accepted generalizations about kinship is the proposition that the greater the urbanization, the smaller the kinship range, and that this apparent result of city life is everywhere the same." He questioned why the kinship basis of French Canadian society had not been radically altered by urbanization, feeling that the differences "are not due to more extensive rural survivals among the French Canadians, or to longer urban conditioning in the United States, but in each instance seem to be part of the established urban way of life, with its cultural values." The differences are due also, thought Garigue, to the presence of "a cultural complex which included the French language as spoken in Quebec, a specific system of education, membership in the Catholic church, and various political theories about the status of French Canadians in Canada." "*It seems,*" he says, "*that the crucial factors in diminishing kinship recognition are the cultural values of the society, not its degree of urbanization.*"[32]

Marcel Rioux, a leading French Canadian sociologist, took issue with Garigue's assumption of French Canadian cultural immunity to the effects of urbanization. He argued that French Canada is less urbanized than the United States, and that "owing to the partial physical and cultural isolation of French Canada in the Nineteenth century, urbanization processes have been at work over a shorter period than in the rest of North America; this society has only started since 1940 to become more individualistic and secularized."[33] Rioux demonstrated that a great deal of rural-urban variation existed within French Canada with respect to kinship recognition and that on this basis it was unwise to view French Canadian-American variation exclusively in terms of cultural values.

Noting that wider recognition of kinship had almost certainly existed in the past, Rioux concluded from his study of the Acadian community of Chéticamp, Cape Breton, that it continues to exist in isolated and/or rural areas of French Canada today. In Chéticamp, he found that 20 surnames make up 90 percent of the parish population (such limited patronymic variety is also the rule for rural Quebec). In order to identify an individual, one usually has to name his father or grandfather.

Paul Chiasson would not be recognized by anybody unless he is called Paul-à-Timothée-à-Joseph. Sometimes the fourth generation has to be reached before the individual is properly identified . . . When somebody phones, he should properly identify his party by saying "Placide-à-Paul-à-Lubin Aucoin." A local Acadian weekly, published in New Brunswick, prints a social column about Chéticamp, often omitting the genealogical ties of the individuals. The result is that practically nobody knows which individuals the newspaper is talking about.[34]

One of Rioux's informants, who acted as a *défricheur de parenté* (kinship clearer-upper), for his family, possessed an oral kinship recognition vocabulary of some 2,000 individuals—including members of his patrilineage back to 1785 and many secondary relatives—which was verified as far as possible through local parish records. Other *défricheurs* displayed a similar capacity. Rioux estimates that the average individual knows about 500. He concludes

that there are extensive spatio-temporal variations within French Canada on the question of kinship recognition and that these variations are due primarily to a difference in the degree of urbanization in the various segments of this socio-cultural whole; cultural values might be affected by the social transformations that urbanization brings about, but in the case of kinship recognition it seems that the urbanization factor is primordial.[35]

Is it not possible, however, that the reduced importance of French Canadian kinship in the wake of urbanization, recognized by Rioux, serves to mask an original cultural base? After all, a recognition level of over 200 in Montreal as compared to just over 30 for American college students does represent a major difference.

It would seem wise to seek an analogous geographical region in the United States and investigate the importance of kin-based inter-action there. In the southern United states, for example, there is a marked tendency to maintain regular kin interaction with relatives classed as second-cousins and even beyond. While the basis for this interaction could be classified as "cultural" or "subcultural," the principal factor accounting for it is undoubtedly the lack of spatial and vertical mobility of the region. People still tend to live and die in the place and status in which they were born. Regular contact is thus maintained with large numbers of relatives, so that one's second-cousin's personality as well as his name and relationship can be easily brought to mind. Today, a change can clearly be seen in the region, as many individuals—reluctant to move to the north, for it is often viewed as a cold, ruthless environment where one's very linguistic capacity is likely to be called into question—have moved from small towns and farms of the south to its major cities, Atlanta, Birmingham, and New Orleans. But even in the cities, patterns of visiting and maintenance of other kin contact appear with sufficient strength to suggest that recent urbanization is a major factor in their persistence.

Most interesting from the standpoint of Garigue's culture-based argument is the case of the Louisiana Cajuns (whose cultural base is identical to that of French Canada), who have also begun to move to the cities and suburbs of the south. Clyde Collard's discussion of the state of today's Cajun family is a familiar one:

> The extended family has loosened the hold it once had on the various members of the kinship group. In its place, the nuclear family, consisting of husband, wife, and their children, now takes precedence. Young couples are less dependent on the older generation or on other family members in their age group. Consequently, they are now more independent in decision-making and in choosing their own way of life. They are inclined to move farther away from family localities and to broaden friendship groups beyond family ties. Interactions between kinship groups are less often authoritive and economic but restricted to social/emotional relationships.[36]

Thus it seems apparent, from comparisons of rural and urban French Canada, not just Vassar students and urban Montrealers, that the extent of kinship knowledge does decline with urbanization. In rural French Canada, maintenance of elaborate genealogies seems to be reinforced by more sedentary life styles; there even distant kin are encountered frequently enough to give them a real existence. In Montreal, as in other North American cities, spatial and vertical social mobility remove extended kin from frequent contact.

Yugoslavia

During the nineteenth century, rural Serbian social order focused on a patrilineal corporate family group known as the *zadruga*, which held farmland in common as a kin-based collective. United by the performance of a common task, the *zadruga's* composition was determined by claim to a share in the land and not necessarily by direct relation to an individual. Within the *zadruga*, however, there was frequent discontent—arising primarily from feelings that certain members were not contributing their share of work or from quarrels between unrelated female spouses of members—which provided pressure for division of the land and the consequent dissolution of the group. That dissatisfaction was widespread became apparent upon the passage of a law in 1870 permitting division of *zadrugas*: a virtual epidemic of dissolutions took place, so that by World War I *zadrugas* were scarce. Today the *zadruga* has vanished from Yugoslav life, and average household size has declined from that of ten to a hundred members, sometimes including second-degree patrilineal cousins, to that of an average in 1961 of slightly less than four persons.[37]

From the Yugoslav experience, Barić postulates two levels of kinship: (1) a "substratum level" of recognized relatives outside the nuclear family that is common to a degree in all societies; and (2) the grouping of certain kin into a "structural corporate unit" super-imposed on the substratum level, peculiar to some societies only. In Lorraine Barić's estimation, the disappearance of corporate kin groups has not eliminated the importance of extended kin, even in the cities of what is today a largely industrialized society, but has placed the focus of kinship upon the individual, emphasizing such factors as personal feeling in determining which extended kin are important to him.[38]

In Yugoslavia's cities, the presence of extended kin groups is reinforced by the need for assistance networks to ease adaptation to urban life. Another reinforcement to kin groups is the common pattern—at least for rural-urban migrants who have been in the city for less than a decade—of reciprocal aid and economic exchange between urbanites and their country kin. In the city, kin networks are promoted and continually reinforced by a crucial urban problem: shortage of housing. Solution to a housing need is invariably sought through kin. Once an apartment has been located and its new resi-dents settled, an extended relationship is often furthered by contact with the kinsmen who found the apartment.[39]

Many urbanites maintain strong ties to their villages. These are manifested by frequent visits and by sending children to spend vaca-tions with rural relatives—an exchange often reciprocated by country kin, whose children sometimes spend vacations discovering the world of the city. Eugene Hammel found that in 1965 over half the men in a sample of 350 Serbian industrial workers spent the annual vacation in their native villages.[40] Primary in importance in the maintenance of rural-urban kin networks is the symbiotic nature they often acquire. The urbanites, who frequently own or have an interest in village land, return to check on their holdings and to bring produce back to the city. Most urban families spend the majority of their net income on food—Andrei Simić estimates *at least* 70 percent[41]—so that visits to rural relatives often serve a crucial need of replenishing the larder. On the other hand, just as "urbanites may be seen arriving daily in Belgrade by bus and train, returning from visits with rural kin laden with sacks filled with eggs, meat, cheese, vegetables and other farm produce,"[42] visits to the village are made laden with such cash-purchased products as shirts and scarves, coffee and sugar, and occasionally more expensive items like televisions or farm equipment.

Thus, in Yugoslavia certain urban pressures towards restricted kinship exist—such as a scarcity of housing that usually limits a residence to members of a single nuclear family, and an emerging industrial society that emphasizes individual achievement and restricts the role of kin in helping an individual find employment. But these restrictive pressures are countered by economic necessities that reinforce the importance of extended kin relationships.

India

Research into the impact of urbanization and industrialization upon extended families in India is complicated by the tremendous caste, class, and ethnic diversity of that enormous subcontinent. An individual's birth-ascribed position as a member of a certain caste, or *jati*, has traditionally limited his marriage and occupational possibilities, as well as defined appropriate behavior towards those of other castes. In addition to Hindu-sanctioned divisions of caste, myriads of other divisive factors exist in India—such as language group, region of origin, and religion—that divide its peoples into an immense patchwork. Chief of all the factors that complicate discussion of kinship in urban India is the fact that strong caste barriers make each kindred a minicultural unit with a strong cohesive ideology. On one extreme the family can be defined as fellow members of one's caste or subcaste, which makes it virtually an ethnic group, while on the other hand it could be described on a conjugal or nuclear basis, ignoring the crucial binding force of Hindu traditions to larger caste units.

The traditional corporate family residential unit of most of India's population, the joint family, undoubtedly gains much of its strength from the religious and cultural sanctions surrounding the *jati*. These sanctions promote a strong in-group sense in extended families, although they are often divisive at the societal level. Such joint families, consisting as they often do of brothers, their children, occasionally, their children's children, and often other patrilineally related agnates, are most viable where the family's economic resources are sufficient to provide support and employment for all. Not surprisingly, those best able to maintain the ideal of such a large co-resident family often have large rural landholdings.

Today in the cities of India, the lament that the joint family is rapidly breaking up is frequently heard. Such a belief appears to rise not so much from desire for this to occur so that individuals can gain greater personal independence, but from realization that urban employment and housing frequently make co-residence difficult to achieve. Thus, 71 percent of the 106 workers and foremen interviewed by Michael Ames in the industrial steel city of Jamshedpur stated a preference for patrilineal, patrilocal extended family residence with at least three generations of relatives and their spouses under the same roof, sharing property and meals. Only 12 percent of the sample—most "middle-class" foremen—expressed a desire for conjugal family residence. But preference for joint residence was rarely achieved: 83 percent of the workers and foremen lived in conjugal households, while only one respondent resided in a true joint family.[43]

A similar situation is reported for residents of a village located across India from Jamshedpur, on the outskirts of Delhi. Here, too, a strong preference for joint family living—82 percent of the sample expressed a desire for it—was coupled with the evident inability of many to achieve their ideal: only 37 percent of the families were actually joint, although joint families accounted for 52 percent of the population.

Not surprisingly, *the major factors prohibiting the actualization of higher levels of joint family residence appear to be economic.* Strong support for this interpretation emerged from the Freeds' research, in which they found only a slight and insignificant tendency of joint families to be headed by "village-oriented" rather than "urban-oriented" men, when caste, landownership, and literacy were held constant. Interestingly, all low-caste literate men were urban-oriented, and of them only 15 percent headed joint families. For these individuals, who had achieved literacy despite the handicap of caste, continued strong and intimate association with kin might well reduce the opportunities for achievement which they undoubted sought. Landownership, however, tended to be strongly correlated with joint family residence. This is apparently both because land-holdings permit the support and utilization of the labor resources of large families, and because it is frequently much easier and more efficient to retain ownership and working of land in common than to divide and farm it with a diminished labor force.[44]

Superficially at least, it often appears that India's urbanization has strongly affected the future of the joint family. S. N. Sen, for example, reported that one-fifth of the Calcutta city population lived in single households, and that between 52 and 62 percent of all Calcutta households were single member ones.[45] But the problem in predicting the effect of urbanization upon the joint family is that the high levels of single and nuclear family residence of the city's population are often not perceived by those involved as a breakaway from the joint family. This is probably true both for long-term residents and for recent migrants. The presence of the latter in the city in such large numbers as single individuals paradoxically points to the great strength still enjoyed by joint families: it is need of the village joint family for additional income that often propels its members outwards with the dual purpose of gaining individual livelihood and adding to the income of the family. Adding credence to the assumption that urban single person households often result from an attempt to maintain rural joint families is the fact that a great number of these single residents are married men whose wives and children have stayed behind in villages. As Edwin Eames suggests from his study of the north Indian village of Senapur, "knowing that the nuclear family will be taken care of by the joint family in Senapur, or the wife's family in her parental village, is an important factor enabling the individual to leave Senapur without having to take his nuclear family or worry about their well-being."[46] Additional support for the conclusion that the economic gains of urban employment often permit the maintenance of joint families in home villages is the fact that 82.9 percent of families with migrant members had some form of joint family, while only 48.8 percent of non-migrant families were joint.[47]

In another study, "Caste, Kinship, and Association in Urban India," William Rowe discovered that over 35 percent of the total income of the Saltworker caste of Senapur took the form of cash brought into the village by out-migrants who had left, chiefly for Bombay, in search of employment. The significance of migration—and the cash which such migrants provide—is enough to have made families and villagers who have large numbers of migrants *nouveau riche*. The social impact of the remittances is illustrated by the comments of a Senapur village elder on one such household: "Oh yes, now they are sahibs, but only yesterday they were so poor that when X (of their house) died, they secretly carried the body to the river since they could not afford funeral ceremonies." Rowe concludes that, "in direct contradiction to the claim that 'the city will destroy the village,' it is our finding that, in economic terms at least, the city makes the continuance of the North Indian village possible."[48]

Thus, it appears that most Indians prefer some form of joint family residence and often migrate great distances to urban employment, not in a desire to establish independent households, but with a goal of increasing the viability of their co-residence. As Ames remarks, "if we look only at household structure in Jamshedpur we would mistakenly conclude that the Indian joint family is breaking up and dying out," but if we look at property owning and ideal residence patterns we conclude "that the Indian joint family is thriving rather than dying out."[49]

In time, of course, extended breaks in residence made necessary by the search for employment may lead to the establishment of isolated families as a more common type. Indeed, some evidence exists to suggest that such a pattern may be emerging among middle-class individuals.[50] Sylvia Vatuk suggests that despite the professed ideology common to many urbanites that one's "true home" is in the husband's village, a shift may be occuring away from strong patrilineal joint family ties to a bilateral pattern in which the wife's relatives are also counted as significant members of the nuclear family. In the West, research frequently demonstrates a trend towards "matrilineal asymmetry," or an interactional emphasis of the wife's over the husband's kin, emerging from the wife's tendency to devote more of her own time to the maintenance of family ties than does her husband. While matrilineal asymmetry cannot currently be said to exist in urban India because the husband's family ties continue to be strong, evidence exists to suggest that removal of a wife from residence with her husband's extended family offers a greater opportunity to maintain ties with her own family. Visiting with her own relatives is often easier in cities in comparison to traditional village living situations in which a wife's relatives are generally reluctant to stay with her husband's family, and in which a woman's mother-in-law has the prerogative to prevent her from visiting her native village. The conclusion that urban residence, with its tendency to lessen direct control over the young couple by the corporate patrilineal family, may be promoting bilateral reckoning of kin is also indicated by Vatuk's discovery that a wife's kinsmen or matrilineal relatives were as likely to have helped an individual secure urban employment as was a patrilineal relative.[51]

Urbanization in India seems to have the effect of reducing the size of co-resident kin groups and of increasing the day-to-day isolation of many urban residents from their extended kindreds. Initially, at least, such isolation appears to result more from economic pressures than from desire for independence from larger kin units, although in time it is likely that those who remain in cities will tend to approximate nuclear patterns of residence.

Southeast and East Asia

The paucity of research on urban Southeast Asian families makes it difficult to draw conclusions about the effects, if any, of urban life on kinship. In Thailand and the other countries of Theravada Buddhist Southeast Asia (Burma, Cambodia, and Laos), extended families have not traditionally had the same significance as in China and Japan. Instead, the family has tended more towards the Western nuclear or stem family patterns. Theravada Buddhism emphasizes the individual's isolation, rather than reinforcing the role of the family as Hinduism, Confucianism, Mahayana Buddhism, and Islam do. Thai use of surnames, for example, which are to a degree indicative of concern with extended kin, is an innovation of this century mandated by the King as part of a royal policy of modernization.

Inconclusive as the evidence is, it is clear that the rapid growth of Bangkok in the past several decades has not yet produced major changes in Thai family structure, especially towards breakdown. Indeed, from most reports of the nuclearity and instability of rural Thai families it is difficult to imagine that Thai kinship *could* become significantly less important in the city.[52] Robert Textor reports, for example, that northeasterners who migrate to Bangkok to become *samlor*, or pedicab drivers, often stay with kin, and that "friendship groups serve much the same needs as kinship groups, and are hardly less important."[53]

It can be argued with considerable justification that the recent elaboration of a relatively large Thai bureaucracy and urban middle class, placing a premium upon extended kin networks as vehicles for the distribution of patronage, may actually be increasing the importance of kin among certain of Bangkok's classes. It is quite likely, for example, that marital stability is actually stronger among members of the urban middle class, especially in marriages with the character of interfamilial alliance, than among rural peasants and lower-class urbanites. Here, as elsewhere, economic factors often favor maintenance of close ties with extended kin. Such a development might also be related to the influence of Bangkok's Chinese population—roughly half of the city's population is of Chinese ancestry—which has traditionally valued large corporate kin groups.

Southeast Asia's Chinese population is largely descended from emigrants who left southern China in the nineteenth or early twentieth centuries. Most continue to emphasize the primacy of kin ties in the generally held assumption that kin must rank first in an individual's priorities. Even today Chinese university graduates frequently remit a substantial portion of their income to their families. Most obvious of the bases of family solidarity in the urban setting is the institution of the Chinese family shop, which in many ways provides the urban equivalent of the farm in its support of the family and utilization of its members' labor. Over three-quarters of those working in west Malaysian retail establishments in 1968, for example, were members of the owning families, most of whom live and work on the same premises. They serve as Donald Willmott notes, as "the personnel core of most Chinese businesses [which] is either one family or a single family and one or more satellite families."[54]

Despite the persisting importance of extended kin among overseas Chinese there are indications that emigration from China and settlement among alien peoples have had their impact on the family. Traditional Chinese social organization has emphasized as ideal residence patterns two forms of extended family, the *stem* and the *joint* family. These are distinguished by the residence of parents and one of their sons, his spouse, and children in stem families, and of parents and two or more sons or daughters and their families of procreation in joint families. Joint and stem families are still considered ideal by some overseas Chinese, but there seems to be an increasing preference for conjugal households.

As part of his study of Chinese in the Indonesian city of Semarang, Willmott interviewed fifty housewives to elicit their household preferences. Somewhat surprisingly, forty-seven favored conjugal families. A major concern, expressed even among two of the three respondents who preferred some form of extended family, was that cooperation was very difficult among co-resident extended kin. As one said: "In Chinese families there are too many quarrels if the family sticks together . . . [especially] between mothers-in-law and daughters-in-law and between sisters-in-law. So they separate if they can."[55] Despite the strong preference for conjugal family residence, actual patterns of the sample families were divided equally between conjugal and extended families: 50 percent were conjugal, 40 percent stem, and 10 percent joint.

Comparison with earlier studies of mainland China suggest that although there may have been a shift of residential *preference* among Semarang's Chinese, little shift in actual patterns seems to have occurred. Traditionally, stem families—which serve to pass on the family farm to one of the male offspring—have been most common among small peasant landholders; the larger joint family could only be supported by gentry. Surveys from the 1930's show that the percentage of conjugal families varied from 54 for farm laborers to 12 for landholders in northern Chinese villages, and from 58 for wage-earners to 50 among the middle class in cities. Another survey, from central China, reported that 66 percent of urban families and 45 percent of rural were conjugal.[56] It thus appears likely that there has been a much less significant increase in conjugal family households than might be implied by comparing the ideal family of China's past and the actual family of today's urban overseas Chinese, and that in the past usually only the well-to-do could sustain large co-resident joint families.

Two significant changes in overseas Chinese family patterns do seem to have occurred. Traditionally, stem families were formed by addition of a son's wife to a nuclear family. Of the nineteen stem families in Willmott's sample, eight included a husband and wife, their children, and the mother of either the husband or wife (in one case, both mothers). Thus, in contrast to the traditional stem family, a significant portion of Semarang families were formed by the addition of an aged parent rather than of a young daughter-in-law, a situation noted by Willmott as of social and psychological significance because it makes a great deal of difference "who comes as the outsider to the original unit."[57] Additionally, it seems that members of the Chinese community have begun to place so much greater emphasis upon recognition of the wife's kin that the system is shifting from its traditional patrilineal, patrilocal character to one that is bilateral and bilocal or neolocal (that is, to one recognizing the kin of both husband and wife, and permitting residence with either of their families or establishment of separate residence). Willmott believes that the increasing status of women in men's eyes underlies this change. The rise in status is directly attributable to the bargaining power overseas Chinese women have had by virtue of their scarcity, on the one hand, and by the importance of native women as intermediaries between their Chinese husbands and the local community.

Similar changes in traditional Chinese social organization have been observed among Singapore Chinese. Rural organization in the southern Chinese provinces of Fukien and Kwangtung, from which much of Singapore's population has come, was strongly oriented around agnatic corporate groups formed by common descent through male ancestors. Overseas, the principle of agnation shifted from emphasis on local corporate groups based on traceable kinship—for at most only a few members of each agnatic group were likely to emigrate—to frequent "surname associations," in which those of one surname pooled their resources for mutual aid (for example, the Lim family association). The importance of patrilineally traced descent was modified by the fact that brides no longer moved from the location of their agnatic group of procreation upon marriage and often shifted residence within the city. As locally born generations began to mature and marry, proximity to relatives permitted more emphasis upon the wife's relatives. This, coupled with the fact that many family friends were likely to be nonkinsmen, has helped reduce the importance of agnatic groups. Consequently, such former concerns of the extended kin group as marriage and the worship of family ancestors have tended to become the province of individual families rather than of the entire agnatic, or even surname group. Joint families, too, are significantly absent in Singapore, and a strong tendency exists to dissolve units of married brothers after the death of their parents.[58]

In his research into the impact of urban residence upon the traditional culture of the Batak of Sumatra, Edward Bruner reports that the traditional social organization, or *adat,* has remained strong in the city. Despite the fact that many urban Batak have acquired a Western education and served in the Dutch colonial and later the Indonesian governments, kinship ties have remained a crucial interpersonal component. Undoubtedly, a major factor underlying the retention of close ties between Batak settled in the coastal Sumatran city of Medan and their village cousins of the interior is the fact that both are Christians on a predominantly Muslim island. In an area where religion is the primary source of individual identity, religious differences give the urban Batak community the character of a somewhat dispersed ghetto and emphasize the importance of maintaining rural ties that permit urbanites to withdraw to the country in times of urban economic collapse or sectarian strife.

Although the Batak will be discussed further later, it is worth mentioning here that the relative urbanity of the Batak of Medan had not at the time of Bruner's research produced significant alterations in kinship obligations or in traditional beliefs and ceremonies. Belief in sorcery and other supernatural agents has not disappeared in the city, although some doubt of their efficacy is occasionally expressed (a skepticism probably also found in the countryside). Even traditional Batak ceremonial life persists in Medan, though in somewhat modified form. In the city, for example, the two-part marriage ceremony of the countryside—a Christian church service in the morning followed by a traditional *adat* ceremonial feast in the afternoon—is supplemented by a recent Western innovation, the wedding reception. In general, the church affair is open to the entire Christian community, the *adat* ceremony to urban and village relatives, and the reception to high-status urban Batak and non-Batak friends and business associates.

Most illustrative of the strength of Batak social organization is the fact that, at least at the time of Bruner's research, kin ties were still sufficiently strong to override great experiental differences. This is exemplified in the case of continuing kin contacts between an urban government official, fluent in four languages and the author of a French grammar text, and his uncle, who supported two wives, worked his own fields, chewed betel, and reminisced of his earlier cannibalistic practices.[59]

In completing this survey of Asian family ties, we must consider Japan, which has experienced the region's most radical residential and economic alterations. The question of whether Japanese culture has been forced to change in accomodation to a new industrial order, or whether it has merely incorporated new technological and economic systems in ways congruent with traditional Japanese society, has usually been answered with evidence that points to the minimally disruptive effects of industrialization upon traditional society. Takeo Yazaki provided a generally accepted formulation when he argued:

> there is no justification for regarding contemporary Japanese urban civilization as being generally forced by the requirements of the industrial system into the standardized Western mold, hindered only by lingering traditional elements. Rather, it would seem plausible to conclude tentatively that Japan has been able to exercise alternative options which may produce different long-term solutions—options derived from her own cultural experience and therefore not necessarily available to other countries, but nonetheless options which raise fundamental questions about the range of alternative choices in contemporary urbanization and justify rethinking many rooted assumptions.[60]

Not all researchers have fully concurred with a perspective that denies the potential primacy of universal industrial processes over the incorporative capabilities of Japanese culture. Jitsuichi Masuoka, in an early postwar study tracing the historical evolution of Japanese households, reported that residential family size had declined from an estimated range of 14 to 25 in the eighth century, to 3.82 for urban and 4.68 for rural areas in 1920. Concluding that "the modern family is relatively simple in organization and less inclusive in membership,"[61] and that the size of the family declines with increase in city size, Masuoka deduced that the most common modern family type consists of husband, wife, and children; blood relatives more than one link removed from the family head and affinals other than the head's spouse have largely disappeared from family membership. In restricting his definition of family to co-residents, Masuoka provides evidence that household size has declined, but he says nothing of the importance to urban families of nonresident extended kin.

Though research available in English has not focused on patterns of maintenance or severance of ties with non-nuclear kin, the literature on postwar Japanese families clearly indicates that significant changes are under way. Two factors pointing to probable decline in the significance of extended kin are: increase in the solidarity of the conjugal family, and the growing tendency for business to assume extended family functions.

Enhanced solidarity of the conjugal family is evident in much Japanese sociological literature pointing to a decline in arranged marriages, coupled with a growth in "love marriages" and an apparent tendency for development of greater intimacy between husband and wife.[62] A surprising and telling, bit of evidence of the importance of the marital relationship is revealed in Japan's divorce rates: far from increasing as the society has urbanized and industrialized, they have actually *declined* from 1887 to 1958, from 3.0 to 0.8 per thousand population![63] Such a significant drop is probably best explained by a concomittant decline in the significance of extended families, so that retreat to kin from an unhappy marriage is a less viable option.

The tremendous success of Japanese industry has been coupled with assumption of many extended family functions by employers. Having been engaged as an employee, for example, it is unlikely that one will ever be fired. The relation between company and employee is expected to be a lifelong one, in which the company usually provides not only employment but medical, retirement, recreational, and educational programs for the employee and his family in return for a high level of employee loyalty. Thus, many difficulties of such crises as illness and death are handled by the company. Increasingly, even marriage arrangements—often of two people working for the same organization—are handled by superiors in the company.

One result of the changes undergone by the Japanese family is the increasing loss of a clear social role for the aged. Whereas aged parents once occupied a respected position in a son's house, today the three-generation stem family has become rare. Children are no longer brought up in the same households with grandparents who shower them with affection and transmit traditional Japanese customs often neglected by working parents. Occupational mobility, too, has removed much of the importance of grandparents, whose former role in transmitting vocational knowledge has become more and more irrelevant in a society stressing universal extrafamilial education and achievement. "The ideal of following in a father's footsteps," R. P. Dore reports, "is replaced by the ideal of doing better than the father."[64] These changes, especially the shift of traditional functions of kinship away from actual kin have resulted in what Masuoka has termed the "rolelessness of the aged."[65] Neglect of the elderly has not yet reached the level it has in American society, but the rapid shift in scarcely one generation from a society that venerated its aged to one that often regards them as superfluous has been confusing and painful for many who have passed their productive years. A manifestation of their dilemma can be seen in the growth of *pokkuri* (peaceful end to life). As many as 2,000 men and women journey weekly to a Buddhist shrine near the ancient capital of Nara, to hear a priest discuss the importance of a peaceful end and to have their undergarments blessed, in the belief that the goal of *pokkuri* might thus be achieved. The growth of this temple and others like it is clearly the result of the coupling of life-extending medical techniques with a society in which old people merely exist without a useful role, as a burden on their children. In the words of one old woman who has faithfully journeyed to the Nara temple for years: "Young people don't want to take care of old people . . . and if the old have no one to care for them, they have to go to institutions for the aged. I would rather die."[66]

It is evident that recent changes in Southeast and East Asian families with the growth of urban and/or industrial life styles have been intimately connected with the peculiarities of each cultural tradition and the specific nature of alterations to which these traditions have been exposed. But a careful review of the literature makes it difficult to concur wholly with Bruner's certainty that in Asia "society does not become secularized, the individual does not become isolated, kinship organizations do not break down, nor do social relationships in the urban environment become impersonal, superficial and utilitarian."[67] In the nations of Southeast and East Asia, as elsewhere, economic considerations seem to determine the role of kinship in urban areas. In general, the position of the conjugal family seems to have been enhanced by the processes of urbanization and industrialization.

Latin America

Traditionally, post-conquest Latin American societies have not emphasized large corporate kinship units. Kinship has tended to be ego-centered and coupled with a strong individualistic ethos which generally favors conjugal family residence even in rural areas.[68] Isolated nuclear family household units are not uncommon in either urban or rural areas, although their peculiar nature varies somewhat from place to place.

Hammel, in contrasting the family cycles of a Peruvian village and an urban slum, reports that young adults from both city and village regard the independent nuclear family as the ideal household organization and seek to achieve it as quickly as possible after marriage. Married slum dwellers are more likely than villagers to establish such a residence because the typical absence of other kin strongly encourages co-residence of spouses, especially for women with young children. But formation of a truly independent nuclear family is frequently inhibited by economic pressures that force couples to incorporate other wage-earning adults into their households to help care for children and bear expenses of urban residence like rent, water, and fuel.

Peruvian slum, in contrast to rural, families are more likely to exist as "less-than-nuclear" families broken by the husband's desertion, which gives many of them a matricentric focus. Such matrifocal families appear to result from conflicting male-female goals. Thus, in both urban and rural areas women regard co-residence of husband and wife as ideal. For women, the primary benefit is undoubtedly support by a working male. For men, the urban setting tends to facilitate mobility by removing them from constraints of the village, where the responsibility for real and productive property and the pressure of family attitudes inhibits a husband's decision to desert his wife.[69] An additional factor encouraging matrifocal patterns in low-income urban families is the difficulty of many slum dwellers in earning enough to support a family.[70] Rather than openly admit their inability to meet an important part of their male role, many men desert their obligations.

A recent study of a Lima *barriada* (squatter settlement) suggests that a common feature of many urban families is the presence of relatives, especially aged parents who act as caretakers of the residence and children while the husband and wife work. A great deal of tension often exists in the parent-child relationship, centered around fear that parents' efforts to care for their children may not be reciprocated in their old age.[71]

Several researchers have remarked the importance that Mexicans tend to place on kinship as a basis for continued close interaction, both in cities and villages. Joseph Kahl, in contrasting "modernism" in Brazil and Mexico, felt that the conjugal family of Rio de Janeiro was more "modern" than that of Mexico City. In Brazil, interaction with nonkin tended to be more relaxed and less formal than in Mexico, where such relations were often entered into with suspicion and reserve evidenced, for example, in a tendency not to address others by their first names. The preference of urban Mexicans to rely upon relatives, and their distrust of strangers, was illustrated by responses to a survey administered to samples in Brazil and Mexico. Mexicans indicated a significantly greater tendency to agree with such statements as "it is always better to hire a relative than a stranger" and "people always help persons who have helped them not so much because it is right but because it is good business." In short, "more confidence in nonfamily ties, less dependence on relatives, and less emphasis on male dominance" in Brazil as opposed to Mexico seem to have facilitated an urban Brazilian conjugal family structure which approximates Parsons' anticipated urban mode.[72]

Lewis, too, in making the important point that researchers need to be more careful in distinguishing between the extended family as residence unit and as social group, reports that even though the nuclear family is the most common residence unit for both rural and urban Mexicans, the extended family remains an important social group in both locations. Both extended family bonds and the *compadre* system, with adoptive kin ties from one individual's becoming godfather to another's children, seem compatible with Mexican industrial and urban life. In either situation, though, Lewis suggests that the peasant's emphasis on kinship represents a shallower interpersonal grasping at ascribed ties than do friendships in Western cities. "I suspect," he says, "there are deeper, more mature human relationships among sympathetic, highly educated, cosmopolitan individuals who have chosen each other in friendship, than are possible among sorcery-ridden, superstitious, ignorant peasants, who are daily thrown together because of kinship or residential proximity."[73]

Kemper, in his study of Tzintzuntzan migrants to Mexico City, found the proportion of nuclear, joint, and truncated households roughly the same for both Tzintzunteños resident in their village and in Mexico City. Nuclear households accounted for 70 percent of Tzintzuntzan households and 66.2 percent of those in Mexico City. But further investigation convinced him that, while extended family ties are invariably weak and sometimes nonexistent in Tzintzuntzan, residence in the city seems to actually strengthen them. Frequently, close relatives live in the same *vecidad* (group of apartments), sharing many daily activities and much leisure time, yet pay their own rents and regard themselves as residents of separate households. In reanalyzing his data and checking for patterns of quasi-joint family residence, Kemper found that the number of nuclear households with no significant ties to extended family fell to only 32.5 percent of migrant households, while extended families increased to 41.9 percent when the strict co-residence criterion was eliminated. It is evident not only that many extended family ties have been reinforced by residence in Mexico City, but that they often "serve as significant adjuncts to the nuclear household in easing urban adaption."[74]

Residence in Mexico City has often had what can be regarded as positive effects on the Tzintzuntzan nuclear family in increasing its cohesiveness and improving interpersonal rapport. The compatible but tension-producing roles of male *machismo*, or hypermasculinity, and *la madre abnegada*, the suffering mother, seem less important in the city—to the improvement of the entire family environment. Additionally, the relative economic success enjoyed by most of the migrants engenders greater unity within the family[75] —a condition of marked contrast to that of many urban migrants to Lima, Buenos Aires, and elsewhere whose family lives are frequently disrupted by conditions of poverty.[76]

Numerous writers have noted the prevalence of poverty-based sexual promiscuity, prostitution, and consensual unions in Latin America's urban slums. But much of this undoubtedly grows more out of unwillingness to undergo the cost of a legal civil or religious marriage than from desire to form a free union. Both Mangin and Ugalde, on the basis of research in Lima and in Ciudad Juárez, Mexico, respectively, agree that the percentage of consensual unions is often high but argue that a formal union could not be assumed to make the marriage more stable.[77] Another problem, also more apparent than real, is the frequency of illegitimate children from consensual unions. From a superficial examination of formal marriage rates, rather than of the relative stability of common-law marriages, it often appears that many more children live in truncated families than is in fact the case. Poverty creates a great many human problems; but the assumption that urban poverty leads to sexual promiscuity and family disintegration is often overdrawn, as proven by close analysis. In some instances poverty may actually press kin closer together so that institutions such as the family and *compadrazgo*, uniting the father and godfather of a child in a fictive kin tie, are strengthened in the urban slum.

Oscar Lewis: "Urbanization Without Breakdown"   One of the most influential studies of the impact of rural-urban migration upon the family and traditional culture has been Oscar Lewis' "Urbanization Without Breakdown." This study, based on Tepoztecan migrants to Mexico City, was undertaken at a time when reports of the effects of urban living among migrants invariably emphasized "the negative aspects, such as personal maladjustment, breakdown of family life, decline of religion, and increase of delinquency," presenting an image of "disorganization, sometimes referred to as culture shock incident upon city living."[78] But few earlier studies attempted either to investigate urban migrant families in detail or to compare them with rural counterparts.

With the aid of some graduate students, Lewis located 100 Tepoztecan families in Mexico City—a number he felt represented approximately 90 percent of the total residents in the capital. Each of the 100 families was interviewed at least once, 69 were interviewed twice, and 10 were interviewed ten times. Not surprisingly, Lewis found that a diverse set of motivations, centering around desire for educational and economic advancement, underlay the original decisions of migrants to leave Tepoztlan.

What was surprising was that the study evidenced family cohesiveness as greater in the city than in the village. Extended family co-residence, for example, tended to be slightly more common in the city than in Tepoztlan, while in striking contrast to the village— where 7.4 percent of all households were occupied by isolated individuals or unrelated families living together—neither isolated individuals nor co-residence of unrelated families were found in Mexico City. Undoubtedly, such family co-residence was fostered by greater economic pressures attendant upon finding housing in Mexico City than in the village, where extended family members who wished to reside apart from the others could often find a rent-free empty house. The institution of *compadrazgo* also helped reinforce extended

Kinship Composition by Households:
Tepoztlan, 1943, and Mexico City, 1951

Type	Families in Mexico City: 69 (percentage of all families)	Families in Tepoztlan: 662 (percentage of all families)
Simple Biological family	66.6	70
Biological family with married children and grandchildren	17.2	13.5
Married siblings with their children	2.9	2.1
Persons living alone	0	6.7
Unrelated families living together	0	.7
Miscellaneous	13.3	7.5

Note: Reprinted, by permission, from Lewis 1952:37.

family ties in Mexico City because urbanites without nonrelated friends were more likely to. choose a relative as their child's godfather.

The general standard of living of Tepoztlan families in Mexico City was superior to that of the village: 78 percent of city families had radios, in contrast to 1 percent of Tepoztlan families; 54 percent had sewing machines as opposed to 25 percent; 3 of the 69 city families owned a car and no one in the village owned one; in the city all slept in beds, while only 19 percent of villagers did. As would be expected, city dwellers were more likely to own clocks or read newspapers regularly. The diet of those in the city was similar to but more varied than that of the villagers. Only in terms of crowding did the economic features of city life compare unfavorably with Tepoztlan. In Mexico City sometimes ten people lived in one room, sharing only two beds, and as many as fifteen families might share a single toilet.

In the religious sphere, urbanization had evidently produced not secularization, but rather some shift from the folk catholicism of the village to a greater convergence with accepted Roman Catholic traditions. Many villagers, for example, believed that the mythical village culture hero, El Tepozteco, was the son of Mary. This belief, regarded as superstitious by urbanites, was no longer held by them. Sunday school attendance and veneration of shrines seemed more important in Mexico City, as did general identification with the larger Roman Catholic community. The latter was illustrated by such events as the draping of doorways with black crepe by city dwellers to mourn the death of a bishop. "In Tepoztlan," Lewis felt, "it is doubtful whether the death of the Pope himself would lead to such action."[79]

Lewis' early study helped alert researchers to the likelihood that urbanization was a much more complex phenomenon than originally assumed, and that its impact upon traditional family and culture apparently varied with cultural and economic environment.

Sub-Saharan Africa

The fact that African ethnology has been primarily the preserve of British social anthropologists has guaranteed that social structure, especially kinship, would be a core concern of both tribal and urban research in Africa. Indeed, the very concept of the extended family emerged from anthropological research in rural African societies where, with only slight exaggeration, the individual has been said to be "important only as he contributes to the extended family unit."[80]

With the exception of the Union of South Africa, little industrialization has taken place in African cities south of the Sahara. Consequently, most of the effects upon extended family relations which have occurred in the city can probably be attributed to the urban situation alone, although contact with European institutions from the colonial period on has undoubtedly had profound influence, especially among urban elites.

Not surprisingly, evidence from the numerous studies of urban African families is somewhat contradictory. Kenneth Little, for example, reports that even among urban elites the tendency to perceive social relations in an ethnic (or tribal) context tends to reinforce the importance of maintaining extended kin ties, for it is only within one's own ethnic group and especially among kin that an individual can find ultimate security. Thus, the successful urbanite must live up to the "big man" role with kin: even if he is wealthy and highly educated, room must be available in his house for poor and illiterate relatives. His educated wife, on visits to her home village, will be expected to defer to elders and perform the customary chores of a junior female.[81]

Gary Ferraro, too, in an analysis of Kikuyu rural and urban kinsmen in the East African city of Nairobi, Kenya, has noted a "dearth of differences in kinship interactions between urban and rural peoples,"[82] a phenomenon which he feels is primarily due to the economic insecurity facing both urban and rural Kikuyu. In the absence of a national welfare system, the urban population has continued to give principal importance to kinship networks, knowing that in times of crisis only kin can be counted on. In another particularly interesting study of urban African kinship, Enid Schildkrout demonstrates that kinship often provides the basic structure within which *all* peoples of the city are subsumed. Thus the idioms of consanguineal, or "blood" kinship are used to express solidarity with those of the same ethnic group, whether or not they are actually related, while affinal (or "in-law") idioms, with the joking behavior that is usually appropriate, are extended to those of different ethnic communities.[83]

But many African urban researchers have been concerned with Southall's generalizations that "in the new situations, the scope of kinship rights and duties has narrowed and become more uncertain and the body of kin included in them become reduced."[84] Young people in the Upper Volta capital of Ouagadougou, for example, are generally ignorant of traditional kinship systems. This is especially true for the urban born and educated children of civil servants, who often use French kinship terms; thus traditional terminological distinctions between the children of one's mother's or father's brother or sister are often blurred through use of the broader French category *cousin*. Even more revealing is the embarrassment of many urban youth when forced to use higher-status traditional kin terms with rural kinsmen. Elliott Skinner reports one case involving a father's younger sister who had come from her rural home to perform chores in her brother's household. Rather than refer to her by the respectful term of *pogodoba* (father's sister), the informant preferred to either address her by her Christian name or call her "cousine." Additional attenuation of the importance of non-nuclear kin is also apparent in the fact that, although extended family residence persists among many Ouagadougou families (even among elite civil servants), such families are often transitional ones in which eventual nuclear residence is anticipated.

Occupational diversity in Ouagadougou seems to provide a

major source of strain in maintenance of extended family relations. Often clerks and civil servants find that few common interests remain with their agricultural kin. With ties limited to such areas as the performance of traditional religious ceremonies—which have become less important for the urban group—visits, which are increasingly rare, are often strained and formal. It is not unusual for well-to-do urbanites "to be teased with the term *sana* (stranger)" when they visit their rural village. Rural relatives, who often rely upon urban kin for city produce and to provide lodging and support for children sent to Ouagadougou for education, "more frequently recognize, and take greater interest in, higher-status urban kinsmen than vice-versa." Urban relatives, naturally enough, find that their hours of employment conflict with expectations of rural kin that the city hosts will drop other activities during a visit. In general, the diversity of occupations and interests that emerges from city life has produced a situation in which "kin relations in Ouagadougou are losing their generalized and reciprocal nature and are fast becoming specific, intermittent, and manipulative."[85]

Conflicts between the conjugal family and the lineage in sub-Saharan Africa were traditionally won by the stronger authority of the lineage. This is less true today. Formerly, Northern Rhodesian conjugal families might be broken by divorce and remarriage while the pull of the lineage remained constant. Now, in copper belt towns, the traditional economic functions of the lineage have been largely supplanted by nuclear families in which, because the husband is the sole wage earner, his wife and children are more dependent upon him than ever. The decline of polygamy, the increasing opportunities for personal choice of spouse, and the rise of the conjugal family as a complete economic unit has given the family a closeness not found in the tribal past.[86]

In the Aboure and Bete tribes of the Ivory Coast, 82 percent of Aboure and 56 percent of Bete females marry shortly after puberty. Such early marriages are contracted by the families; the future bride has at best a minimal voice in choosing her spouse. In the city of Abidjan, however, marriage tends to be contracted at a later age, with a consequent increase in freedom to choose a partner. One indication of the decline of family control over selection of a child's spouse is seen in the increase of interethnic marriages in Abidjan. These account for one-fourth of all urban Aboure marriages (as opposed to 2 percent in rural areas) and 8 percent of Bete city alliances (in contrast to 1 percent in the village). But, although the nuclear family's impact upon the choice of spouse appears to have declined in the city, extended family connections have often become more important in selecting a mate.[87]

Urban life in the Ivory Coast, while it has increased the importance of the husband's role as controller of the family income, has also helped free women of both tribal groups from the husband's authority. In response to the question "if you were in a boat with your mother and husband and the boat sank, which one would you save if you were the only one able to swim?" rural wives, perhaps from fear of the sanctions in-laws could bring if the husband was not saved, indicated a strong preference for saving him—a response given by 84.1 percent of Aboure and 79.5 percent of Bete women. Urban women of both groups were more likely to choose to save the mother, a choice taken by 31.9 percent of urban Aboure and 40.9 percent of urban Bete women.

Urban women also seem to have increased their authority in the family—vis-à-vis their children, at least—by virtue of the husband's typical marginality in the urban labor market and the more frequent and extended absences necessitated by his work or search for work. Thus, urban residence in the Ivory Coast seems to have had its primary impact upon the family by providing women with increased freedom, both in the choice of husbands and in relation to the husband's authority over the children. In the case of the Bete, residence with the husband's family tends to reinforce his authority in the villages, while city life has clearly increased the woman's position within the nuclear family. Just the reverse has occurred among urban Aboure, where the wife's removal from her relatives (rural Aboure postmarital residence is typically matrilocal) and her greater economic dependence upon her husband has reduced her dominance: 54 percent of rural Aboure wives reported that their husbands usually yielded in quarrels, while only 27 percent of urban Aboure women felt that they usually gained the upper hand in domestic arguments.[88]

The fact that many West African women support themselves and their children through trading in the marketplace has also had a significant liberating effect. In rural areas, the typical division of labor in the Akan society of Ghana required that men clear the fields of trees and undergrowth and women plant, weed, harvest, and transport produce from the fields, as well as keep house, cook, and care for the children. Each wife was allocated land from her husband's lineage to grow food for the support of her family. Food produced from such plots was under control of the husband, who decided where and how it would be consumed in keeping with the general rule of male dominance and control of the wife. Women could, however, farm land from their own lineage and sell the produce at market, controlling the sums realized from such additional work.

As cities in Ghana grew and the number of landless women increased, more women concentrated their activities in trade. Gradually, women assumed dominance in the commercial sector, as markets in the men's traditional trading commodities of gold, ivory, slavery, and monkeys collapsed and men turned to clerical and other employment for which their easier access to education prepared them. In turn, the majority of women, especially "stranger" women from distant regions, ceased farming altogether in favor of supporting themselves through trade Indeed, many without farmland were "under a compulsion to trade [as] there is an expectation that women will support themselves even after marriage and that they will contribute to the support of the children."[89] In contrast to profits from agricultural produce, trade profits remained with the wife as if they had been realized from farming her own land. The ability to support herself and the emotional support of other women in the marketplace have clearly had an impact upon the structure of family authority. In contrast to rural areas, where "the husband-wife relationship was one of superordination-subordination," the rise of towns has given women a great deal of independence and "diminished the dominance of the husband both in regard to his ability to control his wife economically and sexually."[90]

Diana Azu, discussing the urban family in Ghana, indicates that the solidarity of traditional lineages has been undermined by the dispersion of family members and by the increasing emphasis upon literacy. The nuclear family appears to be emerging as the basic residential unit and polygamy is on the decline, while the increased importance of the conjugal family seems to be coupled with a marked increase in romance as a basis for marriage. Formal education, which has become critical in gaining social position and wealth, has contributed to the diminution of position of lineage elders, both by removing their economic importance and by undermining the traditional knowledge upon which much of their authority was based. Today, elders often look to wealthy and educated young lineage members for monetary aid.[91]

A common problem affecting family and societal stability in many newly urbanized African nations is the tendency of men to migrate to towns without their families in search of employment. The resulting shortage of women in the city tends to keep the migrant from accepting the city as his home, especially if he is already married with a wife and children back home. Additionally, this numerical disparity between sexes and the lack of moderating influence of a co-resident family encourages prostitution and other social problems such as gambling, alcoholism, and drug use.

Abner Cohen's study of Hausa migrants to the Sabo quarter of Ibadan, Nigeria, provides an excellent example of some of the effects that a shortage of women can produce. Unlike many migrants in other regions of the world, Hausa men seem particularly reluctant to establish liaisons with local non-Hausa women. Such liaisons are regarded both as a potential source of death or illness (through magical means) and as a kind of treason to one's group. Consequently, the shortage of Hausa women in the quarter, together with a housing shortage that discourages those bachelors who find eligible women from marrying, has promoted prostitution. So much in demand are women that, even in this predominantly Islamic society, they seem to move rather fluidly from the seclusion of marriage to the independence of prostitution and back again, without the stigma carried by the title "prostitute" in the West. Of the 950 Sabo housewives reported on by Cohen in 1963, many had been employed as prostitutes; all of the 250 active prostitutes were former housewives. Not surprisingly, the status of urban women seems to have been enhanced vis-à-vis their rural Muslim sisters. Male-initiated divorce, for example, is common among rural Hausa, but in urban areas women have gained the upper hand in its initiation. Although Islamic law makes it relatively easy for men, women often have a great deal of difficulty initiating divorce. But in the city a woman can ask her husband to pronounce the divorce formula, *anti taliq* (thou art dismissed), three times, and if this fails ask others to pressure him, go to court herself, or as a last resort desert him and pose as a prostitute. One interesting but not surprising consequence of the demand for female sexual services has been an apparent increase in the status of those who choose to remain housewives. Although they are secluded and have little of the interpersonal freedom of a divorcée-prostitute, husbands must treat them with greater consideration than might be shown in the village lest they desert and enter the world of prostitution.[92]

In a study of two areas of the Ugandan capital city of Kampala, Southall and Gutkind have also remarked upon the manner in which urban life has led African women "to expect more equal and personal relationships in marriage."[93] Concomitant with the growth in female expectations and the demand of better treatment in the form of clothes and entertainment, most of the productive value of a woman's labor is lost to her husband in the city. In contrast to the village, where a woman performs a great deal of the basic agricultural labor, most of the few employment opportunities available to women in the city (becoming a bargirl is a common option) carry the aura of prostitution. Indeed, urban working women are generally classified as actual or potential prostitutes—a taint that applies somewhat more generally to all town women, since the first women to come to towns were prostitutes. This classification is especially common in East African towns, which often lacked the earlier female role of petty trader or beer-brewer common to West African cities.

The absence of agriculture in the town and of opportunities to perform such traditional tasks as carrying firewood and water have left most urban women with little to do. "Good" women are expected to remain at home in their husband's room, performing light domestic chores and avoiding contact with strangers. Not surprisingly, under these circumstances the sexual satisfaction of the wife has become a more and more important aspect of marriage. Sexual dissatisfaction often leads to desertion in families where the husband's economic position is not strong enough to bind his wife to him. Men have mostly themselves to blame, however: on the one hand their moral demands place women in a position of having virtually nothing to do with their time, and on the other, the value men attach to their own love affairs continually undermines the families of other men.[94]

The changes beginning to emerge in kinship patterns among urban educated elites are especially interesting. Members of the Lagos, Nigeria, elite—those who work in banks, government offices, and foreign firms and who spend much working and leisure time in institutions modeled on European ones—have begun to live in isolated households away from extended family. The establishment of "housing estates," most suitable for single conjugal family residence, has promoted values hitherto almost unknown such as privacy and independence. For many, this independence is unwanted because it interferes with the maintenance of kin ties. But for an important emerging minority, the insulation from kin obligations is welcome. "Such divergent reactions," Peter Marris feels, "suggest that there may be a growing divergence in Lagos society, between those who still depend upon traditional family loyalties, and those who are increasingly frustrated by them: a divergence in styles of life related to a corresponding divergence in wealth and status."[95]

Evidence of conflict between the traditional lineage system and the new elite is widespread. In a period of rapid change, in which children frequently have different occupations from their fathers and in which the nature of the work itself has changed beyond recognition, traditional patterns of respect for elders are undermined by situations in which old values are repudiated. Thus, for example, an upwardly mobile man is likely to be reluctant to entrust his children to his mother—something traditionally granted to her as a right—for fear that she may transmit to them a "backward" and unsophisticated view of the world. Similarly, many men and women today base their marriages upon ideas of companionship and relative equality, in contrast to the mores of the past which placed a woman under authority of her husband's family; the reluctance to conform to tradition undermines lineage affiliations. Finally, and perhaps most importantly, the new elite often find themselves the victims of exhorbitant demands for aid from relatives. No longer are they contributors to a family welfare system to which they, too, can expect to turn in time of need. Instead, "to their poorer cousins, their wealth seems so great as to be inexhaustible. Faced with insistent, even predatory claims, they may begin to restrict the range of relatives to whom they recognize an obligation. Many of them besides, may have made their own way by government scholarships, or by promotion within their firm, and feel they owe little to their kin."[96] In short, the pressures of kin demands, coupled with the increasing gulf between life styles, appears to lead to a situation in which the most successful members of a family detach themselves from their extended families. This will undoubtedly in time lead to the establishment of class divisions in urban Nigerian society.

Thus, in Africa as elsewhere, the character of kin ties in the urban setting is forged by a variety of often contradictory pressures. Extended kinship groups are frequently important for urban individuals to retain because they fulfill, at least initially, recreational, economic, religious, and welfare needs. On the other hand, for those who have achieved success in the city, kin ties may become a burden.

CONCLUSIONS

Much of the confusion surrounding the hypothesis that the urbanization and/or industrialization of a population eventually leads to establishment of isolated nuclear families as the basic kin unit evidently results from use of different criteria to define "kin unit."

If the term is used to refer to residential groups, then most available evidence from world urban patterns suggests there is indeed a tendency for co-residence groups to approximate nuclear or conjugal family patterns. This also appears to be the case if kin unit refers to corporate groups of relatively fixed membership. Movement to the city not only serves to remove individuals from close proximity with their patrilineages (as in the case of Indians, many Africans, and overseas Chinese) and matrilineages (in certain areas of Africa, Malaysia, and Indonesia), it also serves to diminish the ties of migrants and their descendants to ancestral lands that formerly provided the economic base for lineage cohesion. However, if we extend the meaning of kin unit to extraresidential, noncorporate, socializing and aid units, then it is evident that neither urbanization nor industrialization work to fully isolate nuclear families from the larger group of kin. Such kin ties outside the conjugal family are habitually maintained by urbanites, although their character often appears to be more voluntary and restricted in scope than in rural areas.

Although the impact of urbanization and industrialization on families is shaped and given special character by specific cultures, certain worldwide uniformities can be seen. During a society's initial stages of urbanization, kin ties are frequently strengthened by the uncertainties of urban life and by the inadequacy of public welfare services. In time, with prolonged residence in the city or the development of public educational, health, and welfare institutions, extra-familial ties tend to attenuate and become somewhat restricted in scope, concentrating on recognition of such life crises as birth, marriage, and death. Another particularly interesting effect upon the world's population is the widespread trend towards marriages of love, which appears to be associated with the forces of urbanization and industrialization. The decline of the authority of extended kin groups often associated with urban residence encourages young couples to select their own partners and to rely upon one another for emotional support. Additionally, weakening of the influence of lineages as corporate groups in cities has encouraged bilateral reckoning of kin, so that children are likely to maintain ties with both paternal and maternal relatives.

In short, it appears that the long-term trends of both urbanization and industrialization are to increase the residential and emotional importance of conjugal families and to give the formation of close extranuclear kinship ties some of the voluntary character of friendships.

⊛ NOTES

1. Wirth 1938:20-21.
2. Parsons 1943:27-28.
3. Smelser 1959:406.
4. Smelser 1966:115.
5. Bott 1957; Young and Willmott 1957; Firth 1956.
6. Axelrod 1956:15; Sussman quoted in Adams 1970:575.
7. Adams 1970:578.
8. Jitodai 1963.
9. Litwak 1960:390.
10. Goode 1963:76.
11. Codere 1955:65.
12. Codere 1955:68.
13. Coult and Habenstein 1965a.
14. Adams 1970:575.
15. Coult and Habenstein 1965a:2, 4.
16. Goode 1963:70.
17. Goode 1963:369-370.
18. Strauss 1969:483.
19. See Laslett 1973, Lasch 1975.
20. Anderson 1971.
21. Furstenberg 1966:327.
22. See Parsons 1943; Linton 1949.
23. Furstenberg 1966:329.
24. Frances Trollope quoted in Furstenberg 1966:331.
25. Furstenberg 1966:331.
26. Furstenberg 1966:332.
27. Furstenberg 1966:333.
28. Both quoted in Furstenberg 1966:333.
29. Furstenberg 1966:335.
30. Rapson 1973:202.
31. Furstenberg 1966:337.
32. Garigue 1956:370-372; emphasis mine.
33. Rioux 1959:379.
34. Rioux 1959:382.
35. Rioux 1959:385.
36. Collard 1975:116-117.
37. Hammel 1969:193; Barić 1967:9.
38. Barić 1967:4.
39. Barić 1967:13-15.
40. Hammel 1969:194.
41. Simić 1973:115.
42. Simić 1973:115.
43. Ames 1969:67.
44. Freed and Freed 1969.
45. Sen cited in Eames 1967:165.
46. Eames 1967:170.

47. Eames 1967:171.
48. Rowe 1973:226-227.
49. Ames 1969:69.
50. Ames 1969:65, 69.
51. Vatuk 1971:293.
52. See Phillips 1965.
53. Textor 1961:21.
54. Willmott 1960:53.
55. Willmott 1960:261.
56. Willmott 1960:263.
57. Willmott 1960:264.
58. Freedman 1957:225-227.
59. Bruner 1961:508.
60. Yazaki 1973:161.
61. Masuoka 1947:537.
62. Vogel 1963:216-224.
63. Masuoka, et al., 1962:4.
64. Dore 1958:113.
65. Masuoka, et al., 1962:5.
66. Krisher 1976.
67. Bruner 1961:508.
68. Goode 1970.
69. Hammel 1961.
70. See Liebow 1967; Gonzales 1965.
71. Mangin 1973:339.
72. Kahl 1968:81-82, 87.
73. Lewis 1973:133.
74. Kemper 1974:28.
75. Kemper 1974:41.
76. Hammel 1961; Germani 1961.
77. Mangin 1970:26; Ugalde 1974:36.
78. Lewis 1952:31.
79. Lewis 1952:38.
80. Aldous 1962:7.
81. Little 1965:142-143.
82. Ferraro 1973:214.
83. Schildkrout 1975.
84. Southall 1961:31.
85. Skinner 1974:108.
86. Powdermaker 1962:316.
87. Clignet 1966.
88. Clignet 1966:395-396.
89. McCall 1961:291.
90. McCall 1961:287, 298.
91. Azu 1974:115.
92. Cohen 1969:51-70.
93. Southall and Gutkind 1957:88.
94. Southall 1961:46-66.
95. Marris 1962:133.
96. Marris 1962:139.

134 URBAN ANTHROPOLOGY

REFERENCES

Adams, Bert N.
1968   Kinship systems and adaptation to modernization. Studies in Comparative International Development 4, 3:47-60.
1970   Isolation, function, and beyond: American kinship in the 1960's. Journal of Marriage and the Family 32:575-597.
Aldous, Joan
1962   Urbanization, the extended family, and kinship ties in West Africa. Social Forces 41, 1:6-12.
Ames, Michael M.
1969   Class, caste and kinship in an industrial city of India. Asia 15:58-71.
Anderson, Michael
1971   Family structure in nineteenth century Lancashire. Cambridge: Cambridge University Press.
Axelrod, Morris
1956   Urban structure and social participation. American Sociological Review 21:13-18.
Azu, Diana Gladys
1974   The Ga family and social change. Cambridge, Eng. African Studies Centre, African Social Research Docs. vol. 5.
Barić, Lorraine
1967   Levels of change in Yugoslav kinship. In Maurice Freedman, ed., Social organization. Chicago: Aldine Publishing Company.
Berkner, Lutz K.
1973   Recent research on the history of the family in Western Europe. Journal of Marriage and the Family 35:395-405.
Bott, Elizabeth
1957   Family and social network: Roles, norms, and external relationships in ordinary urban families. New York: Free Press.
Bruner, Edward M.
1961   Urbanization and ethnic identity in North Sumatra. American Anthropologist 63:508-521.
Clignet, Remi
1966   Urbanization and family structure in the Ivory Coast. Comparative Studies in Society and History 8:385-401.
Codere, Helen
1955   A genealogical study of kinship in the United States. Psychiatry 18:65-79.
Cohen, Abner
1969   Custom and politics in urban Africa: A study of Hausa Migrants in Yoruba towns. Berkeley: University of California Press.
Collard, Clyde V.
1975   The Cajun family: Adjustment to modern trends. In Steven L. Del Sesto and Jon L. Gibson, eds., The culture of Acadiana: Tradition and change in South Louisiana. Lafayette, La.: University of Southwestern Louisiana.
Coult, Allan D., and Robert W. Habenstein
1962   The study of extended kinship in urban society. The Sociological Quarterly 3:141-145.

1965a   The function of extended kinship in urban society. Kansas City, Mo.: Community Studies.

1965b   The prediction of inter-family ties in the American kinship system. Kansas City, Mo.: Community Studies, Inc.

Dore, R. P.
1958   City life in Japan. Berkeley: University of California Press.

Eames, Edwin
1967   Urban migration and the joint family in a north Indian village. Journal of Developing Areas 1:163-178.

1970   Corporate groups and Indian urbanization. Anthropological Quarterly 43:168-185.

Ferraro, Gary P.
1973   Tradition or transition?: Rural and urban kinsmen in East Africa. Urban Anthropology 2:214-231.

Firth, Raymond, ed.
1956   Two studies of kinship in London. London: Athlone Press.

Frazier, E. Franklin
1942   The Negro family in Bahia, Brazil. American Sociological Review 7:465-478.

Freed, Stanley A., and Ruth S. Freed
1969   Urbanization and family types in a north Indian village. Southwestern Journal of Anthropology 25:342-359.

Freedman, Maurice
1957   Chinese family and marriage in Singapore. London: Her Majesty's Stationery Office.

Furstenberg, Frank F., Jr.
1966   Industrialization and the American family: A look backward. American Sociological Review 31:326-337.

Garigue, Philippe
1956   French Canadian kinship and urban life. Reprinted in Rioux and Martin, eds., French Canadian society. Toronto: McClelland and Stewart.

Germani, Gino
1961   Inquiry into the social effects of urbanization in a working-class sector of greater Buenos Aires. In Philip M. Hauser, ed., Urbanization in Latin America. New York: International Documents Service.

Gonzalez, Nancie L. Solien De
1965   The consanguineal household and matrifocality. American Anthropologist 67:1541-1549.

Goode, Judith G.
1970   Latin American urbanism and corporate groups. Anthropological Quarterly 43:146-167.

Goode, William J.
1963   World revolution and family patterns. New York: Free Press.

Greven, Philip J., Jr.
1973   Family structure in seventeenth-century Andover, Massachusetts. In Michael Gordon, ed., The American family in socio-historical perspective. New York: St. Martin's Press.

Hammel, Eugene A.
1961   The family cycle in a coastal Peruvian slum and village. American Anthropologist 63:989-1005.

1969　Economic change, social mobility, and kinship in Serbia. Southwestern Journal of Anthropology 25:188-197.

Jackson, James C.
1976　The Chinatowns of Southeast Asia. Pacific Viewpoint 17:45-77.

Jacobson, Helga E.
Urbanization and family ties: A problem in the analysis of change. Journal of Asian and African Studies 5, 4:302-307.

Jitodai, Ted T.
1963　Migration and kinship contacts. Pacific Sociological Review 6:49-55.

Kahl, Joseph A.
1968　The measurement of modernism: A study of values in Brazil and Mexico. Austin: University of Texas Press, Latin American Monographs no. 12.

Kemper, Robert V.
1974　Family and household organization among Tzintzuntzan migrants in Mexico City. In Wayne A. Cornelius and Felicity M. Trueblood, eds., Latin American urban research. Vol. 4. Beverly Hills: Sage Publications.

Krisher, Bernard
1976　Praying for death. Newsweek, Feb. 16, 1976.

Lasch, Christopher
1975　The family and history. New York Review of Books 22, 18:33-38.

Laslett, Peter
1969　Size and structure of the household in England over three centuries. Population Studies 23:199-223.
1973　The comparative history of household and family. In Michael Gordon, ed., The American family in socio-historical perspective. New York: St. Martin's Press.

Lewis, Oscar
1952　Urbanization without breakdown: A case study. The Scientific Monthly 75:31-41.
1973　Some perspectives on urbanization with special reference to Mexico City. In Aidan Southall, ed., Urban anthropology. New York: Oxford University Press.

Liebow, Elliot
1967　Tally's corner. Boston: Little, Brown.

Linton, Ralph
1949　The natural history of the family. In Ruth Anshen, ed., The family: Its function and destiny. New York: Harper.

Little, Kenneth
1965　West African urbanization. Cambridge: Cambridge University Press.

Little, Kenneth, and Anne Price
1974　Urbanization, migration, and the African family. Reading, Mass.: Addison-Wesley Module in Anthropology no. 51.

Litwak, Eugene
1960　Geographic mobility and extended family cohesion. American Sociological Review 25:385-394.

McCall, D.
1961　Trade and the role of wife in a modern West African town. In Aidan

Southall, ed., Social change in modern Africa. London: Oxford University Press.

Mangin, William
1970   Tales from the barriadas. In W. Mangin, ed., Peasants in cities: Readings in the anthropology of urbanization. Boston: Houghton Mifflin.
1973   Sociological, cultural, and political characteristics of some urban migrants in Peru. In Aidan Southall, ed., Urban anthropology. New York: Oxford University Press.

Marris, Peter
1962   Family and social change in an African city: A study of rehousing in Lagos. Evanston, Ill.: Northwestern University Press.

Masuoka, Edna Cooper, et al.
1962   Role conflicts in the modern Japanese family. Social Forces 41:1-16.

Masuoka, Jitsuichi
1947   Urbanization and the family in Japan. Sociology and Social Research 32:535-539.

Matthiasson, Carolyn J.
1974   Coping in a new environment: Mexican Americans in Milwaukee, Wisconsin. Urban Anthropology 3:262-277.

Parsons, Talcott
1943   The kinship system of the contemporary United States. American Anthropologist 45:22-38.
1949   The social structure of the family. In Ruth Anshen, ed., The family: Its function and destiny. New York: Harper.

Phillips, Herbert P.
1965   Thai peasant personality. Berkeley: University of California Press.

Powdermaker, Hortense
1962   Copper town: Changing Africa. New York: Harper and Row.

Rapson, Richard L.
1973   The American family in socio-historical perspective. In Michael Gordon, ed., The American family in socio-historical perspective. New York: St. Martin's Press.

Reader, D. H.
1966   Tribalism in South Africa. Scientific South Africa 3, 4:15-18.

Rioux, Marcel
1959   Kinship recognition and urbanization in French Canada. Reprinted in Rioux and Martin, eds., French Canadian society. Toronto: McClelland and Stewart.

Rowe, William L.
1973   Caste, kinship, and association in urban India. In Aidan Southall, ed., Urban anthropology. New York: Oxford University Press.

Schildkrout, Enid
1975   Ethnicity, kinship, and joking among urban immigrants in Ghana. In Du Toit and Safa, eds., Migration and urbanization. The Hague: Mouton.

Shanas, Ethel, and Gordon Streib, eds.
1965   Social structure and the family: Generational relations. Englewood Cliffs, N.J.: Prentice-Hall.

Simić, Andrei
  1973   The peasant urbanites: A study of rural-urban mobility in Serbia. New York: Seminar Press.
Skinner, Elliott P.
  1974   African urban life: The transformation of Ouagadougou. Princeton: Princeton University Press.
Smelser, Neil J.
  1959   Social change in the industrial revolution. Chicago: University of Chicago Press.
  1966   The modernization of social relations. In Myron Weiner, ed., Modernization: The dynamics of growth. New York: Basic Books.
Southall, Aidan, ed.
  1961   Social change in modern Africa. New York: Oxford University Press.
Southall, Aidan, and P. C. W. Gutkind
  1957   Townsmen in the making: Kampala and its suburbs. Kampala: East African Institute of Social Research.
Strauss, Murray A.
  1969   Social class and farm-city differences in interaction with kin in relation to societal modernization. Rural Sociology 34:476-495.
Textor, Robert B.
  1961   From peasant to pedicab driver: A social study of northeastern Thai farmers who periodically migrated to Bangkok and became pedicab drivers. New Haven: Yale University Southeast Asia Studies, Cultural Report Series no. 9.
Ugalde, Antonio
  1974   The urbanization process of a poor Mexican neighborhood. Austin: University of Texas Press.
Vatuk, Sylvia J.
  1971   Trends in north Indian urban kinship: The "matrilateral asymmetry" hypothesis. Southwestern Journal of Anthropology 27:287-307.
Vogel, Ezra F.
  1963   Japan's new middle class. Berkeley: University of California Press.
Willmott, Donald E.
  1960   The Chinese of Semarang: A changing minority community in Indonesia. Ithaca: Cornell University Press.
Wirth, Louis
  1938   Urbanism as a way of life. American Journal of Sociology 44:1-24.
Yazaki, Takeo
  1973   The history of urbanization in Japan. In Aidan Southall, ed., Urban anthropology. New York: Oxford University Press.
Young, Michael, and Peter Willmott
  1957   Family and kinship in East London. London: Routledge and Kegan Paul.

Migrants and Urbanites: The Problems of Personal Adaptation and Adjustment to Cities

5 The migrant's arrival in the city rarely isolates him from the constraints and support of close personal relations. Generally, those who leave their homes to find work in cities follow friends and relatives from their home towns and villages, relying upon them for aid in finding employment and a place to live. But the migratory labor movements of which most early arrivals to Africa's colonial cities were a part tended to remove individuals from rural lineage groups without providing substitutes for the functions of those groups. For oscillatory and first-generation migrants, the effects of residence away from corporate kin bodies could be mitigated by visits home and by contact with relatives in the city. Still, the inadequacy of relying upon a greatly attenuated cluster of kin for needed aid and companionship was generally apparent to migrants, whether or not they anticipated extended urban residence. Kin-based associations had to be supplemented by ties formed on other criteria.

A common devised solution to the needs of urban dwellers for wider contact, in Africa as in the West, has been the formation of voluntary occupational, friendship, and entertainment associations. Exposure to others who share ethnicity, employment, or age status through such associations helps provide a niche for recent or long-term urbanites. The development of such associations is essentially an urban phenomenon, clearly derived from the need for adaptive mechanisms in the situation of social change common to cities.[1]

A unique phenomenon of African urbanization has been the fashion in which needs for financial protection, entertainment, and brotherhood have been woven into a variety of "mutual aid" societies. Little and Skinner report the importance of so-called entertainment and recreational associations in other spheres of life.[2] Associations such as the *gumbé* of Ouagadougou, Upper Volta, not only sponsor large outdoor dances for their members, but also have a well-organized structure which provides mutual aid and an interethnic authority base. *Gumbé* members pay monthly dues to the association which are used for the dances, a major source of entertainment, and to aid members in meeting marriage expenses or during periods of illness. Most important, the associations provide a norm-setting institution which cuts across ethnic lines. Most *gumbé* members are men and women between the ages of twelve and thirty, for whom membership provides controlled access to members of the opposite sex. The organization, with dual male and female presidents and vice-presidents and such male officers as a commissioner of police, helps replace rural corporate kin groups in structuring the interaction of unmarried youth. Female members, for example, are chaperoned at the dances and escorted to their homes afterwards; during the dances, men and women segregate themselves on separate benches. Under such organizations, some of the potential for "moral decline" of youth is kept in check, while intersexual contacts that are established often lead to marriage.[3]

Voluntary associations help provide individuals with a sense of belonging. Often this is accomplished through a proliferation of association offices and titles, many of which involve the performance of only minor tasks but which help cement even the least influential members to the group. Little describes one such entertainment association, the dancing *còmpin* of Sierra Leone, devoted to the performance of traditional music and dancing plays and the raising of mutual benefit funds. Weekly monetary subscriptions are collected to pay association expenses and to build a fund providing aid to members during bereavement. The payment of funds to members who have lost their spouses serves as a focal point for association officers' performance of their duties. After a death, the bereaved spouse must notify the Reporter, who requests the Doctor to investigate the death and circumstances surrounding it. If it is discovered that the dead person had been ill and that the association was not notified (so it could provide the sick with individual attention), the relative is fined. The Doctor washes the body of the deceased and mobilizes the Prevoe (provost) to inform association members to meet that evening and pay their contributions. If anyone refuses to pay without adequate explanation, the Bailiff seizes property of equal value. At the evening meeting, organized by the Manager, the Commissioner or Inspector serves as disciplinary officer to arrest or remove anyone who creates trouble. The Clerk or Secretary keeps records of accounts and the Cashier receives the group's funds from the Chief Executive, or Sultan, for safekeeping. The Sultan's female counterpart, the Mammy Queen, supervises the female members. Those who hold such other posts as Sister, Nurse, Solicitor, or Lawyer have various responsibilities. Clearly, the "dancing *compin*" has developed into a complex, multifaceted institution which not only provides its members with entertainment and security but rewards them with something equally important: a structured sense of belonging, especially appealing to those otherwise marginal to city life.[4]

In a sense, voluntary associations provide a transition from birth-ascribed village corporate kin groups to the achieved relations generally associated with urban life. Many associations have behavioral codes prohibiting such antisocial activity as seduction of the wife or daughter of another member. Such structures and rules facilitate adaptation by redefining the urban context in the light of familiar village patterns, by "substituting for the extended group of kinsmen a grouping based upon common interest which is capable of serving many of the same needs as the traditional family or lineage." Equally important is the way in which social achievement forms the basis for authority within the association and the way in which women participate in societies with male-female memberships, which "involves them in a new kind of social relationship with men, including companionship and the opportunity of selecting a spouse for oneself."[5]

Despite the modification of kinship and other traditional supportive mechanisms to fit urban conditions, many migrants experience great difficulty in adapting. The source of pressure is often the immigrant's personality: sometimes migrants are too inflexible to adjust to the altered environments, while in other cases the same maladaptive personality characteristics that pressed them to emigrate from their homes also render them unsuccessful in the city. Frequently, too, the newcomer is unprepared for all but the most menial of city occupations, so that he enters and may remain on the lowest social rungs. Migrants may find themselves thwarted in their aspirations as entire groups through isolation and discrimination because of ethnic or class origin. Finally, failure of migrants to adapt to city life may be the consequence of scarcity of opportunity for even the lowest employment. In some regions—India and certain cities of Southeast Asia, for example—migrants often leave depressed rural homelands for an overcrowded labor market with stiff competition for a few low-paying jobs. Too often such migrants settle in makeshift shanty-towns and scavenge for income to survive.

Many migrants and permanent city residents have, of course, found successful niches in the city—positions which provide prosperity and an enlarged view of the world generally unavailable to non-urbanites. The successful adaptation of these elites has not been studied with the intensity with which anthropologists have studied marginal urban communities. That this is so is a criticism of urban anthropologists, who have often emphasized human pathos and neglected careful studies of those who manage and control developed and underdeveloped countries. It is also a criticism of elites, who have generally been less receptive to studies of their lives than the poor, who either desire the opportunity to tell their story or feel unable to prevent the researcher's intrusion.

Anthropological writings on urban adjustment and adaptation often focus on personal and societal pathology: racism and ethnic conflict, squatter settlements, alcoholism, crime, begging, and the "culture of poverty." One might prefer here to analyze the totality of urban adaptation, for all levels of society; but this book must be about what urban anthropology is, not what it could be. This chapter will treat five interrelated adjustive and adaptive issues that have most concerned urban anthropologists: (1) crime, mental illness, and other social problems; (2) begging; (3) the culture of poverty; (4) overcrowding; and (5) urban slums and squatter settlements. The reader is cautioned to remember that what appear to politicians and urban planners as social "problems" are often viewed by those involved as adaptive "solutions" to the demands of urban life.

CRIME, MENTAL ILLNESS,
AND OTHER SOCIAL PROBLEMS

Psychological adjustment [from rural] to Bangkok life is complex and often difficult. The first few days in Bangkok are bewildering to the point of causing stomach upset and sleeplessness. Never before has the newcomer seen such an enormous and confusing place where it is so easy to get lost. He soon develops a fear—not without some justification—that the Bangkokians are looking down on him as a rustic bumpkin who cannot even speak "proper" Thai. His Bangkokian (pedicab) customers seem quick and slick, and often strike bargains that the new migrant senses to be to his disadvantage—yet sometimes it is better to accept a bad bargain than to face ridicule. Soon, however, the newcomer decides that he must learn to "fight" for his living; for now, more than ever before he is on his own. There is no family rice storage bin to rely on. If he does not make money, he does not eat, or such is his exaggerated fear.[6]

The stress of adjustment to a sprawling metropolis like Bangkok, or even to a small city, is often severe for the migrant. He arrives in a fast-paced world which he finds difficult to understand. Sometimes his contacts in the city are too immersed in their own lives to provide him more than a cursory orientation. Often, the up-country migrant arrives unexpected in Bangkok by bus with only a vague idea of where to find his city relatives. He may not have brought an exact address; confronted with an immense, metropolis for which his background has not prepared him, he must wander in search of a stranger who will give him aid. Every day young girls arrive in the Thai capital carrying cardboard luggage and wearing the bewildered expression of an up-country girl new to the city. Usually they make contact with the relatives or friends they seek to help them in the initial period of adjustment. But occasionally such a naive girl falls prey to a smooth-talking male who offers aid in finding her relatives or a job with the real intention of luring her into prostitution.

Evidence indicates that the uncertainty and tension which novice urban dwellers often have to face are frequently internalized, with negative consequences for physical and mental health. Urban Zulus, for example, tend to have higher blood pressure readings than do tribal members who remain in rural reserves.[7] A significant body of literature suggests that urban life either promotes or is associated with higher levels of suicide, crime, and mental illness than exists in nonurban areas.

Nutrition and Diabetes

The variety of food available in most city markets is far greater than that generally available in the countryside. Although many of the poorest urbanites cannot afford to supplement the staple of their diet—whether it be bread, rice, or potatoes—with meat or fish, most citizens can, and city dwellers in general probably have access to more varied diets than peasants. Unfortunately, increased choice does not always mean better nutrition. Diet-related health problems such as obesity and diabetes are often more common in cities than in rural areas. Diabetes, especially, is so much an urban phenomenon that it has been called "a disease of urbanization."[8] This is undoubtedly due to the large proportion of urbanites' total caloric intake that is provided by refined carbohydrates, especially sugar. Diabetes among black South Africans, for example, is apparently rare in rural areas; yet in one black township of Pretoria whose residents are primarily rural migrants it occurs in 2 percent of all people over ten years of age. In the city of Durban, one clinic cares for no fewer than 11,000 nonwhite diabetics in a total white and nonwhite population of only 560,000. These statistics are even more remarkable considering that the incidence of diabetes, primarily a disease which emerges with age, is most common among the elderly—an age group not well represented among the city's nonwhites. In a study of Durban rural migrants, G. D. Cambell suggests that the onset of diabetes follows a "rule of 20 years," in which the first appearance of the disease in 55 percent of all cases occurs after sixteen to twenty-three years of urban living and peaks at twenty years. This conclusion is roughly confirmed by other research in Ireland and Israel.

The chief difference between the diets of urban and rural peoples grows out of the shift from unrefined foods in rural areas to refined foods in the city. Dramatic increases in the intake of refined sugar and white bread—both of which seem to be associated with the development of diabetes—are generally found in urban, as opposed to rural diets. Among urban Indians in Natal, South Africa, for example, annual per capita consumption of sugar is 106 pounds, whereas for all of India it averages only 11 pounds. Considering that an intake of 70 pounds per capita per year apparently marks the dividing line between groups in which diabetes is common and those in which it is not, it seems likely that diabetes will not be a major health problem in India in the near future, while it should continue to be common among urban South African Indians.

Such medical problems as obesity, coronary thrombosis, gout, appendicitis, gall bladder disease, peptic ulcers, and infections of the urinary tract "are almost exclusively urban disorders." Dental disease especially, Cambell notes, is an example par excellence of the diseases of civilization: "in Northern Natal, the dentists tell me the quickest way to find out if a Zulu has been to the mines is to tell him to open his mouth, and the rotting teeth are eloquent evidence of residence in the urban areas."[9]

Urban Psychopathology

Data on relative rural-urban and industrialized-nonindustrialized levels of psychopathology often seems contradictory. The annual suicide rate in such advanced nations as Denmark, Switzerland, West Germany, Austria, and Japan hovers around 20 per 100,000, but suicide levels in England and the United States are roughly half this level and that of the Netherlands is lower still.[10] Clearly, because all these countries are similar in degree of development, arguments based on relative urbanization, increased sociocultural complexity, or more advanced industrialization are insufficient to explain the differing suicide rates.

An even more telling dissociation of a simple correlation of suicide and urbanization can be seen in Raoul Naroll's survey of "suicide wordage" in ethnographic reports.[11] Lacking absolute cross-cultural data on levels of suicide (which if available would provide a useful index of relative levels of societal stress—albeit a somewhat rough one, since suicide frequency would still be strongly influenced by different cultural traditions) Naroll was forced to rely upon the frequency of mention of suicide in ethnographic accounts of the world's peoples. Clearly, such a measure is likely to involve the bias of preoccupations of individual ethnographers, but it should also provide at least an indirect measure of suicide frequency. Analysis of some fifty-eight societies, ranging from primitive tribes to such relatively advanced groups as the Burmese, Italians, Irish, and Dutch, provided no indication whatsoever that suicide is associated either with complexity of social organization or with relative urbanization. Indeed, the highest levels of suicide wordage are recorded for tribal groups: the Iroquois, the Gond of India and the Luo of Kenya. Suicide level is undoubtedly a good measure of societal stress upon individuals and may even prove useful in differentiating relative degrees of rural-urban stress within the same culture. But obviously, contrasting suicide levels of urban societies of Europe, for example, with primitive or peasant societies elsewhere tells us much more about cultural fashions for coping with anxiety than it does about rural-urban differences.

The notion that cities are dangerous to the emotional and physical health of their populations is an ancient one. A good deal of evidence does exist to suggest that for a long time cities were centers of disease where life was sometimes incredibly short. In 1841, for example, the life expectancy of the average Londoner was 36 years and that of residents of the industrial cities of Manchester and Liverpool only 26, compared to 41 for England and Wales as a whole! Even as recently as the decade 1901-1910 the death rate of English urban residents was 33 percent higher than in rural counties.[12] Under such conditions, Thomas Jefferson's fear of the consequences of an urbanized America is understandable: "When we get piled upon one another in large cities, as in Europe, we shall become corrupt as in Europe, and go to eating one another as they do there . . . In solving this question . . . we should allow just weight to the moral and and physical preferences of the agricultural over the manufacturing, man."[13] Almost a century later a physician to the Royal Asylum of Aberdeen, Scotland, in a summary of the available data on "insanity" concluded that

> the most remarkable medical phenomena in our time has been the alarming increase of insanity. Crime has been diminishing; prisons, here and there, have been shut up; but who hears of an asylum being shut down anywhere, or even of its numerous inmates decreasing? Are we but changing lawlessness for incapacity, cunning for weakness, and are we better because fools accumulate and thieves decay?[14]

But, although many researchers have reported an increase of mental illness with a society's urbanization or industrialization, others have told of declining rates.[15] The problem in reaching any clear determination is complicated by numerous issues, chiefly the difficulty of defining the severity of psychological disability in a comparative fashion. Other factors that must be held constant include the age and sex composition of the population, ethnic composition, relevant social class, values (including willingness to accept professional treatment), educational level, occupation type, and environmental stress (wars or epidemics for example).[16]

High levels of urban psychiatric morbidity cannot be denied: the classic midtown Manhattan study, *Mental Health in the Metropolis*, reported an "impairment rate" of 23.4 percent of those surveyed in contrast to a "well" frequency of only 18.5 percent and a combined "mild-moderate" rate of 58.1 percent.[17] Interestingly enough, however, work by Alexander Leighton in rural Sterling County, Nova Scotia, reveals similarly high rates: 31 percent of those surveyed displayed almost certain evidence of psychiatric disorder, 26 percent "probably" had some such disorder, 26 percent were doubtful, and only 17 percent were placed in the category "almost certainly a psychiatrically well individual."[18] The frequent notation of higher incidents of psychic disability in cities[19] is probably the result of what we might term the "differential exposure mechanisms" of city and countryside. Thus, the pressures of city life may reveal inadequate individual psychological structures with greater frequency than does rural life. Rural situations may generally tend not only to provide less test of one's psychic health but may also be more likely to offer protective niches for those who cope poorly with stress.

The same basic conditions of urban life that may produce a sense of anomie in some individuals offer to others stimulation and freedom to develop talents that might be inhibited in a less cosmopolitan setting. We often regard cities as cauldrons for social problems, losing sight of the fact that they are also the chief source of innovation in any society. San Francisco, for example, has one of the highest rates of alcoholism, drug addiction, street crime, divorce, and suicide in the United States. Yet it is justly regarded by many as a point of cultural renaissance to which some of America's most creative thinkers have gravitated.[20]

Even in day-to-day life, the problems of adaptation to cities often seem greatly exaggerated. Tilantongo Indian migrants to Mexico City seem to drink less there than at home and express unanimous agreement that life in the capital is better than in Tilantongo.[21] As Mangin and Cohen have remarked in their investigation of mountain migrants to Lima:

> There is a considerable body of folklore, mostly false or distorted, concerning the barriada residents. It is generally held in the nonmigrant Lima population, and also among many of the migrants themselves, that the barriadas are centers of illness, vice, crime, family disorganization, child neglect, communism, radicalism, anarchy, resistence to progress, and that these

conditions are mainly due to migration. An analysis of police records from the barriada—and the neighboring long-settled district of Rimac in Lima—indicates a much lower crime and vice rate in the barriada. The Cornell medical index was administered to 65 individuals in Mariscall Castilla, and the incidence of sickness was found to be high, but not as high as Rotondo found in Mendocina, a slum in Lima. Judging from conversations with physicians, observations in hospitals, and four years' field work in Peru, there is no reason to assume that the rate of sickness is higher in barriadas than in the general lower class population, and good reason to suspect that the rate is much higher in the provinces than in Lima . . .

The literature of the social sciences has frequently depicted the migrant as a victim of extreme social, psychological and biological stress and has attributed this stress to the conditions surrounding migration itself—that is, movement from one social-physical space boundary to another strange and unwelcome area.[22]

A Lima psychoanalyst, Carlos Sequin, has coined the term "migrant syndrome" to refer to the frequency with which migrants appear to display stress-related symptoms of severe psychological and psychosomatic disturbances. The problem with such assumptions is simply that they are not generally supported by intensive study of both urban migrants *and* their fellows who remain in the home villages. Indeed, as Mangin and Cohen suggest, the migrants themselves "seem to feel subjectively 'better off,' and may actually be found to be in better circumstances than they were prior to their migration."[23] Evidently, much general impression of despair and anomie is not based on contact with the migrant slum dwellers themselves but is the result of fearful projections of intellectuals and other members of the urban middle and upper classes.

Leaving aside concern about whether urban living is more productive of individual and social disorientation than village life, it is obvious that the complexity of factors involved is too great, and our data too weak, to support any firm conclusions—an interesting literature on problems of urban adjustment exists that is useful in itself to discuss. A fascinating example is Marc Fried's "Grieving for a Lost Home," discussing the impact of forced dislocation in urban renewal projects of Boston's West End slums. Again and again during intensive interviews of those who had been forced to move from lifelong homes in the renewal area, Fried encountered reactions of intense grief. People told him: "'I felt as though I had lost everything,' 'I felt like my heart was taken out of me,' 'I felt like taking the gaspipe [or, even] 'I had a nervous breakdown.'"[24] Of 250 women interviewed two years after they had moved, 26 percent reported that they still felt sad or depressed and another 20 percent that they had experienced long periods of grief which lasted for six months to two years. Only a slightly smaller percentage of the 316 men interviewed (38 percent, as opposed to a total of 46 percent of the women) reported the same intense, long-term feelings of grief.

Clearly, much of this grief may have been chronic, grafted upon the renewal experience. Fried feels that all of us—even those who live in crowded, poverty-stricken slums—develop a *sense of spatial identity* that is an important emotional component of our lives. Familiar sights, as mundane as an old tree or a corner store, and familiar people, some of whom one may not know but only recognize on sight, subtly enter into our sense of self so that their removal can leave us emotionally stranded and segmented. Additionally, relocation for West Enders often disrupted social networks by making it difficult to continue relations with close friends who live nearby. The impact of Fried's study is obvious for highly mobile urban populations and those most mobile within them: movement of any kind is likely to be a stressful experience, even if it is anticipated and eagerly awaited; when it is the result of external pressure beyond one's control, it is likely to be particularly debilitating.

Juvenile Delinquency

In addition to mental illness, increased levels of alcoholism, crime, and sexual deviation are often thought to be common concomitants of city life. Graves and others have remarked on the high levels of drunkenness among urban American Indians; Wagner and Tan have suggested that Western-inspired urbanization and culture changes in Malaysia have led to an increase in homosexuality.[25] Weinberg, in his study "Urbanization and Male Delinquency in Ghana," feels that the increase of juvenile delinquency in Ghanaian cities over rural areas is due largely to initial effects of urbanization like disproportionate age concentration of the young, uneven male-female ratio, and lessened influence of traditional kinship controls. Delinquent gangs of the city limit themselves primarily to petty theft of food and and other small items. Theft for them has both an instrumental (subsistence) and an expressive (excitement) dimension, which Weinberg feels can best be understood "as an adaptation by youths who have become alienated from the family and school and are thrust into a marginal social position for which the urban community lacks the institutions and agencies to channel the youngster's needs into conventional outlets. In this anomic state, some boys become attracted to deviant peers in the street society and look to them for guidance."[26]

The shift to peer-dominated gang groups is aided by a tradition of placing children in the care of relatives or nonrelatives. In villages, such placement often merely moves the child to another relative, while his behavior remains under supervision of an extended kin group. In the city, it generally removes him from larger kin control so that "what constituted in a village a minor readjustment for a child in an extended family could become in an urban setting a very profound change in a conjugal family."[27] A comparison of the family situation of delinquent and nondelinquent groups in Accra (see chart below) reveals a startling frequency of nonresidence with parents among both groups: 38.9 percent of nondelinquents and only 11.2 percent of delinquents lived with both parents! Residence with nonrelatives or with the mother only was more typical of delinquents than nondelinquents while, not surprisingly, all who were "on their own" lived as delinquents.

Resident Arrangements of Male Delinquents and
Nondelinquents in Accra, Ghana

Resident Arrangement	Percentage of Delinquents (N=107)	Percentage of Nondelinquents (N=95)
Both parents	11.2	38.9
Father only	17.8	21.1
Mother only	17.8	9.5
Sibling	6.5	7.4
Grandparent	9.3	7.4
Aunt or uncle	15.0	12.6
Distant relative or nonrelative	7.4	3.1
On their own	15.0	0.0

Note: Reprinted, by permission, from Weinberg 1965:90.

Residence patterns alone, of course, are insufficient to explain delinquency. The reasons children are sent to relatives differ between families with delinquent and those with nondelinquent children. Delinquent children are often shifted for negative reasons—parental illness, breakup, or disinterest—while nondelinquents are usually entrusted to relatives for such positive reasons as enabling a child to more easily attend school or learn a trade. Weinberg's work confirms the salience of such unfavorable/favorable motivation for change: 42.9 percent of delinquents had experienced an "unfavorable" shift, whereas only 13.9 percent of nondelinquents were sent to live away from their parents for similarly negative reasons.

The Bureau of Social Affairs of the United Nations has compiled reports from India, Japan, and other Asian nations confirming that delinquency rates are strongly associated with urbanization. In the first six months of 1964, the index of crime in small Japanese villages was only 1.2 per 100,000 inhabitants; in the largest cities it was 2.67. Juvenile delinquency especially appears to be an urban phenomenon, and one especially common to countries undergoing rapid urbanization and economic development, where direct adult control is often lacking. Migration and the partial-family composition often associated with it is undoubtedly a more potent factor in encouraging juvenile delinquency than income level. Children of permanently settled urban families of even the lowest economic position are generally much better supervised and given better schooling than migrant children. Consequently, even though delinquency may be more common among them than among children of wealthier families, it at least tends to be lower than that found among recent migrants.[28]

Prostitution

Street prostitution and brothels are largely urban phenomena that are especially widespread in cities with large migrant male populations. Large-scale rural migration common to such countries as India places a great burden upon the urban labor market, driving wages down. Women especially find themselves limited in job selection by traditional social attitudes, so that often they have little choice other than bare survival as a domestic servant—if indeed, such a position can even be found—or earning a living as a prostitute. Many women, especially if they have children to support, turn to prostitution, choosing to sacrifice their reputations and suffer the exploitation of pimps or brothel-owners in exchange for a modicum of financial security. Young Asian girls are sometimes engaged as *amahs* (maids) with the understanding that they will provide "full [sexual] services" for their employers. Others in Burma, Thailand, the Philippines, and elsewhere are lured from the countryside by promises of employment or marriage and manipulated into prostitution when they arrive in town. In certain poverty-striken communities of northern and southern Thailand today, and in prerevolutionary rural China, young daughters are sometimes sold into prostitution to provide the family with desperately needed cash or a water buffalo; others are recruited by gangs who subject them to multiple rape and then press them into prostitution.[29] The stigma involved, and the feeling that since one is already a prostitute one might as well continue to at least gain the living it offers, make it difficult for women to extricate themselves from the situation.

Although it is often overstressed, economic necessity is clearly a precondition to prostitution. An extensive survey of prostitutes in Beirut, Lebanon,[30] revealed that 81 percent had had no formal schooling; of the remaining 19 percent, total schooling ranged from 1 to 8 years and averaged 4.3. Most prostitutes came from families in which the father's occupation was lower-class: 48 percent of fathers were peasants, unskilled laborers, or small merchants, while only 15 percent were skilled laborers, white collar workers, property owners, or government employees. Surprisingly, 34 percent said they did not know or did not remember their father's occupation, indicating that they either left home early or grew up without a father. Most of the respondents entered prostitution when they were quite young: 71 percent before their twenty-first birthday, one-third between the ages of eleven and sixteen. Undoubtedly, entry into prostitution and the tendency to begin at early ages are facilitated by urban residence: 73.1 percent of the women interviewed had spent all or most of their lives in a large city, 12.3 percent were from medium-sized towns, and only 13.8 percent were from small villages.[40]

Coupled with poor educational preparation for respectable occupations, 63 percent of the prostitutes had been married at least once, and exactly half were unwed mothers at some time before becoming prostitutes. Most husbands seem to have been of low socioeconomic status. Thus, in both their families of orientation and of procreation, few of the women knew anything but economic marginality.

Still, it is a mistake to assume that the prostitutes interviewed were forced to choose between starvation and prostitution. Economic factors are not determinates; they become relevant only when other factors such as family disorganization, early sexual experience, and male deception are present. Equally important as economic necessity, if not more important, is desire for material comfort, pretty clothes, and freedom from traditional social controls. For an uneducated, lower-class woman with children, only prostitution offers a possible path to leisure. Once in the profession, habituation to a relatively easy income makes it unlikely that she will leave. Many of the prostitutes interviewed were quite old—more than half were over 36, and 7 percent over 51—and 56 percent had been prostitutes for over 16 years. Despite such evidence that the vocation is often lifelong, most said they expected to leave the profession entirely one day: 81.5 percent indicated that they expected to quit after saving enough money to retire or once they found a husband or an "honest job."

One of the paradoxes of prostitution is that even though it appears to offer the opportunity for a relatively easy life, negative social attitudes towards it, attitudes shared at least partly by prostitutes and clients, often make it a very lonely and unpleasant job. Almost 71 percent of the Beirut prostitutes answered the question "what do you like about your work and life here?" with the response "nothing at all." 21.5 percent said they like "the money," 12.3 percent the "shelter and security," and 3.8 percent other prostitutes; 1.5 percent indicated that they appreciated the "opportunity to meet a man." The question "what do you dislike about your work and life?" was generally answered with an indication that everything (63.1 percent) was disliked. Next in order of expressed dislike (24.6 percent) were the "sexual intimacies and abuses of clients," a core of the occupation. Particularly resented was the fact that the women had little or no choice of clients but were forced to submit to whomever could pay the price, no matter how drunk he might be or how late he arrived. Thus, although prostitution often seems the only avenue open to many poor and uneducated women, and prostitutes often justify themselves by arguing that all women are really prostitutes in their relations with men but at least prostitutes are astute enough to make this pay, the prostitute's world is often characterized by resentment toward her clients and society as a whole.

Political Corruption

Political corruption is a widespread urban phenomenon. The taking of what some Asians refer to as "tea money," or bribes ("coffee money" in such coffee-drinking countries as Malaysia and Indonesia), by government officials is not limited to cities but is most prevalent in urban centers where large concentrations of wealth and criminal activity are confronted by government regulation. Corruption can be viewed as serving useful social functions when kept within limits. It can maximize an individual's flexibility of action by permitting him to pass over a minor criminal record through paying a small sum to official record-keepers and by helping him at least partially re-create his identity.

In many cases, minor corruption permits underpaid local officials to gain an adequate living from people who use their services, so that those who place the greatest demands upon the bureaucracy pay for the services they require. In many countries officials do not view themselves as public servants, but as franchise-holders, permitting them to exact a portion of the wealth of those who pass through their offices. Whether customs agents, immigration officials, or policemen, they insist on payment for services just like dentists or carpenters.

An illustration is the recent case of a Bangkok automobile dealer, who received a 200,000-baht ($10,000) cashier's check drawn on a local bank in payment for an automobile. To his surprise, he discovered the check was forged. In hopes of regaining the car he immediately went to the police, where he was met with expressions of sympathy but told that the backlog of cases was too great to permit them to concentrate on his problem. After a few minutes of conversation, he pressed a small cash payment into an officer's hand to encourage him to look for the stolen vehicle in his "spare time." Several days later a police detective visited his office with the information that he "thought" the car "could" be located if the dealer would be willing to pay $1,000 to a police "informant." Knowing full well that this informant was a composite group of which the detective was a member, the dealer paid the money and his automobile was returned. Is this corruption? Undoubtedly, but corruption that helped provide a number of officers with a significant supplement to official salaries, which are too low to support a family in Bangkok.

In a sense, the payment of tea money, unpleasant as it may seem to Americans and infuriating as it was to the automobile dealer, is fairer to the population as a whole than broad taxation. To use Bangkok as an example again, many of its poorest people make few demands upon the government apparatus and cannot afford to pay taxes of any kind. Corruption helps free them from some of the burden of supporting an oversized bureaucracy that provides them few services.

Unfortunately, the pattern of supplementing government salaries in this manner lacks effective internal correction to keep it in bounds. The massive infusion of United States military and economic aid in South Vietnam, for example, helped push corruption to such ludicrous extremes that officials with incomes of only a few hundred dollars a month were able to amass fortunes. Consequently, their interest in serving the great majority of Vietnamese who could not afford their services was minimal. In time, as the influx of American money grew, only foreigners and wealthy local businessmen, politicians, and other public officials were able to gain effective access to the government. Many, if not most Vietnamese came to fear contact with officials whose expectations for payment far surpassed the ability of local people to pay. Worst of all, many officials did not scale down their demands after American withdrawal but turned upon some of the most powerless members of their society—peasants, workers, and prostitutes—arresting them or forcing them to meet strict but meaningless government regulations, not out of desire to enforce the laws, but in an effort to extort bribes to supplement their own incomes.

URBAN BEGGARS

Begging is a worldwide phenomenon that is not limited to impoverished nations. The United States has long had hobo populations who routinely supplement occasional work with requests for handouts of money, food, or clothing. Recently, begging has even spread to unemployed "hippie" youths of largely middle-class origin who have discovered that an adequate income can be gained in affluent America by panhandling for "spare change." Most of this type are only temporary beggars. After a short time they tire of begging and turn to supporting themselves with skills gained through education. Others, caught by physical disability or lack of salable skills, have no alternative to a life sustained by the largesse of passersby.

In most nations of the third world no adequate social welfare programs exist to care for orphaned, aged, crippled, blind, leprous, or demented individuals who cannot rely upon relatives for care. For limbless Vietnamese veterans and half-caste street urchins of Saigon, abandoned by unknown GI fathers and prostitute mothers, begging is often the only alternative to starvation. To Westerners who have been surrounded and clawed by desperate, hungry people who view the clothes of the average American as a conspicuous display of wealth, contact with true beggars—those who cannot provide for themselves and for whom no other source of sustenance exists—becomes a disquieting, indelible memory. These people cannot easily be compared with Western middle-class beggars of convenience.

Despite the ubiquity of beggars in much of the world, little effort has been made to study them intensively. A major reason is undoubtedly the sense that a beggar's position is too obvious to merit research: he or she usually presents himself as an individual who cannot provide for himself as a result of obvious disability, relying upon public sympathy in lieu of a structured welfare system. One attractive young Bangkok girl, for example, has begged successfully for several years by displaying the severed fingers of her hands, provoking sympathy and money from women who realize that her missing fingers will make it difficult for her to find a husband.

Another problem in studying beggars is the difficulty of gaining information from these marginal, generally inarticulate individuals, who fear arrest should their presence attract too much attention. And finally, inquiries into begging are likely to be thwarted by government officials reluctant to have distasteful aspects of their society studied. Malaysia, for example, is one of the under-developed world's most prosperous and intelligently administered nations. But even there, certain city streets are lined by day by beggars with out-stretched hands and at night by beggars sleeping on the "five-foot ways" (sidewalks) in makeshift beds of torn cardboard boxes. While teaching urban anthropology in a Malaysian university, I required all students to complete year-long urban research projects. One student, Chan Lean Heng, whose work will be discussed below, chose to study beggar culture. Although the presence of numerous beggars was obvious to even the most casual and least sensitive visitor to the city of Penang and occasionally prompted newspaper exposes, Chan's efforts to study the problem intensively were countered on one hand by uncooperative social welfare officials and on the other by a local university professor who maintained that "there are no beggars in Penang."

Reports of beggars are most frequent in brief newspaper or magazine articles, or peripherally in ethnographic discussions of urban social problems. Often these reports suggest that the majority of beggars are healthy, able-bodied individuals who turn to begging as a more lucrative alternative to regular employment.

> A common feature in many bazaars, as well as in the central shopping areas, temples, and railway stations, is the inevitable beggar who makes his rounds in all Indian cities. Mendicancy

has become institutionalized due to chronic unemployment and the lack of organized charity or public relief. One survey reported that in the city of Bombay alone there are about 10,000 beggars, some 47 per cent of whom are able-bodied. Of the remainder 18 per cent are aged and infirm, 12 per cent are lepers, and 10 per cent blind and crippled. The total beggar population of Delhi has been estimated at about 3,000, of whom 44.5 per cent are able-bodied. Many beggars earn a rupee or more a day, which is almost equal to, or in excess of, the daily wage of some workers. It has been estimated that Bombay citizens spend some 3,500,000 rupees annually on indiscriminate charity to beggars, and Delhi citizens 918,000 rupees. If such sums were to flow through welfare channels, adequate care and rehabilitation services might be provided not only for all beggars, but for many others also. While many cities have various types of legislation against begging, institutional facilities are not adequate to cope with all beggars even if they are arrested.[31]

A detailed and thorough inquiry, *The Beggar Problem in Metropolitan New Delhi* conducted by the Delhi School of Social Work, found that about 60 percent of the city's beggars were able-bodied people "who should normally be working for their livelihood," although most were illiterate and completely unskilled.[32] A significant portion (29 percent), however, had been forced to begin begging when they or their source of support became handicapped by accident or disease, especially leprosy. Average income (often exaggerated by the press) appeared to be below that of an unskilled manual worker.

A similarly detailed and impressive study of Bombay beggars reported that a much greater proportion are disabled than is generally assumed.[33] Census estimates classify 64 percent as able-bodied workers; but the detailed street survey found only 38 percent to be truly able-bodied. The discrepancy is apparently due largely to census judgments, (which are made by sight and consider only obvious disabilities). Actually, the Bombay study found "no able bodied beggars in the proper and full connotation of the term,"[34] for a large number of the so-called able-bodied were malnourished and afflicted with various psychic, emotional, and physical ailments. That most beggars were not truly able-bodied in the psychological sense should be apparent from the fact that begging itself is often hard work. The beggar has a certain independence which employed individuals do not have, to be sure, but long hours of begging—especially if an acrobatic or musical performance is involved—can easily be as taxing as ordinary work.

Chan's report concluded that most Penang beggars were genuinely needy and that they were physically, socially (for example, an aged widow without children to support her), or psychologically handi-capped.[35] But for some, begging was simply a relatively lucrative occupation the income from which could not be matched elsewhere. While sickness and inability to obtain and continue employment were the most common preconditions to begging, some beggars, especially the aged, begged to pass the time and supplement meager existences. Chan found that some residents of a welfare home took leave from the home several days a week to beg, both to escape the boredom of institutional life and to allow indulgence in such occasional luxuries as eating a bowl of *mee hoon* (a spaghetti-like dish), smoking opium, or gambling. Some of Chan's informants con-fided that "without food they can die but without gambling they can't live." More frequently, of course, aged beggars beg to survive. One of Chan's informants explained simply that "she has to beg because she has no other means of a livelihood because no one wants to employ her anymore but she refuses to kill herself."

In addition to "genuine" beggars, pressed by poverty and handicap to beg, and "professional" beggars who have mastered the art of gaining a living from begging, young children often beg for their own and their family's support. These child beggars sometimes begin before the age of five, roaming city streets with their peers, often with no adult supervision or care of any kind. Parents en-courage child begging to relieve themselves of the burden of pro-viding food and shelter. A typical case is that of a ten-year-old Penang Indian boy who has begged as long as he can remember. He spends his days begging and his nights with his widower father sleep-ing on sidewalks. Aside from small expenditures for *roti* (bread), he gives all he receives to his father.

Finally, many individuals engage in either occasional or "dis-guised" begging, supplementing income without acquiring a self or societal definition as a beggar. In Malaysia, occasional begging is common during religious celebrations, especially after mosque services and during the festival of Hari Raya (when Muslims give to beggars outside the mosque to satisfy one of the five tenets of Islam, giving charity), and also during the Malaysian Indian festival of Thaipusan. Individuals who beg only during such periods do not regard themselves as beggars and are not subject to arrest.

Disguised beggars, too, avoid some of the stigma of definition as a beggar by providing a "service" in exchange for charity—though such services are generally unproductive and unwanted. In Malaysia, disguised begging centers around such so-called services as guarding automobiles or providing a religious blessing. The automobilist, for example, is met at a public parking area by a youth who guides him to a parking place, opens the door, and rolls up the driver's window; later, he rolls down the window and directs the driver out of the parking lot. In exchange, he expects at least ten to twenty cents, which is usually given out of guilt at the disparity of wealth and fear that if money is not offered the car will be damaged or the driver insulted. Beggars who use the religious blessing method often go from door to door chanting prayers, rubbing ashes on doorways, or giving individuals slips of red paper on which good wishes have been written, in expectation that few will reject the expressed goodwill by refusing payment.

It is sometimes asserted that begging results from lack of information on welfare services. Not surprisingly, few beggars interviewed in Penang had any understanding of the state welfare department beyond fear that contact with it would mean incarceration in a home. Their perception of the welfare office as a place where no real help can be expected is generally correct. Of those Chan interviewed, the only one who had hoped that the welfare department could aid him was quickly disappointed. Realizing that he could not care for himself, he attempted to enter the state welfare home, only to be informed that he could not do so without police referral. He arranged for a police constable to arrest him, in hope of gaining quick admission to the home. Instead, he was transferred to a home in another state. After a short, homesick stay, he fled his new home and returned to Penang to resume begging.

The marginality of beggars was clearest in two of Chan's major findings: (1) beggars tended to be true loners, who lived isolated, encapsulated, uncommunicative lives; (2) few beggars begged in a manner that would maximize their incomes. The habitual silence of beggars and the paucity of contact impressed Chan deeply. "A good number of them seem to be verbally dead," she noted, without "any form of contact even with their own kind." Only once in her year-long study of dozens of beggars did she note any conversation among them. This was between two female Chinese immigrants who begged part-time in a temple compound. The atypical character of such communication was illustrated even in this instance, for neither woman gave the slightest acknowledgement to a neighboring beggar.

Maximization of income is achieved through a "positive" begging strategy which involves constant movement and direct approach to prospective alms-givers. Of the beggars studied, few followed a positive strategy; most merely sat on sidewalks hoping alms would fall their way. "Positive" beggars were most likely to be able-bodied, professional beggars.

The most revealing segment of Chan's study resulted from her assumption of the role of beggar as a participant observer (which I observed, in order to intervene in case she was arrested). Dressed in a disheveled fashion and looking much the part, she at first emulated professional beggars by moving from place to place and making direct approaches for aid. Such a strategy produced results: she earned approximately three (U.S.) dollars an hour. Adoption of the "negative," or passive approach to begging used by most real beggars, however, produced little: after about fifteen minutes of squatting on the pavement with outstretched hands and vacant eyes in one of Penang's most active areas, during which time not a single passerby paused to give her alms, she returned to active begging. Evidently such a passive approach makes it easy for others to ignore the beggar without feeling guilt at their lack of charity.

Finally, Chan's research showed that individuals who were on the margin of economic well-being were most likely to give to those only slightly beneath them. Concluding that it "is the poor who help the poor," Chan suggests that:

> Maybe it is because they, having undergone hardship, understand and are aware of what hardship and difficulties are like. That is why they are the ones who seem most generous, most willing to help. Though none of this category has given me a big sum in terms of money, I do greatly appreciate the little token of their kindness—maybe more than the boss who gave me [Malaysian] $1.00. It is not the actual amount received that touched but the sacrifice incurred. Being in pretty difficult situations themselves, they are still aware of my plight. Take, for example, a stall owner in front of a coffee shop. I didn't bother to ask anything from him at first, thinking that I would only be disappointed. But as I passed him, he stopped me and offered something of his own accord, without my pleas.

Begging in much of the third world capitalizes on this interpersonal relation between supplicant and alms-giver largely because such a one-to-one relation is more effective than institutional succor. Most of the populace might resent taxes to support the unseen needy; but personal interaction with a beggar often gives an individual a sense of virtue, even a feeling that good fortune may come his way from the beggar's blessing. A conservative estimate is that in 1959 the people of Bombay gave over (U.S.) $750,000 to beggars. This sum might have been difficult to collect institutionally because the feelings and sympathies that provoked its donation in the begging situation are absent in the institutional one. In this context, Moorthy feels "it may be true to say that organized charity and institutionalized assistance are characteristic of advanced societies."[36] For nations without effective institutionalized expressions of concern, begging serves as a final, often effective appeal to one's fellowman.

One Solution: A Japanese Beggars' Cooperative

Koji Taira's study of urban poverty and Tokyo ragpickers demonstrates that even such lowly occupations as the gathering of waste items for reprocessing, which is considered begging and on the borderline between employment and vagrancy, may provide the basis for general improvement in economic condition and social outlook.[37] Ragpickers and other scavengers have long occupied the lowest stratum of Japanese society. Most are either outcastes[38] or considered marginal in other ways.

> The contempt of the general public for ragpickers has always been deep. The police have maintained close watch over ragpickers as potentially dangerous vagrants, while the public health authorities have regulated the location and standards of the rag business from a sanitary point of view. If the general community regards ragpickers as of no more value than the junk they pick, ragpickers themselves tend to accept this lowly status and social role. How to help these social failures "up and into" the ordinary world is a great social problem. The story of the "Ants' Villa" in Tokyo . . . is one of the few examples of psychological rehabilitation, spiritual growth, and economic success among ragpickers.[39]

Occasionally people classed socially as beggars share ties that permit them to go beyond isolated scavenging for existence. The Ants' Villa is a community of fifty households that occupy a tract of reclaimed land on the Tokyo waterfront. Its members gain a livelihood by scavenging for all kinds of junk—cans, glass, paper rags— which they resell. Life in the Villa is organized on a communal basis centered around a Catholic chapel. In contrast to the isolated, marginally productive scavenging techniques generally followed in the past, the community's work is highly organized. Members collect junk from business concerns in Tokyo, transport it to the community workshops in trucks, sort it by teams of worker-residents, machine pack it, then deliver it to commercial processors for recycling. The community compound is large (16,700 square meters) and contains in addition to the chapel and workshops four residential structures, a children's playhouse, a guest house, and a restaurant where residents have their meals. "The community is clean, quiet, and prosperous," Taira says, and "its standard of living is above the social minimum in every sense." But such prosperity is recent. Fifteen years ago the community, located elsewhere, "was 'subminimum' in every sense, verging in fact upon the underworld of vagrants and criminals."[40] Its members were mere ragpickers and must have been regarded as out-castes.

Past surveys of such groups, like that conducted by Japan's Ministry of Home Affairs in 1911, have shown that—unlike the poor as a whole who tend to blame their poverty on "acts of God," economic factors beyond their control, illness, and old age—ragpickers and others on the borderline of begging explain their status principally as the result of personal failings such as laziness, debauchery, excessive drinking, and lack of skills or education.[41] The internalization of personal inadequacy common to long-term depressed outcaste groups makes it very difficult for them to improve their condition. But a series of events helped release dormant personal energies which reshaped the Villa community and gave its members a vital sense of self-esteem.

In 1950, Motomu Ozawa, a successful businessman who lost everything in World War II, took charge of fifteen unemployed rag-pickers who had just been dismissed by a retiring rag dealer. To establish them, he subleased a deserted lumberyard and, with the aid of a former director of Taiwan's Theatrical Association who had also been displaced by the war, organized a ragpickers' cooperative. At about the same time the young daughter of a professor, a university graduate and a convert to Catholicism, took an interest in the community. She set up a special tutoring program for the children, to encourage them in their studies and help counteract the effects of other schoolchildren's contempt on their self-images and schoolwork. Soon she, too, began to pick rags; she entered the community, where she remained until she died of tuberculosis in 1958.

Under the influence of this woman and the former theater director, the ragpickers gradually began to turn to Christianity. As despised people in Japan they readily identified with the beggars, lepers, thieves, and prostitutes befriended by Jesus. Most important for their conversion to Christianity, Ozawa, the Villa Chief, saw in Christianity an example of extension of principles similar to the ideal organization of a Japanese family, in which Jesus watched over his children and would make any sacrifice for them. Ozawa's acceptance of Catholicism was a turning point in the community; within a few years all had become Christian. Self-esteem and community organization had become so strong that the group—which at this time, in 1958, was squatting on a public park—resisted eviction from the land until the metropolitan government agreed to sell them the site of their present location for fifteen million yen, which, given the community's financial standing, was an extraordinarily large sum.[42]

The successful transition from a group of thieves and beggars to a self-reliant and prosperous community was due largely to the peculiar circumstances of postwar Japan. Individuals like Ozawa and the theater director, who in ordinary times might never have come in contact with such marginal people, were reduced to a similar state by the fortunes of war. Their participation with members of the community led to a common effort to rebuild all of their lives, further aided by the enthusiasm of the professor's daughter to put into action the precepts of her new religion. Finally, conversion of the entire community to Catholicism helped solidify their unity and enhance their sense of self-worth by casting off the outcaste status for which traditional Japanese religion is largely responsible.

The example of the Ants' Villa is unique. But its importance lies in highlighting the fact that the lives of such people can be remade, but that something more than aloof bureaucratic concern is required. What such situations call for—and what is usually overlooked by government policymakers everywhere—is a "'psychocultural policy' to regenerate and strengthen the personalities, outlook, and will to live of the hard-core poor."[43]

THE "CULTURE OF POVERTY"

The case of the Tokyo ragpickers is atypical. More often than not, poor individuals and poverty-stricken communities pass their poverty to succeeding generations. In his studies of Puerto Rican poor in San Juan and New York, anthropologist Oscar Lewis was so struck by the endemic, pan-generational quality of poverty that he coined the term *culture of poverty*. In his conception, the culture of poverty is a common coping mechanism of the urban poor in cash economies characterized by wage-labor employment, profit-oriented production, and high levels of unemployment and underemployment. It offers ready-made adaptive responses to life situations typically encountered by those at the lowest ranks of the social system, and is thus in his conception truly a culture, or subculture, in the traditional anthropological sense.[44]

Lewis hypothesized that there are some seventy traits that can be isolated as characteristic of the culture of poverty, that develop initially as spontaneous attempts by members of marginal communities to cope with the realization that they will never be able to achieve the life styles deemed successful by the dominant group. In time, however, what begins as spontaneous attempts to cope become entrenched and form the core of the culture of poverty. The relation of this subculture of poverty with the larger society is characterized primarily by a "disengagement" in which its members generally do not participate in such social institutions as labor unions and political parties and underuse banks, hospitals, department stores, and educational and cultural facilities. Contact with larger social institutions when it occurs is largely negative, through prisons or welfare institutions.

Life tends to be led on a day-to-day basis without much future planning. Lack of steady employment and low wages connect with an absence of property, savings, and food supplies to encourage the purchase of small quantities of food at the economical loss such purchases involve. Scarcity of money presses people to makeshift solutions of frequenting pawnshops and borrowing at exorbitant interest rates.

Middle-class values are known and often accepted, but reality places them beyond reach. The police, as enforcers of an alien code, are often despised, as are government officials. Indeed, recognition of the legitimacy of any organization beyond the residential family unit is usually weak and sporadic. Marriages are frequently avoided in favor of the freedom and flexibility of consensual unions which give the wife greater claim to the children and control over her own property and eliminate the legal complications of divorce. Family instability tends to produce female-centered households and a situation that "does not cherish childhood as a specially prolonged and protected stage in the life cycle," so that sexual activity begins early. Those who grow up in this culture have a strong sense of fatalism, helplessness, and inferiority, as well as a tendency to exhibit a high incidence of weak ego structure, orality and confusion of sexual identification, all reflecting maternal deprivation; a strong present-time orientation with relatively little disposition to defer gratification and plan for the future, and a high tolerance for psychological pathology of all kinds. There is widespread belief in male superiority and among the men a strong preoccupation with *machismo*, their masculinity.[45]

Lewis' description of the *culture of poverty,* and its vivid portrayal in such widely-read books as *Children of Sanchez* and *La Vida,* has struck a strong chord of recognition among anthropologists who immediately recalled many of its characteristics from their own fieldwork. But many have felt discomfited by the concept, especially by the notion that such a culture or subculture is everywhere similar, overriding the diverse character of the world's cultures. Others have taken Lewis to task for failing to emphasize the diversity of life styles common to poor people, the fact that the poor *do* contribute to the larger society and economy, and, most important, the fact that mere poverty does not necessarily consign one to a "culture" of poverty. Still others have felt use of the term *culture of poverty* to be dangerous to well-being of the poor themselves, since it could discourage efforts to help them by suggesting that—while the original basis for long-term, cross-generational poverty rests in political and economic systems of the society as a whole—once the adaptive mechanisms of the culture of poverty have taken hold they are extremely difficult to overcome.

The logic of the culture of poverty can quickly become circular: it is argued that people behave in a characteristic manner because they are poor and that they are poor because they act like poor people. The culture of poverty, Rolland Wright states, is "an idea conceived by one kind of man and applied to another ... [consisting] largely of the first man trying to imagine the impact of poverty on people he assumes are like himself, without realizing it might mean something quite different to the poor themselves, because they are different men." Wright suggests that Lewis has approached the problem of poverty from the wrong direction: "rather than imagining that the poor are the way they are because they are poor ... [we should consider the possibility] that they are poor because of the way they are."[46]

Some of these criticisms are excessive and a bit unfair, as Lewis points out in his own defense.[47] He disposes of criticism that the term *culture of poverty* should be replaced by *subculture of pov-*

erty[48] by noting his repeated emphasis that he is actually speaking of a subculture but that, since his books are meant for a wide audience, he chose to use the term culture to avoid confusion and the possible assumption that subculture means an inferior culture.[49] Although he perhaps has not emphasized sufficiently the diversity of adaptation he found in slums, he argues that he "had no intention of equating an entire slum settlement with the culture of poverty . . . In my experience, the people who live in slums, even in small ones, show a great deal of heterogeneity in income, literacy, education, political sentiments, and life-styles." Indeed, a distinction between economic poverty and a culture of poverty can definitely be seen, and the latter "is found only in approximately 20 percent of the families who live below the poverty line." Finally, in response to the criticism that emphasis on an entrenched, pathological adaptation of the poor to their poverty constitutes a kind of "blaming of the poor" for perpetuating their own poverty by inability to defer gratification and to lift themselves and their children from a vicious poverty cycle, Lewis protests that, in his view,

> in the long run the self-perpetuating factors are relatively minor and unimportant as compared to the basic structure of the larger society. However, to achieve rapid change and improvement with the minimum amount of trauma one must work on both the "external" and "internal" conditions. To ignore the internal factors is to ignore and distort the reality of people with a subculture of poverty. In effect, this is harmful to their interests because it plays down the extent of their special needs and the special programs which are necessary to make up for the deprivations and damage which they have suffered over many generations.[50]

Not all critiques of the *culture of poverty* argument can be easily dismissed. Perhaps the most serious critique is provided by Lewis himself in his statement that the culture is found "only in 20% of the families who live below the poverty line." Equally serious is Mangin's objection—reminiscent of the Redfield-Lewis debate over the character of Tepotzlan—that Lewis overemphasizes disorganization, bitterness, and violence, and neglects the close mixture of positive and negative behavior and world view typically found among slum inhabitants. Indeed, from the responses given by seventy-four randomly selected adults in a Lima *barriada* to the Minnesota Multiphasic Personality Inventory (MMPI), it is evident that inconsistencies in world view are common:

Q. The future looks blacker every day.
     Yes 61   No 13

Q. A young man of today can have much hope for the future.
     Yes 59   No 5

Q. Many children are a burden.
     Yes 50   No 23

Q. One should sacrifice all for one's children
     Yes 71   No 3

The same people who see the future becoming blacker every day have hope for the future. The same people who view their children as a burden believe that they should sacrifice for them.[51]

Johnson and Sanday, in their article "Subcultural Variations in an Urban Poor Population," drawn from a detailed study of Pittsburgh poor, suggest that *two* poor subcultures exist: one black and one white. Testing determinants of lack of future orientation, they found that race, not poverty, explained this supposedly crucial characteristic of the culture of poverty: poor blacks demonstrated much less future orientation than did poor whites.[52] Similarly, a California survey of 1,156 male heads of intact families revealed that Spanish-speakers were most likely to demonstrate traits associated with the culture of poverty concept, followed by blacks, then whites. The authors concluded that the most likely explanation for the greater incidence of culture of poverty patterns among Spanish-speakers was not to be found in poverty itself, but in the language handicap and in certain Latin cultural values that promote fatalistic and dependent orientations.[53]

In America, at least, and possibly elsewhere, it is likely that the despair for the future which lies at the base of the concept of the culture of poverty may have its core in racial discrimination rather than in poverty. If this interpretation is correct, Lewis' work with the Puerto Rican poor may have unknowingly led him to a problem whose ethnic component he neglected in favor of purely economic explanation.

OVERCROWDING

Poverty is obviously relative. It is, as Taira notes, "a grave social problem in rich countries, while it is not in poor countries . . .

countries seem to "discover" poverty in their midst at a certain stage of their socioeconomic development."[54] In Japan, "poverty" was first "discovered" in the late 1880's by a small group of young intellectuals whose readings had familiarized them with the social consequences of industrialization in the West. Japan had just begun its emergence from feudalism and its development along Western lines. Alerted to the existence of poverty in industrial societies, the sociologist Gen'nosuke Yokoyama suddenly found it in the midst of Tokyo. Although he had known of isolated pockets of poverty "containing ten, twenty, or at most several tens of poor households," his newly trained eyes discovered three ghettos of poverty so large that their sight "made him rub his eyes twice before he was sure of [their] existence."[55]

Just as poverty has suddenly emerged as a great social problem for many nations in recent years, so has the problem of urban overcrowding. There is little doubt that most countries suffer from a shortage of housing. The United Nations has estimated that the nations of Africa, Asia, and Latin America need to produce ten or eleven dwellings for each thousand inhabitants during the next decade. When one considers that the industrial nations of the West that can best afford residential construction only produce from five to ten housing units per year, the immensity of the problem faced by most nations is apparent.[56]

Inadequate supplies of urban housing sometimes leads to conditions of severe overcrowding. The problem is especially acute in inner city slums, where recent migrants are most likely to congregate because of need to be close to potential employment. Their inability to afford adequate housing, coupled with the need for proximity to downtown areas, generally consigns them to the worst possible rented housing where they must share cramped quarters with other family members and often with strangers. Once they have established themselves with regular employment and have acclimatized somewhat to the ways of the city, slum dwellers often seek land on the city's fringe upon which to squat.

Those who settle and remain in slums are forced to "pile up" in close quarters. Studies of urban American slums have pointed to such social byproducts of crowding as diminished parental control of children, and even the tendency for slum inhabitants subject to frequent disturbance by others to lose sleep. A study of black slum dwellers at the close of World War II, for example, found that most slept less than five hours a night.[57] In the slums of Chicago, Washington, D.C., New York, and other large North American cities young children often return from school to play in the streets, going home only to eat and then drifting back to the streets, where they stay until they return home to sleep or watch television. The lack of the uncrowded living rooms, dens, and separate yards that are common to the suburbs sends even preschool children out to the "living rooms" of the slums: the streets and sidewalks where peer socialization predominates. Additionally, tensions produced in adults of Western cultures by situations of overcrowding tend to be manifested in excessive drinking and frequent family discord.

In India, the problem of overcrowding and its social ramifications sometimes require unrelated housemates to sleep in shifts. In an attempt to provide some kind of accomodation for industrial workers, the city of Bombay built a number of labor *chawls* of about ten square feet, only to find the dark, poorly ventilated structures packed with one or two large families each. At night even the passages were lined with sleeping bodies.[58] City populations of the nation have increased much more rapidly than has living space, so that measurements of available living space per person in such cities as Hubli and Jamshedpur have shown that from 21 percent (Hubli) to 50 percent (Jamshedpur) of the total city population live in situations of "extreme overcrowding," that is, with less than twenty-five square feet per person.[59] Indians who have emigrated to the relatively rich Southeast Asian nations of Malaysia and Singapore sometimes pack upwards of one hundred people into a small two-storey house. Others maximize earning power by working during almost all their waking hours. They may gain a little additional income as night watchmen by sleeping on their rope beds in front of a shop-house in the hope that their mere presence will discourage thieves.

A pre-World War II study of coolie quarters in the Indonesian town of Batavia showed that most of the homes were small (two and a half rooms on average) bamboo and thatch or wood houses with earthen floors. Generally three to four persons occupied each bedroom, with only one *balai-balai* (couch) for every three people. Toilet facilities, too, were meager; only one-eighth of the dwellings had even the most primitive facility.[60]

Probably nowhere has the density of human population remained consistently as high as in the Chinatowns of Asia. Many living quarters above Chinese shop-houses in the central cities of Kuala Lumpur and Singapore have been subdivided into minuscule cubicles, each occupied by a family. The average size of such cubicles in Upper Nankin Street, Singapore, has been found to be ten feet square. Some inhabitants merely rented a narrow bunk under the stairs

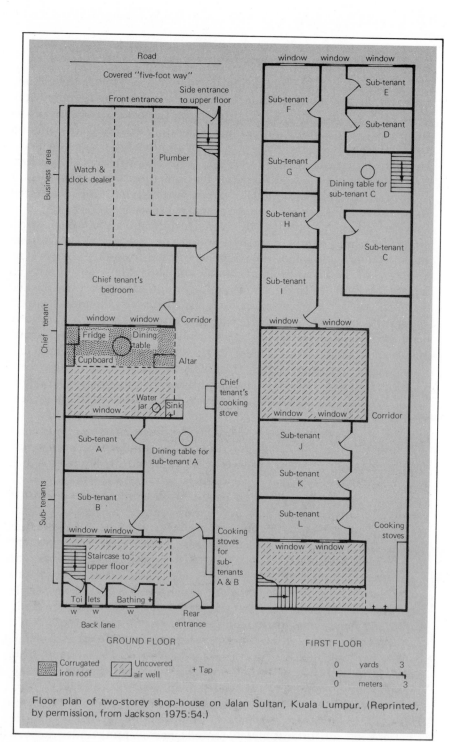

Floor plan of two-storey shop-house on Jalan Sultan, Kuala Lumpur. (Reprinted, by permission, from Jackson 1975:54.)

or slept with the shop assistants in the downstairs business area. The mean number of households (each averaging about four people) in 1970 ranged from three to almost seven per shop in the main areas of Kuala Lumpur's Chinatown; the average for the area was twenty to thirty people per shop-house. As high as this figure is, it represents a considerable decline in preindependence densities, which ranged up to sixty-one people per house on one especially crowded street. The interior upstairs rooms of the houses usually have no windows or other outside openings to provide ventilation or sunlight. Consequently, whole families live in dark, cramped quarters sharing small kitchens, squat toilets, and enclosed water tap areas which serve as baths.[61] Barrington Kaye, in cataloging the household composition and family history of residents of Upper Nankin Street, tells of a not atypical family of four who occupied a 12' x 10½' windowless attic cubicle which could only be reached by ladder. Since the attic rafters came within four feet of the floor at the sides, one could stand only in the center of the room.[62]

Despite what might be unbearable population densities for most Westerners, Chinese slums are not generally centers of social pathology. Considering the overcrowding and the often difficult conditions of life, it is surprising how little crime and obvious mental distress they seem to produce. Population densities as high as 20,000 persons *per acre* in Hong Kong are associated with levels of suicide, crime, and drug use that seem minor in contrast to Western cities such as New York, the population densities of which are not nearly so great. Fights are relatively rare, and when they do take place they are generally between members of different communities or households. Much of the Chinese ability to cope with overcrowding is natural in that crowding, at least to a point (far greater than that generally tolerated by Westerners), is considered desirable. Traditional Chinese culture values the co-residence of a large and cohesive kin group. Personal privacy, so important in the West, is regarded as strange if not pathological; and Westerners who live alone in Chinese communities are viewed with a mixture of curiosity, pity, and suspicion.

In addition to the fact that dense levels of co-residence are often not perceived as overcrowding, the Chinese, as Eugene Anderson discusses, tend to interact in patterns that minimize social friction. Space in a Chinese household is carefully divided into private and public domains. Bedrooms are usually occupied only at night, and then only by family members. Outsiders not only do not enter the bedrooms, they should not even look into them. The kitchen, dining areas, front room, and porch area, as well as the streets and sidewalks, are used for socializing. Several families may share the same cooking area, but each family has its own stove, for practical and religious reasons (the kitchen god, who lives in or around the stove, must make a yearly journey to the other world on the family's behalf). Use of time is flexible, characterized by the irregular working hours of the men and schoolchildren (who often attend split shifts) and the fact that everyone eats when he wishes by serving himself from the family cabinet, where food is placed after it has been cooked in the morning. Meals are consumed quickly, with little lingering.

Noise is not usually viewed as a problem. Anderson notes that he "never heard anyone complain about noise in a Chinese household . . . [it] is the sign of life and action, and the household moves in a shimmering ambience of sound from waking to sleep." I have heard parents and older siblings scold children for talking too loudly; but Anderson is correct in suggesting that noise does seem to be either appreciated—indeed, one common Chinese phrase for a good time is *je nao*, or hot noise—or ignored.[63]

Patterns of status and respect based principally on age and sex provide a consistent hierarchy of authority that obviates much potential disagreement. Most important, however, the emotional aspect of personal interaction is largely based upon the assumption that unrelated persons, especially adults, will not involve themselves in one another's affairs. As part of a general set of cultural expectations, individuals display a capacity for pretending to be unaware of others' problems that do not directly concern them. Unburdening one's mind, even to relatives, is rare and considered deviant, as would be the effort to encourage others to do so. If an individual desires not to interact with others, even for extended periods, his wish is respected and household activities continue around him with only minimal participation on his part.

SLUMS AND SQUATTER SETTLEMENTS

One of the most immediate and obvious results of urbanization and housing shortage has been the spread of dilapidated and substandard housing around the world's cities, in *slums* (where homes are generally rented) and *squatter settlements* (usually owner-occupied on illegally seized land). Known as *villas miserias* (Argentina), *barong-barong* (the Philippines), *bidonvilles* (Morocco), *favelas* (Brazil), *barriadas* (Peru), *ranchos* (Panama), *colonias proletarias* (Mexico), or *bustees*, *jhoupris,* and *jhuggis* (India and Pakistan), they sprawl within and around major cities, sometimes encompassing them like a noose.

Today, roughly half the world's population growth takes place in cities. Fully three-quarters of the total number of these new city dwellers move, not to the well-equipped homes and apartments of their dreams, but to densely packed slums and squatter settlements.[64] The remarkable growth of this ill-housed urban population has not resulted from industrial demand for labor, such as occurred in Europe in the wake of the Industrial Revolution, but is the result of narrowing opportunity in rural areas and the hope that cities will offer better, more sophisticated lives. Few of the world's non-Western cities have the industrial base to absorb their burgeoning populations by providing them the wherewithal to move from makeshift housing to permanent, well-built homes of their own. Consequently, for most of the world's present and future urban population, the relatively short-lived purgatory of slum life experienced by most new immigrants to the industrial cities of Europe or to the Lower East Side of New York, followed by upward mobility out of squalor, is unlikely to occur.

The demands upon urban housing resources seem too immense to be met in the foreseeable future. Even if crash programs were undertaken on a worldwide scale to provide adequate shelter for all city dwellers, the problem might actually be aggravated by continued and perhaps augmented influx of rural migrants entering the cities—not only with hope of employment but also with knowledge that government programs might help them find better housing than in their rural homes. The problems of underdevelopment and inadequate housing are intimately linked in a vicious circle, so that underdevelopment seems to foster the kind of urbanization that results in further underdevelopment. "Instead of standing as a symptom of development growth as it was in the West," Hagmuller states, "urbanization in the third world is both cause and effect of continued underdevelopment and increasing poverty."[65]

McGee refers to the current phase of third-world population expansion, in which urban growth seems to bear little relation to labor demands of cities, as "pseudo urbanization."[66] The problem, he feels, is the common colonial experience of most of these countries: European powers encouraged each nation to specialize in production of raw materials required by industries and markets of that colonial power. Thus countries like Malaysia produced rubber and tin, Burma teak, and Ceylon tea. Such specialization did not cease with independence but is still common. Industry that would help absorb urban migrants has not been developed, both because of lack of adequate capital and because the realities of industrial economies of scale and world tariff restrictions make it difficult for relatively inefficient young industries of the developing nations to compete with those of established industrial states.

Pressed into cities without useful outlets for their energies, many urbanites have had no alternative but to survive by selling their labor at the lowest possible wage. Consequently, shared poverty or patterns of "subsistence urbanization"[67] have developed as people enter marginal, low-paying jobs like hawking food and driving trishaws. Often the net return from these jobs is little more than enough for food, so payment of any rent is difficult. Under such circumstances, individuals and families sometimes crowd into shared quarters, even sleeping in shifts to minimize housing expenses. Not surprisingly, many attempt to seize pieces of land where they can build their own homes.

The resulting shantytowns, Albert Meister claims, provide the only framework of adaptation to urban life for many migrants, serving as the setting for a three-part *arrival, crisis,* and *adaptation* process. During the arrival period, fundamental rural values of family and personal stability, domestic neatness, care for aged parents, and honesty are dominant. But often the man of a family fails to find steady work, the woman feels isolated in her new surroundings, and the children enter a world of peer-socialization. Tensions of adaptation well up during this period—especially in the husband as the result of difficulty in supporting his family—leading to the collapse of family unity. "At this point," Meister says,

> family cohesion disintegrates. The man usually finds a mistress and abandons his wife and children. Family authority is shattered. The children lose respect for their elders and become estranged from them (in a conflict between two concepts of behaviourism), quit school and encounter difficulties in making social contacts outside. The family shack becomes gradually dirtier and more disorderly. Their relationships with the neighbours turn hostile in a projection of their own problems, and are characterized by abuse, brawls, thievery and other malpractices. Sex, stimulated by alcohol and the need for powerful emotional outlets to counter frustrations becomes rampant. Sexual companions are frequently changed.

After experiencing various degrees of adaptive crisis, migrants establish either such "delinquent" adaptations as thievery or prostitution or "socially acceptable" adaptations, characterized by the male's steady employment, increased family cohesion, and attention to personal appearance and improvements in the shack. Occasionally, the migrant achieves active participation and leadership in the community. But too often "the tenuity of the border between delinquency and other forms of adaptation . . . damns [the shantytown] as a desireable centre for adaptation in urban life; a cheap solution, it can turn out only a minimal number of urbanized immigrants who will conform to desireable social norms."[68]

In approaching the study of slums and squatter settlements (or "squatments") it is useful to distinguish between them. The slum dweller, though he often lives in worse conditions than the squatter, pays rent and thus has legal claim to residence. The urban squatter illegally occupies government or private land without paying rent and lacks a recognized right to inhabit the property. His occupancy of the house he has built is tenuous, dependent upon his and his fellow squatters' ability to resist forcible eviction. As Charles Abrams points out, in the West squatting has generally been a rural phenomenon—American frontiersmen often settled rural lands without concern for title—while slums have been characteristic of city life.[69] In much of the rest of the world, however, both are a major part of urban settings. Squatments are preferred, since they generally provide accommodation at least equal in quality to that of slums at much lower cost.

Squatters are far from a homogeneous lot. They vary from those common to the cities of India, who sleep and spend much of their lives on the street, to relatively wealthy families who inhabit well-constructed houses on illegally occupied ground. Street-sleeping squatters represent an enormous urban problem in cities like Calcutta, where it is estimated that they number 600,000.[70]

More common to most of the world are squatters who occupy land illegally in order to build their own homes on it. It is estimated, for example, that one million squatters live in hill shantytowns of Rio de Janeiro,[71] and that in 1961 approximately 25 percent of the populations of Djakarta, Kuala Lumpur, Manila, and Singapore lived as squatters.[72] The term squatter settlement can be somewhat misleading, as it immediately conjures up images of people living in makeshift shanties without running water or adequate sewage. This is often but not always the case. Many squatter houses show evidence of careful and prideful construction, and some squatments in Caracas even include high-rise buildings with elevators. Such buildings are officially ignored by those who enforce public building codes but are often comparable to those in legal urban settlements; some are "far better than considerable portions of the residences often referred to as 'middle class'."[73]

Given the great variety of homes and the diversity of occupations among squatters, the only encompassing statements that can be made with certainty about squatter settlements are:

1) all squatments are under varying degrees of threat of destruction or removal

2) squatments do not necessarily remain shantytowns but evolve, frequently becoming ordered settlements with streets, plazas, schools, and sewers

3) squatments develop primarily as the result of the absence of housing markets willing and able to cater to the needs of low-income people.

Such a definition does *not* state that squatment residents are principally rural migrants, that they are marginal to the life of the city, or that they are permanent residents of the settlement. Most important, it does not state that squatments are centers of disease, crime, psychological maladjustment, or other social problems, because such assertions "are patently false for all or the great majority of these populations or because there is no clear evidence that they are different from other working class, and sometimes middle class, populations of the city."[74]

A crucial distinguishing characteristic with important sociological consequences between squatter settlements and slums is that the former often require community cohesion and organization, at least initially, for success. In cities such as Lima, public authorities are constantly on the alert to prevent squatters from "invading" new areas. For a squatment to be successful it must be planned well in advance and carefully and swiftly executed. Small-scale settlements constructed gradually are likely to be discovered and destroyed before they are completed. Frequently, organizers of the invasion will contact such outsiders as engineering students or lawyers to aid them in selecting sites. Once all plans have been made, the squatters generally move at night with their construction materials to previously laid-out lots. If the plans have been drawn carefully and the invading party is large enough, the government will find itself faced with a fait accompli that would be difficult to reverse without a kind of open warfare. *Barriadas* formed by organized invasions often continue some formal organization to guard against future mass eviction, to seek roads, water, and sewage disposal, and to serve as a court for minor community disputes.[75]

A major side effect of World War II was the spread of squatter settlements in Asian cities. During and immediately after Japanese occupation of East and Southeast Asia, there was not much effective opposition to squatting. Even the return of the European powers to their former colonies provided little stability to the land tenure situation; the presence of two powers—the Netherlands (in Indonesia) and the United States (the Philippines)—was cut short by the granting of independence to their former colonies. The influence of the other two—Great Britain (Malaya, North Borneo, and Hong Kong) and France (Indochina)—was limited by the instability of regimes forced to wage guerrilla wars against nationalists and communists. Coupled with lack of effective governmental control, an influx of rural migrants from depressed hinterlands in much of Southeast Asia and the arrival in Hong Kong of masses of refugees from China's civil war made it impossible to prevent wholesale squatting.

Hong Kong, especially, experienced an influx of unprecedented proportions. Although the British Crown Colony has a total area of only 390 square miles, much of which is mountainous, its prewar population of one and a half million was forced to absorb over one million refugees from mainland China. This, together with natural population growth, has pushed today's population to five million and has placed tremendous demands upon a colony that subsists primarily through the purchase of raw materials abroad and their transformation into manufactured goods for re-export. After World War II, the demand for housing space was so great that roofs were rented and houses built on them; and many families were forced to sleep on the streets. Little space was wasted: the 1961 Hong Kong census included staircases, passages, caves, tunnels, and sewers as residential designations. An official Hong Kong government report stated about the populace that

> their need was so great and so pressing that they had no thought for the ownership of the land and it would have required an army of police to have restrained them. Virtually every sizeable vacant site that was not under some form of physical or continuing protection was occupied, and when there was no flat land remaining, they moved up the hillsides and colonized the ravines and slopes that were too steep for normal development.[76]

Although minor in comparison with the Hong Kong experience, urban squatting became common in Malaysian cities after World War II and during the "emergency" war against (largely Chinese) communist guerrillas from 1948 until 1960. The decline of rural employment opportunities and the bright lights of the towns and cities encouraged migration there. Rentals for even the poorest housing structures in town were and are high, in comparison with both town wages and rural housing expenditures (the latter generally limited to cost of materials for the structure itself). With maximum average wages of M $120 per month in 1970 (U.S. $40 then) earned by unskilled laborers and taxi or trishaw drivers, few migrants with a family could afford to rent a house. If possible, he would find a site on state land on which he could construct a house of cheap cast-off wood with a zinc-sheeted roof. Most of the work would be done at night or on holidays to avoid discovery by the Land Office or the City Council. On completing the house he would usually daub it with dirty motor oil to preserve the wood and to give it an aged look.[77]

In cities such as Penang, squatters have even occupied old piers or jetties, where they were initially tolerated in the hope that a house or two at the land end of the jetty would discourage theft from docked boats. In time, however, the relatives of the initial squatters spread to envelop entire piers, ending their commercial utility. Today dozens of precariously constructed houses, often almost completely occupied by persons of the same surname, extend out onto the waters of the Straits of Malacca.

The logic of squatting is inescapable to many rural migrants who enter cities only to find housing markets that cater to the upper and middle classes. For the urban poor, legally available housing is generally old and markedly inferior. Added to the cost of "legitimate" housing is a speculative cost, based not upon actual construction costs but upon estimated demand. "The anarchic growth of the city," as Frank Bonilla points out, has frequently been dominated by "large-scale profiteering and speculation in real estate and construction [that] simply took no account of the housing needs of the large number of people automatically eliminated from the housing market by their low incomes."[78] Given the state of urban housing markets, it is not surprising that much of the world's population has chosen to trade the expensive security of the slum for the tenuous ownership of a squatter's home.

Public objection to slums and squatments invariably centers upon their supposed high levels of crime, disease, social disorganization, and radical activity. Outsiders generally fear them and their inhabitants, as can be seen in this excerpt from a September 23, 1957, *Time* report on Rio's *favelas:*

> Squeezed by belt-cinching inflation and an influx of some 3,700 newcomers a month, the favelas gangsters have moved into the city's streets, boosting the crime rate alarmingly in recent weeks. In previously safe lovers' lanes, girls are raped, and their boy friends robbed, beaten or murdered . . . In the favelas, where policemen rarely tread, gang lords built up Robin Hood reputations, casually rubbed out rivals and stool pigeons, and treated attempts to catch them with growing contempt.[79]

For squatter settlements, at least, such judgments seem to come more out of ignorance than fact. Although often quite poor, the inhabitants of squatments often display a willingness to struggle for betterment that is reminiscent of America's early immigrants. In reality, they are usually hardworking families who hope to gain better lives. Petty stealing and gambling are common, but both resident and outsider usually have little to fear in squatments.

Mangin reports that the only comparative study of delinquency rates in Lima's slums and squatter settlements showed that the rate of delinquency in one central city slum was "high and varied" (many different types of criminality were represented) while that of a squatter settlement was "low and unvaried," mostly involving wife-beating and petty thievery. Even prostitution and gambling in the Lima *barriada* were relatively rare and, surprisingly enough considering popular stereotypes, neither promiscuity nor broken families were common. Generally it appears that family and social relations are strong and that the greatest number of households are nuclear, with resident fathers.[80]

Interestingly, squatters often see themselves as well-off. Most are concerned with job security, legal title to the property on which they are squatting, and educating their children. Concluding a description of one downtown Kuala Lumpur squatment, McGee says:

> The problems of this kampong were remarkably few, even though its levels of income were low, an average of $100 Malayan per month; job stability was high, unemployment low; and in general, the squatter kampong gave every impression of rapid adaptation and assimilation to the problems of the urban environment. It could by no means be labeled a "settlement of misery," but rather a "settlement of necessity"—a necessity brought about by the lack of adequate city housing.[81]

THE MARGINALITY OF SQUATTER SETTLEMENTS

Squatters have often been viewed as marginal to the established life of the city. Nelson refers to "the growing numbers of unskilled semiemployed and abysmally poor urbanites" in Latin America who

> are economically marginal in that they contribute little to and benefit little from production and economic growth. Their social status is low, and they are excluded from the formal organizations and associations and the informal and private webs of contacts which constitute the urban social structure. To the extent that they are rural in origin, they may also be culturally marginal, clinging to customs, manners, dress, speech and values which contrast with accepted urban patterns.[82]

As we have seen, a major fault with characterizing squatters as "marginal" is the implicit assumption of homogeneity that such a broad categorization carries with it—a conclusion repeatedly contradicted by the literature. The tendency of most studies of squatter settlements to focus on aggregate and synchronic data tends to hide the personal and occupational variety of the inhabitants, as well as the continual mobility out of the settlement of individuals and families.

Rather than view shantytowns as marginal settlements, MacEwen suggests that "it should be more fruitful to assume that shanty towns are transitional zones through which an assortment of individuals and families pass who happen to find themselves in a common economic situation and who for similar reasons are forced at a particular moment in time to reside together in a common locality."[83] Viewed from such a perspective, her detailed study of an Argentine shantytown offers a picture of families strung along a continuum of wealth and sophistication ranging from those with irregularly employed unskilled workers to those with highly skilled regular employees, and from those living in mud huts to those in brick houses with electricity, appliances, and plumbing. Her study of shifting residences over time indicates that a gradual rise in material wealth, coupled with a change in occupation and increased association with other urban-oriented individuals, precedes movement out of the shantytown into the city itself. Rather than resist incorporation into city life, most squatters seek to establish urban identities and achieve an urban life style. Isolation, or encapsulation, of squatters from rural areas seems to occur more as a result of their lack of access to urban communications, chiefly radio and newspapers, than out of reluctance to change. When people begin to attend regularly to urban media it is because they have reached a level of literacy and sophistication at which they seek and can profit from regular exposure to newspapers and nonmusical radio programs.

The assumption of economic marginality, that squatters "contribute little to and benefit little from production and economic growth," is a curious one. In addition to the fact that a great deal of small-scale enterprise exists in squatter settlements, squatters and slum dwellers are for the most part employed within their communities. "Even from the outset," Mangin writes, "the local people begin buying and selling to each other at a great rate. In a Lima barriada of approximately 1,500 houses, we counted more than 100 houses where something was sold."[84] Unemployment statistics in Latin American squatments range from 8 to 27 percent, suggesting that the great majority of inhabitants are regularly working within the city's economic system.

Such statistics do disguise the fact that large numbers of employed individuals are "underemployed"—in positions that do not utilize their labor and talents effectively—or self-employed as hawkers, flower sellers, or vegetable vendors, for example. Most such occupations exist in underdeveloped economic systems and could be performed with much less time and labor if the economy were more highly industrialized. Additionally, entire families are often productive entities in which the father's wages are supplemented by the wife's washing clothes, working as a cleaning woman, or peddling. The children may sell newspapers or chewing gum, or watch automobiles, in exchange for a small payment.[85]

Brasilia, the new capital of Brazil, was constructed largely by squatting migrants who built their homes from waste construction wood. Although the government did not officially recognize the squatters, it evidently had a tacit agreement with them permitting them access to undeveloped public land and surplus construction material. Considering the government's desire to construct its capital at low labor costs, this made good sense: it avoided the need to construct worker housing and held down the cost of labor. A strategy of "insistently proclaiming the illegality and eventual demise of the squatter settlements and denying public services such as street lighting, electricity, sewage, and a permanent water system"[86] may save money for the government and give it maximum planning flexibility. But it also has social costs, in that it discourages squatters from spending free time, earned money, and construction skills on improving their homes and communities.

The fear that squatter settlements are centers of radical, communist activity as expressed by Walsh, is simply not borne out by research.

> In this enormous slum lived some 15,000 people many of whom had come down from the mountains, lured by communist agitators. Why starve on a farm the agitators asked, when well-paid jobs, good food, housing and education were waiting in Trujillo [Peru]? This technique for spreading chaos and unrest has brought as many as 3,000 farmers and their families to the barriadas in a month. Once they arrive (on a one-way ride in the communist-provided trucks) they are trapped in the festering slums with no money to return to their farms.[87]

Rather than being centers of radicalism, squatments usually show more conservative voting patterns than middle-class areas,[88] and an economic ethos congruent with nineteenth-century petty capitalism that emphasizes hard work, saving, and outwitting the government. Blame for failure tends to be accepted by individuals rather than projected upon the state. Indeed, only 7 percent of a Santiago, Chile, sample felt that their initial goals had been frustrated by "the system." Most placed the blame for failures they had encountered upon their parents, themselves, or bad luck. Like the immigrants of America's past, rural migrants generally do not feel themselves entitled to anything which they cannot earn.

> Migrants are foreigners to the city. As such, they are more prone, at least initially, to question the legitimacy of their own presence as audacious newcomers than the general urban order. The city which offers the opportunity of upward ascent also sets its own hard rules. The migrant's decision to come to the city, like the immigrant's choice of settling in a new country, implies a tacit acceptance of these rules.[89]

Blaming the general society for one's failures requires a sense of belonging to the social order and having a legitimate claim upon its resources that few rural migrants, or even long-term squatting residents, have. Just as important, most squatters and rural migrants feel their lives have improved in the city, and they have a sense of community with neighbors. Thus their squatments are "slums of hope rather than slums of despair."[90] Such a frame of mind is likely to be altered only by provocative acts by the larger society, such as forced removal of squatters from their homes without adequate compensation.

Finally, the assumption that squatters are marginal because they are "excluded from formal organizations" neglects the fact that squatters form their own organizations to select and invade a plot of land and to administer and protect it later. They attend church services, sports events and schools, and their children join such groups as the Boy Scouts as their families become more established and prosperous. Participation in organizations for the sake of participation has the greatest value for such people with leisure time as unemployed middle-class women. Time spent at meetings must be weighed against such other uses for it as work, home improvement, family life, and interaction with friends.[91] As Walter Miller queries: "In the United States, there are people who go to PTA meetings and there are people who play the numbers. It's my understanding that there are many more people who play the numbers than there are who go to PTA meetings. Why do we always talk as if learning to come to PTA meetings were joining the mainstream?"[92]

Clearly, fears that squatter and slum settlements threaten established social systems by fostering revolution-breeding conditions of marginality and despair are greatly exaggerated. The styles of dress, housing, and attitude of their inhabitants are much less isolated than most outsiders have assumed. Rather than characterize these life styles as marginal, one might more aptly describe them as "poor people's urban."[93]

A SOLUTION: PUBLIC HOUSING

The major problem in approaching solutions to the "problems" of slums and squatters is deciding *whose* problems are to be solved. If the goal is to relieve anxieties experienced by the middle-class Rio de Janeiro urbanite when he glances at the "unsightly squalor" on the hills above him, then clearly destruction of the squatters' homes and removal of the population will help solve his problem. If, on the other hand, the social goal is to improve the lives of the *squatters,* other solutions may actually be less expensive than forced removal to public housing. Undoubtedly, the least expensive and in many ways the most fruitful approach to squatments would be to provide the inhabitants with legal titles to ownership, which would encourage them to improve their houses without fear that the investment might be lost through forced and uncompensated removal. The building of streets and provision of potable water, sewage, garbage service, and electricity would in most cases result in gradual improvement in the area until it eventually became indistinguishable from other, non-squatter, parts of the city.

Some squatments, however, present severe dangers to their residents. The inhabitants of certain areas of Rio, Buenos Aires, and Hong Kong, for example, are subject to periodic threats to life and property from floods and mud avalanches.[94] Such cases aside, it appears that the best general solution to most squatter problems is to encourage illegal occupation.

If people are not to be forcibly prevented from coming to the city, the "squatter problem" is in essence one of finding low-cost housing for those who cannot afford the city real estate market. The need for cheap housing is universal and overwhelming. Yet builders cannot make a profit from potential squatters, although the city may benefit from their cheap labor. By occupying unused land and building their own houses from scraps of the city's economy, they have provided their own solution to their housing problem. As Peattie has remarked, "it turns out that the development of squatter settlements is one of those regular irregularities through which societies are able to do things which they find necessary while at the same time denying the existence of, or at least any support to, the phenomenon."[95]

Though there is little doubt that squatters have in general found their own best solution, their solution has invariably been rejected by fellow citizens. "The problem" remains in the minds of government officers and "concerned" citizens everywhere, as Sam Schulman writing in *The New York Times Magazine* (January 16, 1966) illustrates:

> There are some men—their numbers are small, but they are growing—of good will and insight who are profoundly disturbed, and passionately concerned with the eradication of these subhuman clusters. Msgr. Ruben Isaza, Bishop Coadjutor of Bogata, has called them "malignant tumors that have grown on my city" and, along with others of his country men, is working for their displacement and for the betterment of the social and economic factors which have created them.[96]

"The problem is," Mangin summarizes perfectly, that "the solution is the problem."[97] Alternative solutions to squatments have had to be found to satisfy the more numerous and powerful non-squatter segments of the community. These solutions usually focus upon destruction of the settlements and relocation of the inhabitants to public housing. Such housing helps remove, or at least reduce, the city's blemishes, often simply by resettling squatters out of the city's central area to its fringes.

For squatters, as for American slum dwellers whose areas have been "renewed," such removal sometimes proves a great burden as their housing costs and commuting time to work increase. Suddenly they find themselves renting a house or apartment they will never own, or buying a home through long-term mortgage payments they cannot afford. Where formerly they had paid no rent and "owned" their homes, relocation often means paying for homes over such a long period that they do not feel any real sense of ownership. The possibility of eviction for nonpayment is convincing enough to most that their legal position has not improved much over what it was in the squatment.

Land which the city is willing to make available to resettlement programs and which architects and construction companies deem desirable is often far from the original settlement. Resettlement in the 1960's of 25,000 Rio squatters to Vila Kennedy (built at a cost of $10,000,000 and partially funded by USAID—consisting of a dense cluster of nearly identical houses which sell for approximately U.S. $2,000 each) helped most of those relocated escape the threat of death through rockslides, which typically result in about a hundred deaths every year. Resettlement, however, also took them thirty-one miles from the center of Rio and as much as forty miles from their former homes. Ideally, each family was to pay approximately 15 percent of its income towards the mortgage and own its house in fifteen years. But more than 60 percent of the residents are habitually behind in payments. A principal reason for the imminent default of so many families is the high cost of commuting: in addition to the four-hour commute to and from city jobs, a man can easily spend one-third of the minimum wage on transportation. Commuting costs, coupled with the 15 percent mortgage, leave only about $18 a month for minimum wage-earners for the family's food, clothing, medical care, and entertainment.

Added to the hardship is the fact that living in Vila Kennedy makes it difficult for women and young people to find jobs. Over half of all those between the ages of sixteen and twenty-five are unemployed. In *favelas* women and young children can find part-time employment selling newspapers or taking in wash and doing housework for well-to-do families. But in the Vila the cost and difficulty of transportation render such minor income supplements unworthwhile. Consequently, youths often loiter, and many people fear to walk the streets at night because they are considered less safe than those of the *favela*.

For women, especially, the move to Vila Kennedy has been unwelcome. Almost half of all the women interviewed by Salmen in Vila Kennedy said they wished to return to their former residences, while only one-third of the men did. Despite the hardships of Vila life many men seem to feel that the possibility of ownership and removal from some of the physical hazards of the *favela*, was worthwhile. The women's discontent was magnified by their sense of lost independence in the Vila. Without the possibility of part-time employment they were more dependent than ever upon their husbands for support, a situation which can sometimes be difficult indeed:

> The husband of this [particular] woman spent so much time on his journey to work that he eventually found it a near necessity to stay in Rio during the week, visiting his wife and two small children in the Vila only on week-ends. After some months of this, the man stayed away from the Vila altogether. It was soon discovered that he had met another woman in the city [and] had started a second family. While an extreme case, modified versions of this story were not uncommon.[98]

Oscar Lewis, in a 1968 article entitled "Even the Saints Cry," tells the poignant story of a Puerto Rican mother. Cruz Rios moved from one of San Juan's oldest slums, La Esmeralda, to Villa Hermosa, a government housing project, at the urging of a social worker. The move seemed a good idea at first. The children were not so likely to be bitten by rats and delinquency was not as great a problem. But the Villa was designed for a middle-class life style in which people plan their lives and budget more carefully for monthly expenses than Cruz Rios was able to do. For her, paying only $6.50 a month rent in the housing project was more painful than meeting the $11.50 monthly rent in La Esmeralda: falling behind on the rent in her former residence did not mean immediate eviction as it does in the Villa. Her old stove had been a kerosene one, and when she "didn't have a quarter to buy a full gallon of kerosene, I got ten cents worth." The project's electric stove, of course, required full payment of the monthly electric bill for the electricity supply to continue unbroken.

Casual supplements to welfare income were also more difficult to arrange in the project. Selling numbers and occasional prostitution provided needed income in the slum. "In La Esmeralda I could get an old man now and then to give me five dollars for sleeping with him. But here I haven't found anything like that at all." In the project such activities are restricted by resident policemen and investigating detectives. Most painful of all for Cruz Rios was her sense of rejection by others in the Villa who visited her apartment to "furnish the place with their mouths" by telling her where a television and a set of furniture she could not afford should go. The others, she felt, strove for a pretentious respectability which few in the slum would claim. "This place isn't like La Esmeralda, you know, where there's so much liveliness and noise and something is always going on," she complains. "Here you never see any movement on the street, not one little domino or card game or anything. The place is dead. People act as if they're angry or in mourning."[99]

Aside from the fact that the location and character of "low-cost" rehousing schemes is often unacceptable to relocated individuals, the cost is *not* always low, even for those who formerly paid rent or devoted significant portions of their incomes to household improvements. So-called low-cost housing ("flats") have been built in Penang, Malaysia, by the state government at a cost per unit (one bedroom, hall, kitchen/toilet, and bath) of approximately M $7,500 (U.S. $3,000), while well-built, comfortable, wooden Malay-style structures can be built for only M $3,000. Rentals for the state units average M $55 per month, including sewage, water, electricity, and maintenance. While the rent in proportion to capital and service cost is reasonable, it is still too high for the poor. Of all households in Malaysia in 1970, 58 percent had an income of M $200 (or less) a month, which was the amount originally set as the maximum income that could be earned and still permit families to qualify for low-cost state housing. But even if the average resident earned the maximum qualifying income, he would pay 25-30 percent of it for rent. Since family clothing, food, and transportation must be bought with the remainder, few families who qualify can actually afford low-cost housing. Consequently, only 27 percent of those living in public housing in Penang actually have incomes below M $200 per month. For many, even the most minimal and reasonable rental or mortgage payment is too much, so that "low cost housing in Penang," as Ong says, simply "does not benefit the poor."[100]

Even if we accept the assumption that inhabitants of public housing must bear all or a major share of its cost, units are often priced out of reach of the poor by insistence upon unrealistically high construction standards. An agency of the United Nations, for example, proposed in 1960 that all public housing in the South and Southeast Asian region have separate toilet and bathing facilities for each unit, as well as a veranda or balcony for escape from interior heat during the hot months. Additionally, the report suggested that a gross area of 40 square meters per unit or an average living space of 70-85 square feet per person be provided per family of five or six. Such a goal fails to take cognizance of the fact that 97 percent of houses in rural India and 44 percent of urban Indian households had no latrine of any kind, 37 percent shared toilet facilities, and only 19 percent had private toilets. Additionally, 93 percent of rural households and 72 percent of urban did not have bathing facilities. Finally, in both rural and urban areas, only a quarter of all households had more than 100 square feet of space per person, while almost half had less than 50 square feet for each member.[101]

The United Nations public housing recommendations are commendable, but they appear unrealistic if the *poor* are to be provided housing. Standards which appear to be "the minimum necessary and low enough to experts fully cognizant with the existing acute housing situation"[102] are so far removed from current standards as to be unrealizable. A more realistic approach to public housing would be one that seeks to approximate, and perhaps slightly improve, the general conditions of those poor who are already housed. Too great an improvement, when its cost is not fully borne by the tenants, invariably results in displacement of the real poor by a more well-to-do group which uses deception or bribery to gain entry to the project. Displacement of the poor by middle-class individuals when project rents are below rents for comparable private accomodation has plagued such housing projects as those of New York City and Nairobi, Kenya. In Nairobi those in the lowest income brackets are *less* likely than those in the highest to occupy public housing units. Three quarters of those earning less than 200 shillings a month live in private housing; but less than 23 percent of those earning 1,000 shillings a month live outside City Council or government housing.[103]

In designing public housing projects, planners often ignore cultural and ethnic differences among resettled populations, treating them as a single entity. In Colombia, two ethnically distinct subcultures, the highland mestizos and lowland blacks, account for approximately 70 percent of the nation's population. In 1969, four years after development of a housing project called Barrio Piloto in the city of Cali, 10 percent of the project was mestizo, 25 percent black, and 65 percent members of Cali's urban working class. Many of the latter entered the project when some of the original mestizo and black families left. By 1969, only 23 percent of the original mestizo units had left the project, while 55 percent of the original black units had departed. The different response of the two groups to public housing is apparently the result of a stronger work ethnic, greater family unity and cooperation, and a greater identification with national institutions among mestizos than among blacks. Most mestizos seem to aspire to the status of urban workers, while the blacks are generally oriented towards rural occupations.

Barrio Piloto was planned by the National Housing Institute and a local elite woman's group. The homes were one-storey units with combined living and dining rooms, two bedrooms, kitchen, and bathroom, which were turned over to their tenants unfinished in anticipation that they would make the final necessary improvements. The occupants' former slum houses were accepted as down payments, with the remainder to be paid over a seventeen-year period and monthly payments to increase 10 percent annually. Meeting mortgage payments requires a monthly income of at least 800 pesos (U.S. $40). Before relocation, 73 percent of the mestizo and 71 percent of the black units earned less than 500 pesos (U.S. $25) a month. In order to successfully survive in the project most families had to find some way to increase their income—at which mestizos were much more successful than blacks: 39 percent of Mestizo households, in contrast to 15 percent of black units, were able to reach an income level of at least 800 pesos a month. Mestizos tended to increase income by shifting occupation, especially by leaving agriculture, and by adding paying relatives to their households. In contrast to the vertical job mobility of mestizos, most blacks exhibited horizontal mobility so that when they did change occupations they remained at the same economic level. Increase in income through sharing household expenses usually came about by renting rooms to nonrelatives, for kin among blacks felt less obligation to pay rent.

On sociocultural levels of adaptation, mestizos seemed to identify with their new residences, devoting more time and money to home improvements than blacks and making greater use of community facilities such as church, schools, and medical center. Apparently many mestizos were ready for, and responded positively to, relocation. Blacks, "on the other hand," Ashton feels, "have not wished to make changes in economic and socio-cultural patterns and continue serial marital unions, frequent leisure-time spending in nearby dancehalls, and employment in largely rural occupations."[104] The major problem in relocating the black population was apparently that the middle-class professionals who planned the project assumed

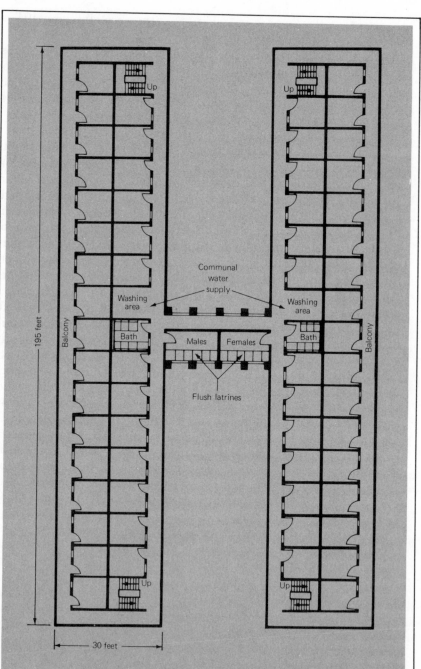

195 feet

Balcony

Up

Communal
water
supply

Washing
area

Bath

Males | Females

Flush latrines

Washing
area

Bath

Balcony

Up

Up

Up

30 feet

Design of a typical floor of Hong Kong public housing (after Dwyer 1964:165)

that future tenants would aspire to urban factory employment, and they priced the units accordingly. Most mestizos shared the orientation of the planners, adapted successfully, and remained in the projects. Blacks continued to hold rural-type occupations and follow rural patterns of hospitality towards relatives and, consequently, were unable to make the mortgage payments. The different experience of the two groups suggests to Ashton that "it is almost as if planners were attempting to build a project for Mestizos and not for Negroes."[105]

Not all relocation projects have had such limited success. Hong Kong, especially, has had a particularly impressive public housing policy—a quite remarkable one considering the immensity of the task. From 1954, when the Hong Kong Housing Authority was created by an initial loan of H.K. $156 million (approximately U.S. $22 million then) until 1968, squatters numbering 1,092,000, more than a quarter of the entire population, were relocated in public housing units. The structure of a loan arrangement with a revolving fund in which loans were amortized over a forty-year period at 3.5 percent interest permitted rentals of 350-square-foot apartments to be kept at monthly levels as low as H.K. $14-18. Today Hong Kong squatments no longer infringe upon the central areas of Victoria and Kowloon, but are peripheral.

The initial Hong Kong resettlement program began as a government attempt to cope with a massive squatter camp fire in December, 1953, that displaced 50,000 people. The pressure of the moment led to a decision to build high-density housing with minimal standards on the cleared site. The basic design consisted of an H-shaped block with separate units for each family arranged on the parallels and the communal water supply, latrines, and clothes-washing areas located in the connecting bar. The small high-rise apartments constructed could be afforded by even the poorest families. The government has been careful to maintain this policy, although the space allocation has increased from approximately 24 square feet per adult to as much as 70. The earlier squatter settlements often had as little as 8 square feet of living space per person, so the space gained in high-rise buildings made the units, small as they were, as spacious or more so than the residents' former homes.

In time, the Authority began to use its experience to design projects with play areas for children, and to orient the units so neighborhoods would be formed. The government's policy of providing the best possible housing that the colony was willing to subsidize and that the population could afford has resulted not only in very low rent delinquency but also in an obvious general identification with and appreciation for the projects, evidenced by the manner in which the occupants help with building maintenance.[106]

The Hong Kong Housing Authority has had support from a vigorous population; but most important has been the Authority's policy of providing massive quantities of *affordable* accommodation, at the sacrifice of what project architects (and middle-class values) would ordinarily demand. Consequently, unlike the situation in so many other public housing projects in various countries, the poor themselves seem truly to have benefitted from Hong Kong's resettlement programs.

CONCLUSION

In this chapter, a wide range of social problems common to the world's cities have been discussed. It would be easy—as many have done—to look at such worldwide urban dilemmas as crime, poverty, slums, and squatter settlements, then despair of hope for the future of an urbanizing world. Indeed, certain problems, such as lack of adequate housing, are certain to become even more serious in the coming decades. Others, like the availability of educational and public health facilities, may actually be improved as the concentration of people in cities eases the tasks of providing public education and health care.

From this discussion it should be evident that cities and complex societies often place strenuous demands on the skills and adaptability of individuals seeking to carve their niches at the most complex level of human social organization. For many, migrants and long-term urbanites alike, cities become arenas of personal failure. But for others, with the advantages of personal ability, interpersonal contacts, or fortune, urban life offers opportunity and hope of personal betterment that exist nowhere else.

⊛ NOTES

1. I use "adaptive" here to mean behavior promoting well-being or survival. My usage blurs Kluckhohn's distinction between "adaptive" (behavior that results in survival) and "adjustive" (behavior that reduces individual anxiety). Thus, according to his definition, "suicide is adjustive but not adaptive" (1944:79). The distinction is often a useful one in psychology but is usually ignored in anthropology.
2. Little 1957; Skinner 1974.
3. Skinner 1974:204-211.
4. Little 1957, 1967.
5. Little 1957:593, 592.
6. Textor 1961:17.
7. Scotch 1960.
8. Cambell 1970.
9. Cambell 1970:315.
10. Hendin 1962:447.
11. Naroll 1969.
12. Davis 1965:12.
13. Plog 1969:288.
14. Plog 1969:290.
15. Jacobs 1938.
16. Hollingshead and Redlich in *Social Class and Mental Illness* provide evidence that the frequency of reported mental illness is inversely related to class status: the higher one's class, the less likely he is to become a mental patient. Members of the highest social class (Class I) accounted for 3 percent of the nonpatient population in their sample and only 1 percent of the patient population. Those of Class II comprised 8.4 percent of the nonpatients and 7 percent of the patients. Class III individuals accounted for 20.4 percent of the total population and 13.4 percent of the hospital population. Class IV contained 49.8 percent of the population and 40.1 percent of the hospital population. The lowest class (Class V) accounted for only 18.4 percent of the total population but 38.2 percent of the patient population.
17. Srole, et al., 1962:213.
18. Leighton 1969:189.
19. Plog 1969.
20. Cook 1963.
21. Butterworth 1962:273.
22. Mangin and Cohen 1964:82, 85.
23. Mangin and Cohen 1964:86.
24. Fried 1963:151-152.
25. Graves 1970, 1973; Wagner and Tan 1971.
26. Weinberg 1965:85.
27. Weinberg 1965:90.
28. Hauser 1957:232-235.
29. Tasker 1976.
30. Khalaf 1965:17-31, 87-88.

31. Clinard and Chatterjee 1962:72-73.
32. Delhi School of Social Work 1959:146.
33. Moorthy 1959.
34. Moorthy 1959:64.
35. Chan 1973.
36. Moorthy 1959:42.
37. Taira 1969.
38. See DeVos and Wagatsuma 1972.
39. Taira 1969:168.
40. Taira 1969:168.
41. Taira 1969:166.
42. Taira 1969:168.
43. Taira 1969:172.
44. Lewis 1966a.
45. Lewis 1966a:23.
46. Wright 1971:315, 326.
47. Lewis 1969.
48. See Valentine's criticism (1968) of the "culture of poverty."
49. Lewis 1959:2; 1961:xxiv, xxv; 1966b:xxxix.
50. Lewis 1969:190-192.
51. Mangin 1967:73.
52. Johnson and Sanday 1971:135.
53. Irelan, et al., 1969.
54. Taira 1969:155.
55. Taira 1969:157.
56. Schorr 1968:231.
57. Schorr 1968:207.
58. Prabhu 1956:62.
59. Bulsara 1961:66.
60. Wertheim, et al., 1958:224.
61. Jackson 1975.
62. Kaye 1960.
63. Anderson 1972:146, 145.
64. Hagmuller 1970.
65. Hagmuller 1970:44.
66. McGee 1967:17-22, 80.
67. Breese 1966:5.
68. Meister 1970:41, 42.
69. Abrams 1964:13-14.
70. McGee 1967:157.
71. Salmen 1969:74.
72. McGee 1967:157.
73. Leeds 1969:48.
74. Leeds 1969:44-47.
75. Mangin 1967:70-71.
76. Dwyer 1964:158.
77. Barakbah 1971.
78. Bonilla 1962:385.
79. Quoted in Mangin 1967:71.

 80. Mangin 1967:72.
 81. McGee 1967:165.
 82. Nelson quoted in Mangin 1967:71.
 83. MacEwen 1972:45.
 84. Mangin 1967:76.
 85. Laquian 1971:193.
 86. Epstein 1972:57.
 87. Quoted in Mangin 1967:66.
 88. Mangin 1967:83.
 89. Portes 1972:284.
 90. Turner quoted in Mangin 1967:82.
 91. Portes 1972:273.
 92. Quoted in Peattie 1974:106-107.
 93. Peattie 1974:104.
 94. Morse 1969.
 95. Peattie 1974:105-106.
 96. Quoted in Mangin 1967:85.
 97. Mangin 1967:85.
 98. Salmen 1969:82-83.
 99. Lewis 1966c.
100. Ong 1973:35.
101. Sovani 1966:21-24.
102. Sovani 1966:25.
103. Harris 1970:45.
104. Ashton 1972:177.
105. Ashton 1972:190.
106. Juppenlatz 1970:57-62; Dwyer 1964, 1970.

▦ REFERENCES

Abrams, Charles
  1964   Man's struggle for shelter in an urbanizing world. Cambridge, Massa-
          chusetts: MIT Press.
Anderson, Eugene N., Jr.
  1972   Some Chinese methods of dealing with overcrowding. Urban Anthro-
          pology 1:141-150.
Ashton, Guy T.
  1972   The differential adaptation of two slum subcultures to a Colombian
          housing project. Urban Anthropology 1:176-194.
Barakbah, Syed Mansor
  1971   The problem of illegal settlers in urban areas of Kedah State, Malaysia.
          Journal of Administration Overseas 10, 3:201-209.
Batson, Edward
  1958   Relative poverty in a peri-urban area: A report from the Cape Flats
          "Vleiland Survey." Journal for Social Research 9:37-49.

Bonilla, Frank
1962   Rio's "favelas": The rural slum within the city. Dissent 9, 4:383-386.
Brand, W.
1958   Differential mortality in the town of Bandung. In W. F. Wertheim, ed., The Indonesian town. The Hague: W. van Hoeve.
Breese, Gerald
1966   Urbanization in newly developing countries. Englewood Cliffs, N.J.: Prentice-Hall.
Bulsara, Jal F.
1961   Problems of rapid urbanization in India. Bombay: Popular Prakashan.
Butterworth, Douglas S.
1962   A study of the urbanization process among Mixtec migrants from Tilaltongo [sic] in Mexico City. America Indigena 22:257-274.
Calhoun, John B.
1962   Population density and social pathology. In Leonard J. Duhl, ed., The urban condition. New York: Simon and Schuster.
Cambell, G. D.
1970   Diabetes in non-white people in Natal: A disease of urbanization. In H. L. Watts, ed., Focus on cities. Durban, South Africa: Institute for Social Research at the University of Natal.
Chan Lean Heng
1973   The wayside loners: "Beggar culture" in Penang, Malaysia. Penang: School of Comparative Social Sciences, Universiti Sains Malaysia.
Clark, Margaret
1959   Health in the Mexican-American culture. Berkeley: University of California Press.
Clinard, Marshall B., and B. Chatterjee
1962   Urban community development in India: The Delhi pilot project. In Roy Turner, ed., India's urban future. Berkeley: University of California Press.
Cook, Donald A.
1963   Cultural innovation and disaster in the American city. In Leonard J. Duhl, ed., The urban condition. New York: Simon and Schuster.
Davis, Kingsley
1965   The urbanization of the human population. In Cities: A scientific American book. New York: Alfred A. Knopf.
Deevey, Edward S.
1962   The hare and the haruspex: A cautionary tale. In Eric and Mary Josephson, eds., Man alone. New York: Dell.
Delhi School of Social Work
1959   The beggar problem in metropolitan New Delhi. Delhi: Delhi School of Social Work.
DeVos, George A., and Hiroshi Wagatsuma, eds.
1972   Japan's invisible race. Berkeley: University of California Press.
Dreikurs, Rudolf
1963   Individual psychology: The Adlerian point of view. In Joseph Wepman and Ralph Henie, eds., Concepts of personality. Chicago: Aldine Publishing Company.

Dwyer, D. J.
 1964 The problem of in-migration and squatter settlement in Asian cities:
  Two case studies, Manila and Victoria-Kowloon. Asian Studies
  2:145-169.
 1970 Urban squatters: The relevance of the Hong Kong experience. Asian
  Survey 10:607-613.
Epstein, David G.
 1972 The genesis and function of squatter settlements in Brasilia. In
  Thomas Weaver and Douglas White, eds., The anthropology of urban
  environments. Boulder, Colorado: Society for Applied Anthropology.
Finney, Joseph C.
 1969 Intercultural differences in personality. In J. C. Finney, ed., Culture
  change, mental health, and poverty. New York: Simon and Schuster.
Fried, Marc
 1963 Greiving for a lost home. In Leonard J. Duhl, ed., The urban condition. New York: Simon and Schuster.
Graves, Theodore D.
 1970 The personal adjustment of Navajo Indian migrants to Denver,
  Colorado. American Anthropologist 72:35-54.
 1973 The Navajo urban migrant and his psychological situation. Ethos
  1:321-342.
Hagmuller, Gotz
 1970 A noose around the city. Ceres 3, 6:44-47.
Hammel, Eugene A.
 1964 Some characteristics of rural village and urban slum populations of
  the coast of Peru. Southwestern Journal of Anthropology 20:346-
  358.
Hanna, William J., and Judith L.
 1971 Urban dynamics in black Africa. Chicago: Aldine-Atherton.
Harris, John R.
 1970 A housing policy for Nairobi. In John Hutton, ed., Urban challenge
  in East Africa. Nairobi: East African Publishing House.
Hauser, Phillip M.
 1957 Urbanization in Asia and the Far East. Calcutta: UNESCO.
Hendin, Herbert
 1962 Suicide in Denmark. In Eric and Mary Josephson, eds., Man alone.
  New York: Dell.
Hollingshead, A. B., and F. Redlich
 1958 Social class and mental illness. New York: John Wiley and Sons.
Irelan, Lola M., et al.
 1969 Ethnicity, poverty, and selected attitudes: A test of the "culture of
  poverty" hypothesis. Social Forces 47:405-413.
Jackson, James C.
 1975 The Chinatowns of Southeast Asia: Traditional components of the
  city's central area. Pacific Viewpoint 16:45-77.
Jacobs, J. S.
 1938 A note on the alleged increase in insanity. Journal of Abnormal and
  Social Psychology 33:390-397.

Jacoby, Erich H.
1970   The coming backlash of semi-urbanization. Ceres 3, 6:48-51.
Johnson, Norman, and Peggy R. Sanday
1971   Subcultural variations in an urban poor population. American Anthropologist 73:128-143.
Juppenlatz, Morris
1970   Cities in transformation: The urban squatter problem of the developing world. St. Lucia: University of Queensland Press.
Karno, Marvin
1965   The enigma of ethnicity in a psychiatric clinic. Paper presented to the Southwestern Anthropological Association annual meeting, Los Angeles, California.
Kaye, Barrington
1960   Upper Nankin Street Singapore: A sociological study of Chinese households living in a densely populated area. Singapore: University of Malaya Press.
Khalaf, Samir
1965   Prostitution in a changing society: A sociological survey of legal prostitution in Beirut. Beirut: Khayats.
Kiev, Ari
1968   Curanderismo: Mexican-American folk psychiatry. New York: Free Press.
Kluckhohn, Clyde
1944   Navaho witchcraft. Boston: Beacon Press.
Laquian, Aprodicio
1971   Slums and squatters in South and Southeast Asia. In Leo Jakobson and Ved Prakash, eds., Urbanization and national development. Beverly Hills: Sage Publications.
Leeds, Anthony
1969   The significant variables determining the character of squatter settlements. America Latina 12, 3:44-86.
Leighton, Alexander H.
1969   A comparative study of psychiatric disorder in Nigeria and rural North America. In Stanley C. Plog and Robert B. Edgerton, eds., Changing perspectives in mental illness. New York: Holt, Rinehart, and Winston.
Lewis, Oscar
1959   Five families. New York: Basic Books.
1961   The children of Sanchez. New York: Random House.
1966a   The culture of poverty. Scientific American 215, 4:19-25.
1966b   La vida. New York: Random House.
1966c   Even the saints cry. Trans-Action 4, 1:18-23.
1969   Comment on "culture of poverty: Critique and counter-proposals." Current Anthropology 10:189-192.
Little, Kenneth
1957   The role of voluntary associations in west African urbanization. American Anthropologist 59:579-596.
1967   Voluntary associations in urban life. In Maurice Freedman, ed., Social organization. Chicago: Aldine Publishing Company.

MacEwen, Alison M.
    1972   Stability and change in a shanty town: A summary of some research findings. Sociology 6, 1:41-57.
McGee, T. G.
    1967   The Southeast Asian city. New York: Praeger.
Madsen, William
    1964   The Mexican-Americans of south Texas. New York: Holt, Rinehart, and Winston.
Mangin, William
    1967   Latin American squatter settlements: A problem and a solution. Latin American Research Review 2, 3:65-98.
Mangin, William, and Jerome Cohen
    1964   Cultural and psychological characteristics of mountain migrants to Lima, Peru. Sociologus 14:81-88.
Meister, Albert
    1970   The urbanization crisis of rural man. Ceres 3, 6:40-43.
Moorthy, M. V., ed.
    1959   Beggar problem in greater Bombay. Bombay: Indian Conference of Social Work.
Morse, Richard M.
    1969   Recent research on Latin American urbanization: A selective survey with commentary. In Gerald Breese ed., The city in newly developing countries. Englewood Cliffs, N.J.: Prentice-Hall.
Nair, B. N.
    1960   Urbanization and corruption. Sociological Bulletin 9, 2:15-33.
Naroll, Raoul
    1969   Cultural determinants and the concept of the sick society. In Stanley C. Plog and Robert B. Edgerton, eds., Changing perspectives in mental illness. New York: Holt, Rinehart, and Winston.
Nelson, J. M.
    1969   Migrants, urban poverty, and instability in developing countries. Cambridge: Harvard University Center for International Affairs.
Ong Ban Seang
    1973   The impact of low cost housing on the employment and social structure of the urban communities: A case study of Penang. Penang: School of Comparative Social Sciences, Universiti Sains Malaysia.
Patrick, E.
    1971   Emotional stress in university students. In Nathaniel N. Wagner and Eng-Seong Tan, Psychological problems and treatment in Malaysia. Kuala Lumpur: University of Malaya Press.
Peattie, Lisa R.
    1974   The concept of "marginality" as applied to squatter settlements. In W. A. Cornelius and F. M. Trueblood, eds., Latin American Urban Research, vol. 4. Beverly Hills: Sage Publications.
Plog, Stanley C.
    1969   Urbanization, psychological disorders, and the heritage of social psychiatry. In Stanley Plog and Robert Edgerton, eds., Changing perspectives in mental illness. New York: Holt, Rinehart, and Winston.

Portes, Alejandro
  1972   Rationality in the slum: An essay on interpretive sociology. Comparative Studies in Society and History 14, 3:268-286.
Prabhu, P. N.
  1956   A study on the social effects of urbanization. In The social implications of industrialization and urbanization. Calcutta: UNESCO.
Press, Irwin
  1971   The urban curandero. American Anthropologist 13:741-756.
Price, John
  1966   A history of the outcaste: Untouchability in Japan. In George DeVos and Hiroshi Wagatsuma, eds., Japan's invisible race. Berkeley: University of California Press.
Qadeer, M. A.
  1974   Do cities "modernize" the developing countries? An examination of the South Asian experience. Comparative Studies in Society and History 16, 3:266-283.
Raymaekers, Paul
  1963   Prédélinquance et délinquance juvenile à Léopold ville. Inter-African Labour Institute Bulletin 10, 3:298-328.
Rodman, Hyman
  1968   Family and social pathology in the ghetto. Science 16:756-762.
Salmen, Lawrence F.
  1969   A perspective on the resettlement of squatters in Brazil. America Latina 12, 1:73-93.
Schorr, Alvin L.
  1968   Housing the poor. In Warner Bloomberg, Jr., and Henry J. Schmandt, eds., Urban poverty. Beverly Hills: Sage Publications.
Scotch, Norman
  1960   A preliminary report on the relation of socio-cultural factors to hypertension among the Zulu. Annuals of the New York Academy of Sciences 84:1000-1009.
Skinner, Elliott P.
  1974   African urban life: The transformation of Ouagadougou. Princeton: Princeton University Press.
Sovani, N. V.
  1966   Urbanization and urban India. New York: Asia Publishing House.
Srole, Leo, et al.
  1962   Mental health in the metropolis. Book One: rev. ed. New York: Harper Torchbooks.
Taira, Koji
  1969   Urban poverty, ragpickers, and the "Ants' Villa" in Tokyo. Economic Development and Cultural Change 17:155-177.
Tasker, Rodney
  1976   Vice squad goes underground. Far Eastern Economic Review 91, 13: 32.
Textor, Robert B.
  1961   From peasant to pedicab driver. New Haven: Yale University Southeast Asia Studies Cultural Report no. 9.

Valentine, Charles A.
   1968   Culture and poverty: Critique and counter-proposals. Chicago: University of Chicago Press.
Wagner, Nathaniel N., and Eng-Seong Tan
   1971   Adolescent problems and treatment. In Wagner and Tan, eds., Psychological problems and treatment in Malaysia. Kuala Lumpur: University of Malaya Press.
Weinberg, S. Kirson
   1965   Urbanization and male delinquency in Ghana. Journal of Research in Crime and Delinquency 2, 2:85-94.
Wertheim, W. F., et al.
   1958   The Indonesian town. The Hague: W. van Hoeve.
Wright, Rolland H.
   1971   The stranger mentality and the culture of poverty. In E. B. Leacock, ed., The culture of poverty: A critique. New York: Simon and Schuster.

Class, Caste, and Ethnicity: The Study of Social Stratification and Pluralism in Complex Societies

6 Inequality seems a basic and inescapable aspect of the human condition. Even the smallest, most primitive, hunting and gathering societies parcel out authority and responsibility according to age, sex, and personal abilities. Greater population densities found in horticultural and agricultural societies tend to be associated with the development of increasingly complex and hierarchical forms of social organization, required by larger populations if the society is to remain unified and integrated.[1]

Cities seem to represent a culmination of the pressures towards human social inequality that result from increased division of labor. In small bands, tasks are performed either by the group as a whole aided by a headman, or by such part-time specialists as curers or shamans. Societies composed of larger agricultural villages or clusters of villages require a more discrete structure of authority—often based around a chief and his advisers—if social cohesion is to be maintained. Larger peasant societies such as those of Europe's recent past, still characteristic of much of Latin America and

Asia, have invariably evolved hierarchies of nobility that govern by virtue of a special religio-contractual relation with the peasant commoners.

The peasant-artisan-ruler axis found in such feudal societies allocates a critical task to the members of each stratum. Peasants farm and provide manpower for public works and the military; and artisans provide utensils, art work, and social services which the group needs; and rulers provide a locus within which arrangements are made for defense, public works, and maintenance of internal stability. Each division usually has religious sanctions, justifying an individual's relative position in the society and, more important, inhibiting the revolt of subordinate groups.

As cities develop, the characteristic hierarchies of peasant societies expand and gain new meaning. Increased size of a city and its hinterland at first usually reinforces control by its religio-military hierarchy. But such urban expansion is often associated with increase in trade both within and beyond the boundaries of the society. The traders typically come from either the artisan class or outside ethnic groups, such as the Jews of medieval Europe and the Chinese of present-day Southeast Asia. In periods of major trade expansion the trading group's power increases at the expense of the nobility, who may soon find their position threatened by the new moneyed elite. Initially, the nobility of most of Europe and Asia responded by establishing bonds of marriage with the most successful traders, assuring themselves and their descendants access to the newly created wealth and providing the merchants with important political allies. In time, however, the emergence of this business-oriented group could not be so easily co-opted; in nation after nation the ruling aristocracy found itself displaced and overthrown, not by peasants or others at the bottom of the social hierarchy, but by a new commercially oriented middle class.

Analysis of any of the world's cities today reveals some aspects of this pattern. The cities of North America, Japan, and Western Europe are virtually free of influence of the old aristocracy. Here the process of economic control has gone farther along the path of differentiation, so that real political and economic power is no longer clearly in the hands of a commercial middle class, but is shared by a nexus of trained technicians, businessmen, scientists, and managers.

The theme of individual achievement is prominent in all of these urban societies. All give their primary rewards of power and status to persons who have developed through education or demonstrated in action their capacity to perform particular social functions.

Even members of an older, inheriting commercial elite must acquire skills and education if they wish to maintain their rank. In contrast, feudal elites still retain great influence in much of Latin America and South and Southeast Asia. Some even have their positions as titular or limited rulers written into the constitutions that proliferated as European colonial powers withdrew. Others maintain influence through control of large areas of land and intermarriage with successful commercial families. Today, most of these aristocratic families have adapted to present-day realities of status and power by using wealth and position to send their children for education in Europe or America—both so that they have the best possible preparation for their future occupations and to gain the status of overseas education.

While feudal aristocracies of much of the world have had to share power and wealth with a newly emerged commercial sector, and often with a military and bureaucratic elite as well, they have often been successful in preventing erosion of their own position. Rarely has an aristocracy been totally wrenched from its position and replaced by an elite that owes its position completely, or even primarily, to individual achievement.

Differences of status, power and wealth have not been the only ones accented by urban life. Cities have always been crossroads where populations of diverse ethnic background come into contact. Foreign communities of merchants and slaves have frequently resided in the midst of indigenous inhabitants. The earliest written records of the kingdoms of Southeast Asia tell of the presence of resident Indian Brahmins and Chinese merchants next to local urbanites, a fact which the first European travelers repeatedly entered into their journals. Similarly, early European records chronicle Greek colonies and settlements throughout most of the eastern Mediterranean; and evidence from the first African cities indicates that Arab traders and other outsiders have long been a feature of African urban life. Today ethnic groups are seldom found in isolated occupancy of ancestral lands. Where ethnic homogeneity is strong, those foreign communities that do exist are usually located in cities.

Urban social diversity has a two-fold dimension of differences: those of intragroup status and those of intergroup culture. Distinctions of status within groups whose members share a cultural tradition are often referred to as *class* distinctions, whereas cultural differences are often labeled *ethnic* differences. Generally, class status is considered to be *achieved* so that, theoretically at least, movement of individuals from one class to another is possible. Ethnic distinctions, on the other hand, are *ascribed* because one normally enters his ethnic group by birth, never to leave.

Further complicating both urban and rural status distinctions is the fact that groups are often distinguished by criteria that cannot properly be considered as belonging to either class or ethnicity. Thus in some societies color, physical features, or attributed characteristics may become one primary focus of categorization. To be black in the United States, for example, entails a particular gamut of relations to majority white society. But the distinction is not one of class. A black scientist is in most situations *black* first, as is a black construction worker. Neither is the distinction truly an ethnic one: American blacks can be considered neither a coherent cultural entity nor a culturally distinct group removed from a larger American society.

Caste as a basis for social distinction can technically be considered a solely Indian phenomenon in its association with Indian occupational reciprocity and Hinduism.[2] Such a view, however, ignores the strong and revealing parallels between caste in India and such caste-like relations as black-white interaction in the United States; or white, coloured, Asian, and African relations in South Africa; or the relations of *burakumin*—the outcaste residents of "special communities," the Japanese euphemism for ghettoes—with ordinary Japanese. Used in essence to describe a birth-ascribed hierarchy, caste involves a set of *criteria* for determining rank and an *idiom* in which a caste's rank is expressed. In India the principal criterion for ranking is usually one of relative "ritual pollution" (those in the priestly Brahmin caste are the least "polluted"), justifying a gamut of idiomatic expressions of rank through patterns of deference in interaction, ritual activity, and life style.

The mark of caste is indelible. As Berreman has remarked about India, a person of shoemaker caste is considered of low status because his assumed association with dead animals and his impure personal habits and defiling social and religious customs make him ritually impure. Even if he should become a schoolteacher or politician, practice vegetarianism, follow orthodox Hindu religious traditions, and never touch a dead animal or make a shoe, he remains of shoemaker caste. "He may be individually esteemed, but in the system he is an untouchable; he is ritually polluted like every other shoemaker and he is treated accordingly."[3] In the United States the basic criterion for ranking is the association of Negro phenotype with a presumption of genetic, intellectual, and moral inferiority that is used to justify the idiom of white behavior toward blacks.

Briefly, then, *complex human societies tend to organize themselves along three more or less distinct lines: class, caste, and ethnicity.* The distinction of class refers to theoretically achieved status distinctions within a common cultural community. Caste, too, suggests intrasocietal divisions but of a birth-determined character, making them more rigid than those of class. Ethnic distinction, in contrast, refers to culture-based intergroup differences.

In reality, our distinctions are not quite so tidy. Class rigidity is often much stronger than definition of class, as achieved status suggests. In much of Europe, notably England, class lines often assume caste-like inflexibility in which upward movement is very difficult. Even in America, with its pervasive ideology of class mobility, behavior appropriate to one's class is learned early in life and quickly forms the basis for clique formation and discrimination against those of different class.[4]

The Lynds' classic sociological study of 1929, *Middletown,* found that opportunities for an adult working-class American male to rise to the business class were very small. They noted, however, that while adults might be bound to their class, many children of working-class families aspired to middle-class status and would undoubtedly achieve it.[5] But even this greater mobility (of income, education, and prestige of position) of children over their parents is frequently exaggerated through failure to correct for a general "mobility inflation." Thus, at a time when most children have greater incomes, more education, and better jobs than their parents, and *absolute* intergenerational mobility may be great, *relative* intergenerational mobility may not be nearly so impressive. The consensus may be that more people are joining the "middle class"; but most apparently mobile individuals probably fall into a similar status position, *vis-à-vis others,* to that occupied by their parents, in comparison with others of the parents' generation. Absolute statistics often give the impression of great mobility, while relative ones indicate that actual upward mobility may be low because the vast majority of individuals merely tread water to keep up with what can be termed "socioeconomic inflation."

Ethnic differences often come to demarcate social interaction between groups. This interaction is subject to varying degrees of restriction, ranging from virtual absence of contact (in situations where interaction is limited primarily to the instrumental areas of politics and economic dealings) to a situation in which minimal barriers exist to intergroup contacts. To the degree that such groups exist side by side with no one of them achieving societal dominance—

although one group may control the political and another the economic sphere of a society, for example—anthropologists frequently label the society *plural*.[6] Societies characterized by clear patterns of dominance and subordination, on the other hand, are often referred to as *caste societies*,[7] even when the "castes" are actually different ethnic groups.

The parallels between systems of caste and ethnic stratification are many, yet a crucial difference remains. As George DeVos has remarked in a personal communication: "A caste cannot escape psychologically because it has no separate culture to harbor to—but an ethnic group can mobilize itself both psychologically and politically in terms of its separateness—rather than fighting lower status within the system."

There can be little doubt that progressive urbanization, and the increasing division of labor which accompanies it, promotes class distinctions. Theoretically, it would seem that systems based upon true individual achievement in which every person is permitted to maximize his personal talents would be most compatible with increased occupational variety and complexity. What is less certain is whether cities, especially industrial cities, tend to reduce the significance of caste and ethnic differences. In short, *do urban situations promote individual mobility and achievement of a class nature, and a concomitant de-emphasis of such birth-ascribed categories as caste and ethnicity?*

Not surprisingly, the literature is scattered, the terms used in discussions are not always the same, and the basic issue of the impact of urban life upon the character and degree of social stratification is often only dimly kept in mind. Since the particular concerns of researchers reflect the cultural areas in which they work, the discussion that follows is ordered geographically. It considers the basic concerns of research in Africa with tribalism, national identity, and class; in India with caste and class; in Southeast and East Asia with ethnicity, national unity, and class; in South America with caste, ethnicity, and class; and in Europe and North America with ethnicity, caste, and class.

SUB-SAHARAN AFRICA: TRIBALISM, ETHNICITY, AND CLASS

No non-Western region of the world has been studied as intensely by anthropologists as Africa. And no other topic has captured the attention of African researchers as has ethnicity. The first European colonists to arrive on the continent were struck by what they perceived as tremendous regional, cultural, and linguistic varieties. Early travelers and missionaries repeatedly remarked the "peoples," "kingdoms," "sultanates," and "customs" of Africa's peoples. Only rarely in this period, however, was the term "tribe" used to delineate what were believed to be culturally distinct groups; later it became the dominant concept by which anthropologists and administrators alike ordered the African diversity.[8]

"Tribes" are often real enough: many a group in Africa has long recognized the closeness of its relation to others who speak a similar language and follow similar customs, sharply demarcating those of the group as a whole from other groups through patterns of intermarriage and loyalty.

But keen awareness of "tribal" differences was often a colonial phenomenon. As large sections of Africa came under British, French, and Belgian control, two processes were set in motion that undoubtedly heightened the salience of such differences:

1) Different groups of Africans, especially those who migrated to cities, came into contact with one another more frequently, often noting a discontinuity between those who spoke their language and followed similar customs and those who did not. Whereas many peoples may earlier have distinguished only between "kin" and "others," contact suddenly made them aware of a gradation between kin, those who were not kin but whose customs were similar, and those who were neither kin nor culturally alike. This conceptual shift was evidently most important for those who came from relatively uncentralized and unstratified societies without chiefs and the relatively clear group boundaries of such groups. Those from stratified and centralized chiefdoms, on the other hand, undoubtedly already held a greater awareness of belonging to a corporate entity, or "tribe."

2) Colonial administrators emphasized tribal categories. This was either out of desire for discrete and manageable administrative units, with native elites who could be held liable for the behavior of their subordinates and used as intermediaries between colonizers and the general population, or from realization that the task of maintaining colonial dominance would be made easier through adherence to a policy that maximized what group differences did exist (the so-called divide and rule policy).

Often tribal distinctions were made simply from ignorance or from projection of one's home situation, for the European world was itself segmented into such categories as Englishmen, Welshmen, Scotsmen, Frenchmen and Germans. It is hardly surprising that men raised in European traditions would quickly note similar differences among African peoples. Often the differences did exist, although sometimes administrative distinctions were made between groups whose distinctness was neither cultural nor recognized by the people themselves.

As Southall has eloquently asserted, most "tribal" identities are hardly "primeval" distinctions but are of relatively recent, post-colonial origin. Certain groups such as the Luyia, Kalenjin, and Mijikenda of Kenya, for example, formally "came into existence" in the 1940's or 1950's, yet are generally regarded as ancient tribes. Numerous tribes of importance today were unknown and unreported by explorers who traversed their home territories during the last century, while others appear simply to represent broad residential, rather than cultural categories: the Bakiga of Uganda are simply "highlanders," while the Nyamwezi and Sukuma formerly meant people from the west and north, respectively.[9] Every ethnic group or category encountered by the British in Nigeria, for example, had to have its own distinct administrative relation with the British except in the case of very small groups incorporated into larger ones for administrative purposes. Once categorized, the group was expected to have fixed geographical boundaries, and its migrations in rural areas were either stopped or controlled. "Ethnic distinctiveness," the British realized, "was one key to orderly administration. And one should work through the existing structure of authority of traditional governments, if the leaders were cooperative. If not, others would be found who were."[10]

Southall feels that the importance of "tribalism" has been exaggerated by Africanists, perhaps exacerbating the continent's ethnic problems, which are as serious as the "American dilemma" of race.[11] As anthropologists, and as members of a group as responsible as any other for reifying the concept of tribe, Southall argues that we have an obligation to set the matter straight. But his own solution is limited: "I have therefore expunged the term tribe from my anthropological lexicon and use instead the concept of ethnicity to denote all differentiation based on a sense of common ancestry and culture among individuals and groups at different levels."[12]

Whatever the conceptual utility of the term tribe, and whether or not its usage represented an accurate reporting of cultural differences or merely maximized what were only slight differences, the phenomena it is used to describe today are real enough. *Tribalism, or adherence to ethnic loyalties and behavior patterns, has been the major stumbling block to the formation of unified African states that today find themselves in control of territory arbitrarily carved out and segmented by colonial conquest.* The tragedy of tribal divisiveness has everywhere been manifest in Africa in the assertion of governmental and political hegemony by certain tribes over others. The semiautonomous regional governments of pre-civil-war Nigeria, for example, followed a policy of discriminatory practices against alien and minority tribes. Each of the three Nigerian Regional Governments favored members of the dominant tribal group—the Ibo in the east, the Yoruba in the west, and the Hausa-Fulani in the north—by denying government jobs, loans, scholarships, and in the north building plots to members of minority groups.[13] This tribalism has sometimes had deadly consequences, as in the 1966 anti-Ibo riots in Jos, where the number of dead was so great that bulldozers from local mining companies had to be brought in to dig mass graves.[14] Similarly, as many as 3.5 percent of the population of the tiny African kingdom of Burundi are estimated to have died in the tribal massacres of 1972.[15]

The influence of urbanization upon African tribalism has been a major concern of urban anthropologists, many of whom have spoken of the *detribalization* that results as urban migrants begin to think of themselves as townsmen rather than tribesmen. This concept, too, has had its various critics. Colonial administrators sometimes resisted the permanent migration of Africans to towns in the practical fear that detribalized migrants might represent a greater threat to their authority.[16] Anthropologists, on the other hand, have objected to the term for its lack of precision. When, for example, can an individual properly be said to be detribalized? Some have seen the process as akin to Durkheim's concept of anomie and the detribalized man as a marginal being without clear cultural loyalties and bearings. For most, the process is analogous to that of *acculturation*—a gradual process of shifting from adherence to the patterns of one culture to those of another (or to a syncretism of the two), in this case a change from tribal ways to town ways.

Gluckman states that

> the moment an African crosses his tribal boundary to go to the town, he is "detribalized," out of the political control of the tribe. And in the town, the basic materials by which he lives are

different: he walks on different ground, eats food at different hours and maybe different food at that. He comes under different political authorities, and associates with different fellows. He works with different tools in a different system of organization . . . an African townsman is a townsman, an African miner is a miner.[17]

Gluckman argues that even newly urban Africans must be viewed as individuals living and behaving within a milieu determined by an urban or industrial setting. He is of course aware that the tribe's influence upon its members persists within the city, but notes that it impinges upon an individual's life in a quite different manner than in the rural homeland. On the other hand, when the detribalized urbanite returns to the political homeland of his tribe, such a perspective holds that he becomes deurbanized and again tribalized.

Use of the term detribalization can be either in Gluckman's geographic sense of a shifting of social fields from rural or tribal to an urban setting, or in terms of culture. Epstein and Mitchell have refined the tribal/urban aspects of an individual's behavior by noting that people in cities generally shift back and forth from traditional "tribal" to "urban" behavior according to a process of situational selection.[18] Thus one may live a tribal life at home, while working in a factory under a set of rules and relations with other employees that is based upon an industrial framework in which tribal customs are irrelevant.[19] Yet even within "modern," multitribal organizations such as the African Mine Workers' Trade Union described by A. L. Epstein, electoral battles have been fought through appeals to tribal loyalties.[20] Schisms within the union frequently appear to be interpreted along tribal lines. Undoubtedly, in some respects the term tribe, with its ambiguity of meaning as either a locational or behavioral concept and its somewhat perjorative connotation of "uncivilized," is an unfortunate nomenclature. Although as William Shack and others have suggested, it might be more fruitful to reserve the term tribe to the rural area and use ethnic group for the city,[21] "tribe" dominates most of past literature and requires circumlocution to avoid.

Often urban residence at least temporarily enhances or maintains tribal identity among people who rely upon such ties for support. Europeans and Indians who were forced by economic necessity to live in the same areas of Kampala, Uganda, as Africans did, kept their relations with black neighbors to a minimum;[22] so, too, do Africans often minimize contact with those outside their own tribes. Jean Rouch noted that awareness of tribal identity is often greatly increased in cities, so that members of some groups who cling to life in a "little regional cell" can be said to be *supertribalized* by urban residence.[23] Plotnicov flatly asserts that "the Nigerians in Jos cannot conceive that one may be both black and detribalized."[24] This often appears to be the case when migrants are confronted with the city's ethnic diversity. Tribalism, Mitchell says, is simply

> a phenomenon arising out of culture contact . . . [that comes] into being when people of different origin are thrown together in industrial areas and other labour centres, in schools, in farms, or similar situations . . . The anthropologist could only be expected to develop an interest in tribalism, therefore, when he set about studying people in modern industrial centres.[25]

African residence in European-controlled cities may result in internal tribal divisions based upon acceptance or nonacceptance of European life ways. Xhosa contact with white-dominated cities in South Africa, for example, has produced a split between members of the group along lines of identification with urban (white) or tribal (Xhosa) values. Thus, Xhosa themselves bisect their entire population into "school" Xhosa and "red" Xhosa. School Xhosa value the "civilized" ways of the city and express such urban aspirations as desire to "belong to the business men in town; to 'sportsmen'; 'those who attend church regularly'; to 'people with professions'." Red, tribally-oriented Xhosa—so termed because of the tradition of smearing their bodies with red ochre—encapsulate themselves by avoiding "the things of the white man" and respond to the query "what sort of people would you like to belong to here?" with stereotyped answers: "'I should like to belong to the Red people in town,' 'Red people who drink kaffir beer,' or more simply, 'Red people from my home place.'"[26]

The Tonga of Rhodesia have encapsulated themselves similarly in the cities of Rhodesia and the Union of South Africa, where they have migrated to find work. The uncertainty of life in European-dominated cities—an anxiety that could also be felt in cities controlled by non-Tonga Africans—encourage Tonga to regard the city as a temporary residence and to funnel the fruits of their labor home. Van Velsen concludes from his experience with Tonga labor migrants that

> the number of years spent in the towns is not a reliable index of that person's "urbanization." . . . It is relatively unimportant whether an African has lived for one, ten, or twenty years, with or without intervals in his tribal area, in the specialized and

industrialized economy of the towns if he relies for his ultimate security on his tribal society, after his limited security of urban employment has come to an end.[27]

Zulu migrant workers to South African cities engage in regular, ritualized intertribal fighting. Before whites had enforced intertribal peace, warfare was an important aspect of a man's identity. Adult men were regarded as mere boys until they had established manhood by proving their fighting ability. Movement of laborers into European-controlled cities did not diminish tribal fighting. At first, in fact, European police permitted and supervised the fighting, to permit the men to "work off steam." Later, tribal fighting became so prevalent that it was banned; fighters had to seek out-of-the-way settings like mine dumps. The ban may have been the result of Europeans' realization that they would be the preferred targets if they were to lay down their rifles and fight hand-to-hand. Indeed, when Albert Luthuli, the Nobel Peace Prize winner and president of the African National Congress, was photographed performing a war dance in full Zulu regalia at a wedding, Zulus took the performance as a "challenge to the white government, and it was generally regretted that Dr. Verwoerd [the South African Prime Minister] could not find the time to accept the challenge in behalf of the white community."[28] Rather than diminish tribal fighting, urban residence and European constraints have only stripped it of some of its surrounding ritual and code of conduct. It has become merely "brutal and cathartic," and "for the truly urbanized, sticks and clubs have been exchanged for more lethal weapons such as knives, iron bars, and even revolvers . . . for the less urbanized, clubs are still in fashion."[29]

But persistence of tribalism in the city is not the same as rural tribalism. Tribesmen in urban areas quickly learn that strict tribal power and the power of chiefs is restricted to their homeland. In the city they encounter new sources of power and prestige, based upon education and the acquisition of special skills, to which many willingly transfer their loyalty. Common tribal or ethnic bonds may still keep members together and may even be enhanced, but as Immanuel Wallerstein has noted: "quite often the group from which the individual is 'detribalized' (that is, the tribe to whose chief he no longer pays the same fealty) is not necessarily the same group into which he is 'super-tribalized' (that is, the ethnic group to which he feels strong bonds of attachment in the urban context)."[30]

Popular and academic studies of African societies frequently focus on the conflict between ethnic and national loyalties. In this context, ethnicity is invariably seen as the greatest threat to national unity. Although the divisive aspects of ethnic conflicts are obvious, such judgments ignore the paradoxically beneficial transitional effects that the development of strong ethnic loyalties may have for national unity. Most important, the formation of large ethnic units helps reduce the importance of strictly reckoned lineages and kin, by providing for the first time for many a nonkinship level of intimate association. Once ethnicity is recognized as a basis for loyalty, it absorbs such family functions as caring for the sick and securing employment for group members. Even the use of ethnicity for political organization—as long as it does not get out of hand and lead to separatist movements—helps solidify the legitimacy of national institutions. The transition to a nation-state is eased by the fact that ethnic alliances tend to focus political opposition onto individuals as members of different ethnic groups, rather than upon the political system itself. Rejection of a Yoruba politician by Ibo in Nigeria, for example, and an effort to replace him with an Ibo official may actually help reinforce the authority of the post, easing the transition to full acceptance of a multiethnic body politic.

An important enhancement of tribal identities is the division between the "owners" of cities and those who have migrated to them as "strangers." In Africa, tribes upon whose traditional homeland a city is placed generally assume, and are accorded by others, the status of owner; outside migrants are regarded as strangers who often live in a special quarter of the city at sufferance of its owners. In most cities queries of who "owns" them receive clear-cut answers: for example, Kano and Ibadan, Nigeria, are owned by the Hausa and Yoruba, respectively. Only rarely does a situation exist such as that described by Plotnicov for Jos, where several competing groups each have geographic or religious claims to the city. It "may well be that it is ideologically inconceivable for Nigerians to think a settlement can belong to *no* ethnic group in particular or that any place can be thought of as the equal possession of all the country's citizens."[31]

The stranger-owner division can be so strong that it overrides even the binding force of adherence to a common religion. Islam especially has had notable success in Africa, due largely to its appeal as a "nonwhite" religion;[32] but common belief in Allah and adherence to Muslim precepts are not necessarily sufficient to ease cross-ethnic interaction. Cohen's study of Hausa-Yoruba relations in Ibadan provides an excellent example of the manner in which such divisions may be so strongly supported by political and economic differences that potential for unification is responded to as a threat. Thus, the Hausa live in a special quarter among Yoruba owners. Although they produce neither commodity, they hold a monopoly on the cattle and kola-nut trades, facilitated by the absence of generally available credit and communication facilities that is common to preindustrial societies. In the course of years of trading they have developed a close network of centers for the purchase, transport, and resale of cattle and kola in Yorubaland, even to the point of establishing enclaves in areas where no Hausa communities had existed. The benefits of tribal distinctiveness are obvious: by keeping themselves aloof from other ethnic groups they can maintain tight lines of trade and prevent the encroachment of others upon them.

During British rule, Hausa tribal distinctiveness and exclusive rights to residence in a separate quarter (Sabo) of Ibadan were recognized. With independence and the development of a nationalist movement in Nigeria, however, Sabo was no longer accepted as a separate ethnic entity and its chief vested with governmental authority over its inhabitants. At the same time as the residential and political aspects of Hausa isolation were being undermined, social interaction between Hausa and Yoruba was encouraged by rapid growth of a Yoruba Muslim community. Detribalization and a gradual loss of the trade monopoly seemed likely. But, rather than succumb to assimilation, the quarter adopted en masse a mystical Muslim order, the Tijaniyya, offering a new and more puritanical version of Islam. Participation in the new order resulted in the full seclusion of women and a marked increase in adherence to such pillars of Islam as the five daily prayers and the performance of the pilgramage, or *haj*, to Mecca. The renewed sense of religion and the "new myth of distinctiveness for the Quarter . . . [as] a superior, puritanical, ritual community, a religious brotherhood, distinct from the masses of Yoruba Moslems in the city, complete with its separate Friday Mosque, Friday congregation, and with a separate cemetery" resulted in a situation in which the Hausa of Sabo have become *"more socially exclusive, or less assimilated into the host society, than at any other time in the past.* They thus seem to have completed a full cycle of 'retribalization.'"[33]

One particularly interesting and promising area of urban research centers on interethnic stereotypes. Clyde Mitchell, in *The Kalela Dance*, discusses the use of such stereotypes by dancers on the Rhodesian (Zambian) copper belt, to mock the supposedly strange customs and sexual habits of other tribes. Interestingly, members of the tribes who are the objects of jest make up part of the audience and appear to enjoy the humor as much as the others.[34] More curiously, the performers (who are laborers) wear European-style clothes and refer to themselves by titles of British officers. Mitchell suggests that they are participating vicariously in the life style of the new African elite that models itself along European lines:

> The European life has become so much a part and parcel of life in the urban areas that the Europeans themselves have faded from the background. *Kalela* dancers do not seek vicarious participation in European society but vicarious participation in the upper levels of African society, from which, by their lack of qualification, they are excluded. The prestige system in the urban areas thus uses "civilization" or "the European way-of-life" as a standard or scale of prestige. To command respect in such a system the African needs to be educated; to occupy a post which accords high prestige; and to draw a salary large enough to enable him to purchase the clothing and other symbols of prestige.[35]

Quite likely, much of the appeal of such dress and demeanor lies in a kind of trying-on and playing with European or upper-class African identity, just as tribal identities and acceptable behavioral boundaries of teasing, hostility, and humor are being tested in the security of the "just joking" situation of the dance.

An interesting approach to interethnic stereotypes and joking has been developed by Enid Schildkrout in her study of urban immigrants in Ghana. Her analysis, closely related to our earlier discussion of tribal boundaries, shows that urban migrants to Kumasi habitually extend consanguineal kinship terms to all members of their own ethnic group, whether or not they are actually related, with the one exception that those who are related by marriage are referred to by their proper affinal term. Affinal kin terms, too, are not limited to actual kin. Members of the Mossi, Mamprusi, and Dagomba tribes have evolved a fictive set of in-law relationships based upon legendary marriages in their tribal pasts. These ties are a basis for joking among individuals of the different tribes, which helps set a framework for interaction that recognizes proximity and distance at the same time. Invariably the joking would be either inappropriate or obscene if it occurred outside the context of fictive kinship. Schildkrout tells of one "joke" played by a man claiming to be a Hausa, who approached a recent Dagomba arrival, called him *Kafiri* (pagan), and suggested he return to his village. The Dagomba, quite naturally, was angered. As he was about to strike the joker, a Mossi observer stepped in and told him that the "Hausa" was really a Mossi. Suddenly, what would have been an act of provocation had the "joker" actually been Hausa, became a joke.

Closer analysis of which groups classify others as joking affines revealed that the Mossi are much closer historically, culturally, and linguistically to their Mamprusi and Dagomba "affines" than they are to the other ethnic groups of the town. Thus joking unites larger groups by affirming cultural solidarity through the idiom of affinity, while continuing to recognize the distinct identities of each group. It occurs, Schildkrout concludes, "precisely in this domain where cultural boundaries are blurred but where ethnicity, and the concept on which it is based, can be used to express status differences."[36] Beyond the range of fictive affines, where clear linguistic and cultural differences exist, no joking occurs to bridge ethnic boundaries.

The Mossi majority of Ouagadougou, Upper Volta, hold a plethora of judgments on the character of the various stranger groups in their midst. Mossi from most other kingdoms, not surprisingly, are held in high esteem, although Mossi from the northern region of Yatenga are considered touchy and haughty. The Gourounsi, whose homeland was being absorbed by Mossi when the French arrived, are jokingly referred to as Mossi *ligidi* (money), in reference to the fact that they were formerly sold as slaves. Other groups, such as the Fulani, are considered clever, while Yoruba men and women are felt to be honest and hard-working. Certain groups are held in ambivalent regard: Songhay and Djerma men of neighboring Niger are considered good traders and hard workers, but their women are looked upon as prostitutes specializing in a lower-status migrant clientele.

Most disliked of all by the Mossi are the Dahomeans, Togolese, and Ghanaians, resented because of their association with the French colonial period, during which they held clerical jobs to which locals aspired. They are remembered for their haughty demeanor and racist attitudes towards the Mossi and are frequently accused of exploiting the country by sending money home. They are also said to practice human sacrifice by devouring children to increase their spiritual powers. In 1964, an unfounded rumor provided the pretext for wholesale expulsion and repatriation of Dahomeans and Togolese civil servants. The shouts of a young servant boy temporarily locked in a Dahomean house were taken by the landlady to be the prelude to a sacrifical ritual. Rumors spread that missing children—whose disappearance was regularly announced on the radio but whose reappearance was not—had died in similar ceremonies. The resulting outburst of fear and hostility was used by the government as a pretext for the firing and repatriation.[37]

Similar problems have occurred elsewhere in Africa as the result of perceptions that certain groups have been given special treatment by Europeans. Groups with whom Europeans first came into contact, especially those receptive to Christianity and Western education, were naturally favored by colonial governments. Often, as colonization proceeded, clerks and low-ranking administrators of a British or French colony would travel to a newer colony and assume posts there, effectively blocking the advance of locals.[38] In contrast to the situation of Ouagadougou, Mossi migrants to the Ivory Coast held many valued jobs by virtue of their position with the French. Here, too, local hostility has occasionally reached dangerous levels. In 1969, widespread anti-Mossi riots erupted and the city of Abidjan was placed under alert for three weeks. Investigation revealed that a Frenchman had visited the local state employment office to request a chauffeur. Rather than leave the selection of candidates to the discretion of office workers, he specifically asked for a Mossi, explaining that they were better workers than Ivoiriens. The Mossi who got the job was killed by enraged Ivoiriens who had been waiting in line for jobs. Several days later a similar incident occurred, provoking one Ivoirien to vow that "we will fight to the death to keep foreigners out of our country. The French help the Mossi by asking for them as manual laborers. The Mossi will be sent back to Upper Volta on shields."[39]

The association of particular groups with special status can cause serious problems, especially when a system of clear ethnic stratification exists or is perceived to exist. The expulsion of (Asian) Indians from Uganda is another example of the problem of relatively well-to-do minorities. Initially recruited by the British as laborers, or having come to Africa as commercial intermediaries between the British and Ugandans, many Indians stayed behind after the British departure. Ironically, their position as intermediaries and their closer approximation to local African physical appearance made them even more of an ethnic lightning rod than the British had been. Whites were clearly distinct in their occupations and color and thus more readily granted elite status. The social pretensions of Indians, on the other hand, and especially stereotypes of them as the post-colonial country-club elite, led to their being made the scapegoats for the country's economic problems at the hands of Idi Amin. Although many Indians had welcomed Amin's 1971 coup, they soon found that he resented them. At a conference held to discuss the "Asian problem," Amin complained that Asians had refused to integrate into Ugandan society: "About seventy years have elapsed since the first Asians came to Uganda, but despite that length of time the Asian community has continued to live in a world of its own to the extent that the Africans in this country have, for example, hardly been able to marry Asian girls."[40] In 1972 Amin ordered the 75,000 members of the Asian community, who in all accounted for only one percent of the nation's total population, to leave Uganda.

Another minority group whose members profited from stability of the colonial period to establish themselves as commercial middlemen, and who today are often resented by local populations, is the Lebanese. The first Lebanese to arrive in West Africa were generally of lower status than their East Indian counterparts of East Africa. They came from poor families, many of which had sent some of their offspring out of the country, especially to the United States. Arriving in West Africa, they at first began their commercial ventures by peddling in marketplaces; later they found largely unexploited niches along railroad lines in the interior, where they learned the local languages and thrived by trading textiles and city products to tribal peoples for local produce. In time the originally humble Lebanese came to occupy mercantile and elite positions out of proportion to their numbers. As with the Jews of Europe, the Chinese of Southeast Asia, and the Indians of East Africa, their highly visible relative wealth—made more obvious by the close proximity to locals demanded by their occupations—has engendered resentment.[41] In the Ivory Coast "the Lebanese are, in fact," M. A. Cohen says, "the most hated non-Africans in the country."[42] In a 1969 meeting with President Houphouët-Boigny they were told to "Ivoirize" their businesses within six months by taking local partners, to keep written records of their accounts, and to renew their immigration cards annually. The posture of the Lebanese in the meeting evidenced their fear of deportation (as later did occur in Ghana):

> You do not cease to give to the world, Mister President, examples of democracy such as that created by the Greeks thousands of years ago . . . The majority among us have passed the greatest part of our active lives here. We are only Lebanese by origin, but Ivoireans of heart . . . we wish to be considered not like foreigners, but adopted Lebanese, perfectly integrated into the modern society of today.[43]

The problem of identity is especially acute for descendants of African and Lebanese unions.[44] Initially, single Lebanese migrants took African women as concubines. The relationship was usually regarded as marriage by the African women and their kin as it conformed to local marital customs and included payment of a bride price. Muslim Lebanese usually formalized their African marriages in an Islamic ceremony. Christian Lebanese, for whom divorce was much more difficult to obtain rarely if ever married African women in a church ceremony. They regarded their relationships with their African wives not as marriages but as a more or less prolonged state of cohabitation. As they achieved prosperity, both Christians and Muslims returned to Lebanon to obtain Lebanese wives. The African "wives" were then divorced or simply discarded, and they and their offspring returned to live with their families. When the woman belonged to a matrilineal group such as the Ashanti of Ghana, the children were readily incorporated into their mother's tribe. But in most cases the local tribes trace descent patrilineally, not recognizing offspring of their sisters as part of the tribe. Since no Lebanese Christians and only a few of the wealthiest Muslims were willing to accept their mulatto children, the African-Lebanese became, in effect, involuntarily detribalized. Spurned by Lebanese, who considered them African, and not recognized by their African kin, who viewed them as Lebanese, they were and are of amorphous identity.

One mulatto attempted to resolve his dilemma by asserting, "I am Lebanese by tribe and Sierra Leonean by nationality," knowing full well that his membership in the "Lebanese tribe" is not recognized by Lebanese and confers none of the rights or duties normally associated with tribal membership. The common treatment of mulattos has made them more conscious of their separate and distinct status. Today, many African-Lebanese have formed closed communities and moved into jobs as technicians or drivers which associate them with neither the agricultural traditions of their mothers' tribes nor the commerce of their fathers'. But the small size of these communities—estimates range from 2,000 to 5,000 persons each in Sierra Leone, Guinea, and Senegal—and marginal character suggest that their future is not in constitution of a distinct "mulatto tribe," but in a blending with the emergent class-based structure of their respective nations.

More important to future ethnic and class relations in Africa has been the relation of Africans with European colonizers. During the colonial period, and continuing today in the white-dominated areas of southern Africa, segments of the African population were called upon to serve as intermediaries in the governing process between rulers and ruled. They occupied what Leo Kuper has termed an "intercalary" position, both separating and coordinating activities of the two groups.[45] From the white viewpoint, having African officials occupy these roles provided a useful device for transmission of communications; for Africans, it offered some chance to air their desires and gave the appearance of participation in their own governance. British everywhere in the empire maximized the utility of this distinction—although perhaps not always consciously—by keeping all colonials at a distance, away from close contact and especially away from "the club."[46] Thus, while the British made education available to colonials in Africa, they never ceased to regard them as Africans. The French, on the other hand, encouraged Africans in their territories to frenchify themselves, giving certain Africans who mastered French language and customs access to their world and the special status of *évolués* (highly civilized people).

Unfortunately for purposes of governance, Africans who achieved *évolué* status invariably lost touch with other Africans. As in Indo-China, African *évolués* who had turned their backs on their fellows in fawning imitation of their French overlords sacrificed what authority they might have had and yet, despite all their efforts, were still regarded by the French as either biologically or culturally inferior. Interestingly, studies by Jahoda in the former British colony of Ghana and by O'Brien in French colonial Africa suggest that there is less resentment of Europeans in former British colonies than there is in regions once governed by the French.[47] This seems to be the case for French and British colonies in general; it is perhaps the result of the fact that the British offered a model and the education to achieve it, at the same time insisting that locals retain their distinct identities. When independence came, the trauma for African elites in British colonies who had been able to select what they found useful from their colonizers without being under pressure to imitate them undoubtedly made the transition from colonial to home rule easier that it was for *évolués* who had developed a psychological dependence upon French culture.[48]

In any event, the experience of colonialism transmitted European models of aspiration and behavior to "modern elite" Africans, providing a fairly uniform, nontribal basis for interaction.[49] Today, members of the elite have largely replaced or joined the remaining Europeans in jobs, homes, clubs, and life styles. As Baeck, Parkin, and Kileff have noted, tribal loyalties have not completely vanished among modern elites; but they have become somewhat blurred, so that they are generally not of primary importance in choice of friends or day-to-day behavior.[50]

Among those at lower socioeconomic levels, in contrast, tribal identity retains its importance and interaction is more likely to be ethnocentric. Undoubtedly this is due to the fact that in most situations the aspirations and desires of the elite are best served by emphasis upon such nontribal concerns as gaining a Western education—preferably abroad, so that one has the status of a "been-to" and almost certain entry into the governmental or professional elite—while most of those in the lower stratum rely upon their fellow tribesmen for aid.[51] Only in special interest situations such as the copper belt labor strikes do class considerations appear to cut across ethnic ties for the urban poor,[52] although, as noted earlier, there is a tendency for city peoples from tribes of similar linguistic, cultural, and regional origin to unite in multitribal units.[53] In Cape Town, South Africa, for example, most important to an urban migrant is his *abakhaya* (home-boys), a group of individuals who come from the same region and who live, eat, and usually work together in the city. *Abakhaya* loyalties are often strong enough to bind together people of different ethnic backgrounds, so that even members of the traditionally hostile Xhosa and Mfengu tribes will form such a tie if they come from the same district.[54]

The importance of continuing tribal loyalties has led some to doubt whether true detribalized or in Kuper's term "depluralized,"[55] class-based elites can actually be formed. One problem with use of the class concept has been that upper-status individuals often maintain close ties with lower-status kinsmen, and males often marry women of their ethnic group but of lower class.[56] Schwab's study of Gwelo in Southern Rhodesia, however, illustrated that, despite a setting in which black aspirations were limited by white control, class-like behavior and aspirations were evident. The symbols of high indigenous status—represented by higher education, Western possessions, use of English to communicate, and avoidance of such lower-status gathering places as beerhalls—had clearly been adopted from Europeans. Parental aspirations for their children's future occupations, as well as the expressed aspirations of grammar school children, indicated an acceptance of a European status hierarchy: 76.3 percent of parents (65.7 percent of children) wanted their offspring to enter professional or other white collar occupations, while roughly equal numbers of parents and children (16.4 percent and 17.3 percent, respectively) saw skilled labor, supervisory, or commercial positions as more desirable. Interestingly, 16.4 percent of the children said they hoped to work in agriculture; none of the parents had such aspirations for their children.[57]

In African nations that have gained independence, evidence of the importance of class among elites is indisputable. The transition of Africans to power, in fact, has generally resulted in elite locals assuming almost unchanged the occupations and perquisites of the former colonizers. As Europeans left their artificially high-salaried posts and large, well-staffed colonial bungalows, Africans moved in. So completely European has been the situation of the elite immediately before and after independence that in Nigeria local Africans were granted "home leave" to the United Kingdom![58]

More recent studies show that the shift from traditional status to modern status systems among the elite is complete enough so that one may conclude that at least large segments of Africa's urban population have accepted a class, rather than an ethnic system of status. Occupation, which is the sine qua non of ranking in the West, has clearly gained primacy,[59] and class divisions cross-cutting ethnic lines are recognized by city populations. While tribal migrants who regularly journey home maintain networks of friendships largely within their own tribe, urban-oriented persons of both lower- and upper-class status place greater emphasis upon maintaining friendships with persons of similar status. For lower-class individuals, such friendships are often forged in beerhalls or informal clubs;[60] upper-status individuals usually have friends of similar occupation who work within the same organization.[61] Of 150 friendships listed by a group of 60 elite Ugandans working for the central government, 120 were in the same occupational organization.[62]

> Ethnicity is of minor importance in the friendship organization of elite Africans. The elite conceptualize an elite and a non-elite between whom there is little or no leisure time interaction and no ties of friendship. In contrast, they suggest that they are unified and that any elite African might have as a friend any other elite African.[63]

Even if the elite themselves are still pulled by tribal ties—most frequently expressed by relatives' requests for aid—their children are often completely removed from such threats to their class status. Adult black suburbanites in Salisbury, Rhodesia, invariably understand and respect tribal custom and seek to balance it with their suburban life style. Their children, on the other hand,

are growing up differently. Most attend multi-racial schools.
They know little about traditional customs. They know TV,
European food, beds, bathrooms, and many luxuries that their
rural relatives do not have. Some parents are embarrassed by
their children's behaviour when they visit in the country.
Children are often ignorant of what is expected of them and do
not know how to maintain the balance.[64]

It appears that the social structure of African towns has shifted
from divisions based almost wholly upon tribe or ethnicity to ones in
which dual ethnic and class systems coexist, with class gradually increasing in importance. The diversity of the various countries, the
problems of such ethnically distinct non-African groups as the
Lebanese and East Indians, and the fact that Africans themselves
have not generally achieved uniform consensus on status criteria
prevent description of a completely satisfactory single pan-African
system of status hierarchies. Nevertheless, by way of summary, it is
useful to put forth a tentative urban-status hierarchy that is more or
less applicable to African cities today:

1) *migrants*
    a) temporary or seasonal migrant laborers who may reside
       in urban areas for extended periods of time but who
       remain tribe-oriented
    b) semi-urbanized immigrant laborers with some education
2) *urban individuals* for whom the town is a permanent home
    a) lower-class laborers and such others as prostitutes
    b) the skilled artisans, small shop-owners, and lower-ranking
       government officials who form an emerging, yet still
       somewhat indistinct, middle class
    c) alien (East Indian, Lebanese, Arab) populations who may
       occupy many of the same occupations of those in group
       2b), although they are often more successful com-
       mercially
    d) elite professionals, civil servants, and wealthy business-
       men (sometimes including prominent European ex-
       patriates and other African aliens)[65]

The major problem with class models—especially in situations
in which social stratification is in such clear flux as is generally the
case for urban Africa—is that no randomly selected sample of individuals is likely to adhere to any single model. Thus, migrants may
view urban society as composed either solely of members of dif-

ferent tribes, or of townsmen and tribesmen with no clear differentiation among townsmen; elites may similarly collapse the distinctions
between themselves and nonelites. Often ruling elites will assert
publicly that no classes exist, preferring even to recognize and stress
tribal differences. Official doctrine in many countries denies the
existence of classes, clearly out of fear that acceptance of such
Marxist models as Samir Amin's for the Ivory Coast, which distinguishes between the "masses" (approximately 150,000 workers), the
"middle class" (some 10,000 people), and the "ruling group" (2,000
families) could eventually lead to class warfare.[66]

M. A. Cohen's evidence for the Ivory Coast suggests that class
does provide a useful and accurate descriptive concept, but that
African conditions require that classes be defined as *"categories of
people sharing common political and economic interests arising from
their access to public authorities and public resources and opportunities which they control."*[67] In other words, in Africa especially,
social mobility usually has political origins. Those who are part of
the political elite can and do promote their interests in a myriad of
ways, ranging from having their own streets paved to arranging
government scholarships and high-ranking civil service positions for
their children. "Distinctions between small shop keepers, considered
by Amin as 'middle class' and 'artisans,' included among the 'masses,'"
Cohen asserts, "are simply less important than the political and
economic differences resulting from access to public authority."[68]

Finally, it should be noted that mixed ethnic and class systems
provide a maximum of opportunity for individuals, especially elites,
to manipulate their own status. Sometimes opportunism thus dictates
that a wealthy, educated, politically powerful individual emphasize
his ethnic background to gain the support of others of similar
origin; in other contexts, it is more fruitful to play upon class ties.[69]

INDIA: CASTE AND CLASS

India is a region of seemingly unremitting diversity. More than 600
million people adhere to a variety of religions (Hinduism, Islam,
Buddhism, and Sikhism, to name a few) speak numerous languages
(Hindustani, Hindi, Bengali, Tamil, and others), and come from a
number of geographically and climatically distinct regions. If there is
any single organizing principle in this diversity it is in the concept of
caste, which although properly Hindu in origin has been applied and

accepted as a categorization for nearly all groups in Indian society. It is caste (*jati*) that provides the structural basis for Hindu social organization.

In its strictest sense, caste involves organization of the entire society into endogamous groups that relate hierarchically to one another in terms of principles based on reciprocal obligation and a conception of the relative ritual purity of each group. Castes are *endogamous*; they are frequently associated with *traditional occupations* that enmesh their members in a network of *reciprocity*; and they carry with them a notion of varying degrees of *pollution*, or position within a ritual hierarchy. According to Hindu scripture, all castes are clustered into four larger units known as *varnas*, the origin of which can be attributed to the primeval being. Out of his mouth came the Brahmana (Brahmins) and from his arms, thighs, and feet the Rajanya (Kshatriya), Vaishya, and Shudra, respectively. Each *varna* is associated with traditional occupations: Brahmins are priests and scholars, Kshatriya rulers and soldiers, Vaishya merchants, and Shudra artisans. At the very bottom of the system, beneath and outside all varnas, are the outcastes or untouchables, the *harijan*.[70]

In reality, the ordering is not nearly so neat. In each of India's linguistic regions there are about 200 caste groups, subdivided further into some 2,000 endogamous subcastes that form the basic unit of social life for an individual.[71] Ranking among these groups is often imprecise. Members of one group claim ritual superiority to others that may or may not be recognized by the society as a whole. Only at the upper end of the hierarchy, for the priestly Brahmins, is rank likely to be granted without great question; but even here one group of Brahmins will sometimes assert its superiority over another sub-caste, or refuse to recognize the group as being Brahmin. Theoretically the system has a good deal of rigidity, based upon the *varna* (which literally means color) hierarchy and the philosophy of *karma* (an individual merits his present caste position as the fruit of his behavior in previous lives) and *dharma* (he must follow a moral and religious code based largely upon behavior appropriate to caste status).

In reality, few low-caste individuals or groups seem willing to follow these basic precepts of acceptance of one's lot. Subcastes frequently claim higher birth than they are accorded, arguing that through error or willful discrimination by others their true genealogy has not been accepted. This genealogical pretense is coupled with an effort to emulate behavior appropriate to the level claimed. Srinivas terms this process "sanskritization," noting that:

The caste system is far from a rigid system in which the position of each component caste is fixed for all time. Movement has always been possible, and especially so in the middle of the hierarchy. A low caste was able, in a generation or two, to rise to a higher position in the hierarchy by adopting vegetarianism and teetotalism, and by sanskritising its ritual and pantheon. In short, it took over, as far as possible, the customs, rites, and beliefs of the Brahmins, and the adoption of the Brahmin way of life by a low caste seems to have been frequent, though theoretically forbidden.[72]

Additionally, outcastes are usually neither truly untouchable nor really outcaste, although in certain areas low castes are expected to remain as far as 124 feet distant from Brahmins.[73] Traditionally, those of outcaste or *pariah* status have had the most menial and polluting occupations of Indian society: sweeping and sewage disposal and occupations such as shoemaking, bringing them into contact with the flesh of dead cattle. In Ceylon there is even an "unseeable" caste, the Thurumbas, who are not supposed to travel by day and are expected to drag a palm branch behind them at night, a requirement variously explained by the need to alert others to their presence or to mark their paths so that high-caste people can see the route by which a Thurumba passed and avoid it next day.[74]

Anthropologists usually define caste either as an ethnographic term applicable only to India[75] or in a broader, cross-cultural sense as *"a hierarchy of groups in a society, membership in which is determined by birth"*[76]—a definition that extends the use of "caste" to many other contexts, among them the racial situation of the United States. Those who wish to limit the term to India argue, for example, that American blacks do not constitute a true caste, because there is no uniform and encompassing religious justification for black-white relations that would place black and white Americans in an interrelated system of privileges and obligations. Their criticism is valid, but ignores the fact that such a definition does not fully apply to any place in India,[77] and that there are strong cultural and psychological parallels to be found, for example, between the outcaste experience in India and the life situations of such groups as American blacks and the *burakumin* of Japan.

It is useful to note that outcastes are generally viewed as impure and defiling individuals with whom one should not eat. Ideally in India, *commensality,* or eating together, should be restricted to members of the same caste; those of superior caste should not accept water or food, especially cooked food, from lower castes.[78] High castes should also avoid any kind of close contact, especially sexual intercourse, with those beneath them. To have such contact is to befoul oneself. Groups so ostracized suffer from intense conflict between desire to express resentment and realization that such behavior will often be met with quick, sometimes deadly, retaliation. In general, they either fully internalize rage by accepting "inferiority" as merited by their defiling outcaste stigma[79] or they direct it against others of their group. Seldom does the dominant group feel the brunt of the outcaste's hostility; when expressed, it is usually in an incoherent and unplanned rage that is easily countered.

Clearly, the association of castes with traditional occupations has been altered by the increasing urbanization and industrialization of Indian society.[80] Most obviously, some castes such as the Tannakaras of Jaffna, Sri Lanka (Ceylon), who traditionally kept elephants, have lost their original occupations altogether; mechanization has left other groups, such as oil-crushers, with little work.[81] The growing dissociation of caste with occupation became important with the establishment of a bureaucratic service under the British, and was accelerated by various other caste-free occupations such as work on the Suez Canal or on the railroads and rubber estates of Malaysia.[82]

At first most Brahmins seemed to regard Western occupations as beneath their dignity. The Englishman who brought these occupations was nearly a paragon of defilement, eating pork and beef, drinking alcoholic beverages, smoking tobacco. Yet many sensed that the future lay in adopting British ways, and a number of the most influential Brahmin families used position to maximize their status in the new order. The result of the Brahmin's Westernization, Srinivas says, "was that they interposed themselves between the British and the rest of the native population . . . [producing] a new and secular caste system superimposed on the traditional system in which the British, the new Kshatriyas, stood at the top, while the Brahmins occupied the second position, and the others stood at the base of the pyramid."[83] Alert Brahmins were not alone in maximizing their positions within the new order. Many low-caste individuals prospered under the British, far surpassing in wealth and education members of higher castes too conservative to sense that education and individual ability were becoming important new criteria for occupation and social status.

In general, evidence suggests that caste is becoming less and less important as a primary source of social status. Reports even from rural India show that remittances returned by migrant industrial workers and the effect of the passage of national antidiscriminatory legislation have placed the old caste-based social stratification in a state of flux. "The new ideology," as Den Ouden says, "pointedly emphasizes the importance of occupation and of income, and, consequently, of political power and all else people can obtain with money."[84] This "new ideology" is not, however, egalitarian. In fact, it seems to be emerging as a more set form of class than is generally found in the West.

Rigid as the new status system may prove to be, ample evidence exists that at least a class-like structure is beginning to dominate in India's cities, although high-caste position may give certain individuals a head start in the new system. Wages of north Indian migrants studied by Rowe averaged rupees 124 monthly for those from the landlord castes (Kshatriya), in contrast to wages of the average artisan caste (Shudra) of Rs 91.59, and Rs 70.82 for low-caste agriculturalists.[85] The Poona factories studied by Bopegamage and Veeraraghavan showed inordinate Brahmin representation in managerial and higher technical and administrative positions, while depressed castes were clustered in unskilled trades.[86]

Still, caste identification seems significantly less important in the urban context. When people from the countryside near Poona in western India were asked, "how would you identify yourself to a visitor in the village?" they tended to give their caste first, then their place of residence. In other words, most said "I am a nao-Buddha," or "I am a Gurav," following this with a locational statement such as "I am from Lake Wadi" or "I am from Malthan." Urban Poona workers, on the other hand, responded to the same question by giving name first, then occupation.

The difference is even more marked if the three most important sources of personal identity are considered: 71.5 percent of all villagers listed caste as one of the most relevant aspects of their identity to a stranger (57.6 percent ranked caste first), while only 6.1 percent of the city respondents mentioned caste. Only 31.8 percent of rural respondents listed occupation as one of the most important parts of their identity, while 49.3 percent of urbanites did so. Finally, only 37.1 percent of the rural population felt their names were one of the three most important aspects of their identity, while 92 percent of city dwellers thought so.[87] In rural areas people still tend to feel that a group, birth-ascribed identity of caste and place of origin is fundamental; in urban areas there is a strong tendency to identify oneself by personal and achieved characteristics.

Responses to the question, "which groups in your town or village have a high status and are there any other groups besides these?" produced similar results. Approximately 80 percent of villagers gave answers in terms of caste, while about 90 percent of the urban industrial group gave occupational answers, such as lawyers, engineers, and professors.

One area in which caste remains of primary importance in the city is marriage. In a Sentence Completion Test administered to the rural and urban Poona samples, 92.1 percent of rural people completed the sentence "I want my daughter to marry a ——" with "own casteman," while only 6 percent responded "any educated person." The urban population agreed that caste was the first consideration in marriage: 70.9 percent completed the sentence with the statement "own casteman," although some expression of noncaste liberalism occurred in such answers as "boy of her liking" (6.1 percent), "progressive young man" (5.4 percent), "educated Hindu boy" (2.7 percent), or other responses such as "engineer" and "factory-owner" (5.4 percent).

The tendency for intercaste liberalism to stop short of marriage has often been noted. Srinivas has astutely discussed the manner in which the increasing division of labor gradually makes certain defiling occupations (like the personal handling of human excrement) unnecessary, and the fact that widespread industrialization can be increasingly expected to break down residential segregation and in other ways defuse intercaste tensions. Coeducation, he feels, is certain to make intercaste marriages more frequent; but he adds, "I would urge reformers to go slow on this [as] marriage is a 'hard-point' and too much propaganda at this stage may frighten the upper castes into taking a stand against all reforms."[88]

Ames's study of the industrial city of Jamshedpur in eastern India produced similar results. "Caste is for the traditional villages," his informants told him, "not for the modern towns." As one worker said, "I live with other workers, eat with them and work with them; I do not move with supervisors or the management, even if they are members of my caste, because they belong to a different class."[89] One should reside in neighborhoods based on class—a type of residence encouraged by company housing—and not concern oneself with fellow workers' castes. Indeed, one should not even ask another person his caste.

In reality, caste is important in filling certain service occupations (for example, sweepers, cobblers, and priests) and often is important in factory hiring and promotion. One entire factory department studied by Ames had been filled by members of the same caste, and certain personnel officers in Jamshedpur factories have been accused of favoring their own kin. The people of Jamshedpur, he feels, maintain a "pluralistic or relativistic ethical system" such that

> there is no inconsistency in befriending or eating with a low-caste man in the city and ignoring that same person in the village. It is a man's duty to adjust his actions to suit time, place and circumstance . . . rather than follow general rules blindly, a man should discover a way of behavior most appropriate for the occasion and most suited to his company. A worker therefore adjusts willingly and easily to the demands of city life, and he readjusts with equal ease to the demands of village life when he returns there for the marriage of his daughter, funeral of his elder, or simply for his annual vacation.[90]

It would be a mistake to conclude that a breakdown in traditional ways has suddenly led to what sometimes seems a cynical manipulation of class and caste patterns of behavior. Caste has itself been vigorously manipulated through the ages. Castes often have claimed higher status and seen their claims accepted or rejected by members of other castes for reasons of expediency. Opportunism often leads to violation of caste laws, especially if the situation can be defined as private. Class and Westernization have aided identity manipulation by adding new dimensions to identity, and by making it possible to conceal caste and ethnic background by wearing Western clothes and participating in organizations in which caste is technically irrelevant. Within a class-based context, however, caste can still be invoked in interpersonal relations when this seems beneficial.

An example of an extreme form of identity manipulation is provided by a traditional entertainer who travels from town to town making his living by assuming various identities (policeman, transvestite, Anglo-Indian, rich man) and fooling shopkeepers with his different guises on separate days. After a series of successful deceptions he reveals himself to those he has fooled and requests payment.[91] The humor rests, of course, on the fact that most urban social interaction (especially for shopkeepers) is based upon confidence that individuals can be quickly categorized by appearances, and dealt with in terms of a set of stereotypes appropriate to their category.

Studies focusing on the influence of class divisions *within* specific castes provide insight into another aspect of the increased differentiation and realignment of the population that modern urban life has brought, along the lines of occupation, income, wealth, and power. In research among the Brahmins of a suburb of Dharwar in northwestern Mysore state, Chekki found that a class structure definitely existed: about 20 percent of the Brahmins belonged to the upper class of professional people, 63 percent were middle-class with white collar jobs, and 17 percent were lower-class, working as factory workers, artisans, priests to the poor, astrologers, and cooks. As elsewhere, education is of paramount social importance. Education of Brahmin girls has become more common as the value of companionship in marriage has risen in importance. Parents often give their daughter a minimum education of high school or some college in the hope of making her a better marital catch and thus reducing her dowry.

The Brahmin upper and middle classes maintain a good deal of social distance from their lower-class caste-mates, generally coming into contact only on ritual occasions when interaction is inevitable. On such occasions, it is still felt that kinship bonds supersede class considerations, but interaction is nevertheless clearly affected by socioeconomic differences. No matter how great the expressed solidarity, those of upper and lower class know that they will tacitly avoid each other's company in ordinary circumstances. Marriage, too, generally follows class lines within caste—70 percent of all Brahmin marriages in the suburb were between individuals of the same class, and most of the rest were between individuals of adjacent classes— and there is some indication that intersubcaste marriages along class lines are becoming more common.[92]

Economic considerations have also had an impact on the composition of families and the exercise of authority within the family unit. In a 1965 Bombay study, the nuclear family was found to be the most common single basis of residency, in both middle- and working-class families. Among the middle class especially, nuclear families predominated: 51.9 percent of middle-class families lived in nuclear households, while only 31.5 percent of the working class had nuclear-type residences. Traditional joint family residence, too, was more common in the middle class (15 percent) than in the lower class (10.3 percent). Only in non-normative residences, including such matrilineal extensions as mother's brother and his wife and children, or mother's mother, did the working-class percentage exceed that of the middle-class group (58.2 to 33.1 percent). Close analysis of the data suggests that lower-class individuals are often pressed into culturally unrecognized living arrangements by economic necessity, a hypothesis confirmed by the fact that those middle-class families who had similar non-normative living arrangements also had the lowest economic resources. Those whose incomes placed them securely in the middle class tended to utilize the choice allowed by such security to opt for the traditionally valued joint family residence.

Responses from 1,211 Bombay seventh-grade children to queries on "who has the final say" in family decisions (questions concerning spending, where a vacation should be spent, and so on) showed that children from middle-class families generally perceived their fathers as less dominant than did their counterparts from working-class families. A strong tendency existed in the middle class for family decisions to be shared by husband and wife. Thus, a wife's entry into the husband's joint family minimizes her authority, while the setting up of a separate and distinct residence places husband and wife in a more egalitarian relationship.[93]

In Indian political life, caste-based interests are generally secondary, although caste has often helped form a strong political power base for both high castes[94] and untouchables—as it did for the respected untouchable lawyer, economist, and first postindependence law minister, Dr. B. R. Ambedkar.[95] Study of the deference and friendship patterns in the city councils of Agra and Poona demonstrated that caste was only one of several factors related to the formation of friendships with and the evaluation of fellow council members. Friendships were formed more along party than caste lines; and expressed respect or admiration for other council members seemed to be based as least as much upon individual personal qualities and leadership as on caste or party affiliation.[96]

Clearly, caste in India has probably always been more flexible than it is usually portrayed. The options of sanskritizing, passing, opting out of the system by becoming a holy man, or converting to a noncaste religion such as Buddhism have always been available for those who find their caste position unacceptable.

But today, more than ever before, caste is in a state of flux. The increasing urbanization and industrialization of India has removed millions from their traditional occupations and placed them in work milieus which no longer favor maintenance of traditional caste idioms. Increasingly for many urbanites, class appears to have taken the place of caste in their lives. Just how far the transition will proceed remains in doubt. Will caste continue to decline in general importance, persisting only in such sensitive areas as marriage and perhaps even declining altogether, or will it perhaps enjoy periodic revivals? While the information from India is as yet too fragmentary to state with certainty that the significance of ascribed status (caste) will eventually decline in favor of achieved position (class), it is useful to take a brief look at the role of caste today among overseas Indians in Malaysia.

Caste and Class among Overseas Indians

Movement of Hindus outside India, especially to Southeast Asia, has an ancient history. For those conscious of their caste status and concerned with avoiding ritual pollution, travel among alien peoples has been a major undertaking. The arrival of the British and the incorporation of India into the British Empire encouraged a quantum increase in emigration—at first to work on the rubber plantations of Malaysia and the sugar estates of South Africa and the West Indies, later as merchants and professionals in these regions. Today, important Indian communities are found in Malaysia, Fiji, Guiana, Surinam, Trinidad, and South and East Africa. Studies of caste organizations there report attenuation of the importance of caste in day-to-day life and increased intercaste marriage, although caste endogamy is still strong.[97]

During my tenure as lecturer at an urban Malaysian university, I had the opportunity to observe the role played by caste among Indian students.[98] Conducting courses in race relations within a context in which ethnic interaction is a particularly sensitive issue, I structured the cross-cultural study of ethnic relations partly within a caste perspective. My purpose was not so much to argue for the primacy of such an approach as to illustrate the widespread distribution of systems of structured inequality, systems that transcend race and ethnicity as such.

I soon realized that many of my Indian students were furious with me for raising the issue of caste, even within what I felt was a relatively detached, academic framework. Searching for explanations, I spoke with many of them at length. The hostility appears to have risen for the several reasons that follow.

1) The low position of most Indians in Malaysian society gives them something of the "virtue of the oppressed": they can recoup some losses in the instrumental sphere of society

through the satisfying accusation that Malays, Chinese, and Europeans—but not Indians—are "racist." Caste-consciousness for most is equated with racism, and devotion of class time to the explanation of caste (a subject fascinating to most Chinese and Malay students, who were largely ignorant of caste-based divisions among Indians) was perceived as tantamount to directing a charge of racism at Indians.

    2) A number of students, as the descendants of immigrants who had come largely to work as estate laborers, were apparently low-caste. Incentives to cling to caste ideology were largely negative for them.

    3) Discussion of the concept threatened to disrupt what unity had been achieved among Indian students by bringing to the surface a sensitive and divisive issue which, by tacit agreement, had been suppressed.

    4) Caste, in the eyes of many students seeking education at a university structured along Western lines, was a "backward" concept, a sore reminder of the lack of modernity of much of the Indian population.

Despite reluctance to discuss caste, its presence was clearly felt on campus. Several students privately related to me an incident in which a female Brahmin student hitched a ride from another female Indian student. The other student, cramped in the small automobile, touched the Brahmin and was severely reprimanded. Another Brahmin student was asked during freshman orientation ceremonies "what" she was. The student who posed the query anticipated the response "Indian," or "Malaysian." Instead, to his annoyance (and the annoyance of those Indians who related the event) he was told: "I am a Brahmin."

The mention of Indian Christians by Hindu students was frequently prefaced by statements indicating that Christian converts are invariably from lower castes. Most Christian students, rather than equanimously accept this charge as irrelevant to the doctrine of Christianity, attempted to refute it. One especially devout Christian student became so incensed at frequency of the allegation that she felt compelled to reveal that her grandfather had converted, not to escape low-caste status, but to ingratiate himself with the ruling British colonialists. "My family are high-caste Christians," she explained. Another telling incident occurred in the course of a small section meeting, in which the sole Indian present volunteered that a group of Indians selling cakes on a city street "must be Muslim." When pressed for the rationale, she burst into tears rather than admit to the caste-based commensal taboos of Indians.

Curious about the reasons for the intense response by Indian students to discussion of caste, when most disclaimed its relevance to their lives, I encouraged one of my students, Rita Sellapah, to collaborate with me in an attempt to discern the actual role of caste among the university's Indian population. At first, Rita met in semistructured interviews with various Indian students and attempted to elicit their views on caste. After several weeks of interviewing, during which she was ostracized by most of the Indian students for her own "caste-consciousness" in undertaking the project, we discontinued this approach.

As caste was clearly a sensitive issue that students were reluctant to discuss, we finally decided that only a carefully distributed blind questionnaire, worded to appeal to the academic commitment of the students, could tap the depths of caste feeling. A majority of the students (38) responded to the questionnaire. In response to the general question, "how important is caste to your life?" 27 students (10 of whom were Christian) indicated it was not important, 5 somewhat important, and 3 very important. When asked how important caste was to their parents, only 5 (3 Christians) indicated it was not important, 18 (5 Christians) somewhat important, and 12 (2 Christians) very important.

The clear discrepancy in stated importance of caste between students and parents is open to varying interpretations. It could be argued that the importance of caste has declined in this generation, or that caste-consciousness declines with greater education (only a small fraction of parents had had any exposure to university education). Or, perhaps the blame for caste-based interaction is being shifted to parents—as a consequence of which, having left the atmosphere of the university, which encourages egalitarian interaction, the students will perpetuate the system in much the same fashion as do their parents.

As demonstrated in other research with Indian emigrant communities, caste-based commensal patterns among the students queried seem to have become relatively insignificant. Only the general proscription against eating beef remains the commensal badge of Indians as a whole. Many of the students gave responses to our enquiries concerning eating habits that indicated they were wholly unaware of Hindu proscriptions on source of cooked foods. Of those students who understood and responded, only 4 stated that their eating habits reflected caste status, while 23 (7 Christians) indicated that they did not follow caste proscriptions in their diet. Again, parents were portrayed in a more traditional mold: 11 students indicated that their parents' commensal patterns followed caste rules, while 15 (6 Christians) stated they did not.

Perhaps the most interesting responses were to the question of whether there were students on campus who were particularly caste-conscious. According to 14 of the students, there were many; 3 students indicated that caste-consciousness was something of a "problem" on campus; 7 said it was not; 12 indicated that they were unaware of any caste-consciousness. Of the latter, however, 11 were Christian or professed no religion. Interestingly, those who felt that caste-consciousness was a problem on campus condemned it with unanimity. The few who recognized the problem but did not directly condemn it tended to excuse the offenders on grounds of socialization.

Not surprisingly, caste was rated most important in the area of marriage. Of the Hindu students, 14 indicated that their parents would strongly prefer them to marry within their caste, or near-caste; 3 said there would be some objection if they violated caste endogamy; only 4 indicated there would be no objection. Of the Christian students, 4 indicated strong parental preference for caste endogamy, 1 some preference, and 4 no preference, or uncertainty about their parents' response.

From class discussions, from our survey, and from in-depth interviews with Indian students, it seems that there is less commitment to caste among the students than their parents. The declining attachment seems largely the result of such factors as need to interact with class elites within one's community—whose paucity of numbers often precludes maintenance of strict caste divisions. With education and entry into the modern sector of Malaysia's economy, the appeal of alignments based upon class—of interaction based upon common economic and educational lot—seems greater than that of those tied to caste.

Caste in the lives of most Indian students appears no longer relevant in day-to-day interactions. Sheer lack of numbers dooms most attempts to form friendship and marriage alliances through matching class and caste criteria. As a result, caste seems confined to a covert, almost embarrassing, role. Its presence often makes itself felt against the student's will in such crucial events as marriage, in which non-university-educated parents—unable to perceive the salience of new, class-based ties—may insist upon a marriage that meets caste proscriptions but does violence to the student's desire to find a mate among members of his own class. The extreme discomfort with which many students relate to caste is undoubtedly the result of its ingrained, but repugnant presence in their own lives.

Caste ideology—at least among the educated Malaysian Indian elite—justifies a hierarchy that is no longer relevant to the bases upon which that elite is formed. Consequently, its end is in sight.

SOUTHEAST AND EAST ASIA: ETHNICITY AND CLASS

The ethnic backgrounds of the peoples of Southeast Asia can best be understood through reference to the two major aspects of the region's geography: 1) its central position between the ancient cultural centers of India and China and 2) its rugged mountain and jungle topography, which segments the mainland into three major mountain ranges (one of which extends past the mainland to provide the backbone of the Indonesian archipelago) and three broad, flat valleys. Historical Chinese influence is most evident in Burma, Laos, Thailand, and Vietnam in the tonal character of the principal languages of each nation and in the physical appearance of most of their populations, whose original homelands are thought to have been in southwestern China.

Vietnam, its lowlands separated from the rest of this general region by its easternmost mountain ranges, was long a province of China and can properly be considered an offshoot of Chinese culture. The lowland cultures of Thailand, Laos, Cambodia, and Burma have been much more profoundly influenced by India, which provided their principal religion, Theravada Buddhism, and many aspects of daily cultural life. South of Thailand, in present-day Malaysia and Indonesia, Indian influence has had a prehistoric time depth that can be seen in the Hindu character of the region's ancient empires and in the more recent dominance of Islam, which arrived via Indian traders.

Both Chinese and Indian influence have been most marked among the dominant, culturally advanced lowland peoples of Southeast Asia. Peoples of the hill and mountain regions have generally lived beyond control of the lowland states, as independent tribes speaking a number of mutually unintelligible languages, living in simpler, less hierarchical societies based upon slash-and-burn (swidden) agriculture.[100]

In recent years, new dimensions have been added to the ancient separation of feudal lowland societies and tribal hill groups by the arrival of European colonialists and the later influx of Chinese and Indians. Small and somewhat socially distinct Chinese trading communities were long a feature of Southeast Asian cities. But with the establishment of colonial empires, millions of southern Chinese emigrated to the "South Seas" in the hope of earning enough to support themselves and send money home to ancestral villages. With the exception of Burma, where Indians occupied many of the middle-man niches, Chinese acted as economic intermediaries between colonialists and indigenous inhabitants. Although not always trusted by the colonizers, Chinese businessmen performed the crucial function of creating wealth and helping to establish "dual economies" without which colonial adventures might well have failed.[101] Chinese workers also developed the tin mines of Malaya and established a large number of small spice- and fruit-producing farms.

Today, some 14,000,000 Chinese descendants of these emigrants live in the nations of Southeast Asia. With the possible exception of the numerous antigovernment hill peoples of Burma (and to a much lesser degree of Laos and Vietnam) who have established de facto independent states, and the Muslim populations of southern Thailand and the southern Philippines, overseas Chinese constitute the region's major ethnic problem. They remain a major component of the plural societies that Furnivall found so characteristic of the region:

> In Burma, as in Java, probably the first thing that strikes the visitor is the medley of peoples—European, Chinese, Indian and native. It is in the strictest sense a medley, for they mix but do not combine. Each group holds by its own religion, its own culture and language, its own ideas and ways. As individuals they meet, but only in the market place, in buying and selling. There is a plural society, with different sections of the community living side by side, but separately, within the same political unit. Even in the economic sphere there is a division of labour along racial lines. Natives, Chinese, Indians and Europeans all have different functions, and within each major group subsections have particular occupations. There is, as it were, a caste system, but without the religious basis that incorporates caste in social life in India.[102]

To reduce Southeast Asian ethnic diversity to a manageable level, this discussion will be segmented first into consideration of the effects of urbanization upon the interaction of indigenous tribal and lowland groups. Then, the relations existing between members of overseas Chinese communities and local peoples with whom they reside will be considered. In Southeast Asia, as in Africa, our major concern is with the strength of the persistence of tribal and ethnic differences, and the impact such diversity has upon the formation of unified national societies.

The best example of the impact of urbanization upon a Southeast Asian tribal people is provided by Bruner's studies of the Batak of Sumatra's Lake Toba region.[103] As discussed earlier, migration of Toba Batak to the coastal city of Medan has not severed their strong ties with rural relatives, despite the tremendous experiential gulf which often exists between them. Several factors are undoubtedly involved in Toba Batak maintenance of tight kin and ethnic loyalties. They are Christian in a Muslim nation; their social organization is based upon geographically specific patrilineages which, coupled with the Christian-Muslim division, makes intermarriage with their principal neighbors, the matrilineal Minangkabau, even less likely; and they have a reputation as crude and aggressive intruders among peoples who pride themselves on politeness.

The Toba Batak, like most tribal peoples, tend "to treat the limits of their tribal group as the frontiers of humanity and to regard everyone outside them as foreigners."[104] For them, people are either kin or nonkin. When two members of the group meet for the first time they go through a process they term *martarombo* and *martutur*: uncovering relational ties which bind one to the other so that a kin basis for interaction can be established. Despite the fact that there are over one million Toba Batak today, and that hundreds of thousands have left their mountain homelands and are living throughout Indonesia, the combination of localized lineages and wife-giving/wife-receiving relations between patrilineages ultimately links all members of the group into some tie of kinship.

In Medan, Toba Batak come into contact with other Batak, Atjehnese, Minangkabau, Malays, Javanese, Chinese, Indians, and dozens of other groups. Since they are not concentrated in any one section of the city, members of several of these groups are often their neighbors. Close proximity, however, has not led to close friendship or cross-ethnic identity. During the early period of Indonesian independence in the 1950's, a number of Batak were killed in conflicts with their Muslim neighbors, undoubtedly as much because they had incurred resentment by occupying prestigious white collar jobs under the Dutch as because of their Christianity.

Urban Batak, of course, quickly realized the inadequacy of the undifferentiated nonkin/non-Batak category for coping with the city's peoples, although it remains the basic and primary division. Even "the most urbanized modernized Batak," Bruner says, "starts with the same basic binary opposition, with the one difference that he has acquired the conceptual equipment to make a multiplicity of finer classifications within the class non-Batak . . . to be urbanized may be equated with or measured by the degree of expansion of the scope of categorizations of non-Batak."[105] These divisions of the outside into finer ethnic distinctions are joined with stereotypes providing behavioral guidelines to direct a businessman, or to tell a teenager when he must back down from a fight. Young urban Batak children are taught by their parents thus:

> one can fight with a Javanese, but the best strategy, they say, is to yell at him, and he will probably retreat. If there is the slightest argument with an Atjehnese or a Minangkabau, the standing instructions are to return home immediately and report it to the parents so as to prevent the conflict from spreading. Regarding the Karo Batak . . . the instructions are to try to avoid them. As one mother over-communicated to her children, "they only think of money, they are heartless, we hate them, they are slovenly and dirty."[106]

The distinctions Toba Batak make between themselves and others can be replicated throughout Indonesia. In west Java, the Sudanese/non-Sudanese distinction is primary, as is the division between Minangkabau/non-Minangkabau in Padang, western Sumatra. Bruner hypothesizes that "the initial differentiation in interpersonal relations in Indonesia is on the basis of ethnicity . . . There may be contexts in which the hypothesis does not apply . . . in which the frontiers of humanity were extended to all others, but I do not foresee that this will occur very frequently in Indonesia in the immediate future."[107]

The ethnic typing among indigenous groups that Bruner finds so persistent in today's Indonesia is also present in Malaysia. Mention of the largely Minangkabau region of Negri Sembilan, or of "Penang Malays" or of Banjarese, immediately conjurs up, to other Malays, physical and behavioral stereotypes of these groups. To refer to another as "Jawa" (Javanese) is to suggest that he is probably a hard worker but also dirty in personal habits. Kelantanese Malays are thought to be passionate people and are renowned for the power of their magic and the beauty and independence of their women, qualities often displayed through prostitution. Somewhat paradoxically, Kelantanese are also considered very pious Muslims. But unlike the situation that pertains in Indonesia, the fineness of distinctions between indigenous peoples of Malaysia is largely overridden by the much more important Malay/non-Malay distinction. All Malays considered together account for only 46.8 percent of the population; 34.1 percent are Chinese, 9 percent are Indian, and 8.7 percent are indigenous non-Malay groups largely native to East Malaysia (northern Borneo).

Distinctions between groups as distinct as the Javanese and Kelantanese collapse into a common Malay category in the face of the single most salient ethnic division: Malays and Chinese. The Chinese are not a homogeneous group. They are divided into numerous mutually unintelligible speech groups, each originating in a different area of China and having somewhat different customs. For the Chinese, too, speech group differences have been submerged by realization of their common Chineseness in the face of Malay political dominance. Indians, as mentioned earlier, are also segmented by religion, language, geographic origin, caste, and increasingly class; but in most situations Indians are either ignored or placed in the non-Malay category.

Malaysia, in seeking to forge its identity as an independent nation, is keenly aware of its race problem. National racial policy calls for the favoring of Malays in scholarships, loans, government, and private employment, in hope that part of the economically based anti-Chinese feeling among Malays will be dissipated by a greater Malay share in the national wealth. The government has also instituted a policy designed to assimilate the Chinese into a national Malaysian culture which is essentially Malay: the national language is Bahasa Malaysia (that is, Malay), the national religion is Islam (the Malay religion), the sultans and king and queen are Malay; even the "national culture," which is supposed to be based on a syncretism of Malay, Chinese, and Indian traditions, is clearly seen by Malay government officials as Malay culture.

The greatest problem facing Malaysia's Malay leaders in their efforts to form a "national culture" is simply the fact that Chinese invariably regard Chinese culture as far superior to Malay. Chinese culture, they maintain, was forged through a long history of civilization, while Malay culture is basically tribal. Becoming Malay and adhering to Malay religion and tradition would be a major step down in the minds of most Chinese. In addition to such attitudes, the structures of Chinese and Malay societies differ radically. Traditional

Chinese social structure is based principally upon localized patrilineages whose members were bound together by common surnames
and religious obligations towards ancestors. Immigration of only a
few members of numerous patrilineages made continuation of this
tradition difficult overseas. Instead, overseas Chinese societies tended
to organize around common speech groups, similar geographic origin,
and the same surname. The Chinese emphasis on patrilineally inherited
surnames has provided a basic cleavage between them and the
region's indigenous peoples. With the exception of the Vietnamese,
the use of surnames had been virtually unknown in the region: Thai
and Javanese knew each other merely by single given names, and
most non-Javanese Muslims followed a pattern of referring to themselves by a combination of given name and father's given name.[108]

A characteristic of early Chinese immigration during the pre-
colonial and early colonial periods was the taking of local wives by
Chinese men. Offspring of these unions were sometimes assimilated
into the population; or as in the case of the so-called Baba Chinese
of Malaya, a distinct language and cultural tradition was developed
from a fusion of Chinese and Malay heritages.[109] Immigration of large
Chinese communities during the colonial period, and especially the
arrival of Chinese women, virtually halted what small steps towards
Chinese assimilation had been achieved in Indonesia and Malaya and
retarded assimilation in Thailand. As the overseas Chinese communities expanded, they developed their own regulatory and governing mechanisms through secret societies (known as Triad, Heaven and
Earth, or Tong societies)[110] and surname and other voluntary associations.

These groups further insulated most Chinese from real contact
with local tradition and political control. In French-administered
areas, the various speech groups dealt with colonial authorities and
indigenous peoples through a *chef de congrégation*, or speech group
leader, chosen by the French from among several candidates elected
by the Chinese business community.[111] In Dutch-ruled Indonesia,
and to a lesser degree in British Malaya, Chinese communities were
administered through an individual known as the Kapitan China, who
commanded obedience of the Chinese because he was usually the
head or a prominent member of a secret society.

Thus, in the colonially administered areas of Southeast Asia,
the Chinese were encouraged to, and did, maintain as traditionally a
Chinese form of organization as possible. Such a policy was effective
for colonial administration; but it helped keep the Chinese doubly
isolated, as most overseas Chinese were far from identifying not only

with the country in which they lived, but even with other Chinese who were not members of their speech group. Common identity as Chinese was not even significantly developed. As W. E. Willmott astutely remarks,

> given the traditional Chinese view of the world, little distinction, apart from relative distance, would have been made between cities in China proper and elsewhere "under heaven." For the villager in Kwangtung, for example, a move to Singapore was in many ways comparable to a move to Foochow or Hangchow. In either case he was entering a foreign milieu where solidarity and fellowship could be sought among emigres from his home district, and where "foreign" officials dealt with associations rather than individuals.[112]

Little wonder that when the 1940's and 1950's brought independence to the nations of Southeast Asia, overseas Chinese carried on their tradition of isolation. Postcolonial Chinese-local relations have been most tense in the Muslim nations of Malaysia and Indonesia. In Muslim eyes the Chinese are doubly detested, first as intruders who have "stolen" the local wealth through business practices contrary to Islam (usury, for example). Second, the Chinese are non-believers who keep dogs and eat pork, repugnant to Muslims. Given such Muslim attitudes and the insistence that Chinese adopt local language, customs, and religion, it is not surprising that the gulf is strongest in these countries. Indeed, even if a Chinese wished to assimilate, he would find the process a difficult one fraught with suspicion about his real motives.

Despite major government efforts to forge a national culture and language (both Malay) for all Malaysia's peoples, the Chinese are likely to remain unassimilated in the foreseeable future.[113] The salience of this division between Chinese and Malays has also helped submerge the development of class as a basis of social organization. Although extreme differences in wealth, access to power, and life style exist within the two groups, members of both Malay and Chinese lower classes identify with others of similar ethnic status.[114] But upper-class Chinese and Malays, as well as Indians, do not always reciprocate; they often recognize stronger ties of affinity with others of their class, regardless of ethnic background. Ironically, this sense of cross-ethnic solidarity is largely the result of university educations that are given in English rather than in the official national language.

Thailand's Chinese experience has been radically different from that of Malaysia. The *total* Chinese population of both countries is approximately the same, although Chinese represent a much smaller proportion of the population in Thailand than in Malaysia. The most difficult problem in calculating the number of Chinese in Thailand is deciding who *is* still Chinese. Unlike the Chinese in Malaysia, Chinese in Thailand seem to eventually assimilate. Today, although Chinese account for about 10 percent of total Thai population, and the population of Bangkok is generally estimated as at least half Chinese in ancestry, the great majority of these people would probably identify themselves as Thai. People who are obviously wholly Chinese in descent will sometimes deny their Chinese background.

Most interesting is the fact that those Chinese who have been most successful in Thailand are precisely those likely to be most assimilated to Thai society. William Skinner, in a superb study entitled *Leadership and Power in the Chinese Community of Thailand*, reports that 94 percent of those rated "most influential" by fellow Chinese are able to speak Thai well, while one-third of the "least influential" leaders speak little or no Thai. In interviewing Chinese leaders in Bangkok, Skinner was impressed

> by a wide variation in the degree of apparent assimilation and acculturation among them. Considerations of ancestry aside (any number of ethnic Thai leaders being as much Chinese in ancestry as many of these Chinese leaders), several of them seemed more Thai than Chinese—in mannerisms, dress, personal and business surroundings. Some Chinese leaders even identified themselves as Thai or stated, usually with pride, that they were considered by many people to be Thai.[115]

One businessman whom Skinner interviewed "boasted that he had 'made a Siamese out of [his] oldest son,' who will take over the family business."[116] Boonsanong's study of Chinese assimilation in Bangkok confirms that Skinner's findings for the elite apply to the Chinese community as a whole. Noting first that "the task of defining a Chinese and a Thai person is not an easy one," he reports that most people who consider themselves Chinese are willing to develop intimate friendships with Thai; those who lack close Thai friends usually have little opportunity for close Thai contact. Indeed, nearly half of the Chinese he surveyed reported that some members of their households were Thai. Boonsanong also found intermarriage common: 24 percent of the less educated nongovernment employees, 39.7 percent of the more educated nongovernment employees, and 64.7 percent of the government employees studied said that they or one of their children or siblings are married to a Thai.[117]

Skinner's and Boonsanong's observations can be easily confirmed by simple comparison of the Chinese populations of Malaysia and Thailand. Most Thai-Chinese seem to have given up even such crucial traditional Chinese customs as the keeping of an ancestral altar. Malaysian Chinese generally adhere so closely to Chinese tradition that a visitor to the streets of many Malaysian cities might conclude that he was in China, or at least Taiwan.

The question, of course, is why Chinese have been so willing to assimilate to Thai society. Several factors seem to be involved:

(1) Thai society has traditionally incorporated foreign peoples and recognized them as Thai if they speak Thai, behave as Thai, and profess adherence to Theravada Buddhism (although one can be Muslim or Christian and still be Thai).

2) Thais are proud of Thai culture and grace. Many Thai who resent the Chinese presence in their country seem to feel that it is the *Chinese* who possess an inferior culture, with their toleration of loud speech and what Thai consider disgusting personal habits (such as clearing one's throat in public).

3) The Thai government has carefully and methodically followed an assimilative educational policy by requiring that Chinese children be educated in Thai. It has expressed a carrot-and-stick economic approach to the Chinese by giving certain business concessions to those with Thai business partners or those who have become Thai citizens, at the same time taxing aliens and restricting certain occupations to Thai.

Of all these factors, the most important is doubtless the permeability of Thai society, which places no rigid religious or cultural restrictions on foreigners. Unlike "entry into Malaydom," almost an all-or-nothing phenomenon requiring desertion of Chinese traditions, the process of Siamization is gradual and nearly imperceptible. More often than not, it is probably begun and achieved without most Chinese ever having realized that they were becoming Thai.

The notion of class is still poorly developed in Southeast Asia. Distinctions between peoples continue to be principally on the basis of ethnicity, behavior, or rural or urban residence. Thus most Thai, for example, divide others into "good" people and "bad" people; or Chinese, Thai, Lao, Indian, and *farang* (European); or city people and upcountry people. Although outsiders often analyze Thai social structure by distinguishing class groups,[118] Thai themselves usually rank status much more individualistically, distinguishing persons as individuals rather than on a basis of membership in broad, class-like strata.

To the degree that group cohesion based on common interests is felt, it is usually set in a vertical patron-client system of obligations and loyalties. A man's social position can be measured largely by the number and type of clients he has and by the strength of his own patron, so that Thai social organization can be seen as ordered upon the entourages of important men.[119] A sense of community between those of similar occupation but of different entourages is weak. Even individuals of relatively equal rank within the same entourage usually stress personal attachments to their patron and do not feel loyalties and obligations to one another. Emphasis on vertical patron-client connections has led Hanks to characterize Thai social order as being "like a bundle of fine golden chains of varying lengths, with only occasional cross-connections."[120] Powerful chains within the Thai military, if able to gain access to large resources (such as American aid) can develop immense entourages and completely dominate competing entourage chains. Smaller entourages in the customs department and the Bangkok electric company are able to survive through a service monopoly that permits them to hold a few hundred, or at most a few thousand retainers, but which is insufficient to provide a serious challenge to such dominant chains as those of the police and military. Much of the party confusion of Thailand's recent democratic experiment was related to the tendency to view political life as merely a ground upon which different entourages maneuver to maximize access to power and thus opportunity for survival or expansion.

The only social division common to most of Southeast Asia that approaches the horizontal stratification of class is that of royalty versus commoner. Such a division is, however, conceived in caste-like terms by peoples of the region. As one Malay university student said— in a discussion of Chinese complaints that Malaysian royalty is really just Malay, not *Malaysian*, royalty because Chinese and Indians cannot become sultans—"We can't either." For her, and for the other Malays who nodded in assent, royalty was a group above and beyond Malay society. The idea of class is clearly present among the educated, wealthy, and professional populations of Southeast Asia, but it is not yet generally recognized by the masses, who tend to incorporate elite government officials into the category of royal retainers.[121] Such an interpretation is logical when one considers, for example that until recently all three factions of the Laotian civil war were nominally headed by royal princes; that Prince (formerly King) Sihanouk was the titular leader of the Khmer Rouge; and that the recent prime ministers of Thailand have been members of the aristocracy, as were Malaysia's first two prime ministers, who directed the nation from independence in 1957 until 1976. Even in Burma, Vietnam, and Indonesia, where royal rule did not survive the colonial period, leaders generally seek to identify themselves as intimately as possible with the state in a manner reminiscent of royalty.

Even where royalty is still recognized, real power is in the hands of educated and wealthy elites. In Thailand, as a result of the growth of an intellectual elite and a professional civil service based principally upon educational achievement, effective control of the nation was wrested from the King in a constitutional coup in 1932. In Malaysia, too, the government is administered by a professional civil service, and the King and Sultans exist with restricted powers essentially as figureheads to provide legitimacy to the government. Elsewhere, too—in the Philippines, Indonesia, Vietnam, Cambodia, Laos, and Burma—education and achieved status have instigated the development of class systems based principally upon individual achievement, although recent official policy in the latter four is dedicated to the development of classless, egalitarian societies.

In general, Evers is undoubtedly correct, though premature, in his assertion that race and ethnic differences are declining in favor of class-based interest groups in Southeast Asia. Decrease in racial segregation and increasing co-residence of common class groups, he argues, has produced a "change in the social ecology of Southeast Asian cities . . . while race riots and conflicts between ethnic groups plagued Southeast Asian cities from their beginnings, a conflict based on class lines seems to be more likely in the future."[122]

In contrast to the nations of Southeast Asia, Japan is remarkably homogeneous. Its long isolation as an island archipelago has helped produce fairly uniform cultural traditions. Social stratification throughout most of the recorded past has been based upon feudal divisions between the nobility, its retainers (*samurai* and artisans), merchants, peasants, and various outcaste groups stigmatized by their occupations.[123] Today, merchants, peasants, and outcastes still continue as fairly distinct social categories. Industrialization of the nation, however, has helped create a vast array of new occupations. Chief among the effects of industrialization has been the emergence of a new middle class, comprised of white collar employees of large corporations and government bureaucracies, which has gradually replaced in power and influence the old middle class of small businessmen and landowners. Entry into this new group of *sarari* (salary) *men* is theoretically open to all who gain the educational credentials to be hired by a corporation.

The life of the *sarari man*, even in contrast to that of members of the old middle class, is almost unshakably secure. Once hired by a corporation, seniority outweighs individual merit, so an employee can usually predict his salary and position far into the future. But personal security comes at the price of occupational mobility: once an individual accepts a position in a company he is expected to remain with the firm throughout his working life, progressing gradually through its ranks. Even in times of severe financial crisis or depression the company will do all it can to avoid firing idle employees. In times of prosperity, it is expected that such company loyalty will be reciprocated in the working commitment of employees. Only obvious incompetence or misbehavior form proper grounds for dismissal, so the individual who changes companies "soils" his curriculum vitae; his motives for seeking a transfer and his loyalty to a future employer are suspect.[124]

From an external perspective, it seems obvious that Japan has moved from a feudal to a class-based industrial society, with the exception of remaining consciousness of the presence of communities of outcastes and Koreans. A view from the inside, however, shows remarkably little commitment to the idea that classes, or broad strata of individuals with similar background, occupation, education, and life style, truly exist in Japan.[125] The grafting of the model of an ideal and cohesive family upon the larger work world has tended to produce a strong and binding institutional identification that far transcends consciousness of common occupation within different institutions. Thus, printers working for company A tend to identify more strongly with co-workers of whatever rank or occupation than with printers of company B. The primacy of the place of interaction ("frame") as opposed to the character of the interaction ("attribute") was also evident in preindustrial Japan, where village of residence (frame) was a much more important source of personal identity and loyalty than occupation (attribute). Unlike Hindu India, conflicting loyalty between village identity and cross-village occupational identity was not particularly important. Guilds, too, never developed the significance in Japan that they had in many other regions of the world.[126]

What *is* particularly important in defining social status in Japan is the relative ranking of the company or other institution for which one works. Logically, if employment is lifelong and one is likely to occupy a gradual progression of increasingly prestigious positions, the company's reputation is particularly important. To be hired into a respected company, branch of government service, or university is a major, life-determining, goal for young people for which they begin to prepare themselves early in life.

While a great possibility of social mobility exists initially for the Japanese child, determination of his future social position begins in grammar school through the continuing process of "examination hell."[127] Performance in examinations given at each stage of his academic career determines whether or not he will be able to continue and the quality of school he will attend. Eventually, the young adult comes to the end of his academic career with credentials that direct him towards his company and future career. Entry into a company places him in the system of vertical stratification by institution that, Nakane says, forms the basis of the overall structure of Japanese society:

> Even if social classes like those in Europe can be detected in Japan, and even if something vaguely resembling those classes that are illustrated in the textbooks of western sociology can also be found in Japan, the point is that in actual society this stratification is unlikely to function and that it does not really reflect the social structure. In Japanese society it is really not a matter of workers struggling against capitalists or managers but of Company A ranged against Company B.
>
> . . .
>
> [The Japanese care] little about class differences. They are more interested in their relative rank, and so attention is focused upon the self and those in the immediate surroundings. The Japanese in general are virtually incapable of seeing society in terms of strata within which one may locate oneself, yet they will employ delicately graded criteria to distinguish the most minor relative differences between themselves and others.[128]

LATIN AMERICA: RACE, ETHNICITY, AND CLASS

On the eve of the European discovery of the Americas, both continents were populated solely by paleo-Asiatic peoples. The Spanish conquest of the Inca in Peru, the Aztec in Mexico, and other less centralized groups, and the partition of territory that followed, quickly complicated the ethnic situation in Latin America by adding a powerful ultramarine elite. Those born in Europe were known as *peninsulares*, while locally born offspring of European parents were termed *creoles* or *criollos*.

During the first years of colonization, few European women traveled to the New World and most men took Indian concubines and mistresses, beginning a process of phenotypic and cultural intermixture that produced distinct *mestizo* populations throughout the continent. Intermarriage, at least in the beginning, was encouraged by the colonial powers, who saw it as a way of augmenting the numbers of their subjects. The mestizo population increased by continued mestizo-Indian mixture. Through the gradual assimilation of Indians to Spanish language and culture, mestizos quickly became numerically much larger than peninsulares and creoles, often assuming an interstitial position between whites and Indians as small shopkeepers and landowners. Gradually the importance of the peninsulares declined, until the pan-continent independence movements of the early nineteenth century left creoles at the peak of caste-like social hierarchies, followed by mestizos and Indians. Further complicating the social matrix was the presence of large black populations brought to Brazil and the Caribbean to work plantations as slaves in place of Indian populations decimated by disease.

In Latin America—unlike North America, where large numbers of Europeans arrived to settle as farmers—Europeans came to establish mines, plantations, and large ranches worked by Indians and blacks. Consequently, the ratio of Europeans to Indians was low. In Mexico, for example, "at no time did [the white and Negro population] represent more than 1 to 2 per cent of the total population of the country."[129] Creole dominance of Indians in Latin America was a tenuous proposition, in which the development of strong mestizo groups was a crucial element. Mestizos, though mostly Indian in ancestry, emphasized their European background and looked down on Indians as a separate race. Mestizo-Indian relations everywhere assumed the character both of caste—in which Indians occupied the lowest occupations and deferred to mestizos—and plural societies, for Indians maintained distinct cultures that insulated them from much of mestizo depredations.

Ladino (mestizo) and Indian relations in Guatemala provide an excellent illustration of the mixed-caste/plural-society character of the interaction. About one-third of the population of the eastern Guatemalan town of San Luis Jilotepeque is ladino, and the remainder are Indians of Mayan ancestry. Here, as elsewhere, phenotypic distinction between the two groups is often minimal or nonexistent, so that many persons regarded as ladino are physically indistinguishable from others considered Indian. Indeed, Indians who have mastered Spanish and ladino culture can and do pass as ladinos, although the ideology of racial discreteness invariably obliges them to move to another town to be accepted as ladinos.

Ladinos of San Luis Jilotepeque—a town that is typical of much of Latin America—display a good deal of contempt for Indians and monopolize the most important social status symbols. Although strict residential segregation is not practiced, ladino houses usually cluster on the town's central plaza, the traditional location of the upper class of Latin American towns. Social distinction in this Guatemalan town is made primarily on the basis of language, dress, and certain prerogatives reserved to ladinos. Indians are usually bilingual; ladinos speak only Spanish. Indians wear special costumes: the women dress in wrap-around skirts, embroidered blouses, strings of beads, and cloth headshawls, while men wear short-tailed white shirts and loose white trousers that hang below the knee. Indian women go barefoot; men sometimes wear sandals. Ladinos, on the other hand, wear shoes and European-style clothes. Both Indians and ladinos desire land, but each has different motives for ownership. To an Indian, land has a somewhat mystical significance and is willingly worked with one's own hands. Ladinos desire land, on which manual labor is usually done by Indian *peones,* for its use as a source of income.

Indians in San Luis Jilotepeque are expected to treat ladinos respectfully, as superiors. A ladino, for example, may visit an Indian house without prior notice and expect to be served a meal with the family honored by his presence. An Indian will not be invited to dinner at a ladino house; his very entry requires not only permission, but use of the back door. When an Indian encounters a ladino on a sidewalk, he is expected to tip his hat and step into the street to allow the ladino to pass. Similarly, Indians address ladinos as "Senor" without reciprocation. Certain types of amusements are reserved for ladinos. Indians, for example, are not allowed inside the town's two pool parlors, though they may watch ladinos play through the windows. Neither may they use the ladino basketball court or attend dances, amateur theatricals, or drinking parties given by ladinos, although ladinos can and do come uninvited to Indian social affairs.

Interestingly, Indians of this town manifest little evidence of hostility towards ladinos. Even under the influence of alcohol, Gillin reports,

> I never saw an Indian grow aggressive towards *ladinos* . . . In the great periodic Indian fiestas aggression is noticeably absent; Dionysiac release of any sort is practically unknown. Rorschach tests on thirty Indians showed aggression in only 6.7 per cent, although 30 per cent of the thirty ladinos showed signs of a small degree of aggression.

Apparently the cultural distinctness of the Indian group offers them a satisfying refuge from ill-treatment by ladinos. Indeed, Gillin suggests that "in some respects it would seem to be more satisfying to be an Indian than a *ladino*."[130] Prestige for Indians is based largely upon individual character, experience, and wisdom, while ladinos measure status primarily in terms of money and material possessions. Indians maintain a religio-political hierarchy of men who settle community disputes and manage the community's all-important folk-catholic ceremonial life, which centers around fiestas, cults of the saints, and rain-making ceremonies. Work on the land and in handicrafts is valued by Indians, who display great pride in their artistic workmanship. Coupled with ceremonial activity, their productive endeavors leave them very little free time, so that "boredom and idle time are practically unknown among the Indians, whereas they are a major problem among the *ladinos*."[131] Racial or caste tensions between the two groups are thus minimized by allegiance to distinct goals and cultural traditions common to plural societies. Additionally, since Indians can and do become ladino, social tension is also defused by the fact that Indians who become dissatisfied with their lot have the option to move to another town or city and adopt a ladino life style.

The socio-symbolic, rather than the phenotypic, character of the Indian and mestizo categories in Latin America has created a complex continuum in many countries. Sometimes membership in a category is uncertain. Residents of one village in the Andes, for example, have regarded themselves as mestizos, yet have been classified as Indians on comparative grounds by outsiders.[132] In general, however, the postconquest period has seen a steady decline of the Indian proportion of a population in favor of an increase in mestizos. This shift, and a continuum of physical appearance from the usually European-appearing elite to the Indian features of the lower class, has created a class system in most of Latin America in which race appears as only one of several criteria for membership in a given class. The division is not usually rigid, for persons of Indian appearance can and do appear in the higher classes; but looking too completely Indian will bar an individual from upper-class status in almost all of Latin America. In large lowland cities the elite will often claim "pure" Spanish or other European ancestry even when their appearance belies the pretense. Even in Mexico, where *indigenismo* is well developed politically, those of the highest class are usually Caucasian in appearance; the term *indio*, while not necessarily referring to actual physical appearance, is often used to describe those of lower class.[133]

Richard Adams' study of the change from caste to class in a small Peruvian sierra town provides an excellent illustration of accommodation of the typical Latin American class system to the reality of a large Indian population. In this town, Adams reports the emergence of three distinct classes. The upper class is as yet still split into two divisions: old, well-to-do mestizo families, and Indians who have gained status through higher education in engineering, medicine, and other professions. The middle class, although not yet clearly delineated, consists of a mixture of Indians who enjoy financial success and older, unsuccessful but not poverty-stricken mestizo families. The bulk of the Indian population is lower-class, although here, too, there is some mixture with "a few [mestizos] who 'live low as an Indian.'"[134] Gradations of class rest on a number of cultural and occupational variables:

Farming: applies to all classes, though lower and sometimes middle groups provide paid labor; middle and upper classes own land

Mining: workers are lower- or sometimes middle-class, whereas nonmanual employees are middle- and upper-class

Clothing: workers wear mestizo-style shirts and blouses in the lower, middle, and sometimes upper classes, while modern dress is often worn by the upper class and, on occasion, by members of the middle class

Language: all classes speak Spanish, although Quechua is favored by much of the lower class

Education: all classes attend primary school and upper and middle secondary school; some members of the upper class attend university or professional school

Marriage: lower class tends to marry members of same or adjacent class within the town; middle and upper classes more likely to marry outside town

Political leadership in the district: upper-class
Protestantism: middle and lower classes
Attendance of Catholic mass: upper and some middle classes.

Adams suggests that the history of Peruvian social status can be traced from Pizarro's days to the present, in a transition from an original "three caste or class" system of whites (divided between European and American-born), mestizos, and Indians. The whites were a small minority everywhere in Peru, and their numbers in the sierra were insignificant. Here, as elsewhere, the mestizo-Indian caste division carried with it "the seeds of its own destruction . . . [as the] very fact that 'Mestizo' means 'mixed' means that any cross with the lower caste produces a high caste person."[135]

Similarly, nations such as Brazil, with large African populations, evidence a replacement of African with European traditions in a process analogous to mestizoization,[136] although certain African-based religious cults have remained important and have even spread to non-African Brazilians.[137] The tendency for higher-class rank to be associated with greater proportions of European ancestry has also been reported for the Caribbean area.[138] Thus, as Safa reports in *The Urban Poor of Puerto Rico*, "social class . . . supplants skin color as the primary determinant of a person's status in Puerto Rican society." But she also notes that "darker-skinned persons certainly are at a disadvantage in getting jobs, education, and other opportunities for upward mobility . . . most Puerto Ricans would also object to their children marrying a colored person."[139] For Caribbean blacks, as for those with Indian features in most of Latin America, the opportunity for class mobility usually stops short of the top. In the upper class of Martinique,

> the upward advance of the colored people, light mulatto as well as Negro, comes to an abrupt end. Color and racial ancestry exert a much greater influence than the factors of wealth and education. Marriage with the small upper-class white elite, which controls the greater part of the island's agriculture, industry, and commerce, is next to impossible for all persons of Negro descent.[140]

What we find, in Brazil and the Caribbean is not an absence of concern with color, as some have suggested, but an accommodation to the reality of numbers: "pure" Europeans are really mixed and exist almost everywhere in the region, in much too small numbers to attempt to establish a class or caste system based solely on race even if desired. Under such conditions, the sharp racial distinctions common to the United States, in which anyone who has any degree of black ancestry is regarded as black, would be meaningless. Instead of such a caste-like system, systems of class gradation in which color is merely one criterion of status have developed, similar to the color gradations still current among American blacks. Most of the black population of Rio de Janeiro, for example, is located in *favelas*; and few of Brazil's elite could be considered black. Much of the debate over the supposed "color blindness" of Brazilians results from failure of many scholars to note that, despite the alleged absence of racism, color barriers are maintained as far as demographic and historical realities permit.

Class Structure and Attitudes

In Latin America, as elsewhere, the reality of the concept of class has been questioned. Certainly class does not exist in any truly objective sense, and people often appear unaware of their actual class positions. A survey of 2,836 residents of Rio de Janeiro, for example, discovered a good deal of variation between a respondent's own assessment of his class status and a standardized occupational assessment of his actual class ranking. Only 19 percent of those whose occupations clearly placed them in Class One ranked themselves this high. Half of Class One individuals (48.6 percent) placed themselves in the middle of the class spectrum at Class Three, or slightly above in Class Two (24.8 percent), while 7.7 percent actually ranked themselves in the two lowest classes. Similarly, more than half of those assessed as lowest-class ranked themselves higher—although, in general, the lower an individual's status, the more likely he was to make an accurate self-assessment.[141]

Historical circumstance can have major influence on the recognition of class as a basis for urban social organization, as Andrew Whiteford has demonstrated in *Two Cities of Latin America*. In contrasting two long-established medium-sized cities, Popayán, Colombia, and Querétaro, Mexico, Whiteford found that class-consciousness was much greater in Popayán than it was in Querétaro. Class in Popayán was "no theoretical construct conceived by the analyst, but a basic part of the social structure which defined each individual's mode of life and his relationship with the other members of the community." Evidence of the importance of class in the Colombian town was not hard to gather: the term class was commonly used, and "notices might appear telling of the departure for school of a son of a family of the *class alta* (upper class) or an obituary was quite likely to lament the departure from this earth of one 'Ricardo Delgado, a respected member of the middle class.'"

Popayán's upper class was derived directly from a long-standing feudal aristocracy. Most members of the highest class lived close to the town's central plaza; they were educated, worldly, and highly literate. They dressed in the fashions of "the great cities," held most of the city's important offices, and derived at least part of their income from ownership of large cattle haciendas. The lower classes, in contrast, lived on the city's outskirts in small adobe houses with thatched straw or corrugated iron roofs, supporting themselves as laborers. A great many showed strong Indian ancestry in physical appearance and clothing style. Between these two extremes a middle class could be distinguished, in the words of one of Whiteford's informants by the fact that "they have enough to eat but none to waste, they dress well but not with style, they have nice homes which are not fancy, and they live well without pretension."

The citizens of Querétaro, in contrast, expressed little concern with class. Undoubtedly, this was due largely to the relative insignificance of the city's old upper class, which had been decimated in the land reform brought by the Mexican revolution. The old families still existed and were proud of their ancestry, but few could maintain aristocratic luxury. "Although they moved with the knowledge that their words and actions carried weight in the community," Whiteford says, "the traditional regard for the aristocrat had been broken in Mexico . . . [so that] there were even some people who did not know who the aristocrats were." The city was basically a middle-class one of small shopkeepers, clerks, journalists, lawyers, and teachers, who had had at least secondary education and who lived in moderate-sized and comfortably furnished houses. Basically they were more secure, both financially and in attitude, than their Popayán counterparts. More had cars and modern conveniences, and they had "a kind of solidarity and occasionally expressed a critical superiority toward the members of the upper class which was largely lacking in Popayán."

Like its Colombian counterpart, Querétaro had a large lower-class population who performed the necessary manual labor—ditch-digging, field labor, blacksmithing, mechanical repair, and most recently factory work—disdained everywhere in Latin America. The men usually wore coveralls, patched shirts, and woven leather sandals, while the women had sandals or went barefoot and wore their cotton dresses covered in front by aprons and their hair in braids. "Patches, huaraches (woven leather sandals), braids, large hats and aprons were diagnostic features of the dress of the Lower Class," Whiteford reports, "and anyone who regarded himself as above this category exerted every effort to avoid them."

Although references to social class were not common, and social classes in Querétaro "hardly existed," concern with mobility was high, especially among the middle class. Even here there were limits to the possibilities of social mobility for the self-made man. No matter how capable a man, or wealthy he might become, his upward social movement stopped at the lower upper-class. Because in Querétaro, as elsewhere, the nouveau riche of this group were usually wealthier and more influential than the "old" families of the upper upper-class, frustrations of the prevention of further advancement were minimal. "In the minds of most Querétanos, the members of the Lower Upper Class were the top of the social scale, and it was only on rare occasions that a man who had achieved this eminence realized that there was anyone above him."[142]

Increasing industrialization of Latin America and greater educational opportunity has everywhere resulted in substantial growth of the urban middle class. Some of this new class is descended from the older middle class of small property-holders and merchants. But most who are today found in middle-level occupations have risen from families who were lower-class or even rural a generation or two ago.

If class is indeed a real phenomenon in Latin America cities, marked by a similar orientation towards life by those of the same social stratum, then we would expect to find sharp cleavages in the outlook of members of the middle and lower classes. Robert C. Williamson has attempted to test the reality of attitudinal differences between the urban lower and middle classes of the Central American countries of El Salvador and Costa Rica and of Colombia's capital, Bogota.[143] Extensive interviews in Central America demonstrated that members of the middle class: had more social contacts and wider exposure to formal education and mass media; evidenced a greater sense of identification with their jobs and had a sense of advancing towards set goals; had happier and more stable marriages; in general, had a more optimistic view of life than did those of the lower class.

Both men and women in the middle classes were much more likely to approve of the use of birth control to limit their family size. In Costa Rica this difference was especially marked: 64.3 percent of middle-class husbands and 58 percent of their wives approved the use of birth control, whereas only 33.6 percent of lower-class husbands and 30.5 percent of their wives did. In other matters of marriage, however, the middle classes were more conservative. *Unions libres* were quite common among the lower classes, accounting for 52.4 percent of urban El Salvadorean and 20.8 percent of Costa Rican marriages, but they were rare in the middle classes. Only 6.6 percent of the middle-class Salvadorean sample and .9 percent of the Costa Rican group admitted to living in a free union. Undoubtedly, the willingness to formalize marriage was related to a more positive attitude towards marriage in general and towards one's partner in particular among the middle class. Whereas nearly 70 percent of the Salvadorean and 80 percent of the Costa Rican middle-class groups said they would marry the same person if they had their lives to live over, less than half of lower-class Salvadoreans (47.8 percent) and 54.2 percent of lower-class Costa Ricans said they would do so.

Williamson's Bogota study produced similar results. As in Central America, the middle class tended to have wider and stronger networks of both kin and friends than did members of the lower class. Here, too, the middle class was more likely to watch television and attend movies than was the lower class, whose use of communications media was mostly limited to constant playing of the radio. Middle class respondents attributed family problems to failure to develop mature bonds of affection between members, whereas the lower class tended to see economic pressures as the major cause of family disintegration. Lower-class familial attitudes were more authoritarian. Significant differences existed between samples of the lower and middle classes in terms of attitudes towards parental authority. The lower class felt quite strongly that children should not be permitted to talk back to their parents, and 100 percent of the lower-class group agreed that "the most important thing that a child can learn is to obey his parents." Lower-class individuals also expressed agreement with the statement that "women should not be placed in positions of authority over men." Politically, middle-class people gave their highest ratings to a former liberal president, while the lower class strongly preferred a past dictator.

When asked to identify their own class, those rated middle-class correctly identified themselves in 82.5 percent of cases (1.5 percent felt they were lower-class and 16 percent upper-class). Two-thirds of lower-class individuals, however, claimed middle-class status. But the fact that only 18.4 percent of the lower class approved of the existence of class divisions in Columbia (48.9 percent of the middle class approved) suggests that many who rated themselves middle-class were aware that their self-estimation was not generally shared by others. Lower-class individuals tended to have a certain nostalgia for the past:

most felt that people in general were happier a century ago than they are today. Most interestingly, members of the middle class rated themselves significantly higher than those of the lower class in traits of generosity, sociability, optimism, and self-confidence, while those in the lower class saw themselves as moody, introverted, and pre-occupied with their health.

Williamson's work seems to have clearly established the existence both of common middle-class values and of an *awareness* of being middle-class in cities of three Latin American countries. Because social history and ethnic composition vary a good deal among these three countries, it is logical to conclude that research in other countries would yield similar results. Thus we can speak with some confidence of the widespread existence in Latin America of middle classes. The reality of upper classes who are passionately aware of their own existence is, of course, not in serious doubt. What is uncertain is whether a class-conscious lower class really exists in Latin America. Others recognize and respond to a lower class as if it existed, to be sure, but does the lower class recognize itself? Williamson's discovery that scarcely one-third of those in his lower-class Bogota sample rated themselves lower-class suggests that those in the lower classes may tend to have rather fuzzy and ill-formed ideas of systems of social class and their places within them.

Researchers in Latin America rarely report difficulty in eliciting attitudes towards lower classes, whereas they seem not nearly so successful in obtaining lower-class attitudes towards themselves and the other groups. An example is the Hawthorns' study of social class in Sucre, Bolivia.[144] Their description of the city's social classes is thoughtful, detailed, and reminiscent of other Latin American studies in its description of upper classes clustering around the central plaza and the increasing preponderance of mestizos and Indians as one descends the social hierarchy. Ideology among middle and upper classes was easily obtained. Only the attitudes of the lower-class *cholos* (mestizos) remained elusive. The authors' access to the world of the lower class thus proved no firmer than that of the stereotypic understandings of the local elite:

> The lower class ideology of social stratification could not be obtained from direct interviews; political speeches and articles from La Paz newspapers may be cited and indicate economic jealousy as a potent motive. This section of a political speech is ascribed to President Belzu in the last century:
> "Cholos: while you perish from hunger and misery, your oppressors who call themselves gentlemen and exploit your

work, live in luxury. All you see around you belongs to you, for it is the fruit of your labors. The wealth of these so-called nobles is nothing but loot they have taken from you."[145]

That urban lower-class workers are frequently exploited by methods that can be cruel and devious is not doubted.[146] But what is evident from a number of studies of Latin America's urban poor is that the poor themselves, in contrast to the opinions of those who study them, often do not feel exploited. As Safa reports of poor urban Puerto Ricans: they "do not feel oppressed because, in their opinion, the present society offers sufficient opportunities for those who work hard to get ahead . . . they aspire to become members of the new middle class in Puerto Rico." Here, as elsewhere, the poor tend to blame poverty on personal inadequacies rather than on the society's socioeconomic structure. "There is little recognition among the poor," she says, "of conditions in the larger society that perpetuate the system of inequality in Puerto Rico, such as colonialism, a monopolistic agriculture and industrialization, and continued economic and political dominance by the elite."[147]

Michael Whiteford (one of Andrew Whiteford's two sons, who, along with his daughter, have also become anthropologists) has recently described the attitudes of residents of Popayán's poorest *barrio,* Tulcan, towards their social position.[148] The Tulcanese do not recognize a continuum of social class, but divide society into polarities: "them," or those who are economically better off, and "us," the people of Tulcan and Popayán's other *barrios.* Tulcanese are no longer willing to accept their position as "something willed by God," but seem increasingly discontent with their lot, an attitude fostered by the radio and other media that expose them to new ideas. Many Tulcanese seem to sense their engagement in a constant struggle with an elite who cling to the status quo. Tulcanese

> say their poverty forces them into situations they would not have to face if they were rich. Hence, when Lupe de Martinez' son-in-law was jailed on charges of robbing a drunk, she was very perturbed. After a trip to the jail, she decided that it was a clear case of harassment of the poor. If her son-in-law had been rich, she argued, he never would have been arrested, or if by some remote chance he had been, a few well-placed pesos would have settled the issue quickly and quietly. Even after Ernesto confessed to the crime, Lupe was undaunted. This would not have happened in the first place, she maintained, had they not been so poor, and after all, their poverty essentially was the fault of the rich.[149]

Coupled with their awareness of lack of power, which in the instance above assumes the character of a scapegoating of the rich, Tulcanese do not feel that the rich merit their positions by virtue of their training, ability, or hard work. "Given the chance, many feel they could run the country in a better, more equitable manner," as one of Whiteford's informants put it, "than 'the rotating oligarchy which does nothing but eat, fornicate, and sleep while the people slave to support them.'" Yet, despite their evident bitterness towards the elite as a whole, the Tulcanese are caught in the dilemma of many of the world's poor: they usually like and respect those members of the elite for whom they have worked and with whom they have come into personal contact. In speaking of upper-class individuals whom they know as "magnificent people . . . it is almost as if they are saying oligarchs are exploitative people, and we would be very much better off without them. Nevertheless, I have never met one whom I did not like and admire."

Group or class unity among the Tulcanese is minimal. Despite the fact that they are all poor and aware of their lower-class position, they remain aloof one from another, using the formal "usted" address and insisting upon calling each other "don" or "doña," "even if they have known each other for years." When Tulcanese encounter each other on the street, their "greetings are short, verging on being curt," in contrast to encounters of higher-class people who shake hands and embrace. Most tellingly, when Tulcanese interact with those of a higher social class they "shake hands and are very genteel and cordial, exhibiting a type of behavior not demonstrated among lower-class social equals."[150]

Careers and Social Structure in Brazil

Theoretically—and I stress theoretically—ranking by class in industrial societies is achieved through the ability and perseverance of the individual. Rank in agrarian, or preindustrial societies, on the other hand, is (theoretically) caste-like in ascription, so that even when an individual does achieve higher position through his own efforts his success is likely to be reinterpreted in the more generally static context. Such divisions of ranking may have a general, abstract truth to them, but it must be remembered that individual achievement in this area usually plays a much less significant role even in America than our class ideology suggests. By the same token, status ascription even in caste systems, as seen earlier, is not as rigid as the concept of caste implies.

Bearing in mind that ideal types, no matter how useful, remain theoretical abstractions, it is nevertheless worthwhile to consider one such division suggested by Anthony Leeds in his essay "Brazilian Careers and Social Structure." Leeds suggests that the study of social stratification in complex societies can profit from a heuristic division into *static-agrarian societies,* those in which crops constitute the major source of wealth and power, and *expansive industrial societies,* those in which wealth is derived from the industrial processing of raw materials. The former grouping is today represented by most Latin American and Southeast Asian countries; the United States, Japan, and Western Europe are examples of the latter. A third type, *expansive agrarian societies* were formerly found in such nations as China and Thailand and in the early Mesopotamian empires, but they became extinct in competition with the growth of expansive industrial societies in the past several centuries.

We would expect to find vocational and professional schools, coupled with corporations and a contractual basis of social organization, in expansive industrial societies. Static-agrarian societies would be based upon ties of kinship and patronage and a variety of unformalized face-to-face relations.

Brazil has moved rapidly within the past few decades from an agrarian to an industrially-based society. Following Leeds's hypothesis, we would expect to find its initial years of industrialization characterized by the transfer of static-agrarian patterns of social organization to the new order. The gap between old methods of recruitment to agrarian tasks, and the new emphasis upon special skills, is usually obvious in "developing" nations. Brazil is no exception. The initial stages there of rapid, transplanted industrialization are characterized by an administrative vacuum which in the absence of established methods of formal training must be met by importation of foreign specialists, sending students abroad for training, and emphasis upon "self-made" men.

Leeds found that the lack of "curricularized training" in Brazil was most obviously manifested in the frequent reference of Brazilians to *autodidactos* (self-made men), which he says "began to register in my consciousness after many hearings."[151] He also remarked the phenomenon of one individual holding a series of often seemingly unrelated positions, or a *cabide de emprego* (employment hanger), which too results from the lack of specificity of background training requirements. In Brazil as in other developing countries, a background in student politics may lead to a position in journalism, then to politics, then to gradual movement into the top of a rather fluid and interchangeable political-administrative-commercial elite in which one may hold concurrent or successive positions in the civil service and on bank or corporate boards of directors. The key to advancement in such a situation is not training per se, but self-promotion and the cultivation of contacts.

In Brazil, the informal institution of *panelinha* (little saucepan)—which Leeds defines as "a relatively closed, completely informal primary group, held together in common interest by ties of friendship or other personal contact acting for common ends and including a roster of all key socio-political-economic positions"—provides something of a type illustration for social advancement. Through kin ties, school friendships, and movement through social networks, these small, mutually supportive groups acquire members in diverse fields who use their particular niches to help the other members advance from early postuniversity jobs through a series of often quite distinct positions to their final positions in middle age. During the early and middle stages of the career it is important to make a name and create a growing presence, to gain the best possible position in an influential *panelinha* and to be readily accepted for whatever positions (journalist, politician, banker, or corporate director) might become available through the auspices of fellow *panelinha* members. The first ten or fifteen years of a successful career "are characterized by multiplying the sources of support, first, so that there may be no retrogression; second, so that there be a permanent set of trampolins; third, so that there exists variegated sets of connections, among which, for strategic reasons, the careerist may move to advance his later career."[152]

The process of successful advancement by individuals during the initial phases of their country's movement to an industrial society is by no means simple. Those who succeed must be deft and adventurous. "There is an intense selection," Leeds notes, "in favor of those persons with keener perceptions, with sharper abilities to see more meanings behind the cues, and with the energy and drive to follow up and make use of the information so acquired."[153] But such selection, no matter how rigorous at times in promoting those of superior intelligence and ability, is limited to persons for whom position of birth and experiences of early life have paved the future to entry into a *panelinha* in the first place.

On the basis of such presence and absence of opportunity, we can agree with Leeds's suggestion that, instead of using the term class to encompass all of Brazilian social structure—or that of most Latin American, African, and South and Southeast Asian countries—

it would be more appropriate to recognize a transitional, two-tiered system of *classes* and *masses,* with real internal stratification present only in the former. Class in much of the third world has clearly begun to supplant ethnic and caste divisions. But the full force of class ideology is often found only among elites of these societies.

NORTH AMERICA AND EUROPE: RACE, ETHNICITY, AND CLASS

Anthropologists have left the study of social stratification in North America largely to sociologists. With the significant exception of W. Lloyd Warner, few have directed their interest to class, race, or ethnicity in their own culture, even after having done research elsewhere. Most significantly, the acculturation and assimilation of American ethnic groups has received little attention, despite the fact that some of the most impressive instances of acculturation have occurred among immigrants to the United States and Canada.

In 1955, Melford Spiro was able to find only about thirty publications by anthropologists concerned with the acculturation of American ethnic groups. But the work that had been completed suggested that: 1) the least acculturated groups were also the least socially mobile; 2) *intra*ethnic conflict was associated with mobility such that there was a tendency to assume that a member of one's own ethnic group who had "made it" had "sold out" in order to do so; 3) groups who desired social mobility and were refused the opportunity to assimilate tended to exhibit some form of nativism in which exaggerated expression of ethnic pride salved the wounds of rejection; 4) religion tended to be more resistant to acculturation than ethnicity, so that religious "acculturation" was probably better thought of as "deculturation"—that is, there was a tendency to move away from formal religious attachments altogether, rather than transfer allegiance from one religion to another; 5) those who migrated individually without families tended to have greater difficulty adapting to their new environment but also assimilated most readily; and 6) the father's inability to teach his children to cope in a new cultural context tended to make families less patrilineal (the children, especially the eldest, often transmitted knowledge of the host society's cultural traditions to their parents).

These and other tentative conclusions that emerged even from such scanty data convinced Spiro that anthropologists had sacrificed a major opportunity to study acculturative processes at home. The loss, he felt, was heightened by the fact that, in contrast to most acculturation towards Western traditions in other countries, which spreads from a small colonial group to a much larger host society, the situation in North America was one in which minority, migrant groups acculturated to the traditions of the existing inhabitants.

Undoubtedly, Spiro's major conclusion that "the American class system, as it were, prevents the mobility of the unacculturated"[154] is the result of precisely this fact. The overwhelming dominance of older American ethnic groups of the middle and upper strata of an advanced industrial society have made it extremely difficult for immigrant groups to establish parallel and isolated systems of social stratification. Consequently, a major theme of each new wave of immigrants to the United States has been one of translating economic success into social mobility by conforming to the traditions of America's type ethnic group, the WASPs (White Anglo-Saxon protestants).

Sociologists, political scientists, and others have, of course, written profusely about the shift from Polish, German, Italian, and Jewish traditions to some amalgam of what has come to be accepted as standard American culture. The metaphor of the melting pot has often been invoked to illustrate the blending of diverse traditions into a common "Americanness." But today the melting pot ideology has been rejected by those who perceive a strong persistence of distinct ethnic identities in American society.[155] Indeed, a virtual academic industry has emerged to counter the melting pot.[156] The persistence of ethnic identity (and to a lesser degree of distinct cultural traditions) in today's America is real enough. But its importance seems exaggerated by the recent trend to rush the slightest symbols of ethnic distinctiveness into print to prove that we have not really blended into a common pot. Anthropologists who have studied truly plural societies would probably feel, for example, that attendance at Polish-American picnics, membership in a Polish-American voluntary association, and a reluctance to endure Polish jokes does not count for much when the individual probably speaks little if any Polish and shows scant evidence of adherence to Polish cultural traditions. Consciousness of Polish identity in such circumstances seems partial at best.

America has never had a strong, sustained socialist working-class movement based upon class antagonisms. The usual explanation for this is that ethnicity has formed a potent barrier to the development of class-based interest groups. To some degree this is undoubtedly true, although the pattern of development of American industry seems not to have favored the widespread disenchantment of the working class. During the late nineteenth and early twentieth centuries, when factory wages were low and hours very long by today's standards, most industrial workers were separated by their cultural diversity. As American industry grew, so did its ability to compensate its workers. Although the United States and Canada have experienced a few major, bloody strikes, a consistent pattern of labor-owner confrontation has been avoided by the general willingness of employers to meet labor demands.

Unlike many of the world's nations, where a surfeit of labor exists such that the primary goal of workers is to extract wages above what the employer could offer in a labor market in which he could freely replace any one laborer ·with another, labor has in general been scarce in North America. The attraction of millions of immigrants to American industry, and the emphasis upon development of capital intensive industries, both reflect this fact. Throughout most of America's industrial past, large and efficient use of capital meant that workers required to operate plants and assembly lines could be well compensated. The fact that labor was relatively scarce meant that they *had* to be well compensated if they were not to be lost to a competitor. This preciousness of labor is undoubtedly at least as responsible as ethnic divisions for the failure—or, more appropriately, lack of interest—of American workers in establishing a militant socialist movement. Comparison of similar situations in labor-poor postwar Germany and Japan with labor-rich Italy suggests that ethnic segmentation, or "class-cutting"[157] has been overused to explain the marked absence of continued class conflict in the most advanced industrial nations.

What concern anthropologists have demonstrated towards American ethnic groups has been directed primarily towards American Indians, or such non-Western groups as Japanese- and Chinese-Americans.[158] Abel and Hsu have discussed the increasing shift of Chinese-American personality and behavioral patterns towards American norms.[159] Weiss, in a study of Sacramento, California, Chinese reports that they are highly *acculturated* but not yet *structurally assimilated*, in that their life style is strongly American but their friendships and social groupings still tend to be Chinese.[160] But Chinese and Japanese have largely merged into the residential neighborhoods of the larger society; and the barriers to intermarriage heretofore set up by both Asian- and Caucasian-Americans seem to be falling rapidly, although patterns of intermarriage seem biased in favor of Asian-female/Caucasian-male intermarriage.[161] In California, for example, Asian-Caucasian marriages were banned until 1948; by 1972, Tinker's study of the marriages of those persons of Japanese ancestry who lived in Fresno, California, showed that 56 percent were interracial.[162] Undoubtedly, the absorption of Asian-Americans into Caucasian-American society will continue—aided by their strong degree of acculturation, the generally favorable stereotypes held towards them by the larger American society, and the fact that Asian and Caucasian differences are often minimized by the greater distinction made between those groups and black Americans.

Generally, American society is considered a class-based rather than an ethnic-based, or plural, society. Sociology has developed a massive literature on class in America to which only a few anthropologists have contributed.[163] Their contribution has not been insignificant, however. W. Lloyd Warner's return from fieldwork with Australian aborigines to conduct research in "Yankee City" and "Jonesville," for example, has had lasting impact on our understanding of class in America.[164] True to his anthropological training, Warner stressed the importance of basing his analysis of Yankee City upon its natives' conceptions of their world. Using the criteria of (1) *participation* in the social life characteristic of the class of which one is a member and (2) *acceptance* by others as an equal in such social activities, he and fellow researchers reported that six classes existed in Yankee City. There were: (1) the upper upper-class, whose "old money" and breeding gave them the highest prestige, (2) the lower upper group of nouveau riche, (3) the upper middle-class of professionals and successful businessmen, (4) the lower middle-class of small businessmen and white collar and skilled workers, (5) the upper lower-class of the "poor but honest" working man, and (6) the lower lower-class of unskilled workers and never-do-wells.

Warner's system has been criticized for excessive rigidity, and for the fact that it is a composite that few if any members of the community are themselves likely to make. Members of the upper upper-class, for example, are likely to recognize those of their own group and have clear notions of those who fall into the lower upper-class and upper middle-class categories; but they may fuse into a single group people from the lower middle-class and the lower classes. Similarly, those of lower-class and lower middle-class status may not recognize an upper upper-class as distinct from the lower upper-class and upper middle-class groups. Indeed, since class status for those in the lower groups is often based solely upon money, not education or breeding, members of the nouveau riche lower upper-classes are often thought to be at the pinnacle of the community's class system.

Use of such class divisions is also subject to criticism that the divisions are vague and somewhat permeable. Although this is certainly true, and there is frequent disagreement in the assignment of particular individuals to a particular class, class does have social reality in America. The fact that such reality is fuzzier and more imprecise than social scientists might like does not strip it of its veracity.

The research of British social anthropologists on English conceptions of class also emphasizes the prevalent lack of agreement about what constitutes the "proper" basis for class ranking. Differences have often been so great from one individual to another that Bott says "we sometimes wondered if they were talking about the same society."[165] A basic problem in class assessment is the division between *prestige* and *power* class rankings. Although there is generally a good deal of overlap, prestige systems of rating, such as those favored by Warner and others who have studied small communities, differ from Marxist ratings of class as a function of personal power in relation to means of production. Both power and prestige are usually intertwined in individual assessments of position, but certain aspects of the assessor's personal situation can lead him to emphasize one to the exclusion of another.

Bott interviewed one working-class couple, the Jarrolds, of which the wife had had high educational aspirations that were thwarted by ill health. Her husband, too, might have achieved higher occupational status had he not been an orphan and subject to periodic shifts from foster home to foster home. When questioned about class, Mrs. Jarrold laid out a rather elaborate eight-unit division of social class: the "real blue bloods" of the aristocracy; the "leaders of fashion and popular influence," composed largely of intellectuals who had earned their wealth and position; the "professional people" of doctors, lawyers, and higher civil servants; the "poorer middle class" of lesser civil servants and office and clerical workers; the "rich working class," who have televisions, fur coats, and cars; the "poor working class" of factory workers (which, of all the groups considered, had the greatest number of people); and the "floaters," who lived from hand to mouth.

During the time Mrs. Jarrold spoke, Mr. Jarrold added occasional comments, coupled with the frequent query: "What class are we in?" It was a difficult question for his wife to answer. Her greatest respect was reserved for the "leaders of fashion and popular influence" and her greatest affinity was for the "poorer middle class." But in reality she knew that her husband's occupation and income placed them in the "poor working class." The dilemma of personal classification perfectly matched her frustration with class itself. "Class status, she said, *ought* to depend on intelligence and skill; actually it depended on income and occupation."[166] The couple's sense of being misclassed was also related to their own use of class as a vehicle of social interaction. For them, class was relevant only as a preliminary assessment device through which to place people during first meetings. "When you know somebody and like them because of what they are," they said, "you regard them somehow as a person in their own right and you don't think of them as having a class position."[167]

In contrast to the Jarrolds, who preferred a prestige-based system of class, Bott offered the class conceptions of another family of similar income, the Butlers. Mr. Butler was a plumber, and both he and his wife had been raised in tightly-knit working-class neighborhoods. Mr. Butler, who had evidently been strongly influenced by a Marxist-based union movement, saw only two classes: the top class of "utter snobs, the few idle rich, the people who control everything" and the bottom group of "the rest, a very mixed bag." Within the bottom group of woodworkers, miners, engineers, teachers, and others, he was careful to distinguish between "producers" and "administrators." In his view, "the producers really did the work whereas the administrators just supervised and got paid more for it." For the Butlers, class equaled power; those who had it deserved and received their enmity. Discussion of supervisory personnel unleashed a small tirade of resentment: "Mrs. Butler interposed, 'You know as much as all them put together.' Mr. Butler went on to say that he and his mate knew what to do, but had to ask all these people first. 'They do not actually do anything, not even turn a spanner, but we have the pleasure of really doing something.'"[168]

Young and Willmott encountered similar sentiments in their study of working-class east London neighborhoods. Many informants professed to look down upon factory managers and civil servants as people who just "get their money for walking around," while they gave high evaluations to agricultural laborers, coal miners, and bricklayers, who provide obvious and concrete social services. Their concern with productivity and their sense that current societal values are out of step with reality was reflected in the expressed aspirations of one father for his son's future: "I'd like him to take up chemistry. It's completely unproductive and therefore well paid."[169]

The rigidity of Britain's class structure and the sense of treason associated with abandoning one's class was most obvious in the authors' attempt to follow up the lives of girls who had been graduated from two locally important grammar (secondary) schools. In the 1930's, when the girls in the sample were attending grammar school, continuation past elementary school for working-class children was rare. Girls especially were expected to leave school and find jobs to help support their families. Those who scored high on their examinations and gained scholarships to grammar schools met with mixed reactions to their success. Their teachers were, of course, pleased, as were many mothers. But the girls' peers and their fathers usually responded by trying to dissuade them from reaching beyond their status, and with open hostility should they accept the uniform and demeanor of the grammar school student. One of the mothers recounted the family division that resulted from her daughter's scholarship offer: her husband's relatives united against it, telling the mother that she "ought to be ashamed" of encouraging her daughter to rise above the working class; the mother stood firm, saying, "she's going as far as she can go."[170]

The followup by Young and Willmott, fifteen to twenty years after graduation of 24 women who had continued in school found that 6 were still single or were separated from their husbands, 9 had married into a higher social class, and 9 had married into the same class as or a lower class than their fathers. All the single or separated women lived at home with their mothers. For them, the major effect of grammar school education had not been to pull them away from home, but to overeducate them for the potential husbands of their working-class neighborhoods. Those who married into the same class as their fathers, or a lower one, seemed not to have been affected by their education, except insofar as it had helped expand their horizons. Finally, those who married men of a higher class had moved out of their old neighborhoods to suburban surroundings. In spite of the move, and suppression of their Cockney accents and manners, all maintained relations with their parents and saw them twice a month on average.

No society in Europe or North America is completely organized upon class or even ethnicity. Everywhere caste-like differences can be found between the dominant group and certain others. Gypsies, for example, are found throughout Europe and North America as separate, outcaste groups.[171] In France, North African migrants exist at the bottom of the social heap—as do Italian and Turkish migrant workers in Germany, West Indians in Britain, and Sicilians in North Italy. In Canada, French Canadians occupy a separate but clearly subordinate status vis-à-vis English Canadians that gives Canadian society a strong plural and caste-like character at the same time. In both the United States and Canada, American Indians and blacks remain in such a clear birth-ascribed position of inferiority, reinforced by the sense that both are somehow irredeemably tainted by the mark of racial pollution, that they can generally be spoken of as outcastes.

The barrier for blacks to free entrance into the American class system was long ago noted by Warner, who saw that the caste line separated two distinct systems.[172] Generally, the white American class system is superimposed above the entirety of the black system, although of course many blacks have achieved a level of wealth and education beyond that of the majority of whites. These individuals are often caught in the cruellest bind, for a background that would earn unquestioned respect if they were white is sometimes rejected by whites of inferior class but superior caste status. Indeed, much of the intrapsychic conflict felt by middle-class and upper-class blacks undoubtedly has its origin in the realization that individual caste mobility can not be achieved by education or social refinement.[173]

Such studies by anthropologists as Elliot Liebow's classic *Tally's Corner* and Gerry Rosenfeld's *"Shut Those Thick Lips!"* portray distinct and self-perpetuating social systems of black lower-caste adaptation to urban American life. If their settings were typical of the situation of most or all of American blacks (which they are not, as many middle-class blacks have pointed out especially in reference to *Tally's Corner*), it would be difficult to hold out any hope for the disappearance of caste in America. As it is, American blacks are acculturated—the idea of a distinct "black culture" is a chimera—but not assimilated to the larger American society. Feelings of fear and mistrust are much too strongly rooted among both blacks and whites to vanish in the foreseeable future.

At the extreme of structural assimilation to American society also lies the "hard point" of resistance to intermarriage. When it occurs, it does not result in the production of socially categorized "white" or "Eurasian" children, as Asian- and Caucasian-American marriages do, but it merely augments the black lower caste because mixed offspring are categorized "black." At the moment, tremendous improvement in the lot of most black Americans seems to be under way. But it is most likely that such improvement will result principally in a shift of the caste line still further from the near-horizontal direction of the past towards a vertical division, rather than in disappearance of the line altogether. All of the social action towards integration and the amelioration of the lot of black Americans over the past several decades appears merely to be leading America from a separate and unequal society to one which is equal but still separate.

CONCLUSION

The development and spread of urban life seems everywhere associated with a trend away from the dominance of birth-determined social orders to orders founded on individual achievement. Densely populated agrarian societies of the past usually had social hierarchies based on a four-part division of peoples into *religious leaders, aristocrats, commoners,* and *slaves* or *outcastes*. In the early stages of urbanization, religious leaders seem to have dominated by virtue of their assumed direct contact with the gods; but the need for protection from other groups and the common desire for territorial expansion required development of a warrior class, which soon assumed power with the warrior-elite establishing itself as a religiously justified aristocracy. The income and support of this group came from its ability to arrogate large amounts of land and the slaves to work it, as well as to tax commoners in the form of demands upon their labor and produce. Commoners supported themselves through agriculture, and provided the energies and manpower for public works and the military.

In addition to these four major groups of people, cities harbored smaller populations of artisans and merchants who catered to the needs of the priestly and aristocratic elites. As states expanded and absorbed other states their cities grew, and this commercial sector increased in importance until in time the wealth and power of some of its members rivaled that of the aristocrats. Where merchants and artisans enjoyed sustained demand for their services, they developed guilds and associations that forged them into common interest groups. Recruiting their numbers as much on the basis of ability as birth, they formed middle groups between the elite on one hand and the commoners and slaves on the other. In time, in countries as diverse as India, China, Japan, and the nations of Europe, these middle groups either deposed the aristocracy or shunted it aside into a merely symbolic role. With their triumph, the ideology of birth-ascribed social hierarchies gave way to more or less flexible social systems set upon an ideology of individual achievement.

True "class" systems are undoubtedly the products of industrialization. There is, as we have seen, a continuity between the hierarchies of preindustrial cities and those of industrial class systems. But Reissman seems correct in asserting that the ancient Egyptian "middle class" of artisans, priests, and merchants, for example, is "only a very distant cousin of the industrial middle class." He states: "It seems to be abundantly clear that once industrialization begins, when there is an industrial 'take-off' in Rostow's sense of that term, urban growth, a class system, and a nationalistic political philosophy also are evident partners in that process, thereby ending the former state of rural sentiments, a feudal type of landed aristocracy, and a localistic political philosophy."[174] Social forms analogous to class may be found in preindustrial settings, but the opportunities for individual mobility are severely limited in contrast to those existent in industrial societies, where specialized and advanced occupational training for individuals is at the heart of the system.

Territorial expansion of agrarian and industrial empires has never been restricted to peoples of identical cultural traditions. Everywhere, diverse ethnic groups have been incorporated with varying degrees of completeness into larger political and economic units. Where economic factors such as the cattle/kola-nut monopoly of the Hausa of Ibadan, or cultural factors such as Malay-Chinese differences in Malaysia, favored separation, groups coexisted side by side as distinct ethnic entities in plural societies.[175] In other situations, such as that of the Hutu and Tutsi of Burundi, where one group gains dominance over another, systems of ethnic stratification have emerged. In still other regions, acculturated but distinct groups have been incorporated as slaves or outcaste populations at the bottom of caste societies.

The initial phases of empire and the growth of secondary (and to a lesser degree, primary) urbanization heightened the salience of ethnic differences by bringing peoples who may never have felt a strong sense of ethnic loyalty into contact and competition with peoples of different language and customs. For these societies, the challenge has been to integrate their peoples into common political, economic, and cultural frameworks without evolving potentially divisive systems of ethnic or caste stratification. Generally, the problem is to channel people away from ethnic alignments to those formed around personal achievements and common citizenship. The need to override "primordial" alignments is the same, whether the goal is to direct hostile and distinct nationalities into a uniform loyalty to a classless nation-state, as in Burma, or to transform all vestiges of caste and ethnic stratification to a common class system in which anyone can aspire to (and, given ability and drive, can achieve) the highest positions available, as in the United States. "This tension between primordial sentiments and civil politics," Clifford Geertz states,

> probably cannot be entirely dissolved. The power of the "givens" of place, tongue, blood, looks, and way-of-life to shape an individual's notion of who, at bottom, he is and with whom, indissolubly, he belongs is rooted in the non-rational foundations of personality . . . what the new states—or their leaders—must somehow contrive to do as far as primordial attachments are concerned is not, as they have so often tried to do, wish them out of existence by belittling them or even denying their reality, but domesticate them. They must reconcile them with the unfolding civil order by divesting them of their legitimizing force with respect to governmental authority, by neutralizing the apparatus of the state in relationship to them, and by channeling discontent arising out of their dislocation into properly political rather than parapolitical forms of expression.[176]

The shift away from primordial attachments does not remove the human need for distancing from others. In place of ethnic parochialisms, class divisions have emerged based upon the acquisition of economic or political power and social prestige. Even in countries like the United States, where class has been successfully domesticated (for most Americans, the preoccupation of fellow English-speaking Britons with class, and its distant vocabularly, seems alien), the primordial attachments have not vanished. Indeed, they have taken on a peculiar double-edged quality: certain segments of the population of the United States are removed from the mainstream of American society, on the one hand by the marks of their physical features, culture, and language, while others who have been fully assimilated suffer from a sense of emptiness at their loss of ethnic identity. Many of the mass of citizens who can really only identify themselves as Americans have been left to create fictive Italian, Polish, Greek, or Lithuanian identities, long after the customs and language required for true membership in these groups have vanished. Persistence of identity for blacks, Spanish-speakers, and Indians has placed most of the one-sixth of America's population that falls into these groups into lower-caste or lower ethnic-group status.

The twentieth-century city may be at fault for "the loss of identity . . . [that is the] major psychological problem" of twentieth-century man, as Reissman claims.[177] But for many of the world's nations, and for much of the population of Europe and North America, the loss of primordial identities has not yet come far enough.

NOTES

1. Carneiro 1967.
2. See Cox 1948:489-508; Dumont 1970:201-216, 239-258.
3. Berreman 1966:283.
4. See Hollingshead 1949.
5. Lynd and Lynd 1929; see also Tumin 1967:91-93.
6. Furnivall 1948:303-312.
7. Berreman 1966.
8. Cohen and Middleton 1970:2.
9. Southall 1975:274. See Leach 1954 for a similar discussion of the validity of traditional ethnic distinctions of the Burmese hills.
10. Ottenberg 1974:8.
11. Hanna and Hanna 1971:105.
12. Southall 1975:274.
13. Plotnicov 1964:126.
14. Plotnicov 1972.
15. LeMarchand 1974:5.
16. Mair 1963:39.
17. Gluckman 1961:69.
18. Epstein 1958; Mitchell 1960.
19. Mayer 1962.
20. Epstein 1958.
21. Shack 1973:254.
22. Southall and Gutkind 1957:26.
23. Rouch 1956.
24. Plotnicov 1967.
25. Mitchell 1960:2.
26. Mayer 1961:207-208.
27. Van Velsen 1961:232; see Shack 1973 for discussion of the maintenance of ethnic distinctiveness among Gurage migrants to Addis Ababa, Ethiopia.
28. Nkosi 1965:6.
29. Nkosi 1965:8.
30. Wallerstein 1960:131.
31. Plotnicov 1972:011.
32. See Banton 1957:163.
33. Cohen 1969:185-186; emphasis mine.

34. Mitchell 1956. An example of Kalela joking:

> ... What have I heard
> the Nsenga woman slept with what?
> You tell me—you who have heard it
> She slept with a dog ...
> Yesterday I desired an Nsenga woman,
> Why did she refuse me?
> I pleaded with her but she entirely refused
> Saying that I did not know how to copulate ...
> I shall send my dog to the Nsenga woman,
> The one that refused me will then acquiesce (Mitchell 1956:42).

35. Mitchell 1956:15.
36. Schildkrout 1975:257.
37. Skinner 1974:195-199.
38. See Henderson 1966:377.
39. Quoted in Cohen 1974:73-74.
40. Quoted in Twaddle 1975:12.
41. Winder 1962; Little 1974:69-73.
42. Cohen 1974:128.
43. Quoted in Cohen 1974:128-129.
44. Khuri 1968.
45. Kuper 1967:137.
46. See George Orwell's *Burmese Days* for an excellent treatment of British colonial life based upon this theme and the consequences of getting too close to "the natives."
47. Jahoda 1961; O'Brien 1972.
48. Little 1974:56-65.
49. See Plotnicov's useful distinction (1970) between "modern," urban elites, and "traditional," tribal elites.
50. Baeck 1961; Parkin 1969; Kileff 1975.
51. The value of a foreign education is clearly reflected in one song about a girl's hopes for a future husband: "What shall I do to get a man of that type? One who is a been-to, car full and fridge full [possessing a car and refrigerator]? What shall I do to obtain a man like that?" (Busia, quoted in Little 1965:141.)
52. Epstein 1958.
53. See Powdermaker 1962:310-311.
54. Wilson and Mafeje 1963:47-73.
55. Kuper 1969:480-486.
56. Goldthorpe 1961.
57. Schwab 1961:135.
58. Tiger 1967:196.
59. Fallers 1973:210-297.
60. Gutkind 1965.
61. Kileff 1975; Jacobson 1968, 1973.
62. Jacobson 1968:128.
63. Jacobson 1968:133.
64. Kileff 1975:94.

65. The ranking is based on that suggested by Wilson and Mafeje (1963:15) for the South African township of Lancia. The South African situation has, of course, limited class differentiation among urban black Africans, a fact reflected in the distinction of only two urbanized types: the "townee," or *tsotsi* types (divided into *Ikhaba* and *Oomac* on the basis of age), corresponding to our type 2a), and the "decent people" of the respectable lower and middle classes, the *ooscuse-me*, roughly equivalent to 2b).

66. Amin 1967.

67. Cohen 1974:194; emphasis his.

68. Cohen 1974:194.

69. Little 1974:52-54.

70. Basham 1954:240-241; Srinivas 1962:63-64.

71. Ghurye 1957:26-27.

72. Srinivas 1952:30.

73. Srinivas 1952:27.

74. Banks 1960:65-66.

75. See Leach 1960.

76. Berreman 1966:279; emphasis his.

77. See Leach 1960.

78. The significance of eating together for acknowledging equality has undoubtedly been the basis for past white American resistance to integration of restaurants and lunch counters. In India, Mandelbaum (1970:198) says: "Eating together is a sign of equality among individuals and groups, second only to intermarriage. Those who take their meals side by side, eating food from the same cook and kitchen, thereby show that each has equal ritual status with his fellow diners. And those who eat together are apt to act together and support each other, whether as family group, faction, lineage, or jati."

79. See Goffman 1963.

80. Because the focus of this section is the impact of urbanization and industrialization on the role of caste in India's social structure, any more detailed discussion of caste is beyond its scope. Those interested in pursuing some of the rich literature on caste in India should refer to: Basham 1954, Berreman 1972, Béteille 1965, Cohn 1955, Dumont 1970, Leach 1960, Lynch 1969, Mandelbaum 1970, Mayer 1960, Mencher 1974, Rudolph and Rudolph 1967, Srinivas 1952, 1962.

81. Banks 1960:64.

82. See Gough 1960:28-29.

83. Srinivas 1956:85.

84. Den Ouden 1975:233.

85. Rowe 1973:229.

86. Bopegamage and Veeraraghavan 1967:35.

87. Bopegamage and Veeraraghavan 1967:41-42.

88. Srinivas 1962:76.

89. Ames 1969:61, 62 (paraphrased).

90. Ames 1969:63-64.

91. Berreman 1972:577.

92. Chekki 1970.

93. Straus and Winkelmann 1969.

94. See Srinivas 1962:15-41.
95. Dr. Ambedkar, who is revered among untouchables, eventually sought to escape the Hindu caste system by converting to Buddhism. His example, and the mass public conversions he encouraged, have resulted in the conversion of several million untouchables to caste-free Buddhism and a marked revival of the religion in its original homeland. Unfortunately, this effort to escape caste has been hampered by refusal of many Hindus to accept conversion as a legitimate escape from *pariah* status (see Lynch 1969, 1972; Fiske 1972).
96. Rosenthal 1966.
97. Schwartz 1967; Mayer 1967; van den Berghe 1970b:283.
98. This discussion is excerpted from Current Anthropology 16:291-293.
99. Mayer 1967:15-16.
100. For discussion of the tensions between hill and lowland peoples see Anonymous (1974), *The Montagnards of South Vietnam*. For detailed historical and ethnographic discussions of Southeast Asia, see Coèdes 1966, Burling 1965, Leach 1954, Provencher 1975, LeBar 1972, and LeBar, et al., 1964.
101. "Dual economy" refers to an economy with a Western superstructure (based on extraction of resources for the metropolis and resale of manufactured goods in the colony) and an indigenous subsistence sector.
102. Furnivall 1948:304-305.
103. Bruner 1956, 1961, 1973a, 1973b.
104. Lévi-Strauss 1966:166, quoted in Bruner 1973a:373.
105. Bruner 1973a:386-387.
106. Bruner 1973a:388.
107. Bruner 1973a:391.
108. Today, following a royal decree, Thai use surnames. They are not, however, usually considered important, and Thai will often not know the surnames of friends. The Muslim naming pattern avoids the formation of surname groupings by generational shifting of the final name. Thus, Mohammed *bin* (son of) Abdullah might name his son Ibrahim and he would be known as Ibrahim bin Mohammed. Some tendency towards the perpetuation of surnames may be developing among certain members of the Malay elite, who have begun to omit the *bin* and *binte* (daughter of) and refer to themselves simply as, for example, Juhanna Anwar. The importance of surnames to Chinese is most clearly shown by their position at the beginning of a name. Tan Gake Hua, for example, has the surname Tan and the given name Gake Hua.
109. Purcell 1965:248; Willmott 1969:103-116.
110. See Comber 1957; Freedman 1967a:23-25.
111. Willmott 1969.
112. Willmott 1969:299.
113. Rabushka's questionnaire surveys of Malaysian university students (1969, 1971) suggest a more optimistic conclusion, for more students than expected indicated willingness to intermarry. He explains the discrepancy between expressed willingness and actual intermarriage rates by suggesting that there is a "distinction between behavior and attitudes" (1969:61). The problem is more basic than that: the university emphasizes liberal, integrative attitudes, and the students tend to give liberal responses even

if they do not really subscribe to them. Actual marital decisions, too, are a family matter in which ethnic constraints on the choice of partner are usually primary. Undoubtedly, ethnographic research based on close personal relations with a number of students would have alerted Rabushka to the inadequacy of relying solely, or even primarily, upon questionnaire responses for an understanding of student attitudes towards such a sensitive issue.

114. See Bador 1973.
115. Skinner 1958:227.
116. Skinner 1958:236.
117. Boonsanong 1971:47, 54.
118. Jacobs, et al., 1966, separate Thai society into: 1) the aristocracy, 2) the new elite of ranking professional, business, and government people, 3) the middle group of businessmen, civil servants, teachers, technicians, and artisans, and 4) the lower group of unskilled laborers, domestic servants, and street vendors.
119. Hanks 1966.
120. Hanks 1968:30.
121. See Alatas 1972; Bador 1973.
122. Evers 1975:783.
123. See DeVos and Wagatsuma 1972:6-32.
124. Vogel 1963; Nakane 1970.
125. Dore 1958:215-216.
126. Nakane 1970:24.
127. See Kiefer 1970.
128. Nakane 1970:87, 93.
129. Aguirre and Pozas, quoted in Wagley and Harris 1958:50.
130. Gillin 1948:340, 341.
131. Gillin 1948:342.
132. Tschopik 1967:265.
133. Humphrey 1949:140.
134. Adams 1953:243.
135. Adams 1953:224.
136. Frazier 1942.
137. Bastide 1960; Willems 1968.
138. Olien 1968; Safa 1974:68-69; Wagley and Harris 1958:116-117.
139. Safa 1974:68, 69.
140. Wagley and Harris 1958:117.
141. Hutchinson 1963.
142. Whiteford 1960:17-19, 127.
143. Williamson 1962, 1968.
144. Hawthorn and Hawthorn 1948.
145. Hawthorn and Hawthorn 1948:25.
146. See Leeds 1974:85.
147. Safa 1974:104, 105.
148. Whiteford 1974, 1976.
149. Whiteford 1974:170.
150. Whiteford 1974:171-172.
151. Leeds 1964:1324.
152. Leeds 1964:1335.

153. Leeds 1964:1332.
154. Spiro 1955:1244.
155. See Glazer and Moynihan 1970.
156. See Sanders and Morawska 1975, Tomasi 1975, and Kornblum 1974 for some recent sociological perspectives on American ethnic groups.
157. See Hacker 1976.
158. See Walker 1972 for an anthology of writings on American Indian acculturation, and Wax and Thomas 1961 and Braroe 1965, 1975, for discussion of Indian-White interaction. For the literature on Asian-Americans see Sue and Wagner 1973, Caudill 1952, Caudill and DeVos 1956, Hsu 1953, Sandmeyer 1973, Miller 1969, and Light 1972.
159. Abel and Hsu 1949.
160. Weiss 1974 follows Gordon's useful distinction (1964) between cultural or behavioral assimilation to the patterns of the host society (*acculturation*) and the entrance of the minority group into the primary institutions of the host society (*structural assimilation*).
161. Weiss 1973; Fujitomi and Wong 1973.
162. Tinker 1972.
163. See Gordon 1963.
164. Warner 1963; Warner, et al., 1949.
165. Bott 1971:159.
166. Bott 1971:189.
167. Bott 1971:183.
168. Bott 1971:185, 186.
169. Young and Willmott 1957:14.
170. Young and Willmott 1957:147.
171. See Gropper 1975; Rehfisch 1975; Sutherland 1975.
172. Warner 1936.
173. See Kardiner and Ovesey 1951, Elkins 1959, and Crain and Weisman 1972 for especially lucid discussions of the realities of black identity in America.
174. Reissman 1961:41, 51.
175. I do not mean to assert that cultural differences are not important in Ibadan or that economic factors are an insignificant part of Malay-Chinese relations, only that these factors do not appear to me as the sources of ethnic divisions.
176. Geertz 1963:128.
177. Reissman 1961:49.

REFERENCES

Abel, Theodora M., and Francis L. K. Hsu
    1949   Some aspects of personality of Chinese as revealed by the Rorschach test. Research Exchange and Journal of Projective Techniques 12: 285-301.
Adams, Richard N.
    1953   A change from caste to class in a Peruvian sierra town. Social Forces 31:238-244.

Alatas, Syed Hussein
    1972   The grading of occupational prestige amongst the Malays in Malaysia. In Modernization and social change. Sydney: Angus and Robertson.
Anonymous
    1974   The Montagnards of South Vietnam. London: Minority Rights Group report no. 18.
Ames, Michael M.
    1969   Class, caste and kinship in an industrial city of India. Asia 15:58-71.
Amin, Samir
    1967   Le développement du capitalisme en Côte d'Ivoire. Paris: Editions de Minuit.
Bador, A. Kahar
    1973   Social rank, status-honour and social class consciousness amongst the Malays. In Hans-Dieter Evers, ed., Modernization in South-East Asia. Kuala Lumpur: Oxford University Press.
Baeck, L.
    1961   An expenditure study of the Congolese évolués of Leopoldville, Belgian Congo. In Aidan Southall, ed., Social change in modern Africa. London: Oxford University Press.
Banfield, Edward C.
    1968   The unheavenly city: The nature and future of our urban crisis. Boston: Little, Brown.
Banks, Michael
    1960   Caste in Jaffna. In E. R. Leach, ed., Aspects of caste in South India, Ceylon and north-west Pakistan. Cambridge: Cambridge University Press.
Banton, Michael
    1957   West African city: A study of tribal life in Freetown. London: Oxford University Press.
Basham, A. L.
    1954   The wonder that was India. London: Sidgwick and Jackson (Evergreen ed., New York: Grove Press).
Basham, Richard
    1975   On the caste system upside down: Shifting caste and class alignments among Indians in Malaysia. Current Anthropology 16:291-293.
Bastide, Roger
    1960   Les religions africaines au Brésil. Paris: Presses Universitaires de France.
Berreman, Gerald D.
    1962   Behind many masks: Ethnography and impression management in a Himalayan village. Ithaca, New York: Society for Applied Anthropology monograph 4.
    1966   Structure and function of caste systems; Concomitants of caste organization. In George DeVos and Hiroshi Wagatsuma, eds., Japan's invisible race. Berkeley: University of California Press.
    1972   Social categories and social interaction in urban India. American Anthropologist 74:567-586.
Béteille, Andre
    1965   Caste, class and power: Changing patterns of stratification in a Tanjore village. Berkeley: University of California Press.

Blair, Eric [pseud. George Orwell]
    1934   Burmese days. Baltimore: Penguin Books.
Boonsanong Punyodyana
    1971   Chinese-Thai differential assimilation in Bangkok: An exploratory study. Ithaca, New York: Southeast Asia Program Data Paper no. 79.
Bopegamage, A., and P. V. Veeraraghavan
    1967   Status images in changing India. Bombay: Manaktalas Press for UNESCO, Delhi.
Bott, Elizabeth
    1971   Family and social network: Roles, norms and external relationships in ordinary urban families. 2d ed. New York: Free Press. (Original 1957.)
Braroe, Neils W.
    1965   Reciprocal exploitation in an Indian-white community. Southwestern Journal of Anthropology 21:166-178.
    1975   Indian and white: Self-image and interaction in a Canadian plains community. Palo Alto: Stanford University Press.
Bruner, Edward M.
    1956   Primary group experience and the processes of acculturation. American Anthropologist 58:605-623.
    1961   Urbanization and ethnic identity in north Sumatra. American Anthropologist 63:508-521.
    1973a   Kin and non-kin. In Aidan Southall, ed., Urban anthropology. New York: Oxford University Press.
    1973b   The expression of ethnicity in Indonesia. In Abner Cohen, ed., Urban ethnicity. London: Tavistock.
Burling, Robbins
    1965   Hill farms and padi fields: Life in mainland Southeast Asia. Englewood Cliffs, N.J.: Prentice-Hall.
Carneiro, Robert L.
    1967   On the relationship between size of population and complexity of social organization. Southwestern Journal of Anthropology 23:234-243.
Caudill, William
    1952   Japanese-American personality and acculturation. Genetic Psychology Monographs 45:3-102.
Caudill, William, and George DeVos
    1956   Achievement, culture and personality: The case of the Japanese Americans. American Anthropologist 58:1102-1126.
Chabot, H. T.
    1964   Urbanization problems in South East Asia. Transactions of the Fifth World Congress of Sociology, Washington, D.C.: Sept. 2-8, 1962, vol. 3.
Chekki, Dan A.
    1970   Social stratification and trends of social mobility in modern India. Sociologus 20:146-163.
Coèdes, G.
    1966   The making of Southeast Asia. Berkeley: University of California Press.

Cohen, Abner
1969   Custom and politics in urban Africa: A study of Hausa migrants in Yoruba towns. Berkeley: University of California Press.
Cohen, Michael A.
1974   Urban policy and political conflict in Africa: A study of the Ivory Coast. Chicago: University of Chicago Press.
Cohen, Ronald, and John Middleton
1970   From tribe to nation in Africa. Scranton, Penna.: Chandler.
Cohn, Bernard S.
1955   The changing status of a depressed caste. In McKim Marriott, ed., Village India. Chicago: University of Chicago Press, 1969.
Comber, Leon
1957   An introduction to Chinese secret societies in Malaya. Singapore: Donald Moore.
Comhaire-Sylvain, S., and J. Comhaire-Sylvain
1959   Urban stratification in Haiti. Social and Economic Studies 8:179-189.
Cox, Oliver C.
1948   Caste, class and race. New York: Doubleday.
Crain, Robert L., and Carol Sachs Weisman
1972   Discrimination, personality, and achievement: A survey of northern blacks. New York: Seminar Press.
Crissman, Lawrence W.
1967   The segmentary structure of urban overseas Chinese communities. Man 2:185-204.
Dahrendorf, R.
1968   On the origin of inequality among men. Reprinted in Andre Béteille, ed., Social inequality. Baltimore: Penguin Books.
Den Ouden, J. H. B.
1975   De onaanraakbaren van konkunad (The untouchables of Konkunad). Wageningen: H. Veeman and Sons.
DeVos, George, and Hiroshi Wagatsuma, eds.
1972   Japan's invisible race. Berkeley: University of California Press.
Dore, R. P.
1958   City life in Japan. Berkeley: University of California Press.
Doughty, Paul L.
1970   Behind the back of the city: "Provincial" life in Lima, Peru. In William Mangin, ed., Peasants in cities. Boston: Houghton Mifflin.
Dumont, Louis
1970   Homo hierarchicus: The caste system and its implications. Chicago: University of Chicago Press.
Elkins, Stanley M.
1959   Slavery: A problem in American institutional and intellectual life. Chicago: University of Chicago Press.
Epstein, A. L.
1958   Politics in an urban African community. Manchester: Manchester University Press.
Evers, Hans-Dieter
1973   Group conflict and class formation in South-East Asia. In Evers, ed.,

Modernization in South-East Asia. Kuala Lumpur: Oxford University Press.

1975 Urbanization and urban conflict in Southeast Asia. Asian Survey 15:775-785.

Fallers, Lloyd A.
1973 Inequality: Social stratification reconsidered. Chicago: University of Chicago Press.

Fiske, Adele
1972 Scheduled caste Buddhist organizations. In J. Michael Mahar, ed., The untouchables of contemporary India. Tucson: University of Arizona Press.

Folan, William J.
1967 A comment on race, class and status differences in Merida, Yucatan, Mexico. Anthropologica 9:43-50.

Frazier, E. Franklin
1942 The Negro family in Bahia, Brazil. American Sociological Review 7:465-478.

Freedman, Maurice
1957 Chinese family and marriage in Singapore. London: Her Majesty's Stationery Office.

1967a Immigrants and associations: Chinese in nineteenth-century Singapore. In L. A. Fallers, ed., Immigrants and associations. The Hague: Mouton.

1967b Overseas Chinese associations: A comment. In L. A. Fallers, ed., Immigrants and associations. The Hague: Mouton.

Fujitomi, Irene and Diane Wong
1973 The new Asian-American woman. In Stanley Sue and Nathaniel N. Wagner, eds., Asian-Americans: Psychological perspectives. Ben Lomond, Calif.: Science and Behavior Books.

Furnivall, J. S.
1948 Colonial policy and practice: A comparative study of Burma and Netherlands India. Cambridge: Cambridge University Press.

Gallus, Alexander
1972 Cultural plurality and the study of complex societies in anthropology. Studies for a New Central Europe 3, 2:28-47.

Geertz, Clifford
1963 The integrative revolution: Primordial sentiments and civil politics in the new states. In Old societies and new states. New York: Free Press.

Ghurye, G. S.
1957 Caste and class in India. 2d ed. Bombay: Popular Book Depot.

Gillin, John
1948 "Race" relations without conflict: A Guatemalan town. American Journal of Sociology 53:337-343.

Glazer, Nathan, and Daniel P. Moynihan
1970 Beyond the melting pot. 2d ed. Cambridge: MIT Press.

Gluckman, Max
1961 Anthropological problems arising from the African industrial revolution. In A. Southall, ed., Social change in modern Africa. London: Oxford University Press.

Go, Bernard C.
   1972   The Chinese in the Philippines: Facts and fancies. Philippines Socio-
           logical Review 20:385-394.
Goffman, Erving
   1963   Stigma. Englewood Cliffs, N.J.: Prentice-Hall.
Goldthorpe, J. E.
   1961   Educated Africans: Some conceptual and terminological problems.
           In A. Southall, ed., Social change in modern Africa. London: Ox-
           ford University Press.
Gordon, Milton M.
   1963   Social class in American sociology. New York: McGraw-Hill Paper-
           backs, (original 1950).
   1964   Assimilation in American life: The role of race, religion, and national
           origins. New York: Oxford University Press.
Gough, E. Kathleen
   1960   Caste in a Tanjore village. In E. Leach, ed., Aspects of caste in
           south India, Ceylon and north-west Pakistan. Cambridge: Cambridge
           University Press.
Gropper, Rena C.
   1975   Gypsies in the city. Princeton, N.J.: Darwin Press.
Gutkind, Peter C. W.
   1965   African urbanism, mobility and the social network. International
           Journal of Comparative Sociology 6, 1:48-60.
Hacker, Andrew
   1976   Cutting classes. New York Review of Books 23, 3:15-18.
Hanks, Lucien M.
   1966   The corporation and the entourage: A comparison of Thai and
           American social organization. Catalyst 2:55-63.
   1968   American aid is damaging Thai society. Trans-Action 5, 10:29-34.
Hanna, William J., and Judith L. Hanna
   1971   Urban dynamics in black Africa. Chicago: Aldine Publishing Co.
Harries-Jones, P.
   1965   The tribes in town. In W. V. Brelsford, ed., The tribes of Zambia.
           Lusaka, Zambia: Government Printer.
Hassan, Riaz
   1971   Interethnic marriage in Singapore: A sociological analysis. Sociology
           and Social Research 55:305-323.
Hawthorn, Harry B., and Audrey E. Hawthorn
   1948   Stratification in a Latin American city. Social Forces 27:19-29.
Hayner, Norman S.
   1948   Differential social change in a Mexican town. Social Forces 26:381-
           390.
Henderson, Richard N.
   1966   Generalized cultures and evolutionary adaptability: A comparison
           of urban Efik and Ibo in Nigeria. Ethnology 5:365-391.
Hollingshead, August B.
   1949   Elmstown's youth. New York: John Wiley and Sons.
Hsu, Francis L. K.
   1953   Americans and Chinese. Garden City, N.Y.: Doubleday Natural
           History Press.

Humphrey, Norman D.
 1949   Social stratification in a Mexican town. Southwestern Journal of
        Anthropology 5:138-146.
Hutchinson, Bertram
 1963   Class self-assessment in a Rio de Janeiro population. América Latina
        6, 1:53-63.
Jacobs, Milton, et al.
 1966   A study of key communicators in urban Thailand. Social Forces
        45:192-199.
Jacobson, David
 1968   Friendship and mobility in the development of an urban elite
        African social system. Southwestern Journal of Anthropology 24:
        123-138.
 1973   Itinerant townsmen: Friendship and social order in urban Uganda.
        Menlo Park, Calif.: Cummings Publishing Company.
Jahoda, Gustav
 1961   White men: A study of attitudes of Africans to Europeans in Ghana
        before independence. London: Oxford University Press.
Jansen, William Hugh
 1965   The esoteric-exoteric factor in folklore. In Alan Dundes, ed., The
        study of folklore. Englewood Cliffs, N.J.: Prentice-Hall.
Kardiner, Abram, and Lionel Ovesey
 1951   The mark of oppression. New York: Norton.
Khuri, Fuad I.
 1968   The African-Lebanese mulattoes of West Africa: A racial frontier.
        Anthropological Quarterly 41:90-101.
Kiefer, Christie W.
 1970   The psychological interdependence of family, school, and bureauc-
        racy in Japan. American Anthropologist 72:66-75.
Kileff, Clive
 1975   Black suburbanites: An African elite in Salisbury, Rhodesia. In C.
        Kileff and W. C. Pendleton, eds., Urban man in southern Africa.
        Gwelo, Rhodesia: Mambo Press.
Knowlton, Clark S.
 1965   A study of social mobility among the Syrian and Lebanese com-
        munity of Sao Paulo. Rocky Mountain Social Science Journal 2:
        174-192.
Kornblum, William
 1974   Blue collar community. Chicago: University of Chicago Press.
Kuper, Leo
 1967   Structural discontinuities in African towns: Some aspects of racial
        pluralism. In Horace Miner, ed., The city in modern Africa. New
        York: Praeger.
 1969   Ethnic and racial pluralism: Some aspects of polarization and de-
        pluralization. In L. Kuper and M. G. Smith, eds., Pluralism in Africa.
        Berkeley: University of California Press.
Leach, Edmund
 1954   Political systems of highland Burma. Cambridge: Harvard University
        Press.

1960   Introduction: What should we mean by caste? In Aspects of caste in south India, Ceylon and north-west Pakistan. Cambridge: Cambridge University Press.

LeBar, Frank M.
1972   Ethnic groups of insular Southeast Asia. New Haven, Conn.: Human Relations Area Files Press.

LeBar, Frank M., et al.
1964   Ethnic groups of mainland Southeast Asia. New Haven: Conn.: Human Relations Area Files Press.

Leeds, Anthony
1964   Brazilian careers and social structure: An evolutionary model and case history. American Anthropologist 66:1321-1347
1974   Housing-settlement types, arrangements for living, proletarianization, and the social structure of a city. In W. Cornelius and F. Trueblood, eds., Latin American Urban Research, vol. 4. Beverly Hills: Sage Publications.

LeMarchand, Rene
1974   Selective genocide in Burundi. Part 1. London: Minority Rights Group Report no. 20.

Lever, H.
1968   Ethnic preferences of white residents in Johannesburg. Sociology and Social Research 52:157-173.

Lévi-Strauss, Claude
1966   The savage mind. Chicago: University of Chicago Press.

Liebow, Elliot
1967   Tally's corner: A study of Negro streetcorner men. Boston: Little, Brown.

Light, Ivan H.
1972   Ethnic enterprise in America: Business and welfare among Chinese Japanese, and blacks. Berkeley: University of California Press.

Little, Kenneth
1957   The role of voluntary associations in West African urbanization. American Anthropologist 59:579-596.
1965   West African urbanization. Cambridge: Cambridge University Press.
1974   Urbanization as a social process: An essay on movement and change in contemporary Africa. London: Routledge and Kegan Paul.

Lynch, Owen
1968   The politics of untouchability: A case from Agra, India. In M. Singer and B. Cohn, eds., Structure and change in Indian society. Chicago: Aldine Publishing Company.
1969   The politics of untouchability. New York: Columbia University Press.
1972   Dr. B. R. Ambedkar: Myth and charisma. In J. M. Mahar, ed., The untouchables of contemporary India. Tucson: University of Arizona Press.

Lynd, Robert S., and Helen M.
1929   Middletown. New York: Harcourt, Brace and Company.

Mair, Lucy
1963   New nations. Chicago: University of Chicago Press.

Mandelbaum, David G.
1970   Society in India. Berkeley: University of California Press.
Mangin, William
1973   Sociological, cultural, and political characteristics of some urban
        migrants in Peru. In A. Southall, ed., Urban anthropology. New
        York: Oxford University Press.
Mangin, William, and Jerome Cohen
1964   Cultural and psychological characteristics of mountain migrants to
        Lima, Peru. Sociologus 14:81-88.
Mayer, Adrian C.
1960   Caste and kinship in central India. Berkeley: University of California
        Press.
1967   Introduction. In B. M. Schwartz, ed., Caste in overseas Indian com-
        munities. San Francisco: Chandler.
Mayer, Philip
1961   Townsmen or tribesmen. Cape Town: Oxford University Press.
1962   Migrancy and the study of Africans in towns. American Anthro-
        pologist 64:576-592.
Mencher, Joan P.
1974   The caste system upside down: Or the not-so-mysterious East. Cur-
        rent Anthropology 15:469-493.
Miller, Stuart C.
1969   The unwelcome immigrant: The American image of the Chinese,
        1785-1882. Berkeley: University of California Press.
Mitchell, J. Clyde
1956   The Kalela dance. Manchester: Manchester University Press.
1960   Tribalism and the plural society: An inaugural lecture. London:
        Oxford University Press.
Nakane, Chie
1970   Japanese society. Berkeley: University of California Press.
Nkosi, Lewis
1965   Zulu tribal fights. New Society, Feb. 18, pp. 6-9.
O'Brien, Rita C.
1972   White society in black Africa. London: Faber.
Olien, Michael D.
1968   Levels of urban relationships in a complex society: A Costa Rican
        case. In E. M. Eddy, ed., Urban anthropology: Research perspectives
        and strategies. Athens: University of Georgia Press.
Orwell, George. See, Blair, Eric
O'Toole, James
1973   Watts and Woodstock: Identity and culture in the United States
        and South Africa. New York: Holt, Rinehart, and Winston.
Ottenberg, Simon
1974   Ethnicity in a Nigerian town and its environs. Paper presented to
        the Symposium on Ethnic Identity and Adaptation, annual meeting
        of the American Anthropological Association, Mexico City.
Parkin, David J.
1966   Urban voluntary associations as institutions of adaptation. Man 1,
        1:90-95.
1969   Tribe as fact and fiction in an East African city. In P. H. Gulliver,

ed., Tradition and transition in East Africa. Berkeley: University of California Press.

Parthasarathy, V. S.
1958   Caste in a south Indian textile mill. Economic Weekly 10 (Aug. 16) 1083-1086.

Pendleton, Wade C.
1975   Social categorization and language usage in Windhoek, South West Africa. In C. Kileff and W. C. Pendleton, eds., Urban man in southern Africa. Gwelo, Rhodesia: Mambo Press.

Plotnicov, Leonard
1964   "Nativism" in contemporary Nigeria. Anthropological Quarterly 37, 3:121-137.
1967   Strangers to the city: Urban man in Jos, Nigeria. Pittsburgh: University of Pittsburgh Press.
1970   The modern African elite in Jos, Nigeria. In A. Tuden and L. Plotnicov, eds., Social stratification in Africa. New York: Free Press.
1972   Who owns Jos? Ethnic ideology in Nigerian urban politics. Urban Anthropology 1:1-13.

Powdermaker, Hortense
1962   Copper town: Changing Africa. New York: Harper and Row.

Provencher, Ronald
1975   Mainland Southeast Asia: An anthropological perspective. Pacific Palisades, Calif.: Goodyear Publishing Company.

Purcell, Victor
1965   The Chinese in Southeast Asia. 2d ed. London: Oxford University Press.

Rabushka, Alvin
1969   Integration in a multi-racial institution: Ethnic attitudes among Chinese and Malay students at the University of Malaya. Race 11:53-63.
1971   Integration in urban Malaya: Ethnic attitudes among Malays and Chinese. Journal of Asian and African Studies 6, 2:91-107.

Reader, D. H.
1966a   Tribalism in South Africa. Scientific South Africa 3, 4:15-18.
1966b   Detribalism in South Africa. Scientific South Africa 3, 5:29-31.

Rehfisch, Farnham, ed.
1975   Gypsies, tinkers and other travellers. New York: Academic Press.

Reissman, Leonard
1961   Class, the city, and social cohesion. Community Development 7:43-51.

Richards, Audrey I.
1963   Multi-tribalism in African urban areas. In Kenneth Little, ed., Urbanization in African social change. Edinburgh: University of Edinburgh Center of African Studies.

Rodriguez, Clara
1975   A cost-benefit analysis of subjective factors affecting assimilation: Puerto Ricans. Ethnicity 2:66-80.

Rosen, Lawrence
1972   Muslim-Jewish relations in a Moroccan city. International Journal of Middle East Studies 3:435-449.

Rosenfeld, Gerry
1971   "Shut those thick lips!": A study of slum school failure. New York: Holt, Rinehart, and Winston.
Rosenthal, Donald B.
1966   Deference and friendship patterns in two Indian municipal councils. Social Forces 45:178-192.
Rouch, Jean
1956   Migrations au Ghana. Journal de la Société des Africanistes 26:33-196.
Rowe, William L.
1973   Caste kinship, and association in urban India. In A. Southall, ed., Urban anthropology. New York: Oxford University Press.
Rudolph, Lloyd I., and Susanne H. Rudolph
1967   The modernity of tradition: Political development in India. Chicago: University of Chicago Press.
Safa, Helen
1974   The urban poor of Puerto Rico. New York: Holt, Rinehart, and Winston.
Sanders, Irwin T., and Ewa T. Morawska
1975   Polish-American community life: A survey of research. New York: Polish Institute of Arts and Sciences in America.
Sandmeyer, Elmer C.
1973   The anti-Chinese movement in California. Urbana: University of Illinois Press. (Original 1939.)
Schildkrout, Enid
1975   Ethnicity, kinship, and joking among urban immigrants in Ghana. In B. M. Du Toit and H. I. Safa, eds., Migration and urbanization. The Hague: Mouton.
Schwab, W. B.
1961   Social stratification in Gwelo. In A. Southall, ed., Social change in modern Africa. London: Oxford University Press.
Schwartz, Barton M.
1967   The failure of caste in Trinidad. In Caste in overseas Indian communities. San Francisco: Chandler.
Shack, William A.
1973   Urban ethnicity and the cultural process of urbanization in Ethopia. In A. Southall, ed., Urban anthropology. New York: Oxford University Press.
Skinner, Elliot P.
1974   African urban life: The transformation of Ouagadougou. Princeton: Princeton University Press.
Skinner, G. William
1958   Leadership and power in the Chinese community of Thailand. Ithaca, N.Y.: Cornell University Press.
Southall, Aidan
1975   Forms of ethnic linkage between town and country. In B. M. Du Toit and H. I. Safa, eds., Migration and urbanization. The Hague: Mouton.
Southall, Aidan, and Peter C. W. Gutkind
1957   Townsmen in the making: Kampala and its suburbs. Kampala: East African Institute of Social Research.

Spiro, Melford E.
    1955   The acculturation of American ethnic groups. American Anthropologist 57:1240-1252.
Srinivas, M. N.
    1952   Religion and society among the Coorgs of south India. Oxford: Clarendon.
    1956   Sanskritisation and westernisation. In A. Aiyappan and L. K. Bala Ratnam, eds., Society in India. Madras: Social Sciences Association.
    1962   Caste in modern India and other essays. Bombay: Asia Publishing House.
Straus, Murray A., and Dorethea Winkelmann
    1969   Social class, fertility, and authority in nuclear and joint households in Bombay. Journal of Asian and African Studies 4:61-74.
Sue, Stanley, and Nathaniel Wagner
    1973   Asian-Americans: Psychological perspectives. Ben Lomond, Calif.: Science and Behavior Books.
Sutherland, Anne
    1975   Gypsies: The hidden Americans. New York: Free Press.
Thompson, Stephen I.
    1974   Survival of ethnicity in the Japanese community of Lima, Peru. Urban Anthropology 3:243-261.
Tiger, Lionel
    1967   Bureaucracy and urban symbol systems. In Horace Miner, ed., The city in modern Africa. New York: Praeger.
Tinker, J. N.
    1972   Intermarriage and ethnic boundaries: The Japanese-American case. Paper presented to the annual meeting of the Pacific Sociological Association, Portland, Oregon.
Tomasi, Silvano M.
    1975   Piety and power: The role of the Italian parishes in the New York metropolitan area, 1880-1930. Staten Island, N.Y.: Center for Migration Studies.
Tschopik, Harry, Jr.
    1967   On the identification of the Indian in Peru. In Sol Tax, ed., Acculturation in the Americas. New York: Cooper Square Publishers.
Tumin, Melvin M.
    1967   Social stratification. Englewood-Cliffs, N.J. Prentice-Hall.
Twaddle, Michael
    1975   Was the expulsion inevitable? In Expulsion of a minority: Essays on Ugandan Asians. London: University of London Press.
Van den Berghe, Pierre
    1964   Caneville: The social structure of a South African town. Middletown, Conn.: Wesleyan University Press.
    1970a   South Africa: A study in conflict. Berkeley: University of California Press.
    1970b   Race and ethnicity. New York: Basic Books.
Van Velsen, J.
    1961   Labour migration as a positive factor in the continuity of Tonga tribal society. In A. Southall, ed., Social change in modern Africa London: Oxford University Press.

Vincent, Joan
    1971   African elite: The big men of a small town. New York: Columbia
            University Press.
Vogel, Ezra F.
    1963   Japan's new middle class. Berkeley: University of California Press.
Wagley, Charles
    1953   Amazon town. New York: Macmillan.
Wagley, Charles, and Marvin Harris
    1958   Minorities in the new world. New York: Columbia University Press.
Walker, Deward E., Jr., ed.
    1972   The emergent native Americans. Boston: Little, Brown.
Wallerstein, Immanuel
    1960   Ethnicity and national integration in West Africa. Cahiers d'Etudes
            Africaines 1:129-139.
Warner, W. Lloyd
    1936   American caste and class. American Journal of Sociology 42:234-
            237.
Warner, W. Lloyd, et al.
    1949   Democracy in Jonesville. New York: Harper.
    1963   Yankee City. Abridged ed. 1 vol. New Haven: Yale University Press.
Watson, Graham
    1972   Passing for white in South Africa. In P. Baxter and B. Sansome, eds.,
            Race and social difference. New York: Penguin Books.
Wax, Rosalie H., and Robert K. Thomas
    1961   American Indians and white people. Phylon 22:305-317.
Weightman, George H.
    1966   Systems of social stratification in three north Lebanese towns. Asian
            Studies 4:491-499.
Weiss, Melford
    1973   Selective acculturation and the dating process: The pattern of
            Chinese-Caucasian inter-racial dating. In S. Sue and N. Wagner, eds.,
            Asian-Americans: Psychological perspectives. Ben Lomond, Calif.:
            Science and Behavior Books.
    1974   Valley City: A Chinese community in America. Cambridge, Mass.:
            Schenkman Publishing Company.
Wheeldon, P. D.
    1969   The operation of voluntary associations and personal networks in
            the political processes of an inter-ethnic community. In J. Clyde
            Mitchell, ed., Social networks in urban situations. Manchester:
            Manchester University Press.
Whiteford, Andrew H.
    1960   Two cities of Latin America: A comparative description of social
            classes. Beloit, Wis.: Logan Museum Publications in Anthropology
            Bulletin no. 9.
Whiteford, Michael B.
    1974   Neighbors at a distance: Life in a low-income Columbian barrio. In
            Wayne A. Cornelius and Felicity M. Trueblood, eds., Latin American
            Urban Research, vol. 4. Beverly Hills: Sage Publications.
    1976   The forgotten ones: Colombian countrymen in an urban setting.
            Gainesville: University of Florida Press.

Willems, Emilio
    1968   Urban classes and acculturation in Latin America. In E. M. Eddy, ed., Urban anthropology: Research perspectives and strategies. Athens: University of Georgia Press.
Williamson, Robert C.
    1962   Some variables of middle and lower class in two Central American cities. Social Forces 41:195-207.
    1968   Social class and orientation to change: Some relevant variables in a Bogotá sample. Social Forces 46:317-328.
Willmott, Donald E.
    1960   The Chinese of Semarang: A changing minority community in Indonesia. Ithaca, N.Y.: Cornell University Press.
Willmott, W. E.
    1969   Congregations and associations: The political structure of the Chinese community in Phnom-Penh, Cambodia. Comparative Studies in Society and History 11, 3:282-301.
Wilson, Monica, and Archie Mafeje
    1963   Langa: A study of social groups in an African township. Cape Town: Oxford University Press.
Winder, R. Bayley
    1962   The Lebanese in West Africa. Comparative Studies in Society and History 4:296-333.
Young, Michael, and Peter Willmott
    1957   Family and kinship in East London. London: Routledge and Kegan Paul.

Anthropologists in Cities: Urban Ethnography and Ethnology

7 The most basic problem for urban anthropologists has always been that of applying the two central techniques of anthropology, *participant-observation* and *holistic* grasp of the culture at hand, to urban research. The techniques of anthropological methodology were forged for the most part in tribal and village societies where it was often possible to develop personal relations with virtually everyone in the society. After a year or more of living among the people he studied, the anthropologist wrote an ethnography that he hoped would give those of his own society an accurate idea of an alien life way.

In attempting the difficult process of immersing himself in the activities of another culture, the anthropologist is condemned to a greater or lesser degree of failure. Learning the language and customs of others can be difficult and at times discouraging. Even should he fully master them, he can never become a member of the group he studies. Yet, even destined to remain estranged, in becoming a participant he learns to glance long into the perspective of his chosen people. He learns, if his fortune and his work serve him well, to understand what it *feels like* to be a member of the society, to comprehend the affect underlying social relations and to try translating them to his own people in such a fashion that some of his glimpses can be shared.

The experience of studying small-scale societies has led anthropologists to attempt to study the entirety of the "target" culture. This holistic approach, made possible by fairly small populations, has been supported by the feeling of many a researcher that the group he is studying is his very own—for no one else might ever meet them again with the intention of preserving their unique heritage. As part of European colonial expansion, anthropologists were well aware that what was not noted in their records might soon vanish forever. Thus the whole society and culture, or at least everything that one could discover, needed to be understood and preserved.

If anthropology has any unifying thread, other than perhaps the concept of culture itself, it is methodological. Through the intensive and holistic study of peoples, anthropologists have produced ethnographies that, in comparison one with another, provide the basis of ethnology, the cross-cultural study of cultures and societies. Without a methodology designed to help him approach the dual task of understanding individual cultures and the human community as a whole, the anthropologist could no longer truly be an anthropologist. Yet, seemingly by its very nature, the city makes the holistic tradition of participant-observation impossible. Clearly, the size and diversity of even the smallest city makes it impossible for the anthropologist to know each inhabitant except in the most superficial manner; and it casts doubt upon his ability to extrapolate to the city as a whole knowledge gained from the intensive study of a few informants.

What then becomes of the anthropologist in the city, or in the study of what have become known as complex societies? Many anthropologists, as we have seen, have responded to this dilemma by restricting the topical scope of their inquiries to concentration upon rural-urban migration; the effect of urbanization on kinship; some aspect of the adaptation and adjustment of urbanites; or the impact of urban life on social stratification and cultural pluralism. Others, feeling that participant-observation is the hallmark of the profession, have sacrificed holism in favor of *micro-level* traditional or formal ethnographies of clearly segmented urban populations; and some researchers have attempted to trace and analyze urban interactional networks. Researchers have sought to conduct middle-level *community studies*, which retain participant-observation and a restricted holism by limiting themselves to the study of a particular ethnic group or some other clearly isolated section of the urban population. Still other anthropologists have given up the intimacy of research based wholly upon participant-observation of a small portion of the urban population for *macro-level* ethnographies of entire cities, which merge ethnographic, historical, and social survey techniques. Finally, urban anthropologists have found that the problems of scale are not limited to ethnography itself, but seem even more difficult to grapple with at the *comparative*, ethnological level where meaningful generalizations of urban life are sought.

Before examining some micro, macro, community, and comparative urban studies, it must be noted that the methodological problems faced by urban anthropologists are not unique to urban work. Even in small tribal groupings, researchers are forced to extrapolate to the whole from partial information. Close and effective relations are often limited to one or two individuals, whose relating of their own culture comes to occupy an inordinate position in the completed ethnography. Since uniformity is unknown in even the smallest society, these individuals undoubtedly differ from their fellows in knowledge and interpretation of world-views and accepted standards of behavior. For behavior that can be observed by the anthropologist, this is not a serious problem: for example, if he has gathered information on wedding ceremonies he can compare it with actual weddings should any occur while he is in residence. But in other areas, such as knowledge of sexual activity, he must usually rely upon a limited number of informants.

The restricted character of certain cultural areas is vividly described by Gerald Berreman in *Behind Many Masks*.[1] Berreman arrived to study the tiny sub-Himalyan village of Sirkanda, India, in the company of a Brahmin assistant and translator. Unknown to him at the time, the presence of the Brahmin severely restricted his knowledge of certain village activities—such as meat-eating and drinking of alcoholic beverages by high-caste individuals—as villagers tried to impress the plains Brahmin with the orthodoxy of their Hinduism. Such a village might have been all that Berreman saw, had it not been for the paradoxical good fortune of losing his assistant. Berreman was forced to engage a retired middle-aged Muslim schoolteacher to aid him with the local language.

With his new assistant came an entirely new view of the village. The Muslim—in contrast to the respected position guaranteed the Brahmin by his status, and the interest the Brahmin had had in conveying to Berreman a positive image of Hinduism—was an untouchable by virtue of his religion. Suddenly there was no longer quite the pressure there had been for the villagers to keep up their image as virtuous Hindus. Low-caste villagers especially, who had formerly kept their distance from the ethnographer, became less inhibited and visited his house so frequently that soon it "became identified as primarily a low-caste area." Interaction with low-castes— and the increased remoteness of high-castes, whose former presence had kept those of low caste from revealing "village secrets"—made it suddenly apparent that Sirkanda was divided. High-castes tended to see the village in terms of high castes and low castes, while low-castes usually distinguished between high castes, "our caste," and other low castes. Most important, Berreman discovered a great deal of village "backstage" information from his low-caste informants, who did "not feel obligated to protect village secrets to the extent that high-caste people [did] simply because their prestige and position [were] not at stake."[2] In contrast to a fairly orthodox Hindu village, Berreman discovered that brothers often shared wives, that both high- and low-castes held religious observances marked by possessed dancing and animal sacrifice, and that even high-caste village men attended drinking parties. The discovery of any of these activities would have cost the village great loss of status in the eyes of the Brahmin assistant, whereas no pretenses were needed in the Muslim's presence.

> The wealthiest Brahmin in the area, for example, had remarked to Sharma [the Brahmin assistant] and me that while some high-caste Paharis might eat meat and drink liquor, as we had probably heard, he himself never touched these defiling items. Later, when everyone knew that Mohammed (the Muslim) and I knew about and participated in the consumption of these things among high-caste villagers, the same Brahmin shared with us a boiled leg of goat and a quart of liquor which he brought as a gift. He had been uninformative about his family to Sharma and insisted that Paharis were conventional in all respects but he once fed Mohammed and me at his home without concealing the fact that he had three wives. There were, however, facts which he could no more reveal to Mohammed than to Sharma. He would have been disconcerted, to say the least, had he known that we knew of his youthful activities as a member of a notorious woman-selling gang and that he had spent time in prison as a consequence.[3]

The difficulty of gaining an accurate impression of an entire community is not, as Berreman has shown, restricted to larger societies. All research is limited by the researcher's skill and fortune. Additionally, there is the factor of personality. Some anthropologists join ranks with large numbers of missionaries and foreign businessmen in what Shelton terms the "Miss Ophelia Syndrome," in which they refuse to participate in certain symbolic activities—such as eating special foods that Westerners might consider unappetizing—and fail to make close contact with villagers, rationalizing a distance that may be quite costly in terms of understanding by the need to maintain "scientific detachment."[4]

Such methodological problems, part of the profession of anthropology, are encountered in tribal, rural, and urban areas alike. Indeed, in some respects the urban anthropologist has a slight advantage, in that the size of a city offers him a certain privacy that can be utilized for interaction with individuals who come from widely opposed social statuses (such as prostitutes and nuns) without great risk that the relation with one will preclude interaction with the other.

URBAN MICROETHNOGRAPHY

Perhaps the simplest approach to urban research is to cast aside concern with providing a comprehensive description of an entire city, in favor of limiting research to material gathered during participant-observation. For most anthropologists—who tend to regard information gleaned from the lips of an informant as more valuable than reconstructions based on written sources or the somewhat artificial data of survey methods[5]—a microethnographic approach limited principally to material gained from participant-observation is also most appealing.

Although microethnographic methods of necessity limit the arena of research, the goal of such research is usually not nearly so confined. Few, if any, microethnographies are undertaken with the intention of understanding only the individuals studied. Rather, they are grounded in the assumption that intensive study of a few individuals is as productive in comprehending the life of others in similar situations as more extensive ethnographies would be—that intensive research of a few tramps, for example, is at least as worthwhile as wider-ranging holistic studies that seek to study the entire tramp population and its relations with the larger society.

Biographic Techniques

Traditional microethnography—which relies simply upon observation and the eliciting of information from informants, without the special methodology required by formal and network microethnography—at one extreme quickly becomes biography. Indeed, the two best-known traditional microethnographies, Oscar Lewis' *Children of Sanchez* and *La Vida*, are based on the premise that intensive study of the lives of a single family can yield a strong, affective sense of not just their lives but the lives of all those in similar situations. Lewis' introduction to his study of the Sanchez family, in Mexico City, sets as his goal "to give the reader an inside view of family life and of what it means to grow up in a one-room house in a slum tenement in the heart of a great Latin American city which is undergoing a process of rapid social change"[6] through the autobiographies of family members.

Using the innovative technique of encouraging Jesus Sanchez (the father) and Manuel, Roberto, Consuelo, and Marta (his four children) to relate their own life histories into his tape recorder, Lewis was able to provide his readers with an intimate view into a family caught in the "culture of poverty." Their story, like that of the Rios family of San Juan, Puerto Rico, and New York, which is captured by the same method in *La Vida*, is a moving and poignant tale. The vivid portrayal of lives in urban poverty places these works as much in the realm of literature as of social science. Tape-recording has the advantage of letting the principals tell their own stories with a minimum of filtering through the inevitable biases of the ethnographer. Additionally, the limitations of scope and the biases of each family member toward events is corrected to some degree through juxtaposition of the autobiographies. In following the narratives of the Sanchez and Rios families, the reader has the opportunity to assume the role of ethnographer as he assesses each member's tale in the light of those of his immediate kin. He becomes familiar with the personality of each individual and is able to reconstruct events with some correction for situational distortions.

William Mangin modifies Lewis' autobiographical approach by coupling the life history of a Peruvian woman with annotations from his extensive knowledge of *barriada* life that place her recollections in collective context. Thus her tale of being impregnated and abandoned by a married man is seen as a common phenomenon, for, in general, a woman "gets pregnant before marriage, usually by a man who betrays her and turns out to be already married, but often by the man later married." The woman's lament that she worked without pay for the wife of a school director for twelve years is clearly part of a common pattern in which a "large number of women, and many men . . . reported being virtual slaves while working as house servants for middle class families." Mangin further describes this particular woman:

> She felt like one of the family at first, when she worked mainly as a baby sitter, and she travelled all over the province with the family. After a few years, she took on more household duties and seldom left the house. She received no pay for the 12 years. "How could she have fooled me so. I worked very hard. She treated me very badly. When people who had known me saw the way I was working they just shook their heads and said, "huerfanos, pues." (More or less, "That's the way it is with orphans, too bad.")[7]

Student research projects in urban anthropology usually must be microethnographic because concentration on small samples is most appropriate to the time constraints of such projects.[8] A few dozen hours of research are not enough to adequately describe the structure of any city, but if well spent they can capture some particular aspect of it. When teaching at the Universiti Sains Malaysia, I supervised numerous microethnographies. Working alone or in small groups, students explored subjects ranging from trishaw peddlers to Indian breadmen (who deliver bread to homes by bicycle at a commission of approximately two U.S. cents per loaf, and many of whom had made periodic visits to families in India), to unauthorized parking attendants, to teenage prostitutes and dance hall hostesses to social escorts.

Interestingly, the social escort services were studied separately, by a group of three female students who had suggested a study of "naughty girls" and by one male who worked separately. The significance of *who* does the research and *how* it is carried out is illustrated by the two reports. The female students concluded, based on a number of interviews with "escorts," that the "girls" had been unfairly characterized as prostitutes by the larger community, and that in fact they had not lost their moral standards just because poverty forced them to accept socially disreputable employment. The male, on the other hand, was readily offered sexual services at the very establishments where his female classmates had been convinced by managers and escorts that such activity was definitely out of bounds.

Although the traditional microethnographic approach is suitable for projects of limited time, it can be almost infinitely expanded.

Harry Wolcott's *Man in the Principal's Office* focuses upon the activities of a single elementary school principal. It does so partly in reaction to "the manner in which the rapidly expanding body of educational research shows a trend toward huge, costly studies which often yield strikingly unimportant data (for example, that 97 percent of high school social studies teachers talk about politics in class 'always,' 'often,' or 'sometimes'; or that '44 percent of the teachers in metropolitan areas are satisfied as compared to 35 percent of the teachers in small towns')."[9] In focusing on a single occupation among the thousands upon which American society is based, Wolcott provides an intensive view of the world of the school principal, illustrating through careful observation of the principal's day and his formal and informal encounters the compromises required by the expectations of his social role. After shadowing the principal for nearly two years, he was able to describe what a principal does and, more important, how his activities represent a compromise between his own goals and what students, teachers, and the community demand of the job. The principals's remarks on the constraining effect of these expectations are included in the final section of the book, which consists of his reactions:

> He [the principal] particularly pointed out that many of the things which principals do—like chasing dogs off school grounds or tracing a missing sandwich—are done not because principals want to do them but because other people expect it. I think he is absolutely right in linking the limitations of the principal's role with the restraints imposed by constantly having to meet the expectations of a multitude of others. The demands of a position in which "every problem is important" mitigate the opportunity for constructive accomplishment. The principalship is thusly burdened and hampered by the traditions that have grown up around it.[10]

Wolcott's research demonstrates the value of exhaustive analysis of any occupation in highlighting the assumptions of a society as a whole. As such, it is a model for the heretofore underused technique of approaching the study of urban society through careful analysis of the fusion of (1) individual goals and identity with (2) the behavioral expectations appropriate to an occupation.

Ethnosemantic Techniques

A recurrent concern of anthropologists has been whether anthropological descriptive categories accurately represent reality as perceived by those people who are under study. In order to compare societies cross-culturally, anthropologists have developed a vocabulary to categorize apparently similar customs and beliefs. Traditionally, for example, anthropologists have used postmarital *residence rules*— patrilocal, matrilocal, avunculocal, bilocal, and neolocal *rules*—as a basic means of categorizing a group's social organization. Yet, as Fischer and Goodenough have demonstrated in their classic disagreement over how the Trukese should be classified,[11] these rules often seem to have their primary locus in the mind of the anthropologist. Similarly, as Cole argues:

> Few Africans view their societies, let alone understand them, as they are depicted in the monographs of social scientists, many of whom have supposedly spent several years doing field work in the chosen areas. The lack of comprehension on the part of the African is not due to low intelligence, but rather to the rarefied ways in which such studies are written; which leaves a feeling that western social scientists are engaged in a culturally determined, private intellectual game.[12]

One solution to this problem is to approach the study of a culture as a whole through a linguistic perspective. In starting to reduce a foreign language to writing, the linguist encounters an almost infinite number of sounds, many of which have no significance in themselves but are uttered in conjunction with other culturally meaningful sounds. At first, of course, the linguist has no idea which sounds are significant. Consequently, he must attempt to record *every* sound to produce a phonetic transcription of speech utterances. After making the transcription, from the universal categories provided by the International Phonetic Alphabet (IPA), he proceeds to the next stage, phonemic analysis. Here he tries to reduce the number of signs to a manageable level by determining which sounds trigger a difference of meaning in the language and which do not. Thus, for example, a linguist first encountering English would note that English words which begin with the sound *p* have a small puff of air after the *p* known as "aspiration," while words which have the *p* sound imbedded within them do not: the *p* in *pin* is aspirated and written [p'] , while the *p* in *spin* is not and appears in IPA merely as [p] . Comparison of English words with *p* would quickly reveal to our hypothetical linguist that aspiration or nonaspiration may sound strange depending on context but does not trigger a difference in meaning. Wherever it occurs [p] can therefore be written simply as *p*.

In moving from a description of language or any other aspect of culture based on universal to culturally-specific categories, we shift from an *etic* (from phon*etic*) to an *emic* (phon*emic*) level of description, attempting to understand the group we are studying in their own terms.[13] This approach to the study of an entire culture through the categories used by its people is known as *ethnoscience, formal semantic analysis,* or simply *formal analysis.* Theoretically, a formal ethnography—based as it is upon logical extension of the concept of the principle of cultural relativity (every group must be understood and evaluated in its own terms)—should provide a much more accurate indication of the world-view of its subjects than we would expect to find in a traditional, etic ethnography. Unfortunately, ethnoscience has generally failed to meet the expectations of its adherents: the difficulty of rigorously defining and translating the vocabulary of cultural domains has largely restricted it to the study of kinship systems, color, and botanical terminologies where culturally relative classification can be grounded in universal categories.[14]

The problem of knowing whether ethnographic descriptions are psychologically valid for the people they describe is equally a problem for urban anthropologists, even in studying their own societies. As Spradley has shown in his work with tramps: "Those who live in cities may share the same locality but they are actually cultural worlds apart. One important part of *urban* anthropology must be the careful ethnographic description of these cultural worlds."[15]

Nowhere is the separation of "cultural worlds" in America more obvious than in the comparison of tramp and middle-class cultures. Even in their perceptions of tramps, middle-class Americans are often far from the mark. Most would undoubtedly feel that the major, if not the sole, concern of tramps is alcohol. Because most tramps come to attention through arrests for public drunkenness or for such alcohol-related crimes as urinating in public, this is a reasonable assumption. But as Spradley has shown from his careful analysis of what tramps talk about, *making a flop,* or finding a safe and cheap place to sleep, probably occupies more of a tramp's time than any other activity. This is important, if a tramp is not to be exposed to the weather, assaulted, or arrested as a vagrant. Reflecting concern with a place to sleep is the fact that sleep, or *flop,* becomes a noun as well as a verb. Unlike most Americans who usually know where they are going to sleep, for tramps the actual location of a flop is uncertain. Detailed analysis of the taxonomy of flops—paid flops, empty buildings, weed-patches, railroad flops, mission flops, and their sub-units—shows that tramps not only make a noun of their place to sleep, but that they make fine distinctions between types of places based on such factors as expense, comfort, and safety.[16]

As is the case with tramps, most Americans' understanding of heroin addicts is drawn from stereotypes that are seldom based on "inside" knowledge of addict subculture. In an attempt to rectify misunderstandings that have often resulted in law enforcement and treatment strategies that are designed to meet the needs of middle-class Americans rather than addicts, Michael Agar conducted intensive formal analysis of addict inmates at the United States Drug Treatment Center in Lexington, Kentucky. In contrast to most studies of addiction, which "assume the social-psychological failure status of the addict as the problem to be explained," Agar approached his formal microethnography of heroin addicts with the query: "What if such a priori judgements were temporarily suspended and addicts were studied ethnographically as a legitimate community with an alternative culture, different but equally valid if compared to other American subcultures?"[17]

From the beginning, it was obvious to Agar that he was studying a distinct subculture: *junkies* (heroin addicts) of varying age, race, and place of origin could readily converse with one another over a range of topics without being understood by an outsider. As might a linguist, he began his study by noting and gaining definitions of such frequently occurring words as *hustle* (obtain money illegally), *cop* (buy heroin), and *get off* (inject heroin). Gradually, as his knowledge of junkie vocabulary increased to include such terms as *bread* (money), *stuff* (heroin), getting *straight* (in this sense, to have heroin so as to be "not sick"), *dealer* (one who sells heroin), *rip off* (rob), *burn* (getting less heroin than one's money should purchase), *works* (implements used to inject heroin), the *man* (law enforcement officer), and *bust* (arrest), Agar was able to outline a general set of perceptions and the logical relations between them that are central to addict culture.

A *junkie* wants to be able to *hustle* enough *bread* to *cop* some *stuff* from a *dealer* without getting *burned* or otherwise *ripped off* so that he can put the *stuff* in the *works* at his *place* to *get off* and get *straight* without getting *busted* by the *man*. If successful in this strategy, which is merely a summary of a much more complex sub-cultural operation, then the *junkie* can permit himself to relax and enjoy a respite from labor as might any working man. As Agar and others have noted in their descriptions of *the life* (life of a heroin addict), heroin addiction is not simply a craving for a drug, but a way of life. In the words of one addict: "When I'm on the way home with the bag safely in my pocket, and I haven't been caught stealing all day, and I didn't get beat and the cops didn't get me—I feel like a working man coming home; he's worked hard, but he knows he's done something, even though I know it's not true."[18]

The importance of Agar's approach to anthropology should be obvious; it fulfills the purpose of ethnography by providing us with the basic information we need in order to be able to behave like, or at least understand, a heroin addict. For those who would attempt to provide solutions for America's heroin addiction problem, it also suggests that addiction cannot be treated simply as chemical addiction, but that it must be approached with the realization that it is often a *cultural* addiction to an exciting and challenging world that offers meaning to otherwise drab lives.

In another innovative and interesting addition to our body of formal microethnographies, Spradley and Mann have closely analyzed an occupational role, that of the cocktail waitress, in hope that examination of the waitress' position and her interaction with other (female) waitresses, (male) bartenders, and customers might provide "a small window on the world of female and male roles"—and on the well-grounded assumption that answers to questions about what constitutes basic American male and female role stereotypes can best be sought in ordinary situations in which "*manhood and womanhood are defined in the process of social interaction.*"[19]

Particularly interesting and valuable is the authors' segmentation of the ethnographer role into two parts: participant and observer. While Brenda Mann entered the cocktail waitress' world by finding a job at a bar and becoming a participant, James Spradley was the detached observer, who treated the primary researcher (Mann) herself as an informant, to avoid as much as possible "an important phenomenon that happens to every participant observer. Before many weeks have passed the ethnographer *knows* more than she can tell"[20]—a problem made more acute by the fact that she is a member of the wider culture of which the bar culture is a segment.

Network Techniques

Finally, a *network* approach has been used by numerous anthropologists during the past two decades to study the character of interpersonal relations in other societies. Use of the concept of social networks originated with Barnes's study of the Norwegian island parish of Bremnes. In seeking to explain the processes by which crews for the island's fishing vessels were recruited, he noted that:

> Each person is, as it were, in touch with a number of other people some of whom are directly in touch with each other and some of whom are not. Similarly each person has a number of friends; some of any one person's friends know each other, others do not . . . we can often think of the whole of social life as generating a network of this kind.[21]

Barnes's work was quickly followed by Elizabeth Bott's impressive study of "ordinary urban" British families, which demonstrated an association between the character of conjugal relationships and that of the husband's and wife's networks.[22] If the husband and wife had close-knit networks prior to marriage, and if each was able to maintain these networks (unruptured by geographical relocation or other circumstances), then the marriage often seemed just another tie superimposed on preexisting relations, so that each spouse would be continually pulled into other people's activities. Under such circumstances, rigid segregation of male-female roles was common, for a good deal of help and emotional satisfaction came from those outside the conjugal relationship. If, in contrast, both husband and wife entered the relationship with loose-knit networks, or their networks later became loose-knit, they usually sought greater emotional satisfaction and help with familial tasks from one another than from outsiders.

More recently, interest in the analytical use of social networks has spread to such traditional anthropological research locales as Africa. It has been accompanied by the elaboration of network theory, seeking to standardize our understanding of human interpersonal relations through examination of such morphological characteristics of networks as anchorage, density, reachability, and range, and such aspects of the nature of the interaction itself, as its content, directedness, durability, intensity, and frequency.[23]

Epstein has illustrated both "the random character of much of urban social life" and the "elements of regularity . . . within this extremely fluid field"[24] through careful analysis of the contacts of one of his African research assistants over a period of several days. Even in so short a time it was evident that his assistant, Chanda, had a substantial network of friends, relatives, and acquaintances. Chanda's network, of course, in no sense formed a corporate or collective group, for it was the result of his own activities, linking kin with individuals who might well be unknown to one another. Analysis of Chanda's network also illustrated the differing intensity of relations between Chanda and network members, so that it seemed logical to divide it for conceptual purposes into an *effective* network and an *extended* one. The former consisted of individuals with whom Chanda interacted most intensely and regularly and who were also most likely to know one another. Members of the extended network included individuals who were Chanda's acquaintances but who were unknown to one another.

The spread of gossip provides an interesting illustration of the functioning of social networks in urban situations. Gossip not only entertains those who spread it, it also frequently becomes a means of social control by detailing and enforcing behavioral norms. The spread of news of the foibles and failings of others—rarely is "good" gossip greeted with the same interest and excitement as "bad," consequently "bad" gossip travels furthest—helps provide a backdrop for measuring one's own life, as well as an illustration of the dangers of deviation from social norms.

Stories of sexual misconduct seem to be universally the most popular fodder for gossip. Thus, during research interviews in Ndola, Northern Rhodesia (Zambia), one of Epstein's research assistants discovered a household empty of its chief occupant, Charles. In response to his inquiry about Charles, the interviewer noticed that the younger brother left behind was uneasy. Shortly afterwards the cause of Charles's absence emerged: he had been found committing adultery with a woman named Monica, the wife of Kaswende, a truck driver for a local brewery. Wide distribution of the company's beer often took Kaswende on lengthy journeys, and Charles and Monica made use of these absences to carry on a liaison at Kaswende's house. One evening in Kaswende's absence, Charles' younger brother visited the house and discovered the affair. Kaswende, on return, heard of the incident, confronted Charles, and thrashed him severely, warning him that he would beat him in the future whenever he saw him.

Adultery is hardly an unusual occurrence, as Epstein points out. What was interesting in this case was the apparent widespread knowledge and discussion of the affair, evidenced by the wide range of people who knew and related the story. In tracing some of the paths through which the story had spread, Epstein discovered that even the affair itself had mobilized a secretive network of individuals who helped cover for the adulterous couple. The marriage of one of those involved, a woman who let the couple use her house in her spouse's absence, was severed by her husband on his discovery that she had facilitated her friend's adultery—something that made him suspect his wife's rectitude.

The moral message of the spread of news of the adultery seemed to center around the fact that Monica was a very beautiful woman, better educated than her husband, who had married Kaswende after having contracted a venereal disease for which Kaswende had provided medicine. Her parents, in their gratitude, were apparently willing to sanction the marriage; but Monica was less pleased with an arrangement connecting her with an older and evidently impotent man. Clearly, she had married beneath herself to a man who, although he had a well-paying job, dressed and conducted himself like a rustic. Despite her adultery, the prestige he gained from having such a beautiful wife was sufficient to keep him from divorcing her. Thus the gossip, far from condemning Monica, focused upon adultery as an appropriate punishment for a man foolish enough to reach beyond his status.

Implicitly, the tenor of the gossip illustrated the emergence of class as a crucial new component of organization for urban Africans— something violated by the marriage of Monica and Kaswende. As Epstein discovered, "the gossip of [Monica's] friends who made up her own social network (or at least a section of it) provided a re-affirmation of the values which they held in common, and which gave them their sense of identity as a distinct social class."[25] In this light, it is clear that gossip retains its importance as a means of social control, which it has in kin- and ethnic-based societies, but that it now also sometimes articulates norms of behavior defining class distinctiveness.

URBAN COMMUNITY STUDIES

One research strategy that permits the anthropologist to combine participant-observation with limited holism is the community study. By restricting the venue of research, the ethnographer is able to supplement material gained from actual experience with more extensive techniques such as formally interviewing a large sample of the total population. He may reject a questionnaire or some similar approach (as many anthropologists do on grounds that the compilation, administration, and interpretation of questionnaires is a time-con-suming activity fraught with the potential of creating pseudo-informa-tion as an artifact of the structure of the questionnaire) in favor of relying wholly upon participant-observation. But the fact that he chooses to study a bounded community within the city allows him to generalize more readily about the community than he could in a participant-observation study of the entire city.

In effect, a community approach provides the closest possible replication of the traditional tribal study, permitting the anthro-pologist to adapt his techniques to an urban area with a minimum of alteration. Not surprisingly, community studies have been popular among urban anthropologists. They range from studies of American black ghetto communities as a whole[26] to ethnographies of black street-corner men, black gangs, urban blues music and musicians, black Pentecostals, gypsies, Chinese-Americans, a Tokyo ward, and a middle-class Japanese community.[27]

Traditional Ethnographic Analysis

One of the most interesting examples of urban community research is Arthur Hippler's *Hunter's Point: A Black Ghetto*, which combines participant-observation of a San Francisco housing project with analysis of life histories and TAT (Thematic Apperception Test) protocols gathered from members of two fatherless and two intact families, to construct an ethnography of community values, social organization, relations with whites, and the dominant personality patterns of community residents. As a white male engaging in re-search in a black ghetto, Hippler confesses: "I do not feel I truly became a part of the community. I was accepted and adapted to in the way that people come to learn to accept and adapt to other inevitable and somewhat inexplicable phenomena." Denied the possibility of movement as a black in the ghetto, in order to circulate and observe freely Hippler sought to reverse and utilize the oft-noted phenomenon of black "invisibility" in white eyes—in which blacks find themselves ignored by whites in their presence. Two types of invisibility were exploited: that of the high-status person, which "involved such tactics as appearing to be so involved in talking with the 'important' people at places such as the Youth Opportunity Center that 'ordinary' people could afford to ignore one's presence," and that of the low-status person, which Hippler used to similar advantage.

In early stages of my work, and especially on Third Avenue, I often wore very old clothing and in fact did present myself in these situations as a non-communicative and uninvolved "bum." Similarly, someone who spends hours, days, or weeks on end in a record shop doing nothing but listening to records can after a while be ignored. If he is that wrapped up in his own world, he is obviously not interested in yours. Or someone who is busily examining every square inch of a playground fence for "structural defects" clearly can be considered uninterested in the interaction of the children in the yard.[28]

Rather than emphasize the observer aspect of fieldwork as Hippler did, Elliot Liebow attached himself to a group of street-corner men in Washington, D.C. His research strategy already laid out—he planned to do three or four studies of aspects of the lives of lower-class black males—Liebow set out one day merely to "get his feet wet" by spending a few hours in preresearch reconnaissance. He had moved less than a block from his starting point when he stopped to watch the arrest of a kicking, screaming woman; a small crowd had congregated, giving him the opportunity to enter into conversation with two fellow observers. After a brief exchange of police anecdotes one of the individuals, an older man, said goodbye and left. The other man stayed on and accepted the ethnographer's invitation to coffee.

That night, Liebow returned home to write up the day's experience, promising himself that tomorrow he would pursue his original project. But the next morning, walking down the same street, he again encountered a group of men, this time around a puppy. Liebow stopped to admire the animal and went into a "carry-out" (restaurant) to buy milk to feed him. A few minutes later, a newcomer joined the group—of which the ethnographer was by now an established member. When the others took their leave, Liebow and the newcomer, "Tally Jackson," went into the carry-out for a four-hour conversation that began their friendship.

These encounters established both the core of Liebow's approach to his study of black street-corner males and presaged one of the most important conclusions of *Tally's Corner*: that the special circumstances common to lower-class black men in American society, where meaningful employment is generally beyond reach, lead them into a world of quickly made and quickly broken relations. Unable to support their families adequately or to gain positive affirmation of their identities through occupations, these men become involved in both marriages and friendships that are often based on chance and that in time fall victim to the average man's inability to cope with their financial and psychological demands.

Marriage is often doomed to failure because the husband cannot perform the most important role of a male in American society, that of family breadwinner—a failure made even more glaring by the fact that black women are often not only more employable than males but are also eligible for welfare support payments if there is no able-bodied male in the same household. Faced with constant reminder of their failure as men, many husbands seek escape by deserting their wives and children. Friendships, too, are of necessity based upon exaggerated presentations of self granted by each friend to the other to salve his self-esteem. "Friendship," Liebow reports,

> appears as a relationship between two people who, in an important sense, stand unrevealed to one another. Lacking depth in both past and present, friendship is easily up-rooted by the tug of economic or psychological self-interest or by external forces acting against it.
>
> The recognition of this weakness, coupled with the importance of friendship as a source of security and self-esteem, is surely a principal source of the impulse to romanticize relationships, to upgrade them, to elevate what others see as a casual acquaintanceship to friendship, and friendship to close friendship. It is this, perhaps, that lies behind the attempt to ascribe a past to a relationship that never had one, and to borrow from the bony structure of kinship ("going for brothers") to lend structural support to a relationship sorely in need of it. It is as if friendship is an artifact of desire, a wish relationship, a private agreement between two people to act "as if," rather than a real relationship between persons.[29]

Formal Interviewing

In contrast to the transient research population of Liebow, Robert Edgerton in *Cloak of Competence* turned his anthropological training to careful examination of a group of individuals recently discharged from an institution for the mentally retarded. One of the most demeaning labels that can be affixed to a human being is "mentally retarded." It has been said that stupidity is the worst sin a human being can commit. But if this statement is viewed in evolutionary perspective, and the value-laden terms "sin" and "commit" replaced, the statement "stupidity is the worst state in which a human can exist" has firm factual grounding. Nothing is more characteristic of a human being than his ability to reason. Those handicapped in this area are deprived of the core of humanity in a manner in which those who are blind or deaf, for example, are not. To many people retardation is a repugnant subject that conjures up images of salivating, misshapen, subhuman organisms.

This general distaste for the retarded undoubtedly lay behind Edgerton's discovery, at the time he began work with a sample of 110 former inmates of the Pacific State Hospital, that an "outstanding void" existed in the sociological literature. The gap occurred both in the study of the retarded in institutions and, more markedly, in our understanding of how retarded individuals cope outside institutions. In an attempt to fill this void, Edgerton sought to interview individuals in a preselected sample. Of these, 85 percent were eventually located, and approximately half lived within the fifty-mile radius of the hospital that limited Edgerton's territory.

Interviews began with an effort to establish a friendly and informal conversational setting, in which the former patient was encouraged to pursue any subject that interested him at length before an attempt was made to follow a formal interview schedule. In addition to the formal interviews, as much participant-observation as possible was undertaken in ordinary life situations that included trips to recreational areas, supermarkets, and the homes of friends and relatives. Neighbors, friends, relatives, and employees of the subjects were also interviewed when possible, although interviewers were forced to handle delicately the situation of gaining interviews without exposing the subject's past to anyone unaware of it. Fieldworkers were also rotated, so that each former patient was seen by at least two researchers. Rapport was gained with amazing ease: "literally from the first ring of the door-bell, the lives of these former patients were open to us."[30] When problems did occur they resulted from the intervention of a "normal" individual, usually a relative, who did not want the subject to continue with the research.

From the research with discharged patients emerged a picture of individuals whose dominant concern was "passing," by hiding their past as discredited humans and insisting that they were not nearly so stupid as most of the people back in the hospital. "You know, I was worried did they really think I was like them others. The ones that couldn't do nothing or learn nothing. I used to think I'd rather be dead than be like them."[31] The expatients were almost always unsuccessful in passing among those with whom they had repeated contact. But they were often clever in assuming a "cloak of competence" in fleeting encounters, by seeking out familiar situations whose limited permutations had been gone through many times before so that they would not be likely to discredit themselves. Even in situations that demanded abilities they did not possess, such as telling time from a wristwatch, they sought to avoid detection through strategies they hoped would deflect a stranger's suspicions: "I'm sorry, could you tell me the time; I forgot my glasses," for example.

Cloak of Competence illustrates the great utility that a careful blend of participant-observation, directed and nondirected interviews, the gathering of life histories, and especially the relating in their own words of the stories of members of the group—keeping in mind constantly the question, "what are they really trying to say about themselves?"—can offer in providing insight into the nature of any bounded population.

URBAN MACROETHNOGRAPHY

At the opposite extreme from research such as Wolcott's intensive work with a single grammar school principal, we find a macro-approach to urban studies that seeks to describe the city in its entirety through blending ethnographic, historical, and social survey techniques. Inevitably, macroethnographies tend to emphasize social structure rather than to concern themselves with patterns of behavior or cognitive structures common to city residents. As such, urban macroethnography usually seems to resemble more closely sociological, or social anthropological, research than that which cultural anthropologists would be expected to produce.

Social Structure Approaches

Not surprisingly, the bulk of urban macroethnography has been conducted by social anthropologists and set in the context of African cities.[32] Common to all these ethnographies is an attempt to describe the city as holistically as possible. Skinner, for example, in *African Urban Life: The Transformation of Ouagadougou*, titles his chapters the development of Ouagadougou; occupations and economic activities; kinship and kin relations; courtship and marriage; family life and status profiles; ethnic interaction and the role of associations; education; recreation and entertainment; religion; law enforcement; and politics and government—in a fashion reminiscent of ethnographies of tribal societies. Through his long residence in the Upper Volta capital, as both anthropologist and American ambassador, Skinner was able to amass detailed ethnographic and historical information on what seems to be every aspect of Ouagadougou life and each segment of the community. "The methodology used in studying Ouagadougou," he explains,

> was influenced by my belief that African urban life cannot be understood unless all the institutions and aspects of a town are studied. Familiarity with the traditional society and culture of the Mossi people who comprised the overwhelming majority of the town's population facilitated an ethnographic approach. Moreover, the compact nature of the town and its modest population made it possible for me to cover the town myself . . . I was able to observe and to analyze the "social networks" of a key number of individuals from all social strata . . . The existence of a demographic survey of the town obviated the difficult and acutely politically sensitive task of an individual census. Use was made of questionnaires when possible, and when deemed necessary or indeed valuable. The municipal courts of Ouagadougou proved to be a mine of information . . . Municipal and government documents completed the sources of data gathered and used for this study.[33]

In approaching the city holistically, however, Skinner was forced inevitably to gloss over certain topics and to subsume theoretical explanation and problem orientation to description and inclusiveness. In doing so, he has provided us with something that could be termed a study of "culture at a distance up close": he has turned his years of participant-observation towards producing an overview of Ouagadougou rather than fill his text with an assemblage of ethnographic anecdotes.

While the macroethnographic approach to urban study has been found most congenial by sub-Saharan Africanists, others working in the United States, French Canada, Lebanon, and Japan[34] have sought to provide all-inclusive "culture at a distance up close" treatment to their study of urbanized societies. Best known is the work of Warner and his associates during the 1930's in Yankee City, which appeared in several volumes summarized by Warner.[35] The Yankee City series focused upon a number of aspects of the community and included volumes devoted to its social life, status system, and ethnic groups, the social system of its shoe factories, and the symbol systems of its inhabitants.

Although the work resembles sociological studies in its exhaustive team-interview approach to research, its major contribution—delineation of the social class structure of an American community—emerged from Warner's ethnographic training and research experience with Australian aborigines.[36] Warner sought to make his own personal biases explicit before beginning his work on community social structure, and he let his understanding of the community emerge from the categories of his informants. But, coupled with the training in eliciting native categories that came with his background, a tendency also came to generalize too widely. His introduction to *Democracy in Jonesville,* for example, makes expansive claims for the study's scope which few others have been willing to grant: "Jonesville is in all Americans and all Americans are in Jonesville, for he that dwelleth in America dwelleth in Jonesville, and Jonesville in him ... To study Jonesville is to study America."[37] As the sociologist Milton Gordon has argued, "such a claim may well stem from the research techniques and assumptions characteristic of the discipline of cultural anthropology which constitutes Warner's professional training and orientation." He continues: "The ethnologist dealing with relatively self-contained small tribal communities, each of which constitutes its own effective cultural 'universe,' faces no problem of generalizing his results, granted that he has correctly described his community."[38]

Ecological Approaches

Another approach is to view the city as a unit that develops a distinct character of its own as the result of its particular setting and history. Price's team study of Reno, Nevada, for example, approached the study of Reno through certain uniquely integrative features of the city: gambling, prostitution, quick divorces, revitalization of western cowboy culture, and an emphasis on an ethos of personal freedom.[39] His use of a research team to study these aspects of Reno could also have been made within the framework of a modified ecological approach: viewing urban life as a coherent ecosystem within which different individuals exploit occupational niches in order to survive. A portrait of any city as a dynamic system could thus be produced. Members of a research team could be assigned to conduct intensive fieldwork with those who are exploiting the niches, to discover the pattern of exploitation, who is exploited, and how competition in the same or a similar niche is dealt with.

Student research in Penang, Malaysia, for example, revealed that something of a symbiotic relationship existed between prostitutes, trishaw drivers, hotel owners, pimps and gang members, and certain policemen. A sailor or tourist arriving in the city for a vacation would face incessant solicitation by trishaw drivers offering him "a girl" and a needed escort to places of prostitution (somewhat hidden, for prostitution is illegal in Penang). If the visitor responded with interest, he would be taken to a hotel and shown the available prostitutes, who were often enthusiastically introduced by the trishaw driver, who knew that if he were successful in making a connection he would gain a handsome commission. After the arrangements were made, the money was paid to the hotel "manager" (the pimp) whose job it was to dispense it to all who had claim to a portion: the prostitute (who might receive half or less of the standard five-dollar rate for a "short time"), the driver, the hotel owner (the pimp was often a salaried employee), and the Chinese gang members who provided protection against difficult clients and rival gangs. Finally, a portion was set aside for the police officer, who served as a "bag man," collecting money to encourage his fellow officers to ignore the "hotel's" existence. This was difficult, for all such hotels gave clear indication of their true function (a bar usually occupied the entire ground floor, for example, and a steady stream of male clients regularly arrived in trishaws) and most were located within a few blocks of the central police station.

While the ecological approach is a particularly stimulating one around which to organize student research projects, it has obvious advantages and disadvantages. Complete analysis of a city based upon such an orientation probably provides a more accurate description of what a city actually *is* than any other approach, but it does so at the cost of great amounts of time and it requires a number of assistants to conduct primary research and piece together the fragments into a coherent whole.

URBAN ETHNOLOGY

Now that a sufficiently large body of anthropological research in urban areas exists, urban anthropologists have begun to concern themselves with developing an urban ethnology, or comparative urban anthropology. In doing so the hoary issue of coping with the problems of urban complexity and scale has once again emerged.

Recently, an entire issue of the journal *Urban Anthropology* was devoted to the topic "The City as Context."[40] Implicit in the various articles was the problem of defining what a city is and how it is different from other forms of human settlement, and of how any particular study can be set in a context that permits controlled comparison. In his introduction to the special issue, Jack Rollwagen suggests that the relative lack of comparison in urban work is the outgrowth of the anthropologist's earlier tendency to approach the study of peasant villages as if they were self-sufficient units akin to tribes. Concern with the function that the village played in the larger society, or with whether village living had significance in itself, was largely ignored. This "heritage of nongeneralization," he feels "has been passed on to the field of urban anthropology with the result that, by and large, urban anthropologists are wont to 'do a study' of something that interests them and not to spend much (if any) time on function or comparison (which would lead them to attempts at generalizations)."[41] No doubt, Rollwagen is correct.

Indeed, this book is itself an effort to help establish a field of urban ethnology by assessing various studies of rural-urban migration, urban family structure, urban adaptation and adjustment, and urban social stratification and cultural pluralism, with the goal of developing cross-cultural generalizations. One reason urban anthropologists have until now been reluctant to take the next step beyond concrete study to the development of an urban ethnology is, as Rollwagen has suggested, that they have been fixated on the city itself. When they have turned to the broader field of anthropology for aid, the help they have sought has been of an ethnographic (for example, directed towards developing an adequate methodology for the study itself) rather than an ethnological nature.

Recently, movement towards the development of urban ethnology has appeared in Nagata's comparison of two Malaysian towns, James O'Toole's study of identity among urban blacks in the United States and the Union of South Africa, and Roberts' comparison of the interrelationship of city and province in Peru and Guatemala.[42] But Nagata's rejection of the "frequently held or implicit assumption that the city is in itself an independent variable capable of predicting certain social trends and phenomena" suggests that a great deal of debate lies ahead.[43] This ethnological trend will continue, it is to be hoped, both at the holistic level and, more important, at the topical level, where comparison is more likely to produce meaningful insight into urban lives.

Urban anthropologists often have something of an inferiority complex in methodological matters. But, just as the assumption seems questionable that anthropologists who work in primitive societies have an advantage in understanding the group's culture and social structure, so, too, is the notion that good ethnology can be more readily based on ethnographic data drawn from small societies than on that which emerges from urban research. The crucial problem of ethnography, wherever it has been done, has always been—to quote Burling's discussion of anthropological linguistics—this: is the ethnographer "discovering something about the *culture* which is 'out there' waiting to be described and recorded or is he simply formulating a set of rules which somehow work?"[44]

The solution offered by formal analysts, that we truly approach each culture in its own, emic terms, may provide understanding of a group's world-view; but when emic, rather than etic categories are used, the common units required for cross-cultural comparison are lost. In a very real sense all ethnology is based upon ethnographic compromises, whether of translation or of scale. In the end, the criterion for the evaluation of urban ethnographies and ethnology must be the same as for any other research: are they convincing and do they stand the test of re-studies.

CONCLUSION

One of the most incessant, and irritating, queries that anthropologists face in doing fieldwork in third world countries is: "What is an anthropologist doing here?" Because the response "working with you" might be taken as insulting—suggesting that the questioner is a "primitive"—an anthropologist will sometimes take refuge by suggesting he is a special kind of anthropologist or even a comparative sociologist. That stereotype is a strong one, for which anthropologists must accept most of the blame: until quite recently, many of them have regarded the study of urban and complex societies as tangential to the profession and have themselves labeled urban anthropologists as comparative sociologists. It is understandable that others might note the fact that the bulk of past anthropological research has been with so-called "primitive" societies and reach the logical conclusion that anthropologists study "primitives"; but it is disappointing to find that many anthropologists have so little grasp of the basis of their own profession.

The principal goal of anthropology is to gain an understanding of human society and culture that can come only from the study of all human societies; its goal is *not* to study primitive or exotic peoples. As Plotnicov has said of the idea that anthropologists study "primitives," while sociologists, economists, and other social scientists study "civilized" peoples:

> from the time of Tylor to the present, anthropologists have always protested that this is a false or superficial difference, that our framework of observation and discourse includes all known examples of human society and culture, and that our comparative approach has as its ultimate purpose the scientific understanding of *all* human social institutions and behaviors.[45]

Anthropology is not defined by the kinds of people it studies, but by *how* it studies people. It is premised on the assumption that human communities can be understood only in contrast to all other kinds of human societies, and that attempts to understand a community yield maximum success when the researcher lives within it, attempting to share its inhabitants' lives and world-views. Its basic methods have evolved from the conviction that only intense, day-to-day involvement with those one studies can provide real understanding of any human population.

For this reason, the question should never have been whether urban anthropology should or could be done by anthropological methods, but rather how traditional methods could be revised, when necessary, to maximize useful results. Clearly, the answer is not to adopt wholesale certain techniques, such as the sociological survey, from other disciplines. As Hanna astutely notes, the possibilities of misunderstanding that are inherent in such devices are further compounded by cultural differences, so that the "danger of pseudo knowledge is unusually high."[46] Surveys can and have been used with profit by many urban anthropologists, but only because these anthropologists have relied upon insight gained from participant-observation to formulate questions and decipher responses.

"Anthropological sampling" as Margaret Mead has noted, "is not a poor and inadequate version of socio-psychological sampling . . . *It is simply a different kind of sampling,* in which the validity of the sample depends not so much upon the number of cases as upon the proper specification of the informant, so that he or she can be accurately placed."[47] From its use of "anthropological sampling" and intensive study of "sample" members, urban anthropology can offer unique and enlightening view of urban populations, one which contrasts markedly with the sometimes sterile approaches found elsewhere. Anthropologists working in urban and complex societies may wish to improve their descriptions through use of historical, demographic, and survey techniques; but they must retain intensive in-depth interaction with small groups to direct their inquiries and flesh out their conclusions.

Finally, some members of the profession have suggested that much research done by anthropologists in cities is not really urban anthropology but is merely anthropology done within a city. I agree that a great deal of urban anthropological research has the limited focus of studies of "tribes within a city," and that "a major goal of urban anthropology," as Fox has said, should be "to see the city and its behavioral links to the larger society."[48]

But I do not feel that urban anthropology should limit itself to macro or holistic studies, any more than that all anthropologists should rely solely upon what they know as participant-observers. There really is no agreement on how to conduct anthropology in cities and there probably should not be. Embarking upon a micro-ethnographic study, a community study, a macroethnographic study, or comparative research, the researcher invariably gains certain advantages of perspective and sacrifices others. Personality and the vagaries of fieldwork will lead different anthropologists to different insights. By broadly defining urban anthropology as anthropology done within cities, not as a special approach unto itself, the value of these different views of urban peoples will not be lost to it.

 NOTES

1. Berreman 1962,
2. Berreman 1962:xli, xliii.
3. Berreman 1962:xlviii-xlix.
4. Shelton 1964.
5. See Hanna 1966.
6. Lewis 1961:xi.
7. Mangin 1971:60, 64.
8. See Buller 1975.
9. Wolcott 1973:xiv.
10. Wolcott 1973:318
11. Fischer 1958; Goodenough 1956.
12. Cole 1975:ix.

13. Pike 1967:37-72.
14. See Berreman 1966.
15. Spradley 1972:37.
16. Spradley 1970.
17. Agar 1973:1-2.
18. Preble and Casey, quoted by Agar 1973:7.
19. Spradley and Mann 1975:144, 145; emphasis theirs.
20. Spradley and Mann 1975:13.
21. Barnes 1954:43.
22. Bott 1957:52-96.
23. See Mitchell 1969.
24. Epstein 1961:109.
25. Epstein 1969:126.
26. Hippler 1974; Stack 1974
27. Respectively, by subject: Liebow 1967; Keiser 1969; Keil 1966; Williams 1974; Gropper 1975 and Sutherland 1975; Weiss 1974; Dore 1958; Vogel 1963.
28. Hippler 1974:7-9.
29. Liebow 1967:206-207.
30. Edgerton 1967:17.
31. Edgerton 1967:206.
32. See Banton 1957; Pons 1969; Powdermaker 1962; Skinner 1974; Southall and Gutkind 1957; Wilson and Mafeje 1963.
33. Skinner 1974:12-13.
    Du Bois 1955; Warner et al. 1963; Basham 1977; Gulick 1967; Nakane 1970-respectively by area.
35. Warner et al., 1963.
36. Warner 1958.
37. Warner et al., 1949:xv.
38. Gordon 1963:89.
39. Price 1972.
40. Urban Anthropology, vol. 4, no. 1 (1975).
41. Rollwagen 1975:003.
42. Nagata 1974; O'Toole 1973; Roberts 1974.
43. Nagata 1974:021.
44. Burling 1964:27.
45. Plotnicov 1973:250.
46. Hanna 1966:96.
47. Quoted in Kimball 1955:1134; emphasis his.
48. Fox 1972:206.

Anthropologists in Cities 327

 REFERENCES

Agar, Michael
    1973   Ripping and running: A formal ethnography of urban heroin addicts.
          New York: Seminar Press.
Banton, Michael
    1957   West African city: A study of tribal life in Freetown. London: Ox-
          ford University Press.
Barnes, J. A.
    1954   Class and committees in a Norwegian parish island. Human Rela-
          tions 7:39-58.
Barnett, Steve
    1973   Urban is as urban does: Two incidents on one street in Madras City,
          south India. Urban Anthropology 2:129-160.
Basham, Richard
    1977   Crisis in *blanc* and white: Urbanization and ethnic identity in French
          Canada. Cambridge, Mass.: Schenkman Publishing Company.
Berreman, Gerald D.
    1962   Behind many masks: Ethnography and impression management in a
          Himalayan village. Ithaca, N.Y.: Society for Applied Anthropology,
          monograph 4. Reprinted in Gerald D. Berreman, Hindus of the
          Himalayas. Berkeley: University of California Press, 1972.
    1966   Anemic and emetic analysis in social anthropology. American Anthro-
          pologist 68:346-54.
Boswell, David M.
    1975   Kinship, friendship and the concept of a social network. In C. Kileff
          and W. C. Pendleton, eds., Urban man in southern Africa. Gwelo,
          Rhodesia: Mambo Press.
Bott, Elizabeth
    1957   Family and social network. New York: Free Press.
Buller, Lynn M.
    1975   The encyclopedia game. In J. P. Spradley and M. A. Rynkiewich,
          eds., The Nacirema. Boston: Little, Brown.
Burling, Robbins
    1964   Cognition and componential analysis: God's truth or hocus-pocus?
          American Anthropologist 66:20-28.
Cole, Patrick
    1975   Modern and traditional elites in the politics of Lagos. Cambridge:
          Cambridge University Press.
Dore, R. P.
    1958   City life in Japan. Berkeley: University of California Press.
Du Bois, Cora
    1955   The dominant value profile of American culture. American Anthro-
          pologist 57:1232-1239.
Edgerton, Robert B.
    1967   The cloak of competence: "Stigma" in the life of the mentally
          retarded. Berkeley: University of California Press.
Epstein, A. L.
    1961   The network and urban social organization. Reprinted in J. Clyde
          Mitchell, ed., Social networks in urban situations. Manchester: Man-
          chester University Press.

1969 Gossip, norms and social network. In J. Clyde Mitchell, ed., Social networks in urban situations. Manchester: Manchester University Press.

Fischer, J. L.
1958 The classification of residence in censuses. American Anthropologist 508-517.

Fleuret, Anne K.
1974 Incorporation into networks among Sikhs in Los Angeles. Urban Anthropology 3:27-33.

Fox, Richard G.
1972 Rationale and romance in urban anthropology. Urban Anthropology 1:205-233.

Goffman, Erving
1961 On the characteristics of total institutions. Reprinted in Erving Goffman, Asylums. Garden City, N.Y.: Doubleday.

Goodenough, Ward H.
1956 Residence rules. Southwestern Journal of Anthropology 12:22-37.

Gordon, Milton M.
1963 Social class in American sociology. New York: McGraw-Hill.

Gropper, Rena C.
1975 Gypsies in the city: Culture patterns and survival. Princeton, N.J.: Darwin Press.

Gulick, John
1967 Tripoli: A modern Arab city. Cambridge: Harvard University Press.

Hanna, William J.
1966 The cross-cultural study of local politics. Civilizations 16:81-96.

Hauser, Philip M.
1965 Handbook for social research in urban areas. Ghent, Belgium: UNESCO

Hippler, Arthur E.
1974 Hunter's Point: A black ghetto. New York: Basic Books.

Jacobson, David
1968 Friendship and mobility in the development of an African elite social system. Southwestern Journal of Anthropology 24:123-138.
1973 Itinerant townsmen: Friendship and social order in urban Uganda. Menlo Park, Calif.: Cummings Publishing Company.

James, Jennifer
1972 "On the block": Urban research perspectives. Urban Anthropology 1:125-140.

Keil, Charles
1966 Urban blues. Chicago: University of Chicago Press.

Keiser, R. Lincoln
1969 The vice lords: Warriors of the streets. New York: Holt, Rinehart, and Winston.

Kimball, Solon T.
1955 Problems of studying American culture. American Anthropologist 57:1131-1142.

Kornblum, William
1974 Blue collar community. Chicago: University of Chicago Press.

Lewis, Oscar
1961   The children of Sanchez. New York: Random House.
1966   La vida. New York: Random House.
Liebow, Elliot
1967   Tally's corner: A study of Negro streetcorner men. Boston: Little, Brown.
Mangin, William
1971   Autobiographical notes on a rural migrant to Lima, Peru. Sociologus 21:58-75.
Mitchell, J. Clyde
1969   Social networks in urban situations. Manchester: Manchester University Press.
Nagata, Judith A.
1974   Tale of two cities: The role of non-urban factors in community life in two Malaysian towns. Urban Anthropology 3:1-26.
Nakane, Chie
1970   Japanese society. Berkeley: University of California Press.
O'Toole, James
1973   Watts and Woodstock: Identity and culture in the United States and South Africa. New York: Holt, Rinehart, and Winston.
Pike, Kenneth
1967   Language in relation to a unified theory of the structure of human behavior, revised edition. Paris: Mouton.
Plotnicov, Leonard
1973   Anthropological fieldwork in modern and local urban contexts. Urban Anthropology 2:248-264.
Pons, Valdo
1969   Stanleyville: An African urban community under Belgian administration. New York: Oxford University Press.
Powdermaker, Horntense
1962   Copper town: Changing Africa. New York: Harper and Row.
Price, John A.
1972   Reno, Nevada: The city as a unit of study. Urban Anthropology 1:14-28.
1973   Tecate: An industrial city on the Mexican border. Urban Anthropology 2:35-47.
Roberts, Bryan R.
1974   The interrelationships of city and provinces in Peru and Guatemala. In W. A. Cornelius and F. M. Trueblood, eds., Latin American Urban Research, vol. 4. Beverly Hills: Sage Publications.
Rollwagen, Jack R.
1975   Introduction: The city-as-context, a symposium. Urban Anthropology 4:1-4.
Shelton, A. J.
1964   The "Miss Ophelia syndrome" as a problem in African field research. Practical Anthropology 11:259-65, 276.
Skinner, Elliott P.
1974   African urban life: The transformation of Ouagadougou. Princeton: Princeton University Press.

Southall, Aidan, and Peter C. W. Gutkind
1957   Townsmen in the making: Kampala and its suburbs. Kampala, Uganda: East African Institute of Social Research.
Spradley, James P.
1970   You owe yourself a drunk: An ethnography of urban nomads. Boston: Little, Brown.
1972   Adaptive strategies of urban nomads: The ethnoscience of tramp culture. In T. Weaver and D. White eds., The anthropology of urban environments. Boulder, Colo.: Society for Applied Anthropology, monograph no. 11.
Spradley, James P., and Brenda J. Mann
1975   The cocktail waitress: Woman's work in a man's world. New York: John Wiley and Sons.
Stack, Carol B.
1974   All our kin: Strategies for survival in a black community. New York: Harper and Row.
Sugarman, Barry
1974   Daytop Village: A therapeutic community. New York: Holt, Rinehart, and Winston.
Sutherland, Anne
1975   Gypsies: The hidden Americans. New York: Free Press.
Vogel, Ezra F.
1963   Japan's new middle class. Berkeley: University of California Press.
Warner, W. Lloyd
1958   A black civilization: A study of an Australian tribe. New York: Harper and Row.
Warner, W. Lloyd, et al.
1949   Democracy in Jonesville. New York: Harper.
1963   Yankee City. Abridged ed. New Haven: Yale University Press.
Weiss, Melford
1974   Valley City: A Chinese community in America. Cambridge, Mass.: Schenkman Publishing Company.
Whiteford, Andrew H.
1960   Two cities of Latin America: A comparative description of social classes. Beloit, Wis.: Logan Museum of Anthropology, Bulletin no. 9.
Williams, Melvin D.
1974   Community in a black pentecostal church. Pittsburgh: University of Pittsburgh Press.
Wilson, Monica, and Archie Mafeje
1963   Langa: A study of social groups in an African township. Cape Town: Oxford University Press.
Wolcott, Harry F.
1973   The man in the principal's office: An ethnography. New York: Holt, Rinehart, and Winston.

Urban Anthropology:
A Retrospective
and a Foreword

8 URBAN ANTHROPOLOGY THUS FAR

Anthropology is a particularly risky field for those who seek to generalize, as it is a rare ethnologist who cannot find at least one apparent exception to any hypothesis somewhere among the world's cultures. Too often the threat—perhaps I should say certainty—of contradiction intimidates the would-be generalizer. Yet, grounded generalizations should be the goal of any discipline, and urban anthropology has reached the stage where at least a few tentative conclusions can be suggested.

In the important matter of why peoples migrate to cities, it is now clear that while the concepts of rural push and urban pull offer some utility in ordering our thinking, they are much too simplistic to explain such a multifaceted phenomenon. As we have seen, even the concept of migration itself blurs the fact that migrants may be circulatory, oscillatory, or linear, with varying degrees of commitment to long-term urban residence. More important, motivations for migration vary for individual, environmental, and

333

cultural reasons: some migrants may choose to leave rural areas and small towns for personal improvement, while others may combine such a motivation with a desire to help family members left behind.

Perhaps the most important and often noted urban universal is the marked increase in the division of labor that has everywhere accompanied the development of cities and complex societies. Rudimentary divisions of labor based upon sex, age, and specialized knowledge and abilities are found in all societies. But in advanced societies the proliferation of occupational roles far exceeds that found in any other form of social organization. Although kinship and group alignments may at first actually be enhanced by city life, the process of gradual occupational differentiation, which seems inevitably coupled to urbanization, in time undercuts traditional patterns of social organization. The results of this process can be seen in the oft-noted tendency for the influence of large corporate kin groups to suffer decline in urban contexts in favor of the increasing residential and emotional importance of conjugal families. Those extra-nuclear kin ties that are emphasized tend to be of a more voluntary nature and resemble friendships. As Oscar Lewis noted, "There are deeper, more mature human relationships among sympathetic, highly educated, cosmopolitan individuals who have chosen each other in friendship, than are possible among sorcery-ridden, superstitious, ignorant peasants, who are daily thrown together because of kinship or residential proximity."[1] Although his language is harsh, the point that most urbanites have much greater choice of which relatives to see regularly and which non-kin to have as friends than peasants generally do is well taken.

It is evident, too, that images of urban life as centers of human pathology are generally overdrawn. Cities invariably offer better educational, medical, and entertainment facilities than rural areas. Most obviously, from our consideration of the "problems" of over-crowding and squatter settlements, whether or not there really is a problem, and how serious it is, is largely a matter of perspective. The poverty common to most of the world's rural areas, for example, is somewhat masked by its sameness and by low population densities. But in cities poverty that may be perceived by the poor as an improvement over rural conditions is magnified in contrast to the obvious wealth of other sectors.

Finally, it does appear that complex societies place a premium upon social orders founded on individual achievement, although it is clear that even the most flexible class societies still favor offspring of the upper classes. It is not at all certain whether certain phenotypic or racial differences can ever be overriden as bases for the formation of "primordial" loyalties.

The increasing interest of anthropologists in the study of urban and complex societies represents a natural extension of anthropological research into a milieu that is not so different as often imagined from more traditional research among tribal and peasant peoples. But work in urban settings has highlighted certain essentials of human culture and society that have escaped notice in the study of smaller communities. Urban research, for example, quickly alters the meaning of the concept "culture" for the urban anthropologist. The plethora of behavior patterns and their explanations that he immediately encounters make it obvious that the idea of "*a* people's culture" conceived by early anthropologists working in small, relatively homogeneous communities is inadequate to describe the realities of urban life.

One reason for the apparent disintegration of the traditional culture concept among highly urbanized populations is the variety of discrete social roles that characterize all cities. Additionally, the complexity of role juxtapositions makes it unlikely that sufficiently large segments of the community will occupy the same roles and have the same understanding of their positions to give even the idea of a modal cultural pattern consistent utility. And, unlike the situation that appears to pertain to smaller communities, individual role diversity is not truly overcome by adherence to a common cognitive map of the whole. Put simply: urbanites are usually too varied a lot educationally, occupationally, and experientially, to really agree on much of anything.

The realization that no urban person knows the entirety of "his" culture leads us to clearer recognition of what many anthropologists have long known: all people operate with a kind of microculture that exists only as an imperfect replication of those of their fellows. These microcultures invariably contain a conception of an official culture espoused by most—often without real belief or commitment—to facilitate social interaction, which tends to be an effective behavioral guide, especially in situations where the proximity of strangers is most likely to call forth official cultural patterns. Exposure to the varied behavior and belief systems of others, especially those of different backgrounds, serves to expand our knowledge of life strategies and to cast doubt on the correctness of our personal microcultures or identities.

This is true of all human groups, although urban societies—especially those of today, in which mass communications have greatly expanded the knowledge of alien life ways—have enhanced the potential for distancing every man's microculture from those of his fellows. Research on kinship, individual adaptation and adjustment, and ethnicity and social stratification in the city has shown that many constraints of official cultures have become more optional for urbanites as group consensus on what constitutes correct cultural behavior becomes less certain. But maximization of behavioral flexibility seems to come at the cost of increasing transfer of the principal locus of identity from the group to the individual, a transfer that provokes anxiety in many and causes them to seek out or attempt to renew a collective identity.

One apparent effect of urban life is to increase the "backstage" region of urbanites vis-à-vis those not in immediate co-residence and to maximize the potential variety of frontstage performances. Although individuals in all societies, however small and however characterized by face-to-face relations, always conceal parts of themselves from others, the potential to conceal—and to manipulate that which is revealed—is generally maximized in urban contexts. The growth in role potentiality does not, of course, mean that one's family and friends are not privy to much of one's backstage life, only that the relative potential for encountering and maintaining relations set principally in the frontstage region of conscious performance is maximized.

THE FUTURE OF URBAN ANTHROPOLOGY

The problem of what to do with the orienting concepts of "culture" and "society" in a context the immensity of which seems to preclude more than a cloak of ideological and behavioral uniformity provides an illustration of the dilemmas confronting urban anthropologists. Most relinquish any attempt to characterize the city as a whole, devoting themselves instead to particular topical issues, to micro-ethnographies of occupational roles, or to community studies of groups with relatively firm boundaries. There is not yet, and there may never be, agreement on how to conduct anthropology in cities. I believe, however, that urban anthropologists should view such ethnographic diversity as a potential source of new insights rather than attempt to set forth firm guidelines on what should constitute proper urban anthropological research. It seems premature to decide, as has Richard Fox, that "not all anthropology done in cities is urban anthropology. . . . Many studies take the urban environment as a given, a mere location."[2]

But certain problems have emerged in the course of urban research that merit consideration. An inordinate amount of urban anthropological work has focused on "exotic," easily isolated, urban populations, to the exclusion of more detailed descriptions of "normal" urbanites. As a consequence we often have a much more detailed knowledge of squatters than of the elites who wield political and economic power. This is both a criticism of urban anthropologists and of the elites themselves, who have generally been less receptive to detailed studies of their lives than the poor—who provide access to themselves either in a desire for contact with the researcher and the opportunity to tell their story, or because they feel themselves powerless to prevent intrusions. We *do* need more detailed and intensive studies of elites.

Additionally, urban anthropologists are facing with ever-increasing frequency the complaint that all we do is study, not solve, human problems. Whether or not we subscribe to the notion that anthropologists should take a more active role in applying what we have learned to concrete social problems, we must admit that the criticism has validity. Certainly those anthropologists who style themselves as applied urban anthropologists can add as much to our knowledge as those who do not. Of course, the attempt to solve human problems is fraught with potential for failure, and those who try to apply their knowledge risk much more than those who remain aloof to assess the results of others' efforts.

But any effort on the part of urban anthropologists to improve the lot of their informants is worthwhile. Certainly, the insights into the lives and aspirations of others gained through research need not be limited to anthropological publications. Widespread dissemination of research findings should be encouraged. Greater efforts should also be made to facilitate the movement of urban anthropologists between academic and consultative settings, so that city planners everywhere can benefit from the anthropologist's unique perspective, and so that anthropologists can more fully appreciate the practical problems faced by urban administrators.

Methodologically, urban anthropologists have yet to effectively address themselves to the fact that in a complex society neither city nor countryside, *nor any segment of either*, can properly be dealt with as an independent entity. We are quite capable of producing vivid portrayals of the lives of black street-corner men in Washington, D.C., but we have yet to adequately set them into the economic and political realities of American society. One possible solution to this problem that deserves greater consideration is the use of an ecological approach to the study of group interrelationships. As noted in chapter 7, by segmenting the city into various occupational groups and voluntary associations and studying their particular niches of exploitation and adaptation, more thorough and satisfying studies of entire cities and their relations with their hinterlands should be possible. Such an approach almost inevitably requires cooperation of a research team and a consequent loss of independence for the individual anthropologist, something which those imbued with the one man, one tribe, ethos of anthropology's past will not always accept.

Another potentially useful approach to the problem of scale is to combine ethnographic and survey techniques. By carefully blending the intensive and extensive techniques most closely identified with the respective fields of anthropology and sociology, anthropologists can provide vivid in-depth accounts drawn from a limited number of informants with some assurance of how representative those accounts are of the community as a whole. Unfortunately, few anthropologists seem temperamentally suited to use both ethnographic and survey approaches: projects begun with the intention of combining both frequently end with almost complete concentration upon one or the other. Many researchers have entered the world of survey techniques only to become mesmerized by statistical calculations and computers; caught in the intricate passageways of methodology, they have lost sight of their people. The use of survey techniques and other quantitative approaches should not be abandoned; but we must not forget that anthropology's greatest strength has always rested in its efforts to study a people in depth and on their own terms.

Just as cities are deeply enmeshed in their hinterlands, so are they a part of international political, trade, and industrial networks. Few cities today are insulated from events that occur beyond their nation's borders. The recent decision of oil-producing nations to create an oil cartel has had profound effects on political and economic policy in energy-poor Tokyo, Singapore, and Bangkok and in the hinterlands of each. This is not a new problem. During the period of European colonial expansion in the eighteenth and nineteenth centuries, for example, decisions made in London to develop a source of natural rubber within the British Empire had profound effects upon the economic and ethnic makeup of Malaysia. Although cities are clearly outposts of internationalism, this fact has been largely ignored by anthropologists who prefer to continue their tradition of defining tight boundaries around the groups they study.

The need to view cities in their international contexts is becoming more pressing as urban populations in much of the third world continue to burgeon without benefit of industrialization. Unlike the West, where urban growth has for the most part been closely connected with industrialization, cities in much of the world are growing without any real productive reason. In spite of the relative lack of productivity, however, their inhabitants demand access to luxuries to which they have been exposed by urban life and media. Often their demands mean an increase in foreign imports which must be paid for by exporting agricultural goods, so that the life styles of urban consumers are paid for in large part by the labor of peasants.

Much of the peasant revolutionary activity in Vietnam, Cambodia, and Laos can be directly traced to the belief that their cities are draining the countrysides. Few Westerners are sympathetic to the forced relocation of urbanites into rural areas as has occurred in the wake of communist victories in Indo-China. Nevertheless, forced relocation is a viable alternative to the continued growth of large nonproductive populations in cities that lack an industrial base. The problem of how to provide for residents of the third world's "exploding" cities—short of the equally distressing alternatives of peasant exploitation or forced relocation—will not be an easy one to solve. But it is a problem that anthropologists, with their knowledge of cities and peasant communities, are uniquely suited to grapple with.

Still another dilemma that has not been adequately approached by anthropologists, although it has long been on the horizon, is that of the increasing restrictions placed in the path of research in a world increasingly sensitive to the power of communication. Many anthropologists have become virtual "house anthropologists" for the governments of the countries in which they work. Most of us would probably acknowledge the importance of sharing the benefits of our training and research with local scholars and of displaying a certain sensitivity to local traditions. Unfortunately, the more and more common requirement that anthropologists study issues of "national concern" and avoid those which are "officially sensitive," in order to gain visas for fieldwork, favors the impressions that ruling elites wish to foster, but may sacrifice much of the significance and integrity of our research. This problem is unlikely to vanish. Indeed, it will probably become increasingly difficult for anthropologists to conduct truly independent fieldwork in much of the world. Given the realities of international politics, the best anthropologists can probably do is to lobby with nonanthropologists for a freer international research climate.

Finally, some mention must be made of the fact that urban anthropology often implicitly operates from a perspective of rural-urban contrast. We are no longer at the point where we assume that rural peoples exist at opposite poles from the urban world described by Wirth as superficial, anonymous, and characterized by transitory, instrumental relations. Still, much of rural-urban contrast remains implicit in our thinking. Many anthropologists, through temperament or circumstance, have not worked in the rural areas surrounding their urban research venues. Consequently, we are often forced to weigh the effects of urbanization upon any given population by contrasting the rural and urban research reports of two different anthropologists with varying interests. Recently, however, the collaborative work of Foster and Kemper among Tzintzuntzenos in the peasant village of Tzintzuntzan and in Mexico City, as well as the rural and urban field-work of the Gallins in Taiwan, indicates that some researchers are attempting to rectify this situation by studying both urbanites and those who live in surrounding rural areas.[3]

The difficulties encountered by anthropologists in transferring their techniques to urban research are not nearly so great as some have imagined. And although the application of research methods forged in small communities has often required modification in large urban settings, similar and equally difficult problems have confronted fieldworkers in other disciplines everywhere. Considering the large and impressive body of urban anthropological work that has already been amassed—and considering that the alternative to a shift of emphasis toward more complex societies would be for anthropologists to increasingly abandon their fieldwork orientation and assume the role of mere archivists to vanished traditions—the accommodations demanded by larger societies seem slight.

As difficult as some of the conceptual and practical problems of conducting anthropological research are in today's world, they seem clearly outweighed by the potential for insight that lies within our grasp. The recent growth of interest among anthropologists in the study of urban and complex societies represents both a natural extension of the field and an accommodation to present realities.

Urban anthropology is in no sense a threat to the integrity of anthropology. Rather, it is the promise of anthropology's future.

NOTES

1. Lewis 1973:133.
2. Fox 1972:218
3. Kemper 1974; Gallin and Gallin 1974.

REFERENCES

Fox, Richard
    1972   Rational and romance in urban anthropology. Urban Anthropology
            1:205-233.
Gallin, Bernard, and Rita Schlesinger Gallin
    1974   The rural-to-urban migration of an anthropologist in Taiwan. In
            G. Foster and R. V. Kemper, eds., Anthropologists in cities. Boston:
            Little, Brown.
Kemper, Robert V.
    1974   Tzintzuntzeños in Mexico City. The anthropologist among peasant
            migrants. In G. Foster and R. V. Kemper, eds., Anthropologists in
            cities. Boston: Little, Brown.
Lewis, Oscar
    1973   Some perspectives on urbanization with special reference to Mexico
            City. In Aidan Southall, ed., Urban anthropology. New York: Ox-
            ford University Press.

Index

abakhaya ("home-boys"), 225
Abel, Theodora M., 270, 284
Abidjan (Ivory Coast), 125, 221
Aboure, 125-26
Abrams, Charles, 177, 196
Accra (Ghana), 75, 152
acculturation, 213, 268-70, 275, 284
Adams, Bert N., 93, 97, 132
Adams, Richard N., 257-58, 283
Adams, Robert McC., 51-52
adaptation and adjustment: defined, 195; to urban life, 29, 141-94
Africa, 66, 72, 123-30, 141, 207, 210-28, 258, 307, 311-13, 318-19. See also individual countries
Agar, Michael, 309-10, 326
Agra (India), 236
agriculture, invention of, 38-39
Akan, 126
Akkadian city states, 45
Alatas, Syed Hussein, 283
alcoholism, 151
Aldous, Joan, 133
Ambedkar, B. R., 236, 282
America, 23, 49-50, 92-102, 104-5, 148, 170-71, 187, 209, 268-72, 274-76, 278, 306, 308-10, 314-21. See also United States
American family, history of, 99-101
Ames, Michael M., 108, 110, 132-33, 233-34, 281
Amin, Idi, 222
Amin, Samir, 228, 281
Anderson, Eugene N., Jr., 173-74, 196
Anderson, Michael, 99, 132
Angkor, 51
anomie, 10, 213
anthropology: field of, 3-7, 21-30; methodology of, 6-7, 11, 299-325
"Ants' Villa," 163-65
Aranyaprathet (Thailand), 50
Argentina, 174, 182
Ashanti, 223
Ashton, Guy T., 191, 193, 197
Asia. See Southeast Asia and individual countries
Athens, 45
Atjehnese, 243-44
"attribute," 252
Australia, 58